Advertising
Media Planning

2nd Edition

Advertising Media Planning

2nd Edition

Jack Z. Sissors
Professor of Advertising
Northwestern University

Jim Surmanek
Senior Vice President-Executive Media Director
Ogilvy & Mather, Los Angeles

 740 Rush Street, Chicago 60611

Published by Crain Books
A Division of Crain Communications, Inc.
740 Rush Street
Chicago, IL 60611

Library of Congress Catalog Card Number: 82-70975
ISBN 0-87251-057-3

83 84 85 86 10 9 8 7 6 5 4 3 2

Printed in the United States of America

Contents

Preface

This book is an introduction to the subject of evaluating and selecting advertising media in order to meet specific strategic marketing goals. It covers a broad spectrum of decisions that must be made about using media. The book is both theoretical and practical. It includes descriptions of media planning practices as well as explaining selected analytical methods on which to base decisions.

The first edition of the book was written to meet the special needs of those who have little or no knowledge about media planning. This would include college students majoring in advertising; beginners in the media departments of advertising agencies; account executives or other agency personnel who have not been trained in media, but yet need to know and understand media planning principles; and anyone in marketing who needs to know how media decisions fit into the overall marketing strategy.

In this second edition of *Advertising Media Planning*, the authors have made a number of changes in addition to updating and revising the basic material. The material has been completely reorganized to make basic concepts and strategies more accessible to readers—for example, the sample media plan has been integrated into the text (Chapter 10), rather than appearing as a separate appendix.

In addition, methods of planning media and the media themselves have changed more within the last few years than has any other area of advertising. New research methods are becoming available and new ways of analyzing media are replacing existing ones. The media themselves are changing with the advent of cable and the new electronic media. This book recognizes these changes with the addition of such new chapters as the one on computer modeling (Chapter 15) and extra material on the new technology, plus a final chapter looking ahead to the implications of still more changes in the future.

In no way should the value of this book be considered limited because of the changing nature of the business. This is a book that should continue to help the reader understand "how" media are best used and "why" some media were selected and others rejected. The prevailing concepts, practices, and principles covered in this book will continue to be valuable even as techniques and the various forms of media change.

1
An Introduction to Media Planning

What Is Media Planning?

Media planning consists of the series of decisions made to answer the question for advertisers: "What are the best means of delivering advertisements to prospective purchasers of my brand or service?" (Advertisements are delivered by media such as newspapers, magazines, or television.) While this definition is rather general, it provides a broad picture of what media planning is all about.

Some specific questions that a media planner attempts to answer are:

- How many prospects (for purchasing a given brand of product) do I need to reach?
- In which medium should I place ads?
- How many times a month should prospects see each ad?
- In which months should ads appear?
- In which markets and regions of the United States should ads appear?
- How much money should be spent in each medium?

These are only a few of the questions that must be asked. Each one requires a specific answer and decision.

When all questions have been asked and decisions made, the recommendations and rationale are organized into a written document called the *media plan*. The plan, when approved by the client advertiser, becomes a blueprint for the selection and use of media. Once the advertiser has approved the plan, it serves as a guide for actually purchasing the media.

It would be a mistake, however, to think of media planning as nothing more than finding answers to a list of questions about media.

1

Such a view is too narrow to provide the necessary perspective. Rather, it is better to assume that each question represents certain kinds of problems that need to be solved. Some problems are relatively simple to resolve, such as: "On which day of the week should television commercials be shown?" Other problems, however, are much more difficult, such as: "In which media will ads most affect the prospect's buying behavior to result in actual sales?"

Media planning should be thought of as a process or a series of decisions that provides the best possible answers to a set of problems. A planner may find that the solution to a given problem does not guarantee that the solution will work when other factors are considered. Finding the *best* solutions to a set of problems represents the main task of planners, and this is what makes media planning such an intellectually challenging activity.

The role of media planning has changed in advertising agencies. Today, media planning ranks in importance with marketing and creative planning, but in the early days of advertising agency operations media planning consisted of simple, clerical-type tasks. There were fewer media available in those days, and little research on media audiences had been done to guide planners in decision making.

Planning today is an executive function because it has become so much more complex and important than it was years ago. Today's planners must have a greater knowledge base from which to draw to formulate media plans. The planners must not only know more about media, which have increased tremendously in number, but also know more about marketing, research, and advertising than did their predecessors. Most important, planners are called upon not only to make decisions, but to defend them as the best ones that could be made from among many alternatives.

What brought about this change? Foremost was the rise of the marketing concept, which changed media planning from an isolated activity to one closely related to marketing planning. In fact, one way to evaluate a media plan is to measure how effectively it helps to attain marketing objectives. Another cause of the change was the development of new and more definitive media audience research techniques. As a result, there are more research data available to help planners choose from among a myriad of alternatives.

The change was also due to the increase in advertising expenditures by companies with smaller profit ratios to selling expenses. Quite simply, companies of all sizes now spend many more dollars for media. Also, the prices for purchasing ads in the various media have accelerated rapidly— media are very expensive to buy. As a consequence, company managements want better proof than ever before that their money is well spent. The media planner is the one who is responsible for providing detailed and valid explanations for the media decisions.

Media planning, then, is not so much a matter of being able to answer such relatively simple questions as where to place advertisements or how many advertisements to run each week, as it is a matter of proving that optimal decisions were made under a given set of marketing circumstances. Advertisers demand such explanations, and media planners must be able to provide them. Today's media planners have changed as requirements for planning have changed. The new planner must have breadth of knowledge, marketing understanding, research familiarity, creative planning awareness, and media acumen to do the job competently. It is within this framework that media planning now takes place.

Basic Concepts and Definitions

The two most basic words in media planning are *medium* and *vehicle*. A *medium* is a carrier and deliverer of advertisements; media such as newspapers or magazines carry print ads, and media such as radio or television deliver broadcast commercials. The term *vehicle* generally is used to refer to a specific carrier within a media category—the *New York Times* is a vehicle within the newspaper medium—although some persons use the terms medium and vehicle interchangeably. Contemporary usage, however, seems to be settling on rather limited uses of the two terms:

Medium—a broad, general category of carriers such as newspapers, television, radio, magazines, direct mail, or outdoor.
Vehicle—a specific single carrier within a medium such as the *New York Times, Reader's Digest,* or "Dallas."

Mass Media

Mass media, such as newspapers, magazines, radio, and television are especially well-suited for delivering advertisements—as well as news, entertainment, and educational material—to a widespread general audience. Planners find mass media valuable because: (1) such media may be able to deliver large audiences at relatively low costs, (2) they can deliver advertisements to special kinds of audiences who are attracted to each medium's editorial or programming, (3) they tend to develop strong loyalties among audiences who return to their favorite medium with a high degree of regularity. If a planner wants to reach a special kind of audience repeatedly within a certain time period, some media vehicles will be better suited for this purpose than others. Recent research suggests, for example, that certain types of broadcast programs create higher degrees of viewer interest than other program types, thus offering better environments for commercials.

Media planners, however, also know that mass media (like other media) have their limitations in delivering advertising messages. The most serious is that mass media audiences do not see, hear, or read a medium solely because of the advertising content. Media vary in their ability to get both editorial and advertising material exposed.

Newspapers have news, entertainment, information, and catalog values for their readers. A newspaper generally has excellent readership of both editorial and advertising material, serving as a buying guide for readers who are looking for many different kinds of products. House-wives, for example, often check newspaper ads immediately before their regular food shopping day to find the best grocery bargains. For frequently purchased products, where prices are prominently displayed, newspapers can be a very effective selling medium.

Magazines, on the other hand, are much different in their ability to get ads read. Although some people buy a magazine because they are looking for specific product information on a car or a piece of furniture, most magazine readers are looking for interesting editorial material rather than product information.

Broadcast media, such as radio and television, are least sought out by consumers for the advertisements alone. Broadcast commercials have an intrusive character, breaking into the play or action of a program and compelling some attention to the advertising message. Whether any given viewer will or will not watch a particular commercial is determined more by the ingenuity and value of the message than by its appearance on an interesting program.

The effectiveness of the commercial or advertisement obviously affects the impact it will have on the consumer, and the number of consumers who will read, see, or hear it. This is true regardless of which medium is used.

Specialized Media

Special interest consumer magazines appeal to specific reader interests such as skiing, money management, photography, or antiques. These magazines are read as much for their advertising as they are for their editorial content. Therefore, these magazines often attract readers who purchase the magazine not only for the editorial material, but also for information on the kinds of products advertised.

A large category of media also exists to meet the specialized needs of industrial manufacturers, service companies, wholesalers, retailers, and professional workers such as physicians, attorneys, and teachers. These media may take the form of publications that contain editorial matter, as well as advertising, pertaining to the specialized market, but they may also include films, trade shows, convention exhibits, and phonograph records.

Other specialized media exist exclusively for the purpose of delivering advertising messages. They carry no editorial matter and are not sought after by readers as are other forms of media. Such advertising-oriented media include handbills, direct mail, outdoor billboards, and car cards that appear on buses or trucks.

Another special medium is the catalog. Although catalogs are often requested by consumers, they may not be looked at with the same degree of frequency as are mass media. Therefore, the advertising value of catalogs is somewhat limited. A special form of catalog is the telephone book, which carries advertising but also carries editorial matter—telephone numbers. Plumbers, for example, might justifiably use telephone book advertising exclusively because plumbers aren't needed until emergencies arise. On such occasions, the consumer will search ads in the Yellow Pages to find a plumber, but probably will not notice such ads at any other time.

Exposure

One of the most significant measurements used to compare and select media vehicles is exposure. *Exposure* means "open eyes facing the vehicle." While it may be convenient to use such terms as "readers," "viewers," or "listeners" to describe a vehicle's audience, such terms may be misleading. For example, how many pages of a magazine must an individual read before being counted as a reader? Or how long does an individual have to watch a television program in order to be counted as a viewer? Advertising experts are unable to agree on the answers to these questions.

Media planners would prefer to have measurements of how many individuals either read, viewed, or listened to every advertisement within a given vehicle. Using such measurements, planners could compare alternative media choices on the basis of the largest number of prospects reached. But since such measurements are not available on a broad scale basis, planners would settle for measurements of the number of individuals who were *exposed to most of the advertisements* within each vehicle. But even that kind of measurement is not available on a continuing basis nor for all media. Therefore, planners have had to accept exposure to the vehicle itself as a basic measurement.

Most media planners have agreed to use exposure to a vehicle as the basic unit for measuring the size of that vehicle's audience. Exposure, then, is the minimum measurable relationship between an individual and a given vehicle. There is a great difference between being exposed and not being exposed. To be exposed means that a reader or viewer has the *opportunity to see the advertisements* within a particular vehicle. Thus, the number of individuals exposed to a vehicle within a given measuring period constitutes its audience.

Exposure measurements are different for each medium. In magazines, for example, a person exposed to a publication is usually identified by one of two research techniques: (1) by a person's ability to identify editorial material in a particular issue he or she claims to have read or (2) by being able to identify the logo of a magazine he or she claims to read regularly. In broadcast media, a different technique is used. A person is considered a viewer if he or she tuned in to a program for at least five minutes out of a fifteen-minute segment.

With either definition of exposure, the implied assumption is that those exposed to a media vehicle will also be exposed to the advertising in that vehicle. This is obviously an exaggeration that one can disprove simply by recalling one's own experiences of advertising exposure in reading a magazine or watching a television program. Still, exposure measurements continue to be made, and, relative to other kinds of audience research, they are inexpensive to make. Chapter 2 will discuss better forms of media audience measurements.

The term used to designate unduplicated vehicle delivery is *reach*, the ability to deliver ads to consumers based on exposure figures. Considered along with reach is *frequency*, or repetition, which can also be measured in comparing alternative vehicles. Chapter 3 explains reach and frequency in more detail.

Effectiveness

Some media planners believe that vehicles are nothing more than passive carriers of ads. Simple exposure measurements would then be adequate for the purpose of comparing the size of vehicle audiences. The vehicle that delivers the largest number of audience exposures then would be presumed to be best (assuming costs are taken into consideration).

But many planners are dissatisfied with this mode of selecting media. They argue that a vehicle is not a passive carrier of ads. Each vehicle has the power to affect the audience members' perceptions of ads within it, and this ought to be taken into consideration. At first, attempts to go beyond reach and frequency resulted in purely subjective analyses of alternative media vehicles. A planner might select a vehicle that was most "authoritative," or one that had the best "image," or that was the most "believable."

Later, however, such analyses were discarded because they did not truly differentiate between the impacts of various vehicles. Today, a relatively new approach is being tried to bring some of the active elements of a vehicle into consideration in the planning process.

The measurement of advertising *effectiveness* is now widely being considered as a step beyond reach and frequency. While there is disagreement over the definition of effectiveness, perhaps the most widely accepted definition is: the optimum frequency of exposure for a given vehicle reach. *Optimum* means that at a given level of frequency, the recall of ads in a vehicle is highest when compared with other vehicles under consideration. When audience members are able to recall more of the contents of ads in one vehicle than any others, this may signify that the vehicle itself is acting on the audience in some way to help get ads perceived. The use of *effective reach* or *effective frequency* to compare vehicles assumes that media vehicles are *not* passive carriers of ads. Some do a better job than others in getting ads not only exposed, but read or remembered. (See Chapters 3, 6, and 11 for further discussion of effective reach.)

General Procedures in Planning Media

Marketing considerations must precede media planning. Media planning never starts with answers to such questions as "Which medium should I select?" or "Should I use television or magazines?" Planning grows out of a marketing problem that needs to be solved. To start without knowing or understanding the underlying marketing problem is illogical, because the use of media is primarily a tool for implementing the marketing strategy. So the starting point for a media plan should be an analysis of a marketing situation. This analysis is made so that both marketing and media planners can get a bird's-eye view of how a company has been operating against its competitors in the total market. The analysis serves as a means of learning what the details of the problem are, where possibilities lie for its solution, and where the company can gain an advantage over its competitors in the marketplace.

After the marketing situation has been analyzed, a *marketing strategy plan* is devised that states marketing objectives and spells out the actions to accomplish those objectives. When the marketing strategy plan calls for advertising, it is usually to communicate some information to consumers that affects the attainment of a marketing objective. Media are the means whereby advertisements are delivered to the market.

Once a marketing strategy plan has been devised, an *advertising creative strategy* must also be determined. This consists of decisions about what is to be communicated, how it will be executed, and what it is supposed to accomplish. A statement of advertising copy themes and how copy will be used to communicate the selling message is also part of that strategy. Media planning decisions are affected by advertising creative strategy because some creative strategies are better suited to one medium than to any other. For example, if a product requires demonstration, television might be the best medium. If an ad must be shown in high-fidelity color, magazines or newspaper supplements might be preferable. Creative strategy also determines the prospect profile in terms of such demographic variables as age, sex, income, or occupation. These prospects now become the targets that the planner will focus on in selecting media vehicles.

It should be noted that up to this point persons other than the media planner have been making decisions that will ultimately affect the media plan. The marketing or marketing research people were responsible for the situation analysis and marketing strategy plan, though media planners are, at times, involved at the inception of the marketing plan. Copywriters and art directors are generally responsible for carrying out the creative strategy. Sometimes a marketing strategy plan may be as simple as a memorandum from a marketing executive to the media planner, or even an idea in an advertising executive's mind. In such informal situations, media planning may begin almost immediately with little or no marketing research preceding it. Figure 1–1 summarizes the preplanning steps.

The media planner begins work once a marketing strategy plan is in hand. This plan sets the tone and guides the direction of the media decisions to follow.

The first thing to come out of such a plan is a statement of media *objectives*. These are the goals that a media planner believes are most important in helping to attain marketing objectives. Goals might include determination of which *targets*—those persons most likely to purchase a given product or service—are most important, how many of those targets

FIGURE 1–1. The Scope of Media Pre-Planning Activities

Situation Analysis	Marketing Strategy Plan	Creative Strategy Plan
Purpose: to understand the marketing problem. An analysis is made of a company and its competitors on the basis of: 1. size and share of the total market 2. sales history, costs, and profits 3. distribution practices 4. methods of selling 5. use of advertising 6. identification of prospects 7. nature of the product	Purpose: to plan activities which will solve one or more of the marketing problems. Includes the determination of: 1. marketing objectives 2. product and spending strategy 3. distribution strategy 4. which elements of the marketing mix are to be used 5. identification of "best" market segments	Purpose: to determine what to communicate through advertisements. Includes the determination of: 1. how product can meet consumer needs 2. how product will be positioned in advertisements 3. copy themes 4. specific objectives of each advertisement 5. number and sizes of advertisements

MEDIA PLANNING

need to be reached, and where advertising should be concentrated at what times.

Media strategies develop out of objectives. A media strategy is a series of actions selected from several possible alternatives to best achieve the media objectives. Media strategies will cover such decisions as which kinds of media should be used, whether national or spot broadcast advertising should be used, how ads should be scheduled, and many other decisions.

After the strategy is determined, the implementation of the media plan begins. Some planners call all these subsequent decisions *tactics*. Whatever they are called, many decisions still have to be made before tactics culminate in a media plan. As indicated in Figure 1–2, these decisions might include the selection of vehicles in which to place ads, the number of ads to be placed in each vehicle, the size of each ad, and the specific position within each vehicle that an ad will occupy.

Media decisions need to be creative. Yet many of the decisions involved in media planning are based on quantitative analysis of research data, such as audience sizes, costs, product usage habits, and broadcast ratings. But a media plan does not totally depend on such numbers. It must also have a degree of creativity and good judgment. While the research analysis may lead to fairly clear alternatives, the planner's judgment may modify these alternatives in some way. For that reason many advertisers who sell the same kind of product use widely differing media to advertise their brands. What is the correct decision for one brand may be incorrect for a competing brand. A dramatic example of this occurred when Shell Oil Company some years ago selected newspapers exclusively to deliver its ads, while all other major oil companies used a combination of television, radio, magazines, billboards, and newspapers.

The effectiveness of a plan depends to a great extent on the amount of creativity the planner uses. An example of how such creativity might be applied to a media/marketing problem was provided by Leonard Matthews, then vice president of marketing services of Leo Burnett Company, Inc., in Chicago:

> A couple of years ago, we introduced a new product on a regional basis, achieving national distribution in about an 18-month period. . . . Our problem was to advertise in 10 or 12 key market areas and to put extra advertising weight against a very selective local audience in these areas—for example, the factory worker in Columbus, Ohio. All local media are mass in their approach. There are no local magazines beamed at the blue collar worker.
>
> The media planner on this account came up with what I believe was a creative solution to a fairly knotty problem. He isolated the

**FIGURE 1–2. Kinds of Questions That Lead to Decisions about Media Objectives and
Strategies**

The following is an overview of some of the many questions that lead to media objectives
and strategies. Note that strategies grow out of objectives.

MEDIA OBJECTIVES	MEDIA STRATEGIES
What reaction should we take as a result of use of media by competitors?	Should we use same media mix as competitors? Should we allocate weight as competitors? Should we ignore competitors?
What actions should we take as a result of our brand's creative strategies?	Which media/vehicles are best suited? Any special treatments? (Gatefolds, inserts?) Which dayparts?
Who should be our primary and secondary targets?	Which product usage patterns should we consider? Heavy/medium/light users? What distribution of strategic impressions? Which dayparts?
What balance of reach to frequency is needed?	What levels of reach and frequency? What levels of effective reach/frequency?
Do we need national and/or local media?	What proportions should go into national? What proportion in local media?
What patterns of geographical weighting should we use?	Should we weight by dollars or GRPs? Where should we place weights? When should we weight (weeks/months)? What weight levels for each market?
What communication goals (or effectiveness goals) are needed?	Which criteria of effectiveness should we use?
What kind of scheduling pattern do we need? (Continuity/flighting/pulsing?)	Should we use one or the other? When should we weight more heavily?
Does media have to support promotions? How?	What proportion of the budget should be used? What media mix?
Is media testing needed? How should it be used?	How many and which markets? How should we translate (Little USA or As Is)?
Is budget large enough to accomplish objectives?	Do we need to set priorities? Which must we achieve, which are optional? Do we need more money than available?

major factory locations on a map of each market involved. He did some research on where these people lived in relation to where they worked. He worked out an outdoor poster showing which was tailored to the traffic pattern of the factory workers going to and from work. In some cases, he caused boards to be erected opposite plant gates or in plant parking lots.

. . . An obvious idea? A simple idea? Sure. But the outdoor plants, the National Association of Outdoor Advertising, and the client all thought it one of the most creative uses of local media planning they had ever seen.[1]

The decision-making process for media involves not only the use of research as an aid, but judgment and creativity to make the decisions effective. Matthews summed up this combination of talents as follows:

Judgment, then, is the catalyst, the homogenizer which creates a media strategy out of an everglade of facts and opinion. Good judgment is the prime requisite for a good problem solver, and a good problem solver is a good media planner.[2]

As better media measurement techniques and data become available, it will still require that good judgment be used by the decision maker.

Principles for Selecting Media Vehicles

Of all the media decisions made, perhaps the most important is selecting individual vehicles. Planners tend to select one or more vehicles that effectively reach an optimum number of prospects (1) with an optimum amount of frequency (or repetition), (2) at the lowest cost-per-thousand prospects reached (called cost efficiency), (3) with a minimum of waste (or nonprospects), (4) within a specified budget.

These principles apply most when selecting vehicles for mass-produced and mass-consumed products such as food, clothing, or automobiles. Yet even though they may be more difficult to execute, the principles should be the same in selecting vehicles for such products as noncommercial airplanes or yachts where prospects are distributed unevenly throughout the population. It may be less cost efficient to reach those prospects than it would be to reach prospects for mass-consumed products, because planners may have to select vehicles that contain large

---

[1]Matthews, Leonard S., "The Role of Judgment in Media Planning," in *How to Put Media Research Into Proper Perspective in Media Planning,* American Association of Advertising Agencies, Papers from the 1960 Regional Conventions, 1960, pp. 32–33.

[2]Matthews, "The Role of Judgment in Media Planning," pp. 32–33.

amounts of waste to reach such selective markets. There are other times when the principles may have to be modified. For example, if a creative strategy calls for certain kinds of media such as those that produce ads in high-fidelity color, then cost or waste may have to be disregarded in favor of meeting creative goals. Most often, however, these principles are followed consistently in planning.

When planners apply media selection principles, they use media delivery statistics as one piece of evidence that they have achieved the reach required. *Delivery* simply means the number of audience members reached by, or exposed to, a vehicle or a combination of media vehicles.

With the goal of obtaining the highest possible exposure, the planner starts by looking among the many media alternatives that will reach prospects. A planner does this through using media audience research data for individual vehicles. The data are in the form of numbers classified by audience types, and the numbers listed for each medium may be used as proof of audience delivery. In other words, the planner may use this statistical evidence to prove that the best vehicle(s) for reaching the targeted prospects has been selected. Obviously there are other considerations in making this decision. Costs of media may be so high per prospect reached that the planner may have to reject the first choice in favor of other media that reach smaller numbers of prospects at lower costs.

Once audience delivery numbers have been found, they are related to the total number of prospects in the market. If a market consists of 35,000,000 women in the United States who purchased a given kind of product within the last month, then the size of the market is 35,000,000. The planner may select certain magazines that reach 17,500,000 purchasing women, or 50 percent of the market. Is 50 percent enough? It depends on the marketing objectives. If it isn't enough, the planner may select one or more other media vehicles to increase the percentage reached. Because no decision is made in a vacuum, the planner must also take into consideration the creative, promotional, and executional goals of the promotion strategy while evaluating the vehicle's ability to deliver prospects.

Media Plans Are Custom Tailored

A media plan is designed expressly to meet the needs of an advertiser at a given point in time for specific marketing purposes. Today's media plan is usually not a copy of last year's plan, nor is it simply a blank form with spaces that can be filled in quickly with selected dates or times for running ads. Each media plan should be different from preceding ones for the same product.

Why, then, are plans custom-tailored? The answer is that the marketplace is a dynamic center of activity that is rarely the same from year to year. Competitors rarely stand still in their marketing activities. They may be changing their messages, changing their marketing expenditures, introducing new brands, or discontinuing distribution of old brands. Consumers, too, change—moving to different geographical areas, getting new jobs, retiring, getting married, adopting different leisure-time activities, or buying new kinds of products.

As a result, the marketing situation of an advertiser presents new opportunities as well as new problems. The result is a need for a tailor-made media plan to fit a specific marketing situation.

Media planning is not a science with hard and fast rules that can be easily implemented. Because marketing situations change, new approaches to planning are constantly needed to keep up with, or ahead of, competitors. Media planning is also affected by the new kinds of research or analysis needed to keep abreast of a changing business world. Media planning requires a great sensitivity to change. See Case Study 1–1.

Problems in Media Planning

While media planning has become very important within advertising agency operations, it is not performed as efficiently as one might suppose. The planner is faced with many different kinds of problems that make it difficult to arrive at objective decisions.

Insufficient Information

Media planners almost always require more data about markets and media than are available. Some data never will be available, either because audiences cannot be measured or the data are too expensive to collect. For example, no continuing research service measures the audience exposure to outdoor advertising, or to AM or FM radio listening in every market in the United States, or to portable television viewing. Why? Because such services are too costly to provide and because there is no adequate way of measuring these audiences. Both outdoor exposure and local radio listening have been measured—but not on a continuing basis in all cities so as to give the planner comprehensive and up-to-date information. There are also inadequate research data showing the amount of money that competitors spend yearly for outdoor advertising or for local radio advertising.

In television planning, measurements of the audience size for commercial messages are not available. Most television rating services measure the audience size only in terms of individuals or homes tuned in to programs. This does constitute exposure measurement even though there is no assurance that those who keep diaries are actually watching what they claim to have watched. In those homes measured by an

CASE STUDY 1–1
Is There a Best Media Strategy?

Problem: Because there are basic principles by which media strategies are devised, it might seem that these principles would apply to many different marketing situations. The result would be that most media strategies would be alike and that almost every media plan would have about the same strategy.

The following data are presented to study such a situation. They represent media expenditures for the antiperspirant market in 1977:

Media Expenditures in Antiperspirant Market

Brand	Brand Share (%)	Total Dollars Spent (Millions)	Magazines (%)	Network TV (%)	Spot TV (%)
Ban	15	$11.1	13	80	7
Arrid	13	11.1	—	98	2
Right Guard	13	9.5	8	92	—
Sure	13	12.4	10	77	13
Secret	11	12.1	12	70	18
Remaining Brands	35	26.1			
Total Industry	100	$82.3	8	80	12

(Percentage of Advertising Dollars by Medium)

Sources: A. C. Nielsen; Leading National Advertisers.

Comments
1. From the data above, one can see certain parts of strategies common to all brands shown and certain other strategy parts that differ. For example, all brands spent most heavily in network television. But the amounts spent vary from a high of $11,000,000 for Arrid, to a low of $8,500,000 for Secret. On the other hand, Ban spent proportionately more of its budget in magazines than any of the other brands shown. Secret spent proportionately more in spot TV.
2. The implications of these data are that media strategies differ for each company because each sees the marketplace in a somewhat different manner. One must remember that the marketplace represents a battleground where brands vie for high-ranking positions. Some brands may be content to hold their own and not slip in their battle with competitors. Others want to move up the ladder. The strategies they devise are related to their marketing goals.
3. In essence, there is no "best" strategy for everyone. What is best for one company may not work best for another.

Audimeter, it is possible for viewers to turn on their sets and then leave the room. An Audimeter is an electronic device, attached to a television set, which records when a set is turned on, and to which channels. A. C. Nielsen and Arbitron provide this service. When viewers leave the room, the Audimeter will continue to record that the set was tuned in to the program. Even if it could be shown that there were an audience in front of the television sets watching a given program, there is no guarantee that they would watch the commercials. How, then, can the media planner know with any degree of certainty how many people will view or hear a commercial on any given program?

Furthermore, while it may be possible to estimate the size of the audience for a given commercial, there is no way to measure the degree of attention audiences pay to that commercial. As the Audience Concepts Committee of the Advertising Research Foundation pointed out in a report titled *Toward Better Media Comparisons:*

> Television presents . . . difficult problems. . . . Exposure to television, unlike exposure to billboards, is not public and cannot be publicly measured. It is not conceivable that we shall be able to obtain any objective measure of the number of people whose eyes are confronted by a television commercial.

> Television . . . raises another problem. It may be that someone is exposed . . . for only a few minutes. Are we to classify him as exposed to the advertising vehicle or as *not* exposed to it? Clearly we need some criterion for a minimum exposure.[3]

If such data were available, the planner would be able to make decisions about television with a greater degree of confidence than is now possible.

Another problem in television planning is that decisions about the future performance of television programs must be based on data that represent past performance. If the future is radically different from the past, then the data on which a decision is based may be worthless. William E. Matthews, former director of media relations and planning at Young & Rubicam, explained the problem as follows:

> Take spot broadcast ratings. The rating assigned to a station-break spot is an artificial quantity, a sort of average of preceding and succeeding program ratings, which become inapplicable the moment adjacencies change. Suppose you are buying spots in August for late September scheduling. You have no record for the fall because that is in the future, programming is not fully

---

[3]Audience Concepts Committee Report, *Toward Better Media Comparisons,* New York: Advertising Research Foundation, 1961, p. 18.

set, new shows are involved, and you are dealing with a radically different group of factors from those on which you have measurements.[4]

As a result, a decision made on the basis of past data is no more than a rough estimate of what the planner hopes to achieve in the future.

The problem of obtaining sufficient information is especially acute for small advertisers, many of whom cannot afford to buy research data. These companies often do not know how large their own retail sales are because they sell only to distributors or wholesalers. The media planner, then, must guess at the client's sales position in any given market.

Measuring how people read newspapers and magazines is another problem. How much of any given magazine or newspaper is read? How many advertisements are read? How thoroughly are they read? What is the value of placing an advertisement in one vehicle versus another? How does each vehicle affect the perception of an advertisement that it carries? Answers to these and many other questions are not available on a continuing basis, so the media planner must make decisions without knowing all the pertinent facts.

Time Pressures

A problem that affects media planning in an entirely different way is that of the time pressure involved in making decisions. When the agency and advertiser are ready to start their advertising program, the planner often is faced with a lack of sufficient time to solve problems thoroughly. For example, in many cases the planner requires competitive media expenditure analyses showing how much each competitor spends in major markets throughout the country. Gathering such information is a time-consuming task for media analysts, and the planner might have to bypass this investigation in order to write a media plan quickly.

Another time-related problem is the limited number of broadcast times and programs available to be purchased by advertisers at any given time. This problem is compounded if the client is slow to approve the budget, in which case the most desirable broadcast time periods and/or programs may be spoken for before the advertiser enters the marketplace.

In other situations, new research data are so plentiful that there is neither personnel nor time to analyze them. This is especially true for the large amounts of computerized data on media audiences and brand usage. The computer is able to produce masses of cross tabulations at

---

[4]Matthews, William E., "There's Always Another Set of Numbers You Don't Have," in *Hidden Media Values, or Going Beyond the Numbers*, New York: American Association of Advertising Agencies, Papers from the 1961 Regional Conventions, 1961, p. 39.

lightning speeds, but often such data may go unused because there is insufficient time to analyze them.

Variety of Terminology

Still another problem is the inconsistent use of words, phrases, and measurements throughout the advertising industry. Variations in terminology affect understanding and communication. For example, the term *coverage* means something different when applied to network television than it does when used for newspapers. Furthermore, the terms *reach, cumes, cumulated audiences,* and *audience accumulation,* as well as *coverage,* are often used indiscriminately in place of each other.

Another example is the term *market,* which can mean (1) a geographical place, such as the St. Louis market; (2) a group of persons of a certain sex, income, occupation, or education; (3) a special age group, such as the "teenage market," or the "over-45 market"; (4) prospective buyers for a certain product, such as the "television-set market"; (5) consumers of a specific brand, such as the "Kellogg market." Yet few people ever take the time to explain just what they mean when they say "this is our market."

Standards of measurement often differ, too. Two magazines may produce data showing income classes that differ as follows:

Income of Audience Members

Magazine A	Magazine B
$5,000 or less	$3,000 or less
$5,000 to $7,499	$3,000 to $7,499
$7,500 to $9,999	$7,500 to $9,999
$10,000 to $14,999	$10,000 to $13,999
$15,000 to $24,999	$14,000 to $19,999
$25,000 or more	$20,000 or more

Because the breakdown differs, the media planner may find it difficult to compare the audiences of the two magazines. Although more standardization is evolving, the problem continues to exist.

Lack of Objectivity

One of the continuing problems in media decision making is the sterility of thinking about strategy. Planners are not always objective. For example, an over-dependence on numbers may affect objectivity. Media executives often feel that when a decision is substantiated by numbers, such as television ratings, the decision must be valid because the numbers prove it so. It is often difficult to argue with decisions proved by numbers, yet the numbers can be misleading. The methods of measurement may be imprecise, the sample size may be too small, the technique of measurement may be biased or too insensitive to really measure what it is supposed to, or there may be a set of numbers of major significance not available to the media planner—all of which may affect the objectivity of the decision maker. Uncritical acceptance of numbers can be a dangerous practice and may lead to a decision that common sense indicates is wrong. The planner should be wary of over-reliance on numbers.

Objectivity is also affected when a planner accepts relative data as absolute. For example, the sizes of television audiences reported through ratings are not absolute measurements. When a television rating service shows that 15,000,000 homes tuned in to a given television program, this does not necessarily mean that precisely 15,000,000 homes actually tuned in to the program. Since the sample of homes measured was only about 1,200, projections from 1,200 to a total of about 82,000,000 homes means that the margin of error may be quite large. It may be plus or minus a million homes. Such data are to be used for relative purposes only, and the data merely show that Program A probably has a larger audience size than Program B.

On the other hand, a planner cannot ignore the numbers and make decisions entirely on the basis of experience. Clients are certain to challenge the basis upon which media decisions are made.

Measuring Advertising Effectiveness

Because there is no valid way of measuring advertising effectiveness, it is often difficult to prove that media decisions were effective. Consequently, decision making has not been able to advance to the point where there is always substantive proof that one medium is much better than another. Often a media planner has biased preferences in favor of one media class over others and will favor that medium regardless of what statistics or other objective evidence might indicate.

Notwithstanding these problems, decision making is improving and will undoubtedly improve as long as the people in charge realize there are problems that need solutions and make attempts at improving the situation. The Advertising Research Foundation (ARF) and the Association of National Advertisers (ANA) have attacked some of the more pressing problems of research data and methodology. Furthermore, new and more highly qualified personnel within both agency and client organizations have shown a dissatisfaction with traditional methods of decision making and have demanded new and better evidence for decisions. They are critical of the misuse of statistics and have a broad enough background in research, marketing, advertising, and media to set high standards of performance. The era of accountability in which many large companies now operate also will act to improve the decision-making function by demanding better research data and the removal of major obstacles that stand in the way of such data.

QUESTIONS FOR DISCUSSION

1. Why is exposure a relatively crude measurement by which to compare alternative media vehicles?
2. What kind of media vehicle measurements would be better than exposure? Why?
3. Why do most large advertisers prefer to use mass, rather than specialized, media to deliver their messages to their markets?
4. Explain why the media vehicle that reaches the largest number of people is not necessarily the best vehicle for every advertiser.
5. What is meant by the concept of *waste* in media planning?
6. At times a media planner may have to disregard waste in planning. Under what conditions might this happen?
7. Why does media planning require good judgment if the research data on media audiences is considered valid and accurate?
8. What conditions brought about the need to tailor-make each media plan for each advertiser?
9. The consensus of experts is that media are active, rather than passive, carriers of ads. In what ways are media active?
10. What is meant by *accountability* as it pertains to media planning and marketing?

SELECTED READINGS

Advertising Age, "Ostrow on Media: Support Refocus from CPMs: Human Judgment is the Key," Oct. 16, 1978, p.96.

Advertising Age, Editorial: "The Human Element in Media Planning," Sept. 25, 1978, p. 14.

Deckinger, E. L., "Media Strategy and Accountability," *Perspectives in Advertising Management*, Association of National Advertisers, 1969, pp. 159–72.

Deckinger, E. L., "The Magnitude of the Media Problem and What to do About It," *Papers from the American Association of Advertising Agencies Regional Conventions*, 1960, pp. 1–14.

Drexler, Mike, "How to Stay Ahead," *Media Decisions*, August 1978, p. 62.

Greenberg, Joseph, "The Proverbial Forbidden Fruit: Creativity," *Marketing and Media Decisions*, July 1981, pp. 170ff.

Gudrian, H. D., "How to Evaluate and Select Business Media for More Effective Advertising," *Industrial Marketing*, November 1972, pp. 119–20.

Jones, Richard P., "Quiet Revolution in Media Planning," *Media Decisions*, September 1967, pp. 36–40.

Kemp, Frank B.; Rush, Holton C.; and Wright, Thomas A., Jr., *Some Important Things I Believe a Young Account Representative Should Know About Media*, Committee on Client Service, American Association of Advertising Agencies, December 1963.

Keshin, Mort, "The Illusion of Numbers," *Media/Scope*, March 1966, p. 12ff.

Liddel, Robert, "Advertising Doesn't Work Overnight," in *Papers from the American Association of Advertising Agencies Regional Conventions*, 1960, pp. 29–36.

Maneloveg, Herbert, "How Media Men Buy Media—Six Factors for a

Good Plan," *The New World of Advertising, Advertising Age,* Nov. 21, 1973, p. 62.

Martin, Steve, "Taking the Guesswork Out of Media Planning," *Marketing & Media Decisions,* May 1981, pp. 196, 198.

Matthews, Leonard, "The Role of Judgment in Media Planning," in *Papers from the American Association of Advertising Agencies Regional Conventions,* 1960, pp. 23–33.

Matthews, William E., "There's Always Another Set of Numbers You Don't Have," in *Hidden Media Values, Or Going Beyond the Numbers,* American Association of Advertising Agencies, 1961, pp. 37–42.

Surmanek, Jim, "Solid Research Begets Sound Ads," *Advertising Age,* Jan. 18, 1979, pp. 51–52.

Surmanek, Jim "More to Media Buying Than Numbers," *Advertising Age,* May 21, 1979, pp. 64ff.

Surmanek, Jim, "And Now a Word from Our Sponsor," *Chicago Tribune/Sun-Times Supplement,* Oct. 26, 1980, p. 11.

"Systematize the Logic of Media Planning," *Sales Management,* Dec. 1, 1970, pp. 42–43.

Vladamir, Andrew, "No Magic Formula for Media Mix," *Stores,* June 1973, pp. 28–29.

Zeltner, Herbert, "Assumptions, Logic and Media Planning," *Media/ Scope,* August 1963, pp. 8–10.

2
Basic Measurements and Calculations

The purpose of this chapter is to describe and explain basic measurements and calculations used in media planning. These explanations serve as the foundation by which media strategy decisions, to be discussed later, can be understood. The measurements and calculations discussed in this chapter are by no means all that are available. They simply represent those used most frequently. Throughout the chapter, the reader also will be introduced to media terminology not generally found in everyday speech. Terms such as *reach, Gross Rating Points,* or *cost-per-thousand* are examples of unique media language.

The importance of understanding how media audiences are measured and what those measurements mean should be obvious. Media planners can, and sometimes do, make strategy decisions without using measurement data as a guide, but such decisions may be difficult to defend because they tend to be too subjective. Measurement data, on the other hand, provide a degree of objectivity that is hard to refute.

How Media Are Measured

Most media audiences are measured through sample surveys, using data about a small group to find out about a larger universe. The chief reason for measuring samples rather than a vehicle's entire audience is that samples are less expensive to measure. But even if a vehicle's entire audience could be measured, it is doubtful that it would produce data that would justify the extra cost and time.

Sample sizes may vary from as little as 200 to as many as 30,000. Measurements are usually made at specified intervals, not every day of the year.

Network television audiences are measured through national samples of households whose program preferences are recorded by an electronic meter or by diary entries of a family's viewing habits. At present only four markets—New York City, Los Angeles, Chicago, and San Francisco —are measured by electronic meters. The A. C. Nielsen Company calls these devices Storage Instantaneous Audimeters. These meters automatically record the time of day, day of week, and channel numbers tuned in. One meter can record the tune-in data for as many as four different television sets in the household. The meters are connected by a special telephone line to a computer that gathers and tabulates the data.

The value of data from metered households is somewhat limited since they show only the basic tune-in information for a given program. Planners also want to know who the individuals are who are viewing these programs. The answer to *who* is viewing comes from diaries: daily journals in which is recorded additional demographic information such as age and sex of the viewer. Figure 2–1 shows a sample TV diary.

Completed, the diary is mailed to the Nielsen Company, which tabulates the results. Findings from the electronic meters and diaries are then combined into a broad base of information about the audience size and composition for individual television programs.

Local television viewing is also measured through viewer diaries, but the sample size is relatively small, and the findings of these measurements are reported much less frequently than those of network television. The most frequently used data from both network and local market measurements are ratings (to be described later).

Radio measurements are also made through the use of diaries. However, the number of markets measured is smaller than for television. Furthermore, only large markets are measured relatively often (about 70 percent of the time).

At least four different techniques are commonly used to measure newspaper and magazine audiences.

Through-the-book technique for magazines: A sample of readers is selected and interviewed personally. The interviewer shows each respondent a *stripped-down copy*—one in which all the ads have been eliminated, leaving only editorial material—of the magazine to be measured. After qualifying the respondent by making sure that he or she remembers having seen the cover page, the interviewer slowly turns the pages and asks whether each story looks interesting. The ostensible purpose of asking whether a respondent is interested in each article is to subtly determine whether the respondent really did read (or was exposed to) the magazine in question. After going through each article, the interviewer eventually asks, "Now that we have gone through the entire magazine, are you sure that you have looked into it?" Only those respondents who still say that they were sure they had looked into the book are counted. Those

FIGURE 2–1. Sample TV Diary

Here's how to keep your TV Diary:

In columns 1, 2, 3 . . . at the right, **please fill in the first NAMES, AGE and SEX** of all household members (whether they watch TV or not). Include persons away at school, on trips, vacation, etc. If no Male or Female Head of House, write "NONE" in that column.

For each household member, show the approximate number of hours worked per week outside the home. Show a zero (0), for visitors and family members that are not working.

If you have more than one TV, you probably received several diaries. Please write persons names in the same order in each diary, and keep one diary with each TV. (Please see instructions inside the back cover.)

When you have a visitor watching this TV, write "VISITOR" in one of the blank name columns along with visitor's age and sex. (If exact age is not known, put in approximate age.) See example at the right.

If you have more than nine (9) names to write in, please use the column marked "OTHERS" to write in the **number** of additional persons watching.

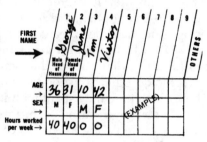

WHEN THE TV IS "OFF"

Draw a line down the "OFF" column for all quarter-hours the TV is off.

WHEN THE TV IS "ON"

Put an X in the "ON" column for each quarter-hour the TV is turned on for six minutes or longer. Please be especially sure to show all **late evening** TV use.

And . . . Write in Station Call Letters, Channel Number and Name of Program. For Movies, please write "Movie" and the Name of the Movie.

And . . . Put an X in the column under the name of each person watching six minutes or longer during each quarter-hour the TV is "ON".

If an entry in a column does not change from one quarter-hour to the next, DRAW A LINE down that column to show that the entry did not change.

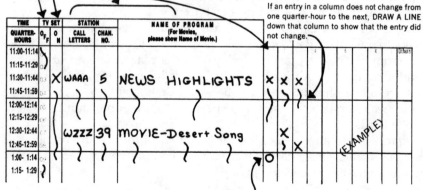

If the TV is "ON" but NO ONE IS WATCHING, fill in the Station and program information, and put a "O" in the first person column.

Thank You!

Source: A. C. Nielsen Company

who are not quite sure and those who reply that they had not looked into the magazine are not counted. Those who say they are sure they have looked into the magazine are then asked demographic questions.

Recent-reading technique for magazines: A sample of respondents is visited by an interviewer who has a specially designed procedure to elicit responses. On individual cards are pasted logotypes for magazines. Respondents are shown one card at a time and then asked if they read the magazine within the last month and where they read it. After this questioning, respondents are asked for demographic information. The interviewer also leaves behind a questionnaire that asks respondents to fill out details about various products they have used and how often they used them. The interviewer returns later to pick up this special questionnaire. On this second visit, the interviewer again asks questions about which magazines have been read over a period of time.

Diary technique for magazines: In this technique, readers are asked to fill out a diary about their magazine reading. In addition to demographic questions, respondents are asked where they read a magazine, how much time they spent with it, and how many pages they looked at.

Yesterday-reading technique for newspapers: Respondents in a selected sample are asked which newspapers they read yesterday. The procedure is much the same as the recent-reading magazine technique. Since there are relatively few newspapers read in any given market, this interview is relatively short.

These techniques are not used equally. The through-the-book and recent-reading techniques for magazines have been combined in the Simmons Market Research Bureau (SMRB) Report. Mediamark Research Inc. (MRI) uses recent reading. The diary technique of measuring magazine audiences is a relatively new idea that is being introduced by Simmons for the Three Sigma Research Center.

Outdoor advertising audiences are measured by asking a sample of drivers to trace their day's travel on a map, indicating routes traveled and destinations. Then a plastic overlay sheet is placed on top of the respondent's map to indicate which billboards have been passed. Tabulations are made showing the numbers and demographics of audiences. These measurements are simply exposures to, or opportunities-to-see, the billboards.

Planners are always looking for better ways to measure audiences. Changes in measuring technology are continually being made as new ideas or methods are developed.

General Uses of Vehicle Audience Measurements

The ultimate purpose of media audience measurements is to enable planners to compare one vehicle with another on a common basis. The objective is to find the best vehicles for delivering the advertising message. Usually, so many different vehicles are available to be used in any advertising campaign that planners depend on measurement data to differentiate one from another.

The result of all these attempts at measurement efforts is a large volume of numerical data, produced at regular intervals. However, the effect of such a quantity of data on media planners and others involved in marketing/media operations may sometimes be a sense of confidence that is perhaps unwarranted. Despite the quantitative aspect, media planning is not scientific in the same manner that physics is. Media audience numbers are the best that can be attained at a reasonable cost, but they do not represent the kind of measurement data planners would ideally like to have, such as information about which media vehicle produces the most sales. Because the numbers may take on an importance that is not warranted, users of measurement data are warned that while the numbers are necessary, they are not absolutes, but rough estimates that need interpretation.

Planners use audience measurement data for the following comparative purposes:

1. To learn the demographics of product or brand users
2. To learn the audience demographics of various kinds of media vehicles—who reads, sees, or hears the vehicle
3. To learn the way purchasers use a product or brand—are they heavy, average, or light users?
4. To learn whether audience members of a particular media vehicle are heavy, average, or light users of the product
5. To learn which media classes and vehicles product users tend to be exposed to.

All of the above information has one basic purpose: to help the planner match media with target markets. The market for any product, from margarine to automobiles, can be identified in terms of certain demographics. What the planner wants to do is to find the media vehicles that best reach the demographic target. Two main concepts guide planners in their use of measurement data. The first is to find vehicles that reach the largest numbers of prospects for a product category or a brand within that category. But planners do not always select the vehicle that delivers the largest number of prospects; sometimes they choose the vehicle that delivers the optimum number of prospects. An *optimum number* means that the number of prospects reached is sufficiently high to achieve some marketing/media goal and yet at the same time allow the planner to attain another goal, such as frequency. The vehicle that delivers the largest number of prospects represents large target reach, while the vehicle that provides a sufficient level of reach with a desired level of

TABLE 2–1. An Example of Matching Media with Markets

Key demographics of the beer market	Time		Reader's Digest		Popular Mechanics	
	Readers (thousands)	Coverage (%)	Readers (thousands)	Coverage (%)	Readers (thousands)	Coverage (%)
Men 18–44	7,881	18.4	8,346	19.5	3,427	8.0
Men in households with $10,000+ income	12,544	20.4	16,245	26.4	8,409	13.7
Beer drinkers	7,677	18.6	9,519	23.1	3,147	7.6

Source: Simmons Market Research Bureau, 1979

frequency would be the optimum. (For a more detailed discussion of the relationship of reach to frequency, see Chapter 3).

Table 2–1 shows how media might be matched with a market using measurement data. Which medium is best according to the matching process in Table 2–1? A tentative answer is the one with the largest audience of prospects. Later analysis may or may not confirm this conclusion, because cost, as well as audience size, is also a consideration. But the first step in making a selection decision will probably center on the matching process.

Various Concepts of Audience Measurements

One of the difficulties in matching markets with media is that no single measurement can be used to determine the audience sizes for all media. Therefore, it is difficult to make intermedia comparisons (such as comparisons between the audience size of a television program and a magazine). Audience size numbers do not mean the same thing from medium to medium because they are measured on different bases.

Actual or Potential Audience Size Measurements

Those who use media audience research should be careful not to confuse data that show the actual size of a vehicle's audience with other data that look similar, but show only potential audience size. The division of audience measurement data into classifications of actual vs. potential (or vehicle distribution vs. vehicle exposure) is the result of new measuring techniques. Before statistical sampling was widely accepted, media owners simply used distribution counts of their vehicles as evidence of audience size. Circulation of print media is one of these older measurements. It represents only potential audience size of the measured vehicle because it does not measure how many people will actually read a given copy of the periodical. As media research techniques have become more scientific, print media have been able to define their readership in terms of numbers of people who actually read the publication, in addition to just pure circulation or distribution counts.

Print Measurements

Print Circulation Measurements. Measurements of circulation are available for most newspaper and magazine vehicles, but these data are of limited use in selection decisions because the data do not provide the planner with information precise enough to select the best vehicles to reach specific people.

Circulation data also do not accurately reflect the number of readers in a vehicle's audience. One unit of circulation means one copy of the periodical distributed, but for every copy distributed, there may be as many as six different readers. One cannot know the size of a vehicle's audience simply by looking at its circulation, yet it is the audience size that is one of the major considerations in media selection. Furthermore, circulation data tell the planner nothing about the demographics of the audience—crucial information when planning is based on reaching precise demographic targets.

As a result, circulation data are seldom used in selecting magazines. However, such data still are often used in making decisions about newspapers because little other audience data are available. Circulation data, while admittedly limited, are still valuable.

When circulation data must be used, measurements verified by the Audit Bureau of Circulation (ABC), as shown in Figure 2–2, are the most reliable. The accuracy of ABC audits is widely accepted throughout the advertising industry. The ABC is a nonprofit, cooperative association of about 1,100 advertisers and advertising agencies; and 2,800 daily and weekly newspapers, business publications, magazines, and farm publications in the United States and Canada. It audits and reports circulations of these publications at regular intervals.

ABC data will include paid circulations categorized for newspapers by city zone, trading zone, and outside areas. In addition, circulation is categorized for newspapers by Standard Metropolitan Statistical Areas (SMSA), making it possible to determine how the distribution of circulation matches selling and marketing areas of advertisers.

Magazine data from ABC show circulation categorized by size of metropolitan areas, by regions of the United States, and by other geographical divisions, all aimed at helping the planner choose the medium that best reaches geographical targets. No demographic data of the reading audience are available from ABC.

Print Audience Measurements. Measurements of the actual size of print audience vehicles can be made by first sampling readers to find an

FIGURE 2–2. Audit Bureau of Circulation Audit Statement

GOOD HOUSEKEEPING

CLASS, INDUSTRY OR FIELD SERVED: The Woman, Her Home and Her Family.

---

1. AVERAGE PAID CIRCULATION FOR 6 MONTHS ENDED DECEMBER 31, 1981:

Subscriptions:	3,494,980
Single Copy Sales:	1,930,810
AVERAGE TOTAL PAID CIRCULATION	5,425,790

Average Total Non-Paid Distribution   44,131

1a. AVERAGE PAID CIRCULATION of Regional, Metro & Demographic editions.

Edition & number of issues		Edition & number of issues		Edition number of issues	
Region #1 (6)	339,039	Region #5 (6)	162,520	Region #9 (6)	319,979
Region #2 (6)	438,730	Region #6 (6)	971,402	Region #10 (6)	226,066
Region #3 (6)	418,203	Region #7 (6)	411,080	Region #11 (6)	617,690
Region #4 (6)	729,937	Region #8 (6)	516,975	Non-Regional (6)	274,169

See Paragraph 12(a)

---

2. PAID CIRCULATION (Total of subscriptions and single copy sales) BY ISSUES:

Issue		Issue		Issue	
July	5,439,920	Sept.	5,329,516	Nov.	5,378,127
Aug.	5,378,584	Oct.	5,292,129	Dec.	5,736,465

---

3. U.S. PAID CIRCULATION BY ABCD COUNTY SIZE based on December, 1981 issue:
February, 1981 issue used in establishing percentages.
Total paid circulation of this issue was 5.73% greater than average total paid circulation for period.

County Size	No. of Counties	% of U.S. Population	Subscription Circulation Copies	% Total	Single Copy Circulation Copies	% Total	Total Circulation Copies	% Total
A	135	41%	1,128,959	33.49	724,900	35.99	1,853,859	34.42
B	271	27%	1,001,871	29.72	629,629	31.26	1,631,500	30.30
C	554	17%	684,657	20.31	413,912	20.55	1,098,569	20.40
D	2,113	15%	555,547	16.48	245,729	12.20	801,276	14.88
	3,073	100%	3,371,034	100.00	2,014,170	100.00	5,385,204	100.00
Alaska-Hawaii	33		15,738		21,530		37,268	
Unclassified					232		232	
TOTAL U.S.	3,106		3,386,772		2,035,932		5,422,704	

FIGURE 2–2. (Continued)

4. GEOGRAPHIC ANALYSIS OF TOTAL PAID CIRCULATION FOR THE DECEMBER, 1981 ISSUE:
Subscriptions and Single Copy Sales figures are based on the percentage for each State Province determined by analysis of February, 1981 issue and these percentages are projected against the total for December, 1981 issue.
Total paid circulation of this issue was 5.73% greater than average total paid circulation for period.

STATE	Subs.	Single Copy Sales	TOTAL	%
Maine	17,107	10,881	27,988	
New Hampshire	17,449	12,965	30,414	
Vermont	10,948	6,482	17,430	
Massachusetts	83,138	58,342	141,480	
Rhode IslandWL	13,685	7,871	21,556	
Connecticut	56,110	37,042	93,152	
NEW ENGLAND	**198,437**	**133,583**	**332,020**	**5.79**
New York	229,913	148,400	378,313	
New Jersey	113,588	68,991	182,579	
Pennsylvania	216,912	117,841	334,753	
MIDDLE ATLANTIC	**560,413**	**335,232**	**895,645**	**15.61**
Ohio	196,384	102,329	298,713	
Indiana	94,771	51,859	146,630	
Illinois	170,382	111,590	281,972	
Michigan	159,092	93,069	252,161	
Wisconsin	111,535	52,785	164,320	
EAST NO. CENTRAL	**732,164**	**411,632**	**1,143,796**	**19.94**
Minnesota	110,167	42,367	152,534	
Iowa	74,243	28,939	103,182	
Missouri	91,349	38,431	129,780	
North Dakota	21,896	7,640	29,536	
South Dakota	19,844	6,714	26,558	
Nebraska	48,241	15,048	63,289	
Kansas	58,162	24,541	82,703	
WEST NO. CENTRAL	**423,902**	**163,680**	**587,582**	**10.24**
Delaware	11,632	6,945	18,577	
Maryland	60,900	39,357	100,257	
District of Columbia	7,869	5,788	13,657	
Virginia	81,770	43,988	125,758	
West Virginia	27,713	15,974	43,687	
North Carolina	70,821	37,042	107,863	
South Carolina	32,845	19,679	52,524	
Georgia	59,189	44,914	104,103	
Florida	110,167	94,226	204,393	
SOUTH ATLANTIC	**462,906**	**307,913**	**770,819**	**13.44**
Kentucky	48,241	23,846	72,087	
Tennessee	52,346	32,875	85,221	
Alabama	40,372	27,087	67,459	
Mississippi	21,212	15,048	36,260	
EAST SO. CENTRAL	**162,171**	**98,856**	**261,027**	**4.55**
Arkansas	23,607	16,901	40,508	
Louisiana	33,871	28,476	62,347	
Oklahoma	42,425	28,476	70,901	
Texas	160,802	114,136	274,938	
WEST SO. CENTRAL	**260,705**	**187,989**	**448,694**	**7.82**
Montana	19,844	10,418	30,262	
Idaho	18,817	9,724	28,541	
Wyoming	9,580	5,556	15,136	
Colorado	47,899	24,309	72,208	
New Mexico	15,738	11,344	27,082	
Arizona	36,950	24,541	61,491	
Utah	21,212	12,270	33,482	
Nevada	9,238	11,113	20,351	
MOUNTAIN	**179,278**	**109,275**	**288,553**	**5.03**
Alaska	5,816	7,408	13,224	
Washington	75,954	45,377	121,331	
Oregon	46,188	27,550	73,738	
California	268,916	193,083	461,999	
Hawaii	9,922	14,122	24,044	
PACIFIC	**406,796**	**287,540**	**694,336**	**12.10**
Miscellaneous		232	232	0.01
Unclassified				
UNITED STATES	**3,386,772**	**2,035,932**	**5,422,704**	**94.62**
Possessions & Other Areas	1,710	3,473	5,183	0.09
U.S. & POSSESSIONS, etc.	**3,388,482**	**2,039,405**	**5,427,887**	**94.62**

	Subs.	Single Copy Sales	TOTAL	%
Canada	**21,554**	**241,237**	**262,791**	**4.58**
Newfoundland	342	2,546	2,888	1.10
Nova Scotia	1,026	12,965	13,991	5.32
Prince Edward Island				
New Brunswick	684	7,640	8,324	3.17
Quebec	1,711	15,974	17,685	6.73
Ontario	10,264	103,950	114,214	43.46
Manitoba	1,026	10,187	11,213	4.27
Saskatchewan	1,711	12,039	13,750	5.23
Alberta	2,395	39,357	41,752	15.89
British Columbia	2,395	36,579	38,974	14.83
Northwest Territories				
Yukon Territory				
CANADA	**21,554**	**241,237**	**262,791**	**100.00**
Foreign	6,159	18,753	24,912	0.44
Unclassified				
Military or Civilian Personnel Overseas	5,132	15,743	20,875	0.36
GRAND TOTAL	**3,421,327**	**2,315,138**	**5,736.465**	**100.00**

3a. CANADIAN PAID CIRCULATION BY ABCD COUNTY SIZE based on December, 1981 issue:
February, 1979 issue used in establishing percentages.
Total paid Circulation of this issue was 5.73% greater than average total paid circulation for period.

County Size	No. of Counties	% of Canadian Pop.	Subscription Circulation Copies	Subscription Circulation % Total	Single Copy Circulation Copies	Single Copy Circulation % Total	Total Circulation Copies	Total Circulation % Total
A	54	61%	12,236	56.77	155,067	64.28	167,303	63.66
B	51	17%	4,078	18.92	41,083	17.03	45,161	17.18
C	65	12%	2,791	12.95	29,600	12.27	32,391	12.33
D	95	10%	2,449	11.36	15,487	6.42	17,936	6.83
TOTAL Unclassified	265	100%	21,554	100.00	241,237	100.00	262,791	100.00
TOTAL CANADA			21,554		241,237		262,791	

FIGURE 2–2. (Continued)

ANALYSIS OF THE TOTAL NEW AND RENEWAL SUBSCRIPTIONS
Sold During 6 Months Period Ended December 31, 1981

5. AUTHORIZED PRICES and total subscriptions sold:

    (a) Basic Prices: Single Copy Par. 12(b)
        Subscriptions: Par. 12(b)... 938,267
    (b) Higher than basic prices: Par. 12(c)...
    (c) Lower than basic prices: Par. 12(d)... 664,899
    (d) Association subscription prices:... None

        Total Subscriptions Sold in Period.. 1,603,166

6. DURATION OF SUBSCRIPTIONS SOLD:

    (a) For five years or more... None
    (b) For three to five years.. 62,601
    (c) For one to three years... 1,531,911
    (d) For less than one year.. 8,654

        Total Subscriptions Sold in Period.. 1,603,166

7. CHANNELS OF SUBSCRIPTION SALES:

    (a) Ordered by mail and/or direct request.. 1,476,158
    (b) Ordered through salespeople:
        1. Catalog agencies and individual agents.. 64,846
        2. Publisher's own and other publishers' salespeople.. 46,984
        3. Independent agencies' salespeople.. 9,125
        4. Newspaper agencies.. None
        5. Members of schools, churches, fraternal and similar organizations.................................... 6,053
    (c) Association memberships.. None
    (d) All other channels... None

        Total Subscriptions Sold in Period.. 1,603,166

8. USE OF PREMIUMS:

    (a) Ordered without premium... 1,598,913
    (b) Ordered with material reprinted from this publication.. None
    (c) Ordered with other premiums. Par. 12(e)... 4,253

        Total Subscriptions Sold in Period.. 1,603,166

ADDITIONAL CIRCULATION INFORMATION

9. ARREARS AND EXTENSIONS: Average number included in PAID (Par. 1) which represents:

    (a) Average number of copies served on subscriptions carried in arrears not more than three months........................ None

10. COLLECTION STIMULANTS:... None

11. BASIS ON WHICH COPIES WERE SOLD TO RETAIL OUTLETS:

    Fully returnable... 100.00%

12. EXPLANATORY:

    Latest Released Audit Report Issued for 12 months ended June 30, 1980.

(a) Par. 1(a): Good Housekeeping is published in a national edition and eleven regional "Match-a-Market" editions. Advertisers can buy any one or combination of these editions. Basic editorial content is the same in all editions.

(b) Par. 5(a): Basic prices: Single Copy: $1.25 per copy with the exception of the December, 1981 issue $1.50 per copy. In single copy price tests 460,216 copies of the July, 1981, 369,140 copies of the August, 1981, 360,145 copies of the September, 1981, 349,731 copies of the October, 1981 and 380,007 copies of the November, 1981 issues were sold at $1.50 per copy. In a single copy price test 74,623 copies of the July, 1981 issue were sold at $1.75 per copy.

    Subscriptions: 1 year $11.97, 2 years $21.97, 3 years $35.97, 4 years $47.97 to July 21, 1981; thereafter, 1 year $11.97, 2 years $21.97, 3 years $39.97, 4 years $53.97.

(c) Par. 5(b): Higher than basic prices: Single copy: All Foreign Countries: $1.25 per copy, to August, 1981; thereafter, $1.75 per copy. 1 year $22.97, 2 years $43.97, 3 years $68.97, 4 years $91.97 to July 21, 1981; thereafter, 1 year $22.97, 2 years $43.97, 3 years $72.97, 4 years $97.97.

(d) Par. 5(c): Lower than basic prices: Special Offers: 1 year $7.97, $8.97, $9.97, $10.97; 2 years $15.94, $18.97; 3 years $31.97.

(e) Par. 8(c): Represents subscriptions sold at basic prices, produced by publisher's own salespeople offering a choice of books in conjunction with subscriptions to this publication and other publications.

We hereby certify that all statements set forth in this statement are true.   04-0375-0

GOOD HOUSEKEEPING, published by The Hearst Corporation, 959 Eighth Avenue, New York, New York 10019.

      WILLIAM S. CAMPBELL   RAYMOND J. PETERSEN

        Vice President & Director of Circulation   Publishing Director

      Date Signed, January 26, 1982.

Source: *Good Housekeeping*

average number of *readers-per-copy*. This figure then is multiplied by the circulation to provide an estimate of the total audience of readers. Most media planners are not interested in the total audience, but only in the numbers of those demographic targets who are the best prospects to purchase their products.

The Concept of Audience Accumulation

Audience accumulation is the build-up of total audiences over time. The time element varies by medium. A major part of the accumulation concept is that audience members are counted only once, no matter how many times they are exposed to a particular vehicle. This is called *reach*. Another measurement, called *frequency*, accounts for repeat exposure. Both reach and frequency will be discussed in more detail in Chapter 3.

Audience Accumulation in Magazines. In magazines, audience accumulates in three ways:

1. Over the issue life of the publication, as the magazine is read by more and more people, passing it along from one reader to another.
2. When advertising is placed in successive issues of the same magazine.
3. When advertising is placed in the same month's issue of different magazines.

The first method of audience accumulation is measured by various researchers who report on the *total audience* of the average issue of a publication. The amount of time it takes for this audience build-up has no bearing on the measurement. A person reading a magazine a month or more after its issuance is counted as a reader to the same extent as the person who reads the magazine the first day it is issued.

The second method of accumulation takes place over different issues. New readers will read a given issue each time it appears.

Quick accumulation is possible when the same ad is run in a given month's issues of different magazines. Some who read one magazine will not read others.

Within a magazine's total audience, researchers distinguish between *primary readers* (those who have purchased the magazine and the members of the purchaser's household), and *pass-along readers* (those not in the purchaser's household). Typical pass-along readers are the purchaser's friends, and/or people reading in doctors' offices, beauty salons, and on airplanes.

In addition to the type of reader (primary or pass-along), a second designator of exposure is also researched: *place* of reading. Syndicated research companies provide data showing where people read magazines. Simmons Market Research Bureau and MRI cite in-home and out-of-home readership for all the publications in their reports.

Several isolated research studies have indicated that the in-home reader, whether a primary or passalong reader, reads more pages of a magazine and spends more time reading than the person outside of the home. Media planners sometimes use this information to give different values, or weights, to each type of reader in order to compare one media vehicle to another.

Audience Accumulation in Broadcast. Audiences also build in broadcast media. Although the concept of accumulation is the same as with magazines, the mechanics differ widely. A television program, with the exception of those recorded on a video cassette recorder, does not have a life beyond its broadcast time. Unlike tangible magazine copies, once a TV or radio program is broadcast, it is finished. Those people who viewed/listened to the show are the only audience the program will have. There is no passalong audience as with magazines. Time *is* a major element in broadcast accumulation.

Nevertheless, TV and radio programs do accumulate audience in three ways:

1. Within the program while it is being broadcast.
2. With successive airings of the same program within a four-week period.
3. With the airing of different programs within the same four-week period.

TV viewers and radio listeners are so designated if they view/listen to five minutes or more of the program. Therefore, if ten people are viewing a program during the first five minutes, then an additional ten people tune in the program in the next five minutes and stay tuned for at least five minutes, the program has accumulated a total audience of 20 people.

Each week that a program is aired, new audience members will tune in for the first time, and thus the accumulation grows. Another way accumulation grows is by advertising on different programs that appeal to the same audience such as women aged 18-49.

In the real world, people tune in and tune out programs at different times during the program broadcast. While ten people might tune in a particular program in the first five minutes, some of them will tune out and some new people will tune in. This phenomenon occurs throughout the program.

Table 2–2 shows how the accumulated total audience of a single episode varies for several programs compared with the audience who viewed the program during an average 15-minute segment. The tune-in

TABLE 2–2. Comparison of Program Ratings:
Average Quarter Hour vs. Total for Entire Program

Program	Telecast Date	Households Viewing (%)	
		Average Quarter Hour	Total Program
Happy Days	1/29/80	22.6	25.4
Eight is Enough	1/30/80	26.4	31.3
Barnaby Jones	1/31/80	18.2	21.0

Source: A. C. Nielsen, NTI, February 1980

TABLE 2–3. Comparison Between One-Week and Four-Week Ratings

Program	Households Viewing (%)	
	Average Quarter Hour	Total of Four Episodes
Happy Days	22.2	25.4
Eight is Enough	24.2	29.0
Barnaby Jones	18.1	21.8

Source: A. C. Nielsen, NTI, January/February 1980

audience in every case is greater in number than those who tuned out. The bucket, therefore, was being filled faster than it was being emptied. This results in a gradual build-up of audience over the entire program.

Table 2–3 shows how successive airings of the same program attract new viewers. The percent of viewers who watch four episodes of "Happy Days," for example, is greater than the average number of viewers watching only one episode.

The Coverage Concept

Audiences can be analyzed in two broad ways: in total numbers of people (e.g., the evening news audience) and as a percentage of the demographic universe of which they are a part (e.g., women aged 35 to 49). One might compare the audience size of ten magazines or television programs on the basis of which delivers the greatest number of people in a target audience, or on the basis of which delivers the highest percentage of the total population in that target audience. Either method will reveal the same relative differences between the media vehicles.

Coverage is a convenient statistical term used to assess the degree to which a media vehicle delivers a given target audience. The higher the coverage, the greater the delivery. Coverage is usually expressed as a percentage of a market reached.

To calculate coverage, the delivery of a specific demographic group (or target audience) by a given media is divided by the total population of that demographic group (the market size). If Magazine X, for example, is read by 2,500,000 women aged 35 to 49, and the total population is composed of 25,000,000 women aged 35 to 49, then Magazine X has a 10

TABLE 2–4. Examples of Coverage Data

Media Vehicle	Demographic Segment	Delivery (thousands)	Population (thousands)	Coverage (%)
McCall's	Women 18 to 49	11,029	49,352	22.3
Parade	Adults with $15,000 or more household income	24,082	75,644	31.8
Benson (TV show)	Households with 3 or more family members	6,211	36,140	17.2

Source: SMRB, 1979

TABLE 2–5. Different Meanings of the Term "Coverage"

Kind of Coverage	Meaning	Uses
General Concept (more accurately called "Market Coverage")	The number of prospects delivered by a given medium. Coverage expressed as a percent of the universe of prospects.	Serves as a goal in planning. Used to determine whether media selected are delivering enough prospects.
Newspaper Coverage	The number of circulation units as a percent of the number of households in an area. If the audience of newspapers in a local market is measured, then coverage is the number of readers in a demographic segment (such as Men 18 to 24) as a percent of all Men 18 to 24 in the local market.	For local markets. A goal to determine whether enough households are reached with one or more newspapers. This represents *potential* audience size.
Magazine Coverage (sometimes called reach)	Same as the general concept. Prospects are demographically defined.	Same as the general concept. This represents estimated *actual* audience size.
Spot TV and Radio Coverage (local market)	The number of TV (or radio) homes within the signal area of station that can tune in to that station.	Serves as a basis for potential delivery in planning. Indicates the maximum size of the *potential* audience of radio or TV homes.
Spot TV Coverage for a national campaign (also for spot radio)	Total number of TV homes in all markets that are part of a campaign, that can tune in (or be reached).	It can show how much of the country's TV homes may be *potentially* delivered by a spot plan. Maximum number and percent of potential exposure.
Network TV Coverage	The number and percent of all stations in a network carrying a given program compared to total TV homes in U.S.	An indication of the maximum *potential* of TV homes that a TV program can reach.
Outdoor Advertising and Transit Coverage	The number of people who pass, and are exposed to a given showing of billboards in a local market, expressed as a percent of the total of all people in the market.	To determine the size of an audience that might look at each showing of billboards.

percent coverage of this target audience. Table 2–4 demonstrates how several media vehicles differ in their coverage of various population groups.

Unfortunately, the term coverage is used in different ways for different media forms. See Table 2–5 for a summary of its meanings.

In magazines, coverage is used in an ideal manner. If there are 12,000,000 households in the United States that own cats and Magazine *A* reaches 6,000,000 of them, then Magazine *A*'s coverage is 50 percent. This 50 percent represents actual exposure to the medium.

But in newspapers and television, coverage may only represent potential degree of reach, not actual reach.

Since coverage can mean a number of different things, it is important for anyone who uses this term to know and understand its alternative meanings. Following is a discussion of how coverage is defined in specific media.

Newspaper Coverage. Most newspapers measure the number of copies sold or distributed and call this "circulation." Newspaper coverage represents the number of copies circulated compared to the number of households in the circulation area.

If the circulation of a newspaper is 500,000 and the number of households in the area is 2,000,000, then the coverage is 25 percent. The assumption is made that each unit of circulation equals one household covered. Coverage represents potential rather than actual exposure since everyone who receives a copy of a newspaper does not read it. No exposure to the medium is necessarily assumed. So coverage based on circulation is only a rough comparison of newspaper audience size related to the market size as measured by the total number of households in that area.

Coverage in newspaper planning, therefore, is not the same as for magazines and other media. The limiting factor is the kind of research that is available.

When using newspaper coverage, planners sometimes suggest that a minimum coverage level in any individual market should be no less than 50 percent. If it can be assumed that not all persons in all households will be exposed to any given edition of a newspaper, then 50 percent is the lowest level that seems practical. Perhaps only two-thirds of that 50 percent will be exposed. Some media planners often set much higher limits on local market coverage, such as no less than 70 percent. In such situations, it may take two or even three newspapers in that community to attain a 70 percent unduplicated coverage.

When a newspaper has research on its total audience size and provides a breakdown of that audience by demographic segments, then coverage will mean something different. It will mean the number of individuals exposed to newspapers compared to the total number of *individuals* (rather than households) in the market. Because such measurements are not always available on a regular basis, newspaper coverage usually means potential exposure.

Magazine Coverage. Magazine coverage, already defined, is the simple ratio of the number of prospects delivered compared with the target market. An example of magazine market coverage is shown in Table 2–6. In Table 2–6, the market is defined as all female household heads who used paper napkins within the last month, or 44,939,000 women. Each magazine reaches a proportion of that market, representing its market coverage. If a market is defined demographically, then coverage by a magazine represents a proportion of a demographic segment base.

Another way to look at magazine market coverage is to look at total users of a given product class. If, for example, one of the syndicated research companies reported that 44,939,000 female household heads used paper napkins within the last month, then that figure would represent the size of the total market. If 9,959,000 readers of *McCall's* used paper napkins within the last month, then that number would represent 22.2 percent market coverage by *McCall's*.

It should be clear from the preceding discussion that planners may define market sizes differently. A market may be defined as all female homemakers aged 18 to 49, or it may be defined as all product users. The subject of defining markets will be discussed in Chapter 4.

Local Television and Radio Coverage. For local radio and television, coverage means the number (or percent) of homes with radio or television sets within the signal area of a given station that can tune in to that station because they can pick up the station's signal. Whether or not they choose to tune in depends on a number of factors such as: (a) whether the programming of the station is interesting enough to attract them, (b) the power of the station, since more powerful stations can cover more homes than weaker stations, (c) the height of a station's antenna and the height of the home's antenna, which affect reception of signals, and (d) the number and nature of obstructions that may prevent the signal from being received, such as bridges, tall buildings, or mountains.

Television stations produce an engineering contour map based on

TABLE 2–6. Market Coverage of Paper Napkin Users of Selected Magazines*

Used Paper Napkins Within Last Month	Number (thousands)	Coverage (%)
Total Users	44,939	100
Family Circle	11,459	25.5
Ladies' Home Journal	8,348	18.6
McCall's	9,959	22.2

*for adult female household heads   Source: SMRB, 1979

their signal strength in a market to indicate how wide an area the station's signal covers. The strongest signal is designated "Grade A" (or one that covers the primary market area surrounding the station). The next strongest signal is "Grade B" (or secondary area coverage). These measurements, however, are not as useful in determining coverage as those that estimate the number of homes covered regardless of whether they are in Grade A or B areas. Research has also shown that some homes outside of the A or B areas can and do receive certain stations.

In order to learn the coverage of a station, research companies send out mail questionnaires to a carefully selected sample of homes located inside and outside the A and B signal areas. These questionnaires ask respondents to list the stations they view regularly. From the returns, estimates are made of how many homes in each county are covered by a station's signal. Such measurements are the starting place for determining the maximum potential audience for a given station. The criterion for being included in a station's coverage statistics is that the home must be able to receive the signal.

Spot Radio or Television Coverage in Multiple Markets. An advertiser who buys spot announcements in a number of markets located in various geographical regions of the United States may be interested in knowing what percentage of all television (or radio) homes in the country the commercial may potentially reach. Perhaps the advertiser has selected 50 of the largest markets in the country. In order to determine the percentage of coverage, it is only necessary to learn the coverage of each station in a plan and add the figures to find the coverage of the entire plan. For example, by buying spot announcements in the top 50 markets, planners can potentially reach nearly 70 percent of the television homes in the country. The planner knows, then, that the maximum audience size (expressed in terms of homes that can tune in to a station's signal) is no larger than 70 percent. Since not everyone in those 50 markets will see the commercials, the exposure will be lower than 70 percent. Table 2–7 lists the percentage coverages of the largest markets.

TABLE 2–7. Coverage of Top U.S. Markets by Using Spot TV

Markets	Coverage (%)
Top 10	32.6
Top 20	45.1
Top 30	53.9
Top 40	60.9
Top 50	67.0
Top 75	79.2
Top 100	86.1
Top 150	95.8
Top 200	100.0

Source: Ogilvy & Mather, Inc.

TABLE 2–8. Network Program Coverage

Network	Program	Household Coverage (%)	No. of stations in lineup
ABC	Barney Miller	98	193
CBS	Archie Bunker's Place	99	201
NBC	Buck Rogers	98	199
ABC	Hart to Hart	94	188
CBS	M*A*S*H*	99	194
NBC	Different Strokes	98	202

Source: A. C. Nielsen, NTI, February, 1980

Network Television Coverage. In network television, coverge is defined as the number and percentage of all U.S. television households that are able to receive a given program. The degree of coverage is affected by the number of stations in a network lineup. The more stations, the more coverage. Table 2–8 indicates the coverage of several network programs.

In broadcast, the term *circulation* is sometimes used to mean the same thing as coverage, but properly used it has a different meaning. Circulation means the number of radio or television households that *can* and *do* tune in to a station a minimum number of times, whether once a month, once a week, or once during a part of the day. Therefore, circulation describes the potential audience size of a network or a station over a period of time. Circulation is a potential audience measurement in that the minimum tune-in required for counting is generally spread over a broad time period, rather than a specific day and time. It is important, then, to remember that both coverage and circulation are measurements of the gross potential audience. *Gross* refers to a crude estimate, and *potential* means that the numbers deal with opportunities rather than actual audience tune-ins to a program. Opportunities for tune-in vary by time of day.

Out-of-Home Media Coverage. Out-of-home media include all media that are located outside a person's home, such as billboards, posters in shopping malls, advertisements in and on buses, etc. Coverage for out-of-home media is the percentage of the population that *passes* the advertisement. Coverage for out-of-home media, therefore, represents the potential for advertising exposure.

Out-of-home media, such as billboards, are still generally purchased by advertisers on the basis of *showings*. A *#100 showing* is the number of billboards needed in a given market to produce the equivalent of 100 percent coverage of the market in a single day. Suppose a market has 100 different billboards erected in and around the city, each of which is passed by an average of 1,000 people each day. If an advertiser purchases

TABLE 2–9. Coverage of Outdoor Showings

	Adults	
Showing	Exposed (%)	Average number of times exposed
#100	87	24
#75	85	20
#50	81	13
#25	73	7

Source: Target Group Index, 1979

ten of these billboards, the equivalent of 10,000 people will pass these boards. If the market has a population of 10,000, then these ten boards would constitute a #100 showing. Other showing sizes can also be purchased, such as a #75 (comprising 75 percent as many boards as in a #100 showing), a #50 showing (half as many boards), and so on.

The outdoor medium is able to generate very high coverage, and therefore reach, over time. Table 2–9 shows the accumulated reach over a 30-day period for different size outdoor showings.

Households Using Television (HUT)

One important television measurement that is frequently used in planning is *Households Using Television* (HUT). It is a coverage figure and represents the percentage of homes tuned into television at a given point in time. Because it includes a *time* consideration, HUT may be classified as a measurement of *net* potential audience size.

Modifying Coverage Data by HUT Data. Coverage data in television represent only audience potential. If a station covers 1,410,000 TV homes, this does not mean that an advertiser will reach all of those homes with a commercial on that station. But what determines how many homes will be reached? To a great extent, the HUT at any time of day will provide a clue to the possible tune-in. As a measure of the net potential audience, HUT indicates what percentage of households with a television set have it turned on at any given time of day, such as morning, early afternoon, late afternoon, primetime, or late evening. The statistics are reported by 15-minute segments to allow a closer examination of tune-ins during various times of the day. Figure 2–3 shows how audience sizes vary by time of day.

Television viewing is affected by living habits. In the morning, tune-in tends to be low, with many men and women at work and children in school. Primary viewers are mothers and small children. When children return home from school about 4:00 pm, the tune-ins rise dramatically, and after 6:00 pm, when many people have returned home from work, the rise in tune-ins is even greater. After 10:00 pm, viewing drops again.

FIGURE 2–3. TV Audience Size by Time of Day

NTI ESTIMATES OF TV USAGE BY DAYPART
(% U.S. TELEVISION HOUSEHOLDS - AVERAGE PER MINUTE)

N.Y. TIME *	MON–FRI 7-10AM			10AM-1PM			1-4:30PM			4:30-7:30PM			MON-SUN 8-11PM**			MON-FRI 11:30PM-1AM			SATURDAY 8AM-1PM		
MONTH	79 80	80 81	81 82	79 80	80 81	81 82	79 80	80 81	81 82	79 80	80 81	81 82	79 80	80 81	81 82	79 80	80 81	81 82	79 80	80 81	81 82
2ND SEPT #	14.0	15.6	15.6	19.9	20.1	20.5	27.8	27.6	27.8	40.8	41.7	42.8	59.9	60.1	58.2	26.1	25.7	26.2	23.4	21.2	22.4
OCT	14.2	15.6	16.1	20.7	20.3	21.3	28.4	27.9	29.2	43.7	43.8	45.6	61.1	61.5	62.1	27.2	27.3	27.5	23.2	23.1	23.1
NOV	16.0	18.3	18.1	21.9	21.8	22.2	29.3	29.0	29.1	48.7	49.5	49.2	62.8	63.8	63.3	27.0	27.0	27.0	25.2	24.3	23.8
DEC	15.9	17.3	17.2	21.4	22.2	22.7	28.4	29.2	29.8	48.9	49.6	50.3	62.2	63.3	63.5	28.6	28.9	29.0	23.6	24.1	24.9
JAN	15.8	18.6	18.7	24.6	26.7	27.4	32.2	32.9	33.9	51.7	53.0	53.1	64.5	64.9	65.3	29.3	29.6	30.4	25.2	25.7	25.9
FEB	17.8	19.3	18.8	25.7	25.3	25.4	32.8	31.6	32.2	51.4	52.3	52.0	65.6	65.4	63.8	27.5	28.0	28.3	25.6	24.7	25.3
MAR	18.4	19.2		24.1	23.6		31.1	30.5		48.8	49.8		63.6	63.4		26.4	26.9		25.2	24.4	
APR	18.0	19.4		23.3	22.1		29.5	28.1		45.1	45.6		60.6	61.0		26.2	26.3		22.2	22.2	
MAY	16.4	16.8		20.6	21.0		26.9	27.3		39.5	41.6		56.4	58.0		26.7	26.8		19.2	20.3	
JUNE	15.5	16.4		22.5	22.8		28.0	28.0		37.7	39.2		52.2	52.8		27.5	27.3		18.8	20.1	
JULY	14.2	15.1		23.0	24.6		28.2	28.9		37.2	38.5		49.4	50.2		27.6	27.6		18.4	18.3	
AUG	14.8	16.1		24.2	25.6		29.2	29.7		38.3	40.3		50.7	52.9		28.2	28.3		18.6	19.2	
1ST SEPT #	14.8	15.7		19.5	21.4		26.7	27.4		39.0	40.8		56.1	55.5		26.5	26.6		21.4	21.4	

1B

* EXCEPT +3 HOURS IN PACIFIC TERRITORY.
UNUSUAL DAYS EXCLUDED (SEE DATES ON PAGE 1A.)

** INCLUDING SUNDAY 7-8 PM.
\# SEPTEMBER REPORTED BY RATINGS REPORT INTERVALS.

Source: A. C. Nielsen Company, Households Using TV Summary Report, 1979

TABLE 2–10. Variations in Viewing by Timer Period and Season

	Total TV Households Tuned In (%)			
	Spring	Summer	Fall	Winter
Daytime (Mon.-Fri.)	25	26	26	29
Early Fringe (Mon.-Fri.)	39	38	47	49
Primetime (Mon.-Sun.)	55	53	62	64
Late Fringe (Mon.-Fri.)	26	27	28	26

Source: A. C. Nielsen Company, Households Using TV Summary Report, 1979

Table 2–10 indicates the variations in viewing for different time periods, as well as by seasons of the year.

The planner can study HUT data and estimate potential audience size better than by studying coverage figures alone. In the early evening hours there are more viewers available than at any other time of day, since both children and adults are usually at home. But there are variations in viewing not only during a single day, but during a given week, and month. During the summer, for example, when persons spend more time out-of-doors, television viewing is much lower in some viewing periods than it is in winter. These variations affect the size of audience that can be obtained.

The media planner, knowing that variations in viewing patterns exist, refines the coverage data to learn the approximate size of an audience that can be reached at various times. Table 2–11 gives an example of how the potential audience size in the Chicago area may be interpreted in the

TABLE 2–11. Potential Audience Size in Chicago Metropolitan Area for Station A

Counties that comprise the Chicago metro area		Number of homes reached at least once a week	Metro area (%)	County Listed (%)
Cook	(Illinois)	147,903	29.0	90.3
Lake		11,400	28.9	88.0
McHenry		4,257	29.2	87.3
DuPage		8,086	30.5	89.0
Will		14,620	28.4	90.1
Lake	(Indiana)	11,848	31.5	93.2
Porter		21,258	31.1	90.8

Source: A. C. Nielsen, NSI Plus County Coverage Study, 1979

TABLE 2–12. Average Number of Homes Reached by Station A

Morning (Mon.–Fri.) 6 am–12 pm	Afternoon (Mon.–Fri.) 12–7 pm	Evening (Sat.–Sun.)	
		7–10 pm	10–10:30 pm
1,038,000	1,141,000	2,468,000	1,879,000

Source: Nielsen Station Index, Viewers in Profile, November 1979

light of tune-in variations by time periods. The advertiser who selects Station A can never hope to reach all of the 2,300,800 households at one time because some of them will prefer other local stations.

From Nielsen or Arbitron, however, it is possible to determine how large the net potential audience is. Table 2–12 shows these data for Station A. These figures would probably be lower if the planner were studying data for the months of July or August, because fewer persons watch television during these months. Furthermore, there are also differences between the net potential audience of Station A and other Chicago stations. In any case, these figures help the advertiser learn about his potential audience size.

After potential audience sizes are examined, program ratings are used to learn the estimated audience size for a given program.

Broadcast Ratings

A *broadcast rating* (television or radio) represents a percentage of some audience base tuned-in, viewing, or listening to a program. For network television, the base is usually all households in the United States that have at least one television set. For local market television, the base is all TV households in the metropolitan area, or some other specially designated area. Radio bases reflect similar geographic areas but include only radio listeners.

Ratings are made both for households and for individuals. The people base for television consists of all persons of a given age group in television households. For example, for women aged 18 to 49, the network program base would be all women aged 18 to 49 in television households in the United States.

Ratings, generally, are a percentage of some specified base, and users of data should know which base is being reported. Such data are provided by research companies.

The Total Audience Rating. The total audience rating represents the percentage of homes (or individuals) in a sample who have tuned to a particular program for a minimum listening period of five minutes. In other words, if individuals in a home have tuned to a program for at least five minutes, they may be counted as having watched the program. These ratings are reported for 15-minute segments of each program, so that if a set in a home has been tuned to a program for a half hour, the measurement will cover at least 10 minutes of that time. The rating is reported as a percentage of the sample tuned to the program. Thus, if 20 percent of the sample tuned in to a given program, this would mean that the program had a 20 rating.

Rating services translate such percentages to whole numbers by projecting the percentage to the total number of television homes in the country or market. For example, if there are 75,000,000 television homes in the United States and a program has a 20 rating, then 20 percent × 75,000,000 would represent 15,000,000 homes estimated to have sets tuned to the program. (See Figure 2–4 for an explanation of how ratings might be made for a sample of 10 homes.) The total audience rating for all programs broadcast on a network at the same time plus the percentage of homes in the sample where the set has not been turned on should add up to 100 percent.

The total audience rating is a measurement of a program's audience size for one telecast. Although ratings may be reported for each week of a given month, the research services will average them to indicate the average tune-in for a typical week in that month.

In studying ratings, one should remember that the measurements are of program delivery, meaning the audience size of the program. There is no measurement of the audience size for a commercial within the program. However, although the placements of commercials may vary, the rating may be assumed to be a rough indication of audience size, because it covers a five- or six-minute tune-in period. Because ratings are used for comparative purposes, the planner will find as many available suitable programs as possible and then make comparisons on the basis of the size of the ratings. Although a rating is a quick way to make comparisons, it is often secondary to a projection that shows the number of homes tuned in (or a simple projection of the rating percentage to the base). Then numbers may be compared and the cost efficiencies calculated.

FIGURE 2–4. Computation of Total Audience Rating for Sample of 10

Home No.	Channel No.	Name of Program
1	2	Program A
2	5	Program B
3	—	Set not on
4	7	Program C
5	2	Program A
6	5	Program B
7	2	Program A
8	—	Set not on
9	7	Program C
10	2	Program A

Summary of Tune-ins

Name of program	Number of sets tuned in	Total audience rating
A	4	40
B	2	20
C	2	20
		(HUT)
Total of homes using TV	8	80%
Sets not on	2	20%
Grand Total	10	100%

The Average Audience Rating. The A. C. Nielsen Company provides a special rating for planners that represents the percentage of homes tuned in to the average minute of a program. It is called the *average audience rating.* Bernard Ober characterized the difference between the average audience rating and the total audience rating as follows:

> Consider a revolving door through which a number of persons pass. A count of the total number of different persons passing through this revolving door might be considered analogous to the total audience rating. . . . In contrast, a count of the number of persons in the revolving door at any time might be considered analogous to the average audience rating of a program.[1]

Table 2–13 illustrates the computation of an average audience rating for a 15-minute program. The average audience rating is particularly useful because it includes not only those who tuned in to the program for five or six minutes (as the total audience rating did), but those who tuned in for only one minute. Many individuals will tune to a program for a few minutes and then switch to another channel in a search for a program more to their liking. Conceivably, however, they may have been exposed to a commercial during those few minutes, so the average audience rating takes such minimal tune-in into consideration and may serve as a measure for a commercial placed somewhere within the framework of a 15-minute segment.

Another advantage of this rating system over the total audience rating is that it better reflects the size of audience when comparing a half-hour program with an hour program. A total audience rating may remain the same or go up during the length of a program; the longer a program is broadcast, the more likely that its total rating will go up. An average audience rating, however, because it is an average, may go up, down, or remain the same during a program. But it does not penalize a shorter program as a total audience rating does. Therefore, the average audience rating is a better measure than the total audience rating for comparing programs of unequal length.

Share of Audience Rating. The *share of audience rating* reflects the percentage of homes tuned in to a program based only on those homes that had their sets turned on, rather than being based on all television homes, as in the total audience rating. If all total audience ratings for a 15-minute time period were added together, the sum would represent the HUT, which always is a proportion of all television homes and is always less than 100 percent. But the sum of all share of audience ratings represents only those homes tuned in at a particular time and always equals 100

---

[1]Ober, Bernard H., *Measuring Television Audiences*, A. C. Nielsen, 1959, p. 3.

percent since homes that had their sets turned off are never figured in the base. The formula for computing share is as follows:

$$\text{Share} \;=\; \frac{\text{Rating}}{\text{HUT}}$$

A comparison of share data with average audience ratings is illustrated in Table 2–14. In Table 2–14, 40 percent of the sets were *not* turned on. When this 40 percent is added to the HUT, the total is 100 percent. Share was computed by dividing the average audience rating by the HUT. The sum of all average audience ratings equaled the HUT, or 60 percent. But the sum of share of audience ratings is 100 percent.

The value of a share statistic is that it enables the media planner to compare two programs broadcast at radically different times of the day, week, or year, or any time where the HUTs for different programs are radically different. To illustrate the use of share data, Table 2–15 shows ratings for a sample program and its shares at different times of the year. If a media planner had made decisions about Program X based only on the average audience rating, he or she might have concluded that this program was losing its audience. After all, ratings were declining. But a study of HUTs shows that they, too, were declining, as might be expected

TABLE 2–13. Computing an Average Audience Rating

Minutes in a program	1	2	3	4	5	6	7	8	9	10	11	12	13	14	15
Percent Tuned in	30	30	30	31	31	31	31	32	32	32	33	33	33	33	33

Total tuned in for 15 minutes = 475
475 ÷ 15 = 31.7; the average percentage tune-in for 15 minutes

TABLE 2–14. Difference Between Average Audience Rating and Share

Programs being broadcast during same 15-minute period	Average audience rating (%)	Share of audience rating (%)
A	20	33.3
B	10	16.7
C	30	50.0
TOTAL	60 (HUT)	100.0

TABLE 2–15. Program X, Ratings vs. Share

Month of year	Average audience rating	HUT	Share of audience rating
January	35.3	72.2	50.3
April	34.2	68.3	50.1
July	28.9	53.5	54.0

when comparing HUTs for January and July. When shares were computed, however, the numbers showed that the program was not only doing well, but actually improving from January to July.

Share is best used when making comparisons based on radically different HUTs. In other words, when the bases for ratings differ, share may be the most appropriate measure.

Figures 2–5 and 2–6 show sample pages from Nielsen Television reports to illustrate the various kinds of ratings used by media analysts. Figure 2–5 shows network delivery for the total U.S., and Figure 2–6 shows delivery in the Chicago TV market for all programs.

FIGURE 2–5. Network TV Audience Delivery in Total U.S.

A-2 *Nielsen* NATIONAL TV AUDIENCE ESTIMATES — EVE.MON. FEB.22, 1982

TIME	7:00	7:15	7:30	7:45	8:00	8:15	8:30	8:45	9:00	9:15	9:30	9:45	10:00	10:15	10:30	10:45
WEEK 1																
ABC TV TOTAL AUDIENCE (Households (000))					17,030				19,480							
TOTAL AUDIENCE (%)					20.9				23.9							
Program					THAT'S INCREDIBLE				ABC MONDAY NIGHT MOVIE OLIVER'S STORY(OP)							
AVERAGE AUDIENCE (Households (000))					13,690				13,200							
AVERAGE AUDIENCE (%)					16.8	16.2*		17.4*	16.2	14.6*		16.1*		17.5*		16.6*
SHARE OF AUDIENCE %					24	23 *		24 *	24	21 *		23 *		26 *		26 *
AVG. AUD. BY ¼ HR. %					15.5	16.9	17.8	17.0	14.4	14.8	15.7	16.6	17.8	17.1	17.2	16.0
CBS TV TOTAL AUDIENCE (Households (000))					16,460				20,460		18,090		19,320			
TOTAL AUDIENCE (%)					20.2				25.1		22.2		23.7			
Program					MR. MERLIN (OP)				M*A*S*H		HOUSE CALLS		SUZANNE SOMERS SPECIAL			
AVERAGE AUDIENCE (Households (000))					12,710				18,830		16,300		14,590			
AVERAGE AUDIENCE (%)					15.6	15.5*		15.7*	23.1		20.0		17.9	18.5*		17.3*
SHARE OF AUDIENCE %					22	22 *		22 *	33		29		27	27 *		27 *
AVG. AUD. BY ¼ HR. %					15.5	15.6	15.6	15.8	22.6	23.7	20.2	19.8	18.5	18.6	18.2	16.3
NBC TV TOTAL AUDIENCE (Households (000))					23,800				24,040							
TOTAL AUDIENCE (%)					29.2				29.5							
Program					LITTLE HOUSE-PRAIRIE (OP)				NBC MONDAY NIGHT MOVIES A WEDDING ON WALTONS MOUNTAIN(OP)							
AVERAGE AUDIENCE (Households (000))					20,540				17,440							
AVERAGE AUDIENCE (%)					25.2	24.5*		26.0*	21.4	20.9*		21.1*		22.1*		21.7*
SHARE OF AUDIENCE %					36	35 *		36 *	32	30 *		30 *		33 *		34 *
AVG. AUD. BY ¼ HR. %					23.7	25.3	25.9	26.0	21.0	20.7	21.1	21.1	22.0	22.2	22.3	21.0
WEEK 2																
ABC TV TOTAL AUDIENCE (Households (000))					18,420				26,730							
TOTAL AUDIENCE (%)					22.6				32.8							
Program					THAT'S INCREDIBLE				ABC THEATRE DIVORCE WARS:A LOVE STORY(OP)							
AVERAGE AUDIENCE (Households (000))					13,530				18,580							
AVERAGE AUDIENCE (%)					16.6	14.9*		18.3*	22.8	21.1*		22.1*		24.2*		24.0*
SHARE OF AUDIENCE %					24	22 *		26 *	35	30 *		32 *		38 *		40 *
AVG. AUD. BY ¼ HR. %					14.5	15.3	17.4	19.1	20.7	21.4	21.7	22.6	23.9	24.4	24.3	23.8
CBS TV TOTAL AUDIENCE (Households (000))					16,710		14,180		18,340		15,080		13,860			
TOTAL AUDIENCE (%)					20.5		17.4		22.5		18.5		17.0			
Program					MR. MERLIN		PRIVATE BENJAMIN (OP)		M*A*S*H		HOUSE CALLS		LOU GRANT			
AVERAGE AUDIENCE (Households (000))					14,590		12,880		16,140		13,940		10,920			
AVERAGE AUDIENCE (%)					17.9		15.8		19.8		17.1		13.4	14.0*		12.8*
SHARE OF AUDIENCE %					26		23		28		24		22	22 *		22 *
AVG. AUD. BY ¼ HR. %					17.8	17.9	15.5	16.0	19.3	20.4	17.1	17.1	14.4	13.6	13.2	12.4
NBC TV TOTAL AUDIENCE (Households (000))					19,560				21,760							
TOTAL AUDIENCE (%)					24.0				26.7							
Program					LITTLE HOUSE-PRAIRIE (OP)				ROY ACUFF-KING CNTRY MUS (BUS-OP)							
AVERAGE AUDIENCE (Households (000))					16,530				14,020							
AVERAGE AUDIENCE (%)					20.4	19.7*		21.1*	17.2	16.9*		17.8*		17.8*		16.3*
SHARE OF AUDIENCE %					30	29 *		30 *	26	24 *		26 *		28 *		27 *
AVG. AUD. BY ¼ HR. %					19.2	20.3	21.6	20.6	16.8	16.9	18.3	17.3	18.0	17.5	16.7	16.0
TV HOUSEHOLDS USING TV (See Def. 1) WK. 1	61.7	63.3	63.8	66.7	69.0	70.5	71.4	71.4	70.2	70.4	69.5	69.2	67.8	66.9	65.6	61.9
TV HOUSEHOLDS USING TV (See Def. 1) WK. 2	62.5	64.0	64.7	66.4	67.2	68.3	69.0	69.9	70.2	70.8	70.4	69.3	65.6	63.4	60.4	58.4

U.S. TV Households: 81,500,000

For explanation of symbols, See page A.

A-3 EVE.MON. MAR.1, 1982

Source: A. C. Nielsen Company

It is important to remember that while ratings may be reported for tuned-in households, they are also reported for people viewing programs. Such ratings usually are broken down by various demographic groups such as age and sex. Furthermore, Nielsen also shows viewer data of programs cross-tabulated by sex and age and other demographic breakdowns. These cross-tabulations allow a media planner to have a better perception of who views each program so that it is possible to better match markets with media.

Measurements of Message Weight

When planners want to know the audience size for a single TV commercial, they use either a program rating or a calculation of the number of viewers exposed to the program. For a single ad in a magazine, they use either a target audience measurement, or a percent coverage of the market figure. But many times, planners want to discuss audience sizes for more than one commercial or ad. To do that they simply add ratings or audience size numbers and disregard the duplication that results.

The sum of ratings is called *Gross Rating Points.* The sum of audience sizes for more than one ad is called *Gross Impressions*. Both numbers are *duplicated*, that is, they are sums of other measurements that may overlap. Gross Rating Points are often abbreviated as GRPs.

Using Gross Rating Points, or Gross Impressions, enables the planner to use a single number to describe the effect of *message weight*. Message weight is a number that quickly tells the planner the duplicated audience sizes for many commercials or ads within a given time period. In spot television, planners often deal with the number of Gross Rating Points per week or per month. But one also can discuss the message weight of an entire year using either Gross Rating Points or Gross Impressions. The user of these numbers, however, must always remember that they represent duplicated audiences.

Gross Rating Points in Broadcast Media

In planning for television, Gross Rating Points are often used to describe the message weight of a week or a month. Shown below is an example of commercials that constituted 90 Gross Rating Points a week:

2 commercials each with a 15 rating	=	30 GRPs
5 commercials each with a 10 rating	=	50 GRPs
2 commercials each with a 5 rating	=	10 GRPs
Total weekly GRPs	=	90

For television planning, one might also want to know how many GRPs per month would be needed to attain a 70 reach. There are appro-

FIGURE 2–6. TV Audience Delivery in Chicago Market

CHICAGO, IL

WK1 2/04–2/10 WK2 2/11–2/17 WK3 2/18–2/24 WK4 2/25–3/03

MONDAY 6.00PM- 8.30PM

TIME PERIOD

TIME PERIOD	STATION	PROGRAM	DMA HH RATINGS WEEKS 1	2	3	4	MULTI-WEEK AVG. RTG	SHR	SHARE TREND NOV '81	MAY '81	FEB '81	DMA RATINGS PERSONS 2+	PERSONS 18+	PERSONS 12-34	WOMEN 18+	WOMEN 18-34	WOMEN 18-49	WOMEN 25-49	WOMEN 25-54	WOMEN WKG	FEM 12-24	PER 12-24	MEN 18+	MEN 18-34	MEN 18-49	MEN 25-49	MEN 25-54	TNS 12-17	CHILD 2-11	CHILD 6-11
			3	4	5	6	7	8	10	11	12	14	15	16	17	18	19	20	21	22	23	24	25	26	27	28	29	30	31	32
	R.S.E. THRESHOLDS 25+% (1 S.E.) 4 WK AVG 50+%		2 LT	2 LT	2 LT	2 LT	1 LT					1 LT	1 LT	1 LT	1 LT	2 1	1 LT	2 LT	1 LT	2 1	3 1	2 LT	1 LT	2 1	1 LT	2 LT	2 LT	4 1	3 1	5 1
6.00PM	WBBM	CH 2 NWS-6	13	14	11	11	12	22	19X	21	19	7	9	4	9	5	6	8	8	9	2	2	8	4	5	7	7	2	2	3
	WCFC	LOVE SPCL	1	<<	1	1	<<		1X		NR																			
	WCIU	ROSA DE LEJOS	1	1	1	1	1	1	1X	NR	2										1	1						1		
	WFLD	H DAYS AGAIN	10	13	11	11	12	21	24X	24	24	8	5	10	5	7	7	6	6	5	14	12	5	8	7	6	5	16	19	21
	WGN	BARNEY MILLER	14	15	14	13	14	25	25X	27	25	9	9	10	9	11	10	9	9	9	9	9	10	11	10	11	11	7	10	7
	WLS	EYEWIT NWS-6	6	11	6	7	8	14	15X	14	17	5	5	3	6	4	5	5	6	5	3	3	5	3	4	4	4	2	2	2
	WMAQ	NWSCENTER 5-6	7	7	10	8	8	14	16X	12	12	4	6	1	6	1	2	3	3	5	1	1	5	1	2	3	3	1		1
	WSNS	ON TV	<<	1	1	1	<<			2	3																			
	WTTW	MACNEIL&LEHRER	2	1	1	2	1	2	2X	2	4	1	1		1								1	1	1		1			
		HUT/PUT/TOTALS *	55	60	55	52	55		56	49	60	37	37	30	38	31	32	33	34	35	32	29	36	30	31	33	34	31	38	37
6.15PM	WBBM	CH 2 NWS-6	13	15	10	12	12	21	19X	20	18	7	9	4	9	4	6	7	8	8	2	2	8	4	5	7	7	2	3	3
	WCFC	LOVE SPCL	1	<<	1	1	1	1	1X		NR																			
	WCIU	ROSA DE LEJOS	1	1	1	1	1	1	1X	NR	2										1	1						1		
	WFLD	H DAYS AGAIN	12	14	14	14	13	23	23X	24	24	10	6	11	6	9	8	7	7	5	15	14	6	9	8	7	6	18	22	25
	WGN	BARNEY MILLER	15	15	15	15	15	25	25X	25	25	10	10	11	10	12	10	10	10	9	10	9	10	11	10	11	11	8	10	7
	WLS	EYEWIT NWS-6	6	10	6	7	7	12	14X	14	16	4	5	3	5	4	4	5	5	5	3	3	5	3	4	4	4	2	2	1
	WMAQ	NWSCENTER 5-6	9	8	11	7	9	15	16X	13	13	5	6	1	7	2	3	3	4	5	1	1	6	2	3	4	4	1	1	1
	WSNS	ON TV	<<	1	<<	1	<<		1	2	3																			
	WTTW	MACNEIL&LEHRER	1	<<	1	2	1	2	2X	2	3		1										1	1	1					
		HUT/PUT/TOTALS *	58	62	58	57	59		58	51	62	38	38	32	39	32	33	34	35	35	33	31	38	32	33	35	36	33	41	41
6.30PM	WBBM	CH 2 NWS-6	12	14	9	12	12	19	15X	18	15	7	8	4	9	5	6	7	7	8	3	3	8	5	6	7	7	3	2	3
	WCFC	LOVE SPCL	1	<<	<<	<<	<<		1X		NR																			
	WCIU	INFORMACION 26	<<	1	<<	1	<<		X	NR																				
	WFLD	MASH 1	11	12	14	13	13	20	19X	16	15	9	8	11	7	9	8	8	7	7	9	11	9	12	10	10	9	11	11	10
	WGN	LAVRN&SHRLY&CO	13	14	14	12	13	21	20X	19	19	10	8	10	9	12	11	9	9	6	16	11	6	7	6	6	6	12	18	19
	WLS	EYEWIT NWS-6	9	10	6	7	8	13	12X	14	14	5	5	3	5	4	4	5	6	6	2	2	5	4	4	5	5	2	2	2
	WMAQ	FAMILY FEUD PM	15	12	16	13	14	23	29X	25	29	9	10	4	12	6	7	8	8	9	5	4	8	3	5	6	7	4	6	6
	WSNS	ON TV	<<	<<	<<	1	<<			2	2																			
	WTTW	WLD-WRLD-ANMLS	6	5	5	5	5	8	9X	10	9	3	4	2	3	2	2	2	3	1	1	1	4	2	3	3	3	1	3	3
		HUT/PUT/TOTALS *	65	62	61	61	62		62	52	64	44	45	37	47	39	40	41	43	40	37	34	42	35	36	37	38	35	46	45
7.00PM	WBBM	MR MERLIN	10	17	14	16	14	22	24	28	21	10	9	10	8	7	7	7	7	8	11	10	9	9	9	10	10	14	13	13
	WCFC	CHICAGO	<<	<<	<<	<<	<<				NR																			
	WCIU	AVG. ALL WKS					<<		1	NR																				
		COLLEGE BKBL	<<	1	<<		<<																							
		CANAS Y BARRO				<<	<<																							
	WFLD	PM MAGAZINE	5	5	6	3	5	7	7X	9	8	3	3	2	3	1	2	2	2	2	1	2	3	2	2	2	2	2	3	4
	WGN	AVG. ALL WKS					8	12	12	16	11	5	6	4	5	5	6	6	6	5	4	4	6	4	5	5	5	4	5	6
		KUNG FU	5		11	7	8	11				5	6	4	5	4	6	6	6	4	3	4	7	3	5	5	5	3	5	6
		SOLID GOLD		9			9	13				6	6	6	6	6	7	7	7	7	7	5	6	5	5	6	5	6	5	
	WLS	AVG. ALL WKS					21	31	25	19	28	16	14	15	14	15	15	16	16	13	12	13	14	15	15	16	16	16	23	23
		ABC MON-MOV	40				40	54				32	28	34	29	35	35	38	35	29	27	27	28	35	33	37	35	30	51	
		THATS INCRDBLE		17	13	13	14	22				10	9	9	9	9	9	9	10	7	8	9	9	8	9	9	9	11	14	14
	WMAQ	HOUSE-PRAIRIE	12	17	21	16	16	24	28X	25	30	11	11	8	15	12	12	12	13	13	11	7	7	4	5	6	6	8	13	13
	WSNS	ON TV	<<	<<	<<	1	<<		1X	1																				
	WTTW	ALL CREATR-SML	4	3	5	4	4	6	9	6	6	2	3	1	3	2	2	2	2	2	1	1	2	1	1	2	2	1	1	1
		HUT/PUT/TOTALS *	74	66	67	61	67		65	56	67	50	48	43	51	45	47	49	50	46	44	40	44	38	39	43	44	47	59	62
7.30PM	WBBM	AVG. ALL WKS					14	21	23	29	24	9	9	8	9	7	8	8	8	9	10	9	9	7	7	8	9	12	11	12
		PVT BENJAMIN	10	16		16	14	20				10	9	8	9	6	8	8	8	9	10	9	9	7	8	8	9	13	11	11
		MR MERLIN			15		15	22				9	9	8	9	9	8	7	7	9	8	7	8	7	7	8	8	8	10	
	WCFC	CHICAGO	<<	<<	<<	<<	<<				NR																			
	WCIU	AVG. ALL WKS					<<			NR																				
		COLLEGE BKBL	<<	<<	1		<<																							
		CANAS Y BARRO				<<	<<																							
	WFLD	YOU ASKED 4 IT	4	4	2	2	3	4	4	6	4	2	2	1	2	1	1	1	2	2	1	1	2	1	1	1	2	2	2	2
	WGN	AVG. ALL WKS					9	12	12	13	10	6	6	5	6	6	7	7	7	5	5	5	7	4	6	6	5	4	6	7
		KUNG FU	5		11	9	8	12				6	6	4	5	5	7	7	6	4	4	5	7	4	6	5	5	3	6	7
		SOLID GOLD		9			9	14				6	6	6	6	6	7	8	7	8	7	5	6	5	6	6	6	6	5	
	WLS	AVG. ALL WKS					22	32	28	21	30	17	15	17	15	17	16	17	17	14	15	16	15	16	16	18	17	18	24	25
		ABC MON-MOV	40				40	53				32	29	35	29	37	36	38	35	29	30	29	29	37	33	37	36	31	50	
		THATS INCRDBLE		19	14	15	16	24				12	10	11	10	10	10	10	11	9	10	11	11	9	10	11	11	14	16	17
	WMAQ	HOUSE-PRAIRIE	12	17	23	17	17	25	29X	26	30	12	12	9	16	13	13	14	14	14	12	8	7	5	5	6	7	9	14	14
	WSNS	ON TV	1	<<	<<	1	1	1	1X	1								1	1	1										
	WTTW	ALL CREATR-SML	3	3	7	4	4	6	9	5	5	2	3	1	3	2	2	2	3	2	1	1	2	2	1	2	2	1	1	
		HUT/PUT/TOTALS *	75	67	70	63	69		68	60	70	51	50	44	54	48	50	53	53	49	46	42	45	38	40	44	45	48	60	63
8.00PM	WBBM	M*A*S*H	12	19	22	23	19	27	32X	33	37	13	14	11	13	11	12	12	13	14	8	9	14	11	12	14	14	12	8	8
	WCFC	BIBLE BAFFLE	<<	<<	1	<<	<<		1		NR																			
	WCIU	AVG. ALL WKS					1	1		NR	1												1							
		COLLEGE BKBL	<<	1	1		1	1					1										1							
		LUCHA LIBRE				<<	<<																							
	WFLD	8 OCLOCK MOV	2	3	4	2	2	3	4X	4	3	1	2	1	2	2	2	2	2	1	1	1	2	2	1	1	1	1	1	1
	WGN	AVG. ALL WKS					7	10	8	8	9	5	5	5	5	6	5	4	5	4	6	6	4	4	4	5	4	6	9	8
		SOLID GOLD	3		10	8	7	10				6	5	6	5	7	6	5	5	4	8	7	4	4	5	5	5	6	11	10
		DE PAUL BKBL		6			6	9				4	4	3	3	2	3	3	4	2	2	3	5	4	4	4	4	4	2	
	WLS	AVG. ALL WKS					26	36	24	28	26	19	18	21	20	23	22	22	22	19	20	19	17	19	19	19	19	20	24	26
		ABC MON-MOV	41	26	14		27	37				21	19	22	20	23	22	23	22	19	20	21	18	20	20	21	21	23	29	31
		ABC THEATRE				22	22	32				15	16	17	20	22	22	22	21	21	21	16	12	14	15	14	13	13	10	
	WMAQ	AVG. ALL WKS					14	19	32	26	26	9	10	6	12	8	9	9	9	11	9	6	7	4	5	5	5	6	7	9
		TV GUIDE SPCL	11				11	14				6	7	3	9	3	5	5	6	7	3	3	6	4	4	4	4	2	3	
		HOUSE-PRAIRIE		18			18	25				12	13	9	17	13	14	15	15	19	15	8	7	5	5	7	7	10	14	
		NBC MON-MOV			16		16	23				11	11	10	14	13	12	12	11	12	14	11	7	7	6	5	4	9	11	
		ROY ACUFF				10	10	15				6	8	3	9	5	6	5	4	5	4	3	7	2	4	5	5	2	2	
	WSNS	ON TV	1	<<	1	1	1	1	2X	1									1											
	WTTW	GRT PERFRMNCES	4	4	5	4	4	6	3X	3	3	2	3	2	3	2	2	3	3	2	1	1	3	3	3	2	2	1		
		HUT/PUT/TOTALS *	76	72	69	69	72		70	66	72	53	54	50	58	54	54	56	57	53	48	47	50	46	47	49	49	49	50	54
			3	4	5	6	7	8	10	11	12	14	15	16	17	18	19	20	21	22	23	24	25	26	27	28	29	30	31	32

MONDAY 6.00PM- 8.30PM

FEBRUARY 1982

NSI AVERAGE WEEK ESTIMATES   CHICAGO, IL

STATION TOTALS (000)

Column groups: **PERSONS** (2+, 18+) · **WOMEN** (18+, 18-34, 18-49, 25-49, 25-54, WKG) · **MEN** (18+, 18-34, 18-49, 25-49, 25-54) · **TEENS** (12-17, GIRLS) · **CHILD** (2-11, 6-11)

HH	2+	18+	W18+	18-34	18-49	25-49	25-54	WKG	M18+	18-34	18-49	25-49	25-54	12-17	GIRLS	2-11	6-11	DAY TIME BREAK STATION
26	48	39	27	26	25	23	23	26	27	27	26	25	6	30	26	38	36	
6	12	10	6	6	6	6	6	7	7	7	7	6		8	7	10	9	
371	583	534	295	60	126	112	133	109	239	51	108	96	117	18	8	31	21	6.00PM WBBM
13																		WCFC
15	26	18	10	5	7	6	6	5	8	4	5	1	2	5	5	3	1	WCIU
378	735	338	182	108	157	93	106	69	156	104	142	87	94	143	86	254	171	WFLD
695	1258	942	470	252	351	244	272	192	472	235	337	247	290	123	51	193	97	WGN
229	369	321	183	49	99	81	99	69	138	41	78	61	67	17	11	31	14	WLS
235	347	336	194	19	51	41	56	64	141	18	48	43	58	6	3	5	5	WMAQ
13	47	21	10	9	9	9	9	5	10	9	10	10	10	2	2	24	17	WSNS
38	51	49	21		2	2	6	2	28	11	12	7	11	2	2			WTTW
1987	3415	2559	1366	502	802	589	686	513	1193	474	741	552	650	316	166	541	327	HUT/PUT/TOT.*
367	573	522	287	58	117	106	127	102	235	53	107	95	115	18	8	32	23	6.15PM WBBM
18																		WCFC
17	29	17	11	6	9	7	7	5	6	2	3	2	2	7	7	4	2	WCIU
432	840	386	206	124	180	111	122	78	181	119	165	104	111	158	93	296	200	WFLD
723	1292	963	480	253	351	245	274	200	483	245	344	251	295	131	59	198	99	WGN
216	342	296	159	46	84	69	87	58	136	43	82	64	71	16	9	30	13	WLS
261	393	375	215	23	58	46	64	65	160	23	58	53	70	6	1	11	7	WMAQ
11	42	20	10	9	9	9	4	1	10	9	10	10	10	2	2	20	14	WSNS
31	40	39	14		2	2	9	4	25	11	12	4	7	1	1			WTTW
2076	3550	2619	1382	520	809	594	694	514	1237	504	780	582	681	339	180	592	359	HUT/PUT/TOT.*
344	551	498	276	62	120	100	120	94	222	58	108	96	110	25	13	27	21	6.30PM WBBM
9																		WCFC
14	40	22	11	9	9	9	9	3	11	1	8	6	6	6	6	12	7	WCIU
421	782	520	242	143	193	126	142	102	278	171	226	153	166	103	34	159	88	WFLD
594	1151	655	388	223	313	209	235	151	268	138	199	141	167	167	124	328	218	WGN
235	369	325	172	47	84	77	102	77	153	47	86	65	76	13	9	31	18	WLS
423	720	608	377	74	142	111	135	117	231	41	98	85	113	33	17	79	43	WMAQ
9	14	6	5	1	1	1	5	4	1	1	1	1	1	1	1	4	3	WSNS
167	286	238	111		47	40	50	19	129	32	55	42	53	11	4	36	17	WTTW
2215	3913	2873	1581	584	908	673	799	551	1292	490	780	590	691	360	203	679	418	HUT/PUT/TOT.*
427	795	516	267	89	155	109	129	98	249	115	169	143	159	117	58	162	103	7.00PM WBBM
3	13	13	4	1	1			1	9	4	5	3	3					WCFC
8	15	15	4		1				11	5	6	3	3			6		WCIU
10																		
3	6	6	3	3	3				3	3	3	3	3					
149	258	200	104	21	39	29	38	33	96	22	37	25	40	17	4	40	29	WFLD
348	614	478	212	98	163	124	133	84	266	102	168	124	141	53	23	83	59	WGN
334	590	467	193	83	150	118	126	70	273	97	167	120	140	43	14	80	58	
387	689	513	207	144	203	139	155	125	243	115	171	136	144			95	64	
612	1263	839	446	198	308	238	272	160	393	180	283	231	255	131	49	293	173	WLS
1175	2581	1685	892	446	702	552	595	360	793	434	636	524	577	247		631	374	
424	824	557	297	115	177	133	164	94	260	95	165	134	148	92	29	175	107	
480	891	663	462	152	236	181	213	165	201	55	100	83	104	68	54	161	97	WMAQ
10	17	12	8	2	3	3	3	1	4	2	4	4	1	1	1	4	1	WSNS
131	191	175	108	21	43	36	43	27	67	17	29	25	36	6	1	13	4	WTTW
2168	4042	2895	1612	582	950	720	836	572	1284	496	794	638	742	393	190	754	467	HUT/PUT/TOT.*
420	762	522	271	91	157	115	133	117	245	88	147	120	142	99	54	141	92	7.30PM WBBM
411	777	521	271	82	157	119	137	118	250	91	152	122	147	111	54	145	92	
449	718	524	295	118	159	105	122	115	230	81	134	113	127	64		130	92	
6																		
6	8	8			1				6	3	4	3	2					WCFC
8	11	11	3		1				8	3	5	3	3					WCIU
<<																		
98	180	143	78	13	30	24	32	22	64	19	31	24	33	13	2	24	19	WFLD
368	663	513	233	107	179	135	143	89	280	106	183	132	148	59	28	92	61	WGN
358	655	510	219	96	170	130	135	76	291	104	186	129	147	54	21	91	62	
396	686	522	275	140	209	152	165	128	247	109	171	140	148	71		92	58	
655	1357	899	471	214	333	248	285	175	428	199	313	250	277	149	56	310	191	WLS
1191	2603	1720	911	472	727	550	591	369	809	455	649	521	580	252		631	374	
476	942	625	325	129	201	148	183	110	300	113	201	160	176	114	39	203	130	
514	968	714	505	172	264	205	238	177	209	58	109	92	114	77	60	177	108	WMAQ
15	23	19	14	3	8	7	13	1	5	5	5	3	1	1	1		1	WSNS
133	192	173	104	24	46	38	46	27	69	20	31	27	40	6	1	13	4	WTTW
2215	4154	2991	1685	625	1018	773	890	615	1306	491	823	653	761	405	201	758	476	HUT/PUT/TOT.*
571	1012	816	424	150	237	183	220	174	392	142	229	196	224	96	28	100	60	8.00PM WBBM
10	1	1	1	1	1													WCFC
16	23	23	8	1	2	2	2	1	15	3	4	6	6					WCIU
20	30	30	10	1	2	2	2	1	20	4	6	6	8					
85	139	125	71	24	38	30	44	18	54	20	30	24	28	6	2	9	8	WFLD
322	649	418	213	109	153	100	114	71	205	90	147	108	120	93	40	138	81	WGN
336	711	432	232	132	177	112	123	80	199	95	155	116	128	107	47	172	99	
279	462	377	156	40	83	65	89	43	221	73	123	81	94	51	34	27		
762	1560	1084	614	293	444	330	374	246	470	234	364	276	308	168	85	308	204	WLS
794	1671	1117	610	294	444	330	377	237	507	252	389	300	339	190	84	364	238	
667	1229	985	626	289	445	332	365	273	359	178	289	203	215	104		140	103	
408	719	582	387	109	135	135	150	134	195	56	98	72	83	46	40	91	65	WMAQ
314	530	447	277	37	95	79	94	85	170	53	74	51	60	20		33	30	
528	998	747	538	164	288	218	252	240	210	55	103	96	114	80		171	109	
477	852	643	450	173	247	170	179	148	193	89	121	71	71	70		138	102	
312	528	492	284	60	111	74	74	63	208	27	72	65	87	15		20	20	
21	21	18	12	3	7	7	12	4	6	1	6	6	6	1		7	6	WSNS
130	200	195	99	21	45	42	51	23	96	32	53	35	40	5	2			WTTW
2325	4326	3263	1830	711	1113	831	964	673	1433	577	931	720	815	418	198	645	419	HUT/PUT/TOT.*
51	52	53	54	55	56	57	58	61	64	65	66	67	68	70	71	72	73	

HH · STATION TOTALS (000)

Column groups: **DMA RTG HH** · **HH** · **WOMEN** (18+, 18-49) · **MEN** (18+, 18-49) · **CHILD** (2-11)

DMA RTG HH	HH	W18+	W18-49	M18+	M18-49	C2-11	STATION
1	26	27	25	27	26	38	
L7	6	7	6	7	7	10	
12	348	269	113	221	103	27	6.00PM WBBM
**	11	1	1			2	WCFC
1	16	9	7	9	6	3	WCIU
11	349	155	133	132	115	246	WFLD
13	627	387	292	348	259	233	WGN
7	220	158	86	143	75	26	WLS
9	265	215	54	166	54	4	WMAQ
**	10	8	7	9	6	20	WSNS
2	70	49	33	28	18	31	WTTW
54	1916	1253	727	1056	640	591	HUT/PUT/TOT.*
12	369	291	121	237	108	31	6.15PM WBBM
**	15						WCFC
1	16	10	8	7	4	3	WCIU
13	405	194	168	169	153	275	WFLD
14	709	475	351	477	340	195	WGN
7	222	171	92	137	80	31	WLS
8	248	204	55	151	53	8	WMAQ
**	12	10	9	10	10	22	WSNS
1	35	18	2	27	12		WTTW
57	2032	1374	806	1215	760	566	HUT/PUT/TOT.*
12	368	291	123	238	114	31	6.30PM WBBM
**	14						WCFC
**	15	11	9	9	6	8	WCIU
13	430	226	189	233	198	230	WFLD
14	642	422	322	370	267	254	WGN
7	218	161	82	141	82	29	WLS
11	329	285	95	189	75	42	WMAQ
**	11	8	6	9	6	15	WSNS
3	95	59	23	75	33	17	WTTW
60	2124	1464	849	1260	781	626	HUT/PUT/TOT.*
12	366	257	129	220	128	90	7.00PM WBBM
**	5						WCFC
**	12	8	6	10	7	6	WCIU
9	293	178	116	191	131	100	WFLD
11	488	312	247	274	188	216	WGN
14	419	305	192	271	182	160	WLS
15	458	424	189	221	101	121	WMAQ
**	7	5	1	1	1	4	WSNS
4	152	112	46	101	42	24	WTTW
65	2201	1600	926	1289	781	721	HUT/PUT/TOT.*
14	430	276	158	253	162	155	7.30PM WBBM
**	4						WCFC
**	7	2	1	7	4		WCIU
3	113	85	32	74	31	28	WFLD
8	353	219	168	269	175	85	WGN
22	646	469	327	418	302	306	WLS
17	501	488	253	206	105	170	WMAQ
**	13	11	5	4	4	3	WSNS
4	132	107	45	68	30	12	WTTW
68	2199	1657	990	1298	813	760	HUT/PUT/TOT.*
17	491	347	195	314	186	123	8.00PM WBBM
**	9	1	1				WCFC
**	10	5	1	9	3		WCIU
3	90	74	34	59	31	18	WFLD
11	348	230	173	245	166	119	WGN
24	704	538	385	446	336	310	WLS
16	469	454	229	206	105	140	WMAQ
1	18	14	9	7	7		WSNS
4	129	100	45	79	40	6	WTTW
70	2269	1762	1072	1364	874	716	HUT/PUT/TOT.*
7	51	54	56	64	66	72	

TIME PERIOD

For explanation of symbols, see page 3.
For RSE explanations, see page 2.

FEBRUARY 1982

Source: A. C. Nielsen Company

priate tables and formulas to make such reach estimates once the number of GRPs is known.

Gross Rating Points in Other Media

In recent years, planners have extended the GRP concept to other media such as magazines, newspapers, and outdoor. In magazines, for example, Gross Rating Points equal the percent of market coverage of a target audience times the number of ad insertions. An example would be as follows:

McCall's target reach of paper napkin users	=	22.2%
Number of ads to be placed in *McCall's*	=	× 5
Gross Rating Points		111

Another way of using Gross Rating Points for magazines (or newspapers) is to add the target coverage for one insertion in a number of magazines as shown below:

Target coverage for *McCall's*	=	22.5%
Target coverage for *Good Housekeeping*	=	20.6
Target coverage for *Time*	=	14.2
Target coverage for *Woman's Day*	=	22.5
Gross Rating Points	=	79.8, rounded to 80 GRPs

One last way to calculate GRPs is to multiply reach times frequency for a given time period.

In January 1973, the Outdoor Advertising Association of America adopted as its basic unit of sale the term "100 Gross Rating Points daily." This basic standardized unit of poster sales is the number of poster panels required in each market to produce a daily effective circulation equal to the population of the market. Other units of sale would be expressed as fractions of the basic unit: 75 Gross Rating Points daily, 50 Gross Rating Points daily, and 25 Gross Rating Points daily. This change in no way alters the 30-day period of sale, and measurement.

Gross Impressions

Gross impressions would be useful in a situation where a planner wants to know, for example, the total weight of four television programs that are being considered for commercials. The audiences of each program (for targets of women aged 18 to 49) are as shown:

Program A:	5,160,000
Program B:	6,990,000
Program C:	4,320,000
Program D:	6,180,000
Gross Impressions	22,650,000

Another use of broadcast gross impressions might occur when someone wants to know the weight of nine commercials that may be purchased on any one program. The gross impressions for nine commercials on Program A (above):

$$9 \times 5{,}160{,}000 = 46{,}440{,}000$$

The use of gross impressions for print media is much the same as it is for broadcast. The following example shows how total gross impressions would be calculated for three magazines with varying numbers of ads:

Magazine	No. of targets reached	No. of ads to be purchased		Gross Impressions
A	5,000,000	× 5	=	25,000,000
B	2,100,000	× 3	=	6,300,000
C	7,000,000	× 2	=	14,000,000
Total Gross Impressions				45,300,000

The number of impressions delivered by a media plan usually runs into the millions, and because the number is so large, it is called a boxcar figure. Its value, however, is debatable. Alone, gross impressions have limited meaning. But if they can be related to some measure of campaign effectiveness such as sales volume, brand awareness levels, or competitive media plan effectiveness, they can be of more value.

How Gross Impressions Are Used in Planning

Gross impressions are useful in comparing the weight given to geographic areas or demographic segments of a market. For example, if the planner wants to be sure that a given media plan reaches a number of different geographic areas in the correct proportions, the gross impressions could be added for each vehicle in the plan and then the proportions of each compared with a weighted goal. Table 2–16 gives an example of how this works. This table indicates that the gross impression distribution of the vehicles selected comes fairly close to the goals set for the plan. It may not

TABLE 2–16. Distribution of Gross Impressions in Media Plan for Brand X

County size	Gross Impressions Delivered (thousands)				Target (%)	Goal set for plan (%)
	Vehicle 1	Vehicle 2	Vehicle 2	Total		
A	308,582	246,972	471,342	1,026,896	51.0	47.0
B	276,980	151,370	471,342	582,331	24.1	26.7
C	187,752	72,764	78,798	339,312	17.3	15.5
D	156,150	60,016	18,796	234,962	7.6	10.8
					100.0	100.0

be worth extra effort to make the gross impression totals come any closer to the stated goals.

Another impression analysis could have been made for targets by age, sex, income, or any other demographic segment desired.

Measures of Cost Efficiency

One of the principles of media planning stated earlier was that media should be selected on their ability to reach the largest audience of prospects at the lowest unit cost. Matching markets with media helps accomplish one part of this principle. The search for media with large audiences of prospects rather than large total audiences recognizes that media costs are too high to permit advertising to those individuals who are not likely to buy the product.

But the other portion of the principle is equally important. This requires that media be selected that reach the largest number of prospects at the most efficient cost. Cost efficiency simply means that audience size must be related to media costs.

Cost-Per-Thousand

Rather than compute a single unit cost, the advertising industry prefers to compute a cost-per-thousand. These may be computed for a printed page or broadcast time, and the audience base may be either circulation, homes reached, readers, or number of audience members of any kind of demographic classification.

Cost-per-thousand is a comparative device. It enables the planner to compare one medium or media vehicle with another to find those that are the most efficient, and it may be used for either intramedia or intermedia comparisons.

Shown below are various formulas that may be used for making comparisons on the basis of cost-per-thousand (abbreviated as CPM):

1. *For print media (when audience data are not available)*

$$\text{CPM} = \frac{\text{Cost of 1 page (black-and-white)} \times 1000}{\text{Circulation}}$$

Since many print media do not have audience research data, this formula is often used. But it tells nothing about the audience.

2. *For print media (when audience data are available)*

$$\text{CPM} = \frac{\text{Cost of 1 page (black-and-white)} \times 1000}{\text{Number of prospects reached}}$$

3. *For broadcast media (based on homes reached by a given program or time period)*

$$CPM = \frac{\text{Cost of 1 unit of time} \times 1000}{\text{Number of homes reached by a given program or time period}}$$

4. *For broadcast media (when audience data are available)*

$$CPM = \frac{\text{Cost of 1 unit of time} \times 1000}{\text{Number of prospects reached by a given program or time period}}$$

5. *For newspapers (when cost of ad is known)*

$$CPM = \frac{\text{Cost of ad} \times 1000}{\text{Circulation}}$$

6. *For newspapers where only circulation is the base, and the agate line rate is used to establish the milline rate*

$$\text{Milline rate} = \frac{\text{Cost of 1 agate line} \times 1 \text{ million}}{\text{Total circulation}}$$

The procedure for using any of the above formulas is to compare media on the basis of the two variables: audience and cost. The lowest cost-per-thousand medium is the most efficient, other things being equal. It is obvious that wherever precise demographic classifications of the audiences are available, that data should be used in the denominator of the formula. Generally, the medium (or media) with the lowest cost-per-thousand are selected, but not always. Whenever a very special kind of target audience is required, and there are few or no media which reach them exclusively, then the cost-per-thousand comparisons may be ignored. In the latter situation, media selections are based on the principle of reaching the largest number of targets, regardless of cost.

For example, there are times when individuals with very high incomes (over $100,000 annually) are target audiences. A few media vehicles reach a small proportion of these audiences, but even if many such vehicles were used, the total number of persons reached might be relatively small. On the other hand, a very large number of these persons might be reached with mass media such as a network television program or a national magazine. It is obvious that either of these two media would also include a large amount of waste, so that when cost-per-thousand are computed, they will seem unduly high. Yet the waste and the high cost-per-thousand might have to be ignored in order to maximize the size of target audiences reached.

Mass produced and consumed products, such as cigarettes, breakfast cereals, and automobiles, usually have target audiences for whom media are selected primarily on a cost-per-thousand basis. Specialized products such as yachts, private airplanes, and classical phonograph records have specialized target audiences that may require that less attention be paid to cost efficiencies and more to audience sizes.

Cost Per Rating Point

Another method of comparing the cost efficiency of vehicles is that of the *cost per rating point* (CPRP). Essentially, a CPRP is a method of comparing alternative broadcast vehicles; relating cost to a rating rather than to an audience number such as in a cost-per-thousand comparison. Both are measurements of relative value, but each uses a different base. The formula for calculating CPRP is as follows:

$$\text{Cost per rating point} = \frac{\text{Cost of a commercial}}{\text{Rating}}$$

If the cost of a primetime spot commercial was $1,000 and the rating for that spot was 10, then the CPRP would be $100.

How does a CPRP compare with a CPM for the same station and commercial? The following shows the differences:

CPRP	CPM
Cost of 30-second commercial: $110	Cost of 30-second commercial: $110
Metro rating, 2:00 pm: 8	No. H.H. delivered, 2:00 pm: 77,000
$110 ÷ 8 = $13.75	$110 × 1000 ÷ 77,000 = $1.43

Is there any preference for using one over the other? Generally, cost-per-thousand is most often used to compare any vehicle efficiency, while CPRP is a tool most often used for quick cost comparisons in broadcast planning.

QUESTIONS FOR DISCUSSION

1. An advertiser is considering using the top newspaper in a given market, but finds that it only has 40 percent household coverage. Why might he conclude that 40 percent is not enough?
2. A planner finds that a television program has 98 percent coverage nationally. Can the planner assume that because the program has a large coverage, it will also have a large audience? Briefly explain.
3. A planner intends to buy 100 Gross Rating Points a week in a given market. Why do 100 Gross Rating Points not equal 100 percent reach in that market?
4. If a planner is considering the use of a magazine that reaches 65 percent of a target market, and intends to buy only one ad, how many Gross Rating Points should be planned for?
5. What, precisely, is the meaning of the following? "We will have a 75 percent coverage in a spot television buy, if we buy the top 60 markets in the United States."

6. What is the relationship between GRPs and Gross Impressions?
7. Why are television ratings not an accurate measurement of the audience size for commercials broadcast within a program?
8. Is it proper to talk about the four-week reach of *Reader's Digest*? Briefly explain.
9. Of what value is it to know the readers per copy of a magazine?
10. Briefly explain why HUT figures for a given time period (such as a Monday evening in February) do not change very much from year to year.
11. Many newspaper columnists who are television critics tend to disparage broadcast ratings with a statement such as: "Well, no one ever called me to ask which program I was watching." Is this statement valid? Briefly explain.
12. In comparing alternative television program ratings, when is the most appropriate time to use share calculations for comparison?
13. What is the value of having circulation audited by the ABC?

SELECTED READINGS

Bogart, Leo, "Isn't It Time to Discard the Audience Concept?" *Journal of Marketing,* January 1966, pp. 47–54.

Broadcast Rating Council, *Maintaining Ratings Confidence and Credibility,* July 1972.

Brooks, Hugh L., "B&W: Still Too Many Unknowns in Magazine Audience Research," *Advertising Age,* July 26, 1976.

Darmon, Rene Y., "Determinants of TV Viewing," *Journal of Advertising Research,* December 1976, pp. 17–20.

Edelstein, Art; Samuels, Gabe; and Tommaney, James J., "Audience Research Debate: Who's Got the Answer?" *Media Decisions,* May 1978, pp. 72–75.

Ephron, Erwin, "Good Media Plans Grow Out of Great Research," *Media Decisions,* October 1970, p. 40.

Ephron, Erwin, "Confused? Six Commonly Held Beliefs About Media Planning That Are Not So," *Media Decisions,* August 1972, pp. 48–102.

Faber, Neil, "Efficiency Is Not Really That Unless Based on Target Demographics," *Media Decisions,* October 1978, p. 84.

Gerhold, Paul, "Seven Fallacies in Audience Measurements," in *Papers from the American Association of Advertising Agencies Regional Conventions,* 1960, pp. 15–22.

Greene, Jerome, "Personal Media Probabilities," *Journal of Advertising Research,* October 1970, pp. 12–18.

Hope, John, "Gross Rating Points Become Official for Outdoor Showings," *Media Decisions,* February 1973, p. 82.

Keller, Paul, "Patterns of Media Audience Accumulation," *Journal of Marketing,* January 1966, pp. 32–37.

Lucas, Darrell, "How Valid Are Media Measures?" *Media/Scope,* January 1960, pp 40–43.

Maneloveg, Herbert, "Media Research Future: Is There Any?" in *Advertising Age,* July 15, 1974, p. 23.

Media Decisions, "Media Research: Where It Stands Today," January 1977, pp. 55–59.

Media Decisions, "Rating Points for Newspapers," April 1971, pp. 44–47.

Media Decisions, "What Is Best for Buying—CPGRP or CPM?" February 1973, pp. 48–49.

Papazian, Ed, "Some Questions About TV Ratings," *Media Decisions,* September 1977, pp. 14–16.

Papazian, Edward, "Setting Priorities," *Media Decisions,* December 1973, pp. 16–18.

Rutens, W. S., "A Guide to TV Ratings," *Journal of Advertising Research,* February 1978, pp. 11–18.

Samuels, Gabe, "A New Proposal for Judging the Goodness of the Data," *Media Decisions,* September 1978, p. 88.

Shiffman, Phil, "A Research Quandary: Problems of TV Audience Measurement Through Nielsen," *Media Decisions,* August 1978.

Shocker, Alan D., "Limitations of Incremental Research in Media Selection," *Journal of Marketing Research,* February 1970, pp. 101–3.

Simmons, W. R., "We Can Believe *Most* of the Numbers *Most* of the Time," *Media/Scope,* September 1967, pp. 46–49.

Smith, Stewart, "Criteria for Media Comparisons: A Critique," *Journal of Marketing Research,* November 1965, pp. 364–69.

Stanton, Frank, "A State of the Art Appraisal of Advertising Research Measurements," *Perspectives in Advertising Management,* April 1969, Association of National Advertisers, pp. 237–45.

Surmanek, Jim, *Media Planning: A Quick & Easy Guide,* Chicago, Ill.: Crain Books, 1980.

Surmanek, Jim, "Coming to Terms with New Media Jargon," *Marketing Communications,* May 1981, p. 6.

Weinblatt, Ira, "Too Much Research?" *Media Decisions,* May 1976, p. 74.

Yergin, Jim, "TV Meters vs. Diaries," *Media Decisions,* December 1978, pp. 122–24.

3

Reach and Frequency

The preceding chapter introduced the concept of audience accumulation along with other measurements. This chapter amplifies the subject of accumulation in terms of reach and frequency, two of the most important considerations in planning media. Reach and frequency are parts of strategy planning and can be manipulated to attain certain marketing and media objectives. Generally, when broad message dispersion patterns are needed, then high levels of reach will be planned. But when a great deal of repetition is needed, then high frequency levels will be planned. Sometimes planning will have to attain both high reach and high frequency.

What is Reach? (in Broadcast Media)

Reach is a form of audience accumulation. It is a measure of how many different households or audience members were exposed at least one time to one or more media vehicles over a period of time (usually four weeks). Reach may be expressed as a raw number, or as a percentage of some universe. (A *universe* is a particular demographic group, such as women aged 18 to 49 or all employed persons.)

Reach differs from Gross Rating Points in that the latter is a duplicated figure, whereas reach is not. The following example illustrates the difference:

A weekly television program has an average weekly rating of 25. Therefore its four-week Gross Rating Points are 100 (25 x 4 = 100). The same television program may have a four-week reach of 65 percent (or 65). Since reach is unduplicated, the statistic will be smaller than the Gross Rating Points. To find this reach, the audience of the television program would have to be measured.

The reason that audience members are counted only once in a reach measurement lies in the history of media research. When early planners were trying to decide what kind of measurement ought to be used to count the size of a vehicle's audience, some felt that an audience member would have to be exposed about three times to a vehicle before ads within that vehicle would have any effect. Other planners disagreed, saying that it could not be known how many exposures would be required. Planners decided to compromise and to count one exposure to a vehicle as evidence of reach, since whether or not the ad was seen, there was a large difference between being exposed and not being exposed. To be exposed at least once meant that audiences then had an opportunity to see ads within the vehicle. There obviously would be no opportunity to see ads if there were no exposure.

Another historical reason for the development of reach concerned the invention of a statistic for radio and television that would parallel the audience reach of a monthly magazine. Planners realized it would be unfair to compare a one-week broadcast rating with the reach of a monthly issue of a magazine. Obviously the magazine reach would be higher. But by using a four-week reach for broadcast media, the planner now had a statistic that was fairly comparable to that of a monthly magazine in terms of audience size.

Table 3–1 illustrates the measurement of reach, using a sample of 10 persons. The sample size for measuring reach is actually much larger, but 10 was used to simplify the concept. While four weeks is the usual measuring period, reach can be measured for almost any period of time. Four weeks happens to have become a standard measuring unit, easily conforming to a monthly accounting period.

Table 3–1 is interpreted this way. Persons 3, 5, 8, and 9 saw the

TABLE 3–1. An Example of a Four-Week Reach Measurement for Program X

Person	Week 1	Week 2	Week 3	Week 4
1	—	—	—	—
2	—	—	—	—
3	⊗	×	—	×
4	—	—	—	—
5	⊗	—	×	—
6	—	—	⊗	×
7	—	⊗	×	—
8	⊗	—	—	—
9	⊗	×	—	×
10	—	—	—	⊗
Ratings each week:	40	30	30	40

For a weekly evening program: × = Viewed the program
⊗ = Counted in reach measurement

program in Week 1, so the one-week reach is four, and the rating is 40 or four out of ten. Because Person 7 was the only new viewer in Week 2, the two-week reach is five. Again in Week 3 only one new viewer, Person 6, was added, making a three-week reach of six; and the same applies to Week 4, when Person 10 was added, bringing the four-week reach to seven. Program X, then, had a reach of seven (out of ten) or a 70 percent reach. Note that Persons 3, 5, 6, and 9 viewed the program more than once in the four-week period, but they were counted only once for the purpose of calculating reach. Also note that the first week of viewing is unduplicated, so it is correct to speak of a one-week reach, although current usage refers to this first-week measurement as either a rating or an audience size statistic.

Kinds of Reach

There are two different kinds of reach that a planner would like to know about in broadcast planning: (a) the four-week reach of an individual vehicle such as a television program, or (b) the combined reach of four or five television programs that would be used as a single package in an ad campaign.

No matter which the planner is interested in, the same principles apply: namely, that audience members are counted only once, no matter how many times they may see the vehicle within a four-week period. In situation (b) where four television programs are being considered for one campaign package, some audience members may be exposed three or four times to only one television program, while other audience members may be exposed to all four television programs a different number of times. But if they see any one of the four programs at least once, they are counted as having been reached in a four-week period.

Suppose, for example, that the reach of four programs was 35,000,000 men, aged 18 to 34. This means that if the planner places a commercial in each of the four television programs, it is estimated that 35,000,000 men, aged 18 to 34, will have an opportunity to see at least one of those four vehicles and, ideally, one of the four commercials within the vehicles. The word "ideally" is a reminder that reach is concerned only with vehicle exposure, not ad exposure. Other measurements can provide ad exposure, but they are not yet available on a syndicated basis.

Table 3–2 shows how the reach of four television programs is calculated. Eight people viewed one of the four programs at least once in a four-week period. A person is counted only once regardless of how many programs were viewed. Therefore Person 1, who watched both Programs A and B, is counted only once, as is Person 7, who watched all four programs. The combined reach of the four programs is eight or 80 percent. Each of the programs also had a reach of its own for the four weeks.

TABLE 3–2. Calculating the Combined Reach of Four Television Programs

Person	Program A	Program B	Program C	Program D	Total 4 Programs
1	⊗	×	—	—	⊗
2	⊗	×	—	×	⊗
3	—	—	—	⊗	⊗
4	—	⊗	×	×	⊗
5	—	—	⊗	—	⊗
6	—	—	⊗	—	⊗
7	⊗	×	×	×	⊗
8	—	—	—	—	—
9	⊗	×	—	×	⊗
10	—	—	—	—	—
Reach	40%	50%	40%	50%	80%

× = Viewed program at least once
⊗ = Counted in reach measurement

The combined reach of all four programs is more properly known as the *net reach* of the four. Other terms that are sometimes used to describe the net reach of four television programs are "cumulative audience," or "audience accumulated by four television programs," or "net undupli-cated audience." Each is correct, but in popular usage people are more likely to say, "The reach of four programs is. . . ."

Relationship of Reach to Coverage

Students and others are sometimes confused about whether to use the term coverage or reach when referring to audience accumulation data. The terms can be interchangeable because coverage sometimes is synony-mous with reach. A better answer is that coverage and reach are quite different because coverage could mean *potential* to be exposed to the advertising, while reach refers to those people who *actually are* exposed. (See Chapter 2 for complete explanations of coverage for each advertising medium.)

Popular usage of these terms provides the basic answer. Coverage *usually* refers to potential audience for broadcast media and to actual delivered audience for print media. Reach *always* refers to the audience actually delivered by any advertising vehicle. Table 3–3 treats the dis-tinction in capsule form.

How Reach Builds Over Time

Reach for television programs accumulates, or builds, in a fairly con-sistent pattern over time. The first time a program is telecast, it accumulates the largest number of viewers. The second time it is telecast, most of the viewers are repeat viewers, although some new viewers are

TABLE 3–3. How to Use the Terms Reach and Coverage

Use Reach	to express a whole number or percentage of people actually exposed to a media vehicle or combination of vehicles.
	Example: Television program X reaches 9 million men aged 18 to 34 within a four-week period.
	Example: Magazine Y has a reach of 25 percent of men aged 18 to 34 with an average issue.
Use Coverage	to express the potential audience of a broadcast medium or the actual audience of a print medium.
	Example: A network television program may have a coverage of 95 percent of TV homes in the U.S.
	Example: Magazine Y has a 25 percent coverage of men aged 18 to 34. (Means same as reach.)

FIGURE 3–1. The Shape of a Typical Reach Curve

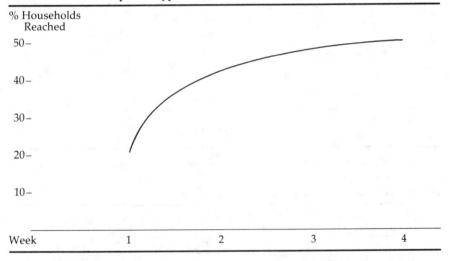

accumulated. The third and subsequent telecasts accumulate even fewer new viewers. If viewing over a four-week period were plotted on a graph, the curve drawn would look similar to that in Figure 3–1. If the same program were telecast over a long period of time, the curve eventually would flatten out and become almost horizontal, though it would never become perfectly horizontal because there would still be some persons, somewhere, tuning in the program for the first time.

An interesting aspect of the reach curve is that when the curve for any single program is compared with that for another program, the curves are similar in shape even though one curve may be higher or lower on a graph than another. Figure 3–2 shows reach accumulated for two television shows over a period of four consecutive telecasts.

FIGURE 3–2. Reach Curves of Two Television Programs

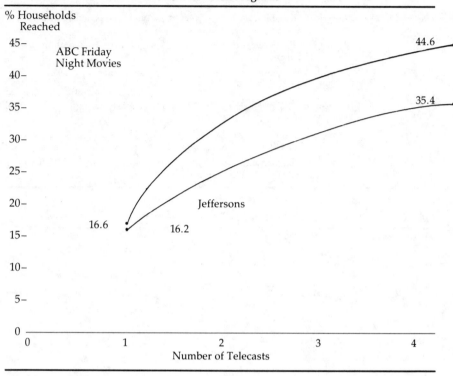

Source: A. C. Nielsen Company, Program Cumulative Audiences Report, April 1979

FIGURE 3–3. Net Reach Curves of Multiple Programs/Commercials for 26 Weeks

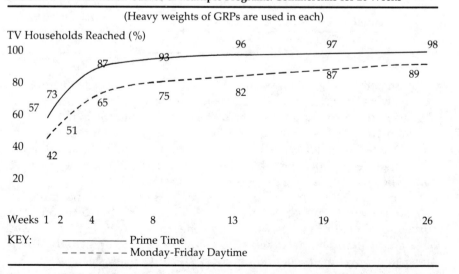

Source: A. C. Nielsen Company

**FIGURE 3–4. Net Reach Curves of Multiple Commercials
for 26 Weeks with Different Weight Levels**

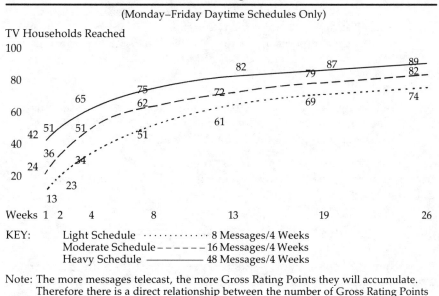

(Monday–Friday Daytime Schedules Only)

TV Households Reached

KEY: Light Schedule ············· 8 Messages/4 Weeks
Moderate Schedule – – – – – 16 Messages/4 Weeks
Heavy Schedule ——————— 48 Messages/4 Weeks

Note: The more messages telecast, the more Gross Rating Points they will accumulate.
Therefore there is a direct relationship between the number of Gross Rating Points
achieved in a four-week period, and the degree of frequency that develops.

Source: A. C. Nielsen Company

Study of the reach curves for multiple television programs or commercials over a period of 26 weeks shows basically similar curves with
only slight variations. Figures 3–3 and 3–4 plot reach curves for a period
of 26 weeks for different parts of the day (called *dayparts*) and for different
weight (GRP) levels.

What is Reach? (in Print Media)

An issue of a magazine or newspaper, not time as in broadcast media,
provides the basic measuring unit for reach measurement in print media.
One does not usually speak of the four-week reach of Magazine A,
although there are measurements that estimate audience accumulation
over time for an average issue of a magazine. Generally speaking,
monthly magazines have a longer issue life than weeklies and general
content magazines a longer life than news-oriented magazines.

Magazine reach can be expressed in a number of ways:

1. Target audience reach of one issue of a magazine. Example:
   the reach of the July 1 issue of *Newsweek* (also may be called
   the total audience of *Newsweek*).

2. Target audience reach of multiple issues of the same magazine. Example: the reach (or net unduplicated audience) of the July 1, July 8, July 15, July 22, and July 29 issues of *Newsweek*.
3. Target audience reach of single issues of different magazines within the same month. Example: the reach (or net unduplicated audience) of July issues of *McCall's, Ladies Home Journal, Reader's Digest,* and *TV Guide.*
4. The reach of single or multiple issues of different magazines occurring throughout the advertising campaign. Example: the reach of *Popular Mechanics* in June and August, *Field & Stream* in July and August, and *Sport* in June and July.

Since there are many qualities expressed in a reach measurement, it becomes important to know them all. Table 3–4 summarizes these qualities.

Frequency in Broadcast and Print Media

Frequency is a companion statistic to reach that tells the planner the average number of times that audience members were exposed to a broadcast program within a four-week period, or were exposed to issues of different print media. Reach is a measure of message dispersion, indicating how widely the message will be received in a target universe. Frequency is a measure of repetition, indicating to what extent audience members were exposed to the same vehicle or group of vehicles. Both reach and frequency are valuable decision tools because they give the planner different options for arranging message delivery in a media plan.

TABLE 3–4. The Meaning of Reach, Summarized

Reach is . . .
1. A measurement of audience accumulation
2. An unduplicated statistic
3. Measured, although it can sometimes be estimated
4. Measured for a single vehicle, or a group of different vehicles
5. Measured for subsequent issues of the same magazine, e.g., the seven-issue reach of *TV Guide* is . . .
6. Reported for a four-week period of television watching
7. Reported for almost any period of time in broadcast measurements
8. Reported by the issue in print media
9. Reported either as a raw number or as a percentage of some universe
10. Reported for households, or for individuals in a demographic category
11. Another term for coverage in print media
12. Measured on the basis of exposure to a vehicle or vehicles
13. Not measured on the basis of exposure to ads in vehicles
14. A measurement that tells the planner how many people had an opportunity to see ads in vehicles

Frequency is usually calculated from measurement data. The formula is the same for broadcast and print media:

$$\text{Frequency} = \frac{\text{GRPs or total duplicated audience}}{\text{Reach}}$$

Example in broadcast: Program X telecast once each week has an average rating of 20 for each week. It has a four-week reach of 43. The frequency is as follows:

$$\text{Frequency} = \frac{20 \times 4}{43} \text{ or } 1.9$$

Example in Print: *TV Guide* has a reach of 54 for six consecutive issues. Its one-issue reach is 29.5.

$$\text{Frequency} = \frac{29.5 \times 6}{54.0} \text{ or } 3.3$$

Frequency Distribution

Persons who use measurement data sometimes forget that frequency is an average and not an absolute number. It is subject, therefore, to the characteristics of all statistical averages. Averages, for example, are affected by extreme scores in a distribution. A few very high numbers may bring up the average of all other scores while a few very low ones may drag down the average. The only way to guard against being deceived by a frequency statistic is to look at a frequency distribution and see whether some segments of a sample are getting disproportionately more frequency than others.

Table 3–5 shows a sample divided into fixed quintiles and each group's reach and frequency. (*Fixed quintiles* means that the sample of audience members exposed was divided into five equal groups, each with 20 percent of the total number exposed.) The distribution of frequency is obviously unequal in Table 3–5. Some of the quintiles received much more frequency than others. This phenomenon is known as *skew*.

TABLE 3–5. Quintile Analysis of Tune-Ins for Program X

Divisions of sample	Reach (%)	Frequency	GRPs
Heaviest 20% viewing	17	11	187
Next 20%	17	6	103
Third 20%	17	5	85
Next 20%	17	3	51
Lightest 20%	17	1	17
TOTALS	85	5.2 avg.	443

Reach of entire sample: 85. Frequency of entire sample: 5.2. Gross rating points: 443.

FIGURE 3–5. Frequency Distribution for Program X

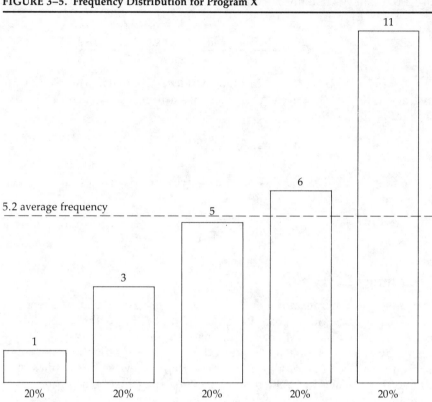

Note: The average number of times each group tuned in to Program X is shown at the top of each column.

Figure 3–5 dramatizes the skew by showing the frequency distribution in graphic form. While Program X had a 5.2 average frequency in Figure 3–5, some segments were receiving more frequency than others. The average frequency of 5.2 does not indicate the disparity. The planner may be deceived by the average frequency level of Program X, thinking that every home in the sample tuned to the program 5.2 times during a four-week period. The illustration shows otherwise. Frequency distributions with a large skew are called *unbalanced*.

Frequency distributions can be arranged according to quintiles, but they can also be arranged according to single increments of exposure, giving the planner a more detailed picture of exposure. Table 3–6 shows a frequency distribution of exposure for all media in a given plan. Subtracting the number reached from the Gross Impressions shows that 8,227,000 of the universe of 29,356,000 did not see any of the vehicles used. Some 3,125,000 were exposed only once out of the 12 opportunities

TABLE 3–6. Frequency Distribution of a Media Plan

		Frequency of Exposure	Number Exposed (thousands)
		0	8,227
		1	3,125
		2	2,269
		3	3,632
Reach	71.97	4	5,235
Frequency	4.01	5	2,474
Gross Impressions	84,749	6	1,201
Number Reached	21,129	7	1,462
Universe	29,356	8	771
		9	622
		10	135
		11	104
		12	98
			21,129 = 71.97%

TABLE 3–7. Four-Week Reaches and Frequencies of Two Media Plans

Frequency of Exposure	Plan A	Plan B
1	24%	20%
2	16	15
3	9	12
4–5	6	13
6–8	5	10
9–12	5	4
13+	5	1
Average Frequency	4	3.6
Total Reach	70	75
Reach at 3+ Frequency	30	40

for exposure, and 2,269,000 were exposed to any two out of the 12 exposures. The number exposed at any frequency is unduplicated, meaning that these people are counted only once. A person receiving 12 exposures would not be counted at any other frequency level.

Frequency distributions therefore provide planners with a method of determining the pattern of repetition that the plan provides. Alternative plans may provide more or fewer repetition patterns. More important, however, is that the distribution will show whether repetition is spread widely, or only among a very few prospects.

The example in Table 3–7 shows how a frequency distribution can help a media planner decide among alternative plans. Plan A has a 4.0 frequency and Plan B, a 3.6. If frequency is important, then Plan A would seem to be the better plan.

Upon studying a frequency distribution such as the one in Table 3–7, however, the planner learns something that could change the decision:

Plan A delivers more audience members at the 1 and 2 exposure level. But for 3–4–5–6–7–8 exposures, Plan B is superior. Plan B reaches more persons than does Plan A at the three or more exposure level. If the advertising effort requires that people receive high levels of exposures (higher levels of frequency), then Plan B is the obvious choice. But only a frequency distribution made it possible for the planner to see why B was better than A.

The Relationship of Reach to Frequency

It is necessary to understand that reach and frequency occur at the same time, but at different rates and in an inverse relationship. Within a given number of Gross Rating Points, as one goes up, the other goes down. Let us first look at the mathematics to understand how these companion terms relate to each other:

$$\text{Reach} \times \text{Frequency} = \text{Gross Rating Points}$$

An advertising schedule composed of a 50 reach with a 2.0 frequency yields 100 GRPs. If these same 100 GRPs were obtained in a different mixture of media, the reach might increase, but the frequency would decline. Conversely, a 100 GRP schedule in still other media mixtures might produce higher frequency, but less reach.

Seymour Banks, formerly vice president of Leo Burnett Company, explained the dynamics of reach and frequency relative to rating size and number of telecasts, as follows:

> . . . Reach is not directly proportional to either ratings or the number of telecasts. Rather, as ratings increase or as the number of telecasts used increases, reach also rises but at a decreasing rate. This is more easily understood when we consider that the companion of reach is frequency. And when the rating or the number of telecasts increases, some of this increase goes towards boosting reach, while some of it contributes toward an increase in frequency.[1]

Up to a certain point, it is relatively easy to build reach. By selecting television programs of a different nature in which to place commercials, it is possible to reach different kinds of people. But there is a point of diminishing returns, where each attempt to build more reach by selecting more and different kinds of programs results in reaching the same persons over and over again, with an increase in frequency rather than in reach. Some homes may never tune in their television sets over an entire month, so they are impossible to reach with TV in that month. Reach will

---

[1]Banks, Seymour, "How to Estimate Reach and Frequency," Leo Burnett Company, 1960, p. 5.

increase as ratings and number of telecasts increase, but it will begin to decline in rate (not total) over time.

The point of diminishing returns mentioned in the last paragraph occurs at about 70 percent and varies somewhat because some target audiences are easier or more difficult to reach. Then frequency begins to rise much faster than reach as additional media vehicles are added to the schedule. The problem can be seen in the following illustration.

Suppose that a media planner has devised a plan requiring the attainment of an 80 percent reach level. The planner selects a number of media vehicles, with a net reach of 75 percent. The question now facing the planner is how to reach the remaining 5 percent. When another vehicle is added to the list, reach may go up perhaps 1 percent, while frequency may go up a great deal. So it may take a large number of additional vehicles to reach the total of 80 percent. Meanwhile, as vehicles are added, frequency rises very fast because every new vehicle adds only a miniscule amount to reach and a large amount to frequency.

Programs That Develop Reach or Frequency

Programs that develop reach are those whose contents tend to change during a given telecast or from week to week. As the contents change, so do audience types. When movies are broadcast, with a drama one week and a comedy the next, two different audiences are likely to develop (with some overlap, of course). Movies, therefore, tend to develop more reach than frequency. But a soap opera broadcast five days a week, or 20 times a month, will tend to draw a relatively smaller audience but one with greater frequency of viewing. An increase in the number of messages delivered also increases the potential for higher frequency.

Table 3–8 indicates that the drama had a much larger reach than did the soap opera, but the soap opera had a much larger frequency than did the drama. Part of the reason for the larger frequency was the frequency of telecasts. The more often a program is broadcast, the more likely it is that it will have a higher frequency.

TABLE 3–8. Comparison of Frequencies for Two Different Kinds of Programs

	Daytime soap opera broadcast 20 times a month	Nighttime drama, broadcast once a week
Total audience rating per telecast	9.7	19.4
Four-week reach	25.4	40.0
Frequency	7.6	1.9
	$\dfrac{9.7 \times 20^*}{25.4} = 7.6$	$\dfrac{19.4 \times 4}{40.0} = 1.9$

*The 9.7 rating is the average rating for a program broadcast 5 times each week (from Monday to Friday) and 4 weeks a month, or 20 telecasts.

FIGURE 3–6. Difference Between Roadblock and Scatter to Build Reach

	Roadblock Indexed to Scatter					
Reach %	114	111	104	104	101	101

Frequency:						
Roadblock	1.0	1.5	2.0	2.5	3.0	3.5
Scatter	1.2	1.7	2.1	2.6	3.0	3.5
GRPs	50	100	150	200	250	300

Source: A. C. Nielsen Company (Prime time, Nov.–Dec. 1977)

Roadblock vs. Scatter Plan

Planning media to build reach can be accomplished in the ways just discussed, but there are two other ways: (a) purchasing commercials on all three networks during the same half hour, called a *roadblock*, or (b) buying a *scatter plan* that places commercials within a number of different program types and time periods, thus bringing in new audience members. Figure 3–6 shows the differences. The chart shows that when the number of GRPs is low, the roadblock produces more reach. When the number of GRPs is high, either technique will produce about the same reach.

Chapter 6 will discuss how to use reach and frequency in planning.

QUESTIONS FOR DISCUSSION

1. If a planner wanted to build reach quickly using magazines alone, which of the three methods of building reach should be used?
2. Which kinds of magazines tend to develop large reach, and which develop large frequency?
3. Why can't one add the ratings for each week in a four-week period to find that program's four-week reach?

4. Which kinds of television programs tend to develop more reach than frequency?
5. Which kinds of television programs tend to develop more frequency than reach?
6. Why is it likely that a television program with a high initial rating (in Week 1) will probably also have a high four-week reach?
7. Why is *unbalanced frequency* possibly a poor media strategy?
8. Briefly explain: Is a rating for one telecast of a television program equivalent to a one-telecast reach?
9. If a television program were measured for 52 weeks (consecutively) what would the shape of the reach curve for that program probably look like?
10. Briefly explain: Of what value is a frequency distribution analysis of a television program?

SELECTED READINGS

Aaker, David A., and Brown, Phillip K., "Evaluating Vehicle Source Effects," *Journal of Advertising Research*, August 1972, pp. 11–16.

Agostini, J. M., "How to Estimate Unduplicated Audiences," *Journal of Advertising Research*, March 1961, pp. 11–14.

Barz, Edward, "A Fresh Look at Cumulative Audiences," *Advertising Research Foundation, 15th Conference Proceedings*, 1969, pp. 8–12.

Bass, K. M.; Pessemier, E. A.; and Tigert, D. J., "A Taxonomy of Magazine Readership Applied to Problems in Marketing Strategy and Media Selection," *Journal of Business*, July 1969, pp. 337–63.

Ephron, Erwin, "Are the People You Want Watching?" *Media/Scope*, October 1967, p. 46.

Forman, Stan, "A Theory of Audience Accumulation," *Journal of Advertising Research*, February 1976, pp. 21–25.

Friedman, Lawrence, "Calculating TV Reach and Frequency," *Journal of Advertising Research*, August 1971, pp. 21–26.

Headen, R. S.; Klompmaker, J. E.; and Teel, J. E., "Increasing the Informational Content of Reach and Frequency Estimates," *Journal of Advertising*, January 1976, pp. 18–21.

Joyce, Timothy, "A Better Way to Measure Magazine Audiences," Axiom Marketing Research Bureau, Inc., 1973.

Kaatz, Ronald B., "Improving Agostini's Formula for Net Audiences," *Journal of Advertising Research*, September 1963, pp. 43–44.

Kamin, Howard, "Advertising Reach and Frequency," *Journal of Advertising Research*, February 1978, pp. 21–25.

Keshin, Mort, "Ins and Outs of TV Audience Cume," *Media/Scope*, May 1968, p. 11.

Mayer, Martin, "A Writer Looks at TV Ratings," *Journal of Advertising Research*, October 1972, pp. 3–10.

Media/Scope, "Cox's Case for Cume," September 1968, pp. 99–140.

Mills, Martin, "How to Estimate Network TV Audiences," *Media/Scope*, March 1966, pp. 90–93.

Lucas, Darrell B., "Can Total Magazine Audience Be Ignored?" *Media/Scope*, November 1964, pp. 64–72.

Marketmath, Inc., "Advertising Reach and Frequency in Magazines," *Reader's Digest*, 1967.

Papazian, Edward, "The Sixth Quintile," *Media Decisions*, September 1973, pp. 12–16.

Towers, Irwin M.; Goodman, Leo A.; and Zeisel, Hans, "What Could Nonexposure Tell the TV Advertiser?" *Journal of Marketing*, July 1963, pp. 52–56.

Twyman, W. A., "A Technique for Measuring Program vs. Commercial Audiences — New Findings from British Television," *Advertising Research Foundation, 15th Annual Conference Proceedings*, 1969, pp. 32–38.

4
Marketing Strategy and Media Planning

There are many ways to start the media planning process, but the best way is by analyzing the situation of a brand in the marketplace. The reason for making such an analysis is to learn how successful a brand has been against its competition, with the objectives of finding "opportunity" areas to exploit or "problem" areas to correct. Ultimately, the findings of a situation analysis should lead to the establishment of marketing objectives and strategies, which in turn lead to the establishment of media objectives and strategies. Although the responsibility for making a marketing situation analysis usually does not rest with a media planner, someone from the agency media department, such as a media researcher, may be involved to some extent in the research activities.

What a Media Planner Needs to Know

To develop a successful media plan, the planner must know as much as possible about the marketing background of the brand being advertised. This background includes product quality, product use, pricing, distribution, packaging, sales promotion, personal selling activities, public relations, and advertising. From a practical standpoint, planners may not need to know every detail, but they should know those pieces of information that contribute to the best planning. Those elements in a marketing situation analysis that most interest a planner are:

History of the market. This deals with sales of all brands in the market, including the brand for which planning is to be done. The analysis includes geographic sales distribution, market size in dollars/units, market shares, seasonal effects, and price effects. The goal is to find out where brands are now in terms of share of market and how they got there. An important item, for example, might be pricing history. What happened to prices for various brands over the years, and how did these price manipulations affect sales? Another concern might be an analysis of cost history and profit related to sales, both for the brand under consideration and for competitors' brands, if known.

Distribution channels. The objective here is to learn how a brand and its competitors distribute products. This includes the following information about each distribution channel: shelf-facings, inventories held, out-of-stock situations, methods of selling, display and advertising allowances, and how and why promotions are used. Problems of selling are sometimes caused by poor distribution, not advertising. Distribution information often affects media strategy because it may help the planner decide where to advertise.

The consumer of the product. This is a profile of who uses the generic product type by personal demographics such as age, sex, income, and occupation, as well as by geographic location. Psychographics—lifestyles and attitudes—should also be included. A consumer profile of those who buy a specific brand versus those who buy competing products is important. Buying habits should also be analyzed in terms of when products are purchased; in which kind of retail outlets; and which sizes, models, and colors are purchased most. How and when consumers use these products also ought to be known. Finally, it would be helpful to know about the *buyer*, the *user*, and the *persons who motivate buyers/users*. All of this information helps the media planner select targets for media.

The product. A history of the product and how it was developed forms this section of the analysis. When and why product changes were made and the effects of such changes for each competitive brand could be important. Consumer perceptions of the values of various brands are also important background information for the media planner.

Advertising and media analysis. An analysis of media expenditures for competing brands would probably be the most important information that a media planner would like to know. This would include media classes used, names of individual vehicles, number of ads used, when advertising ran, and dollar and percentage allocation to each medium and market.

The Marketing Strategy Plan

Once the facts about a marketing situation have been gathered, the data then should be analyzed to learn where problems and opportunities lie. An *opportunity* may be defined as a marketing activity which, if adopted, may result in an advantage over the competitor. An example of an opportunity might be a situation where a manufacturer has improved a brand so that it is superior to competing brands, but this advantage may be known by only 10 percent of the potential consumers. Increased sales may result if the manufacturer is able to communicate this advantage to 50 percent or more of potential consumers.

Problem areas, on the other hand, are those that demand some action to correct the situation. A problem area might be one where a brand does not have a competitive advantage or one where a brand has been steadily losing its share of market for any number of reasons. Finding the causes for the decline is a first step toward changing the situation. Most situation analyses turn up more problem areas than opportunities, but the delineation of each is a necessary preliminary step to marketing and media planning.

Marketing strategy planning consists of setting marketing objectives that will solve the major problems and take advantage of the opportunities. In effect, a *marketing strategy plan* is a blueprint for action geared to selling the product, with the ultimate goal of gaining an advantage over a competitor who, in a sense, is the enemy.

Perhaps the weakest part of many advertising campaigns is the lack of a sound selling strategy. Arthur Tatham, formerly chairman of the board of Tatham-Laird & Kudner advertising agency, once said, "Brilliant copy and art will never make a weak selling strategy succeed. But . . . once there is a sound selling strategy, then good copy and art will multiply its effectiveness." Tatham's statement also applies to media selection and use. Without a sound selling strategy, media planning may represent wasted effort. Media planning does not exist as an activity unrelated to marketing; it is a service function of marketing and selling. The fact that media are often selected and used without being based on a sound selling strategy demonstrates poor logic and inefficient modes of operation. Selling strategy is the heart of a marketing strategy plan.

In summary, the major goals in a marketing strategy plan are:

1. setting objectives that will help solve existing problems and take advantage of opportunity and problem areas
2. deciding how the product should be sold
3. determining to whom the main selling effort should be directed
4. determining what role various elements of the marketing mix should play in the sale of a brand

5. determining what adjustments should be made in package shapes or sizes

6. determining how much should be spent.

Most often, the marketing strategy plan is written by someone other than the media planner. Yet even though the latter may not be directly involved in drawing up the plan, there are a number of reasons why the marketing strategy plan is a significant document to media planners.

The foremost reason is that the marketing strategy plan serves as a unifying and organizing force for all activity within an agency on a given brand's marketing and advertising plans. This means that the market researchers, account executives, and creative people, as well as media planners, are all working from a single source of information. Thus, the plan serves to coordinate all efforts toward the same goals. Large advertising agencies often have so many persons working on so many different accounts that communication becomes difficult. The media planner, especially, needs to know that his or her decisions will be directed toward the same objectives as those of others on the agency team.

Once the plan has been written, it becomes easier to visualize the whole scheme of operations for a given brand. All proposed plans can be evaluated for their logic and completeness to avoid information gaps or contradictions. If a marketing plan exists only in someone's mind or in bits or scraps of memoranda, then errors are hard to locate because no one has an overview of the entire operation.

Perhaps the key to the success of a marketing strategy plan is the degree to which all tactics are spelled out. Herbert Zeltner, marketing consultant, cautioned that many marketing strategy plans are "either glossed over in the rush of hammering together a marketing program, or merely slapped together as a collection of ponderous cliches." He noted:

> To be truly useful, the market strategy statement should not merely reflect some happy generalities about an increase in volume or share of market for the coming fiscal period.

> But establishing the requirement that a specific percent volume increase to be achieved—through the expenditure of a precise sensible sum of money—and that this increase can most realistically be expected through more aggressive development of certain stated territories or segments of the market . . . is the type of statement which gives a properly astute media planner the challenge he needs to create both a perspective and workable media recommendation.[1]

---

[1]Zeltner, Herbert, "Marketing Strategy Statement," *Media/Scope*, August 1964, p. 10.

The media planner needs specific direction, explicitly stated, in order to begin decision making. The media plan grows directly out of the marketing strategy whenever it requires that advertising be used. The various segments of the strategy statement, however, are not all equally significant to the media planner. Foremost in importance are the marketing objectives, the basic selling idea, sources of business, overall sales strategy, and spending strategy. Each of these will be discussed in more detail on the following pages. Figure 4–1 shows an outline of a basic strategy statement.

Marketing Objectives

The marketing goals that the company and agency agree upon may, if achieved, result in the solution of a marketing problem. Marketing goals are measurable in most cases and provide a means of determining whether the strategy employed has been effective. For the media planner, the objectives will undoubtedly affect the kinds of media selected and how media is used. In a sense, then, marketing objectives serve as controls for media planning.

Most marketing objectives relate directly to achieving share of market for a brand; others relate to communication objectives. Here is a sample of marketing objectives for different brands (taken from various strategy statements):

- To increase share in an expanding segment of the X market.
- To regain lost volume—increase sales a maximum of 5 percent and, in turn, shoot for a 14 percent share of market.
- To acquire a 20 percent share of market the first year after national introduction, 25 percent the second year, and 30 percent the third year.
- To introduce the product so that we have at least 5 percent share in each sales division.
- To increase share of market and increase the morale of the sales force in the face of many competitive new product introductions.
- To find and persuade new customers for our product.
- To maintain national coverage.
- To provide regional and local impact where two-thirds of sales are made.
- To increase the overall visibility of the product name against the potential customers and the trade across the country.

Whenever marketing objectives require advertising in specific geographical areas, then media must be selected that best reach those areas. Sometimes the objectives call for added promotional effort in a geo-

FIGURE 4–1. Outline for Basic Marketing Strategy Statement*

Advertiser _____ Brand/Product_____

I. *Major Strategy*

This should be the briefest possible statement of the major one or two strategies you are going to recommend for the planning period, with just enough statement of the problem to explain the strategy.

If you can write this section in one or two sentences or paragraphs, do so. If it takes you more than a single-spaced page, it is probably too long.

II. *Basic Objectives*

A. Short Term (applies to next fiscal 12 months, unless otherwise stated, e.g., six months):

1. Increase share of total market
2. Arrest decline in share
3. Develop added volume
4. Increase total market
5. Profit goal
6. Reduce losses

Translate objectives into approximate sales and/or profit goals.

B. Long Term (applies to any prescribed period beyond the next planning period):

1. Increase share of total market
2. Increase total market
3. Increase profits
4. Position goal, i.e., gain leadership
5. Develop and establish a brand or corporate image
6. Expand line of service or products

Translate objectives into approximate sales and/or profit goals.

III. *The Basic Selling Idea*

A one- or two-sentence statement of the key selling idea. This is the base from which the creative strategy evolves.

IV. *Presentation of the Basic Selling Idea*

This is the creative strategy in its briefest form.

V. *Use or Uses for which the Product Will Be Advertised*

A. Major
B. Minor

VI. *Sources of Business and Relative Importance of Each*

A. Consumer Sources–What are the characteristics of the people who are the best prospects?

1. Regional factors

2. City size
3. County size
4. Income groups
5. Age of housewife
6. Occupation of head of household
7. Family size
8. Seasonal
9. Sex–men, women, children
10. Who is principal purchaser?
B. Dealer Sources–What is relative importance of various types of outlets?
C. Competitive Sources–Important competitive brands or companies–national, regional, local.

VII. *Overall Sales Strategy*
A. Relative importance of price
1. To the consumer
2. To the trade
B. Relative importance of personal salesmanship
C. Relative importance of dealers
D. Relative importance of advertising
E. Relative importance of promotion
F. Relative importance of publicity

VIII. *Product Strategy*
A. The need for product improvement–Analysis of product superiorities and weaknesses compared to competitive products
B. The need for related products
C. The need for adding new sizes or deleting unprofitable sizes
D. The need for improving:
1. Packaging
2. Package design

IX. *Spending Strategy*
A. Is there a need for higher or lower margins? What effect will this have on price, quality, quantity of the product?
B. What is the proper amount to spend:
1. On introduction?
2. On re-introduction?
3. On on-going basis?
C. Is an extended payout plan indicated, and if so, what is the optimum time?

X. *Facts and Documentation*
The pertinent facts needed to define the problems and to document the strategies outlined in the strategy sections.

---

*Reprinted by permission of the Leo Burnett Company, Inc.

graphical region such as the West Coast, or the East Central part of the country. Other times, the objectives may call for a special advertising effort in a given market such as Los Angeles or Cincinnati. Such objectives may limit media choices because few media vehicles are available in some specified areas. The marketing objectives provide direction for the planner in selecting media, but it is up to the planner to find media that best *deliver* the target audience specified.

When marketing objectives call for increases in share of market with special effort directed only at prospects, the media planner may be called upon to increase the number of messages to known prospects. In such cases, media selection becomes secondary to methods of using media. One such method may be to increase the frequency of exposure of advertising messages to prospects.

Occasionally, objectives deal with some area other than market share; for example, the requirement may be "to increase the image of authority among adults." In this situation, it might be felt that adults, especially those aged 21 to 44, are good prospects, yet they are not buying the product. The marketing objective influences the selection of adult-appeal media, such as magazines and Sunday supplements, and perhaps the use of well-known, authoritative television announcers whose personality images are strong in the 21- to 44-year age group.

The Budget

Once the marketing objectives have been stated, it is necessary to know how much money will be required to attain them. It is not realistic to make a grandiose marketing plan and then find that the advertiser is unwilling or unable to provide sufficient funds to make the plan successful. (Budgeting and allocations to markets and media will be discussed in a later chapter.) At this point, the media planner may be called in to help estimate the costs of the marketing strategy plan even before the main portion of the media plan has been started. If enough money is not available to accomplish a given set of objectives, then the objectives may have to be reduced or revised.

Estimating the cost of a marketing plan usually involves two separate activities: estimating media costs and estimating production costs. Media costs may be ascertained by checking published reference books that show media rates or by phoning media representatives to obtain general costs. Production costs may be estimated either by arbitrarily allocating a given percentage of the total budget for that purpose or, if the advertising is relatively simple, by obtaining estimates on specific kinds of production pieces that are needed, such as engravings, art work, typography, videotape, or film. Generally, the media planner is responsible for estimating only the media cost portion of the marketing plan.

The main problem in estimating marketing costs is determining whether any given amount of money spent for advertising will accomplish a given set of objectives. Marketing and media planners most often rely on their experiences with other brands and products as a basis for making these estimates. But other factors also enter in. A new product introduction may require very heavy investments to get it off the ground. Competitors' advertising—where and how much—also may influence the marketing budget. Brands that have to defend their shares of market against the inroads of competitors, or those that aspire to increase market share, may have to spend heavily. Determining the exact amount is by no means a scientific matter. It is based mostly on experience, although there are mathematical models that "predict" the effect of various spending levels. Past experience may show, for example, that an advertiser increased its national share of market by three percentage points by spending $10,000,000. It could then be roughly estimated that it would cost $3,333,333 to raise the share one percentage point. This linear relationship of spending and share of market, however, is seldom witnessed in the real world.

Sometimes the planner recommends spending an amount of money beyond the means of the advertiser. In such cases, either the objectives have to be changed or the advertiser must realize that spending the available budget will not produce the results desired. Sometimes, no matter what sum is recommended, the advertiser has a preconceived notion of the maximum amount that can be profitably spent and will not entertain requests for larger amounts. It behooves the planner, therefore, to establish budget parameters *before* full media plans are devised.

Creative Strategy

A major part of the marketing strategy plan is an explanation of how the product will be sold or a statement of the basic selling idea. From that basic selling idea comes the creative strategy, possibly the single most important influence on the planner during the media selection process. Many times the creative strategy directs the planner in choosing one medium over another or in selecting a combination of media.

Where color is an integral part of the creative strategy, then magazines, direct mail, newspaper supplements, or color television may be required. Newspapers accepting rotogravure printed color inserts (called Hi-Fi or Spectacolor) offer additional alternatives to the media planner. Where the creative strategy calls for the use of cartoon characters, then either comic strips or television may be most appropriate. Again, direction is given to the selection process.

Where a strategy calls for demonstration, one might first think of television; yet it is possible to demonstrate the use of a product in print media through the use of sequential panels showing the various steps in the use of the product. Radio also is capable of demonstration through the use of words that play on the listener's imagination.

Sometimes the creative strategy may call for the use of an announcer or salesperson who can exude a feeling of warmth and sincerity. Either television or radio may be required here, since each excels at conveying emotional impact.

If the creative strategy calls for music, media choices may be limited to radio or television. An alternative is to record the music and advertising message on thin vinyl records and have them inserted into magazines. In this case, however, the creative strategy may have to give way to the budget, which may not tolerate the expense of recording and inserting the record.

Occasionally, creative strategy calls for large and dominating illustrations. This suggests billboards to the media planner, although direct mail or a two-page center spread in newspapers or magazines may be equally acceptable.

Some advertising messages may seem to have more impact on consumers in one medium than they do in another. It should be noted, however, that *impact* is a hazy concept. It is generally assumed to mean that advertising does something to audience members, such as make the message memorable, change attitudes toward the brand, impart significant bits of information, or perhaps serve as a motivating factor in buying. The assumption is not always valid, because there is often little proof that what is claimed to happen actually does. In any case, where creative strategies call for traditional media because of their perceived impact, the planner may find it difficult to break tradition.

So, the creative strategy is an integral part of media planning, perhaps the most important of all. The planner cannot start work without first knowing what is to be said and how it is to be presented to consumers. Only then can media alternatives begin to be considered.

Dealers and Distribution

A major factor in media decision making is distribution to dealers, as it only makes sense to limit advertising to areas where the product is distributed. To do otherwise is to waste effort and money. There are, of course, exceptions, such as when a manufacturer will advertise in an area where the product is not distributed in an effort to "force" distribution on the dealers in that area. Perhaps dealers have refused to handle a new brand because they feel they already have too many similar products on their shelves. Some grocery chains even practice a *one-for-one policy* in which they refuse to take on a new brand unless the manufacturer removes an existing brand from the shelves. By advertising in an area where a product is not yet distributed, the manufacturer hopes that the advertising will create such a demand for the product that the dealers and distributors will be forced to carry the brand. This strategy, however, might sometimes backfire, as consumers who seek the brand and cannot find it might be alienated as future consumers of the brand.

For most products, however, advertising is limited to areas where the product is distributed, and even then only to the markets that produce the most sales or have the greatest potential for sales.

Because dealers are important sources of business, the ability to select media that best communicate with dealers represents another aspect of the planner's job. Most frequently used is the trade press, but a planner may also choose to communicate with dealers through direct mail or trade shows and conventions.

In some cases, the major problem in selling a product is not advertising to consumers, but to dealers. Such a case was discussed by T. Norman Tveter, a marketing expert:

> The problem was to sell a top-quality model train to fathers through boy salesmen, or the sons of those fathers. A sales analysis by the media director, based on sales for the two previous years, was the basis for planning advertising and promotion. Only then did strong points as well as weak show up concerning such factors as availability and rate of sales.

> Using a state-by-state breakdown of two boy age groups . . . as measures of potential, the analysis showed that sales were radically out of line with market potential. Also a breakdown in dollars of shipments to various outlets—such as department stores, specialty chains, and premium distributors—showed that 50 cities accounted for 78 percent of the shipments. Seventeen better-producing cities alone accounted for 62 percent of the shipments, and the two best producing areas, 28 percent to 30 percent. This left about 135 metropolitan areas accounting for approximately 22 percent of the shipments, simply because there were not enough dealers handling the product.

> From this it was concluded that more effective use of media to develop dealers' business was needed. Fewer publications with larger, dramatic advertising to impress dealers were indicated. There were more than 100 metro areas where just one act of getting the right dealer with the proper cooperation could swing all negative factors to positive and score many hundreds of thousands of dollars in new retail sales. In other words, an impressive, primary dealer merchandising campaign in general

media was indicated to take precedence over smaller-copy, more frequency, straight-consumer type of sell.[2]

This case illustrates the role of dealers in getting products sold, and also indicates how media can be used in communicating to dealers.

Dealers also influence media decisions because they are so important in selling at the local level. They are at the firing line and often know which medium works best in their markets. At times they may communicate with the agency indirectly through distributors, wholesalers, or salespeople. Their influence may be very important for their own markets. Furthermore, they often dislike agency media choices, feeling that the media planner is too distant from the scene of action to know which local or national medium works best. In any case, the media planner must pay a great deal of attention to both dealers and importance of distribution in the media plan.

Overall Sales Strategy

The media planner should examine each element of the marketing mix to determine how it might affect media selection and use. Foremost, of course, is the role to be played by advertising. Although one can conceive of a situation where sales promotion, for example, might be more important in attaining objectives, advertising usually plays a significant role in the marketing strategy, and its role should be defined. The more specific this definition is, the better the media planner can plan strategy. Generally, advertising is assigned a communication task that must be accomplished before a product can be sold effectively.

When pricing tactics are important in marketing strategy, a special media effort may be needed either to announce the price or keep the news in front of the consumers. Special prices to dealers also may require special trade media selections and use.

Sales promotion, too, has special significance to media planners. Many promotions call for inserts in magazines or newspapers, such as coupons, booklets, samples of fabrics, tinfoils, or even vinyl records. All of these require careful planning, especially in estimating cost and timing. Marketing or creative plans might also require gatefolds, die-cuts, or special inks, all of which require additional media considerations. Furthermore, the media planner must often select media to announce and keep a special promotion in front of consumers. Contests, cents-off deals, and premiums may lose their impact if they are not noticed by consumers. The general media strategy in such a case is to buy media so as to get the largest reach possible.

---

[2]Tveter, T. Norman, "What the Media Expert Gains from Studying Markets," *Media/Scope*, May 1964, pp. 96, 100.

For other promotions, it may be necessary to tie in local store information with national advertising so that the audience in any given market knows where to buy an advertised national brand. The names and addresses of stores carrying the product are usually listed at the end of commercials or next to or near newspaper or magazine ads.

Other parts of the marketing mix such as personal selling, public relations, or packaging are of less importance in media planning. But the planner should know as much as possible about the whole marketing strategy to maximize the effectiveness of media decisions.

Test Marketing

Whenever a marketing strategy plan calls for test marketing, there is likely to be media involvement. For example, a test marketing situation might use three markets to test whether the following objectives can be attained: (a) to gain a substantial share of each market's sales, (b) to determine whether the total market for the product can be expanded, (c) to determine how many repeat purchases will be made, (d) to accomplish the above objectives within a reasonable length of time at a reasonable profit. Special media planning will be required in this situation.

To carry out the test, the new brand may be introduced in each of the three markets using different marketing tactics. In Market A, 50 percent of the households may be given a free sample; in Market B, 100 percent of the households may be given a free sample; while in Market C, local newspapers could carry a coupon redeemable for a free sample at local stores. In each case, local advertising may be required to call attention to the offers, especially to the coupon offer. Measurements of sales would then be made and compared market-by-market to see which performed best.

Another example of how test marketing could affect media planning would be if media weight varied in each of the three test markets. (*Weight* refers to the number of dollars spent, or GRP levels, in each market.) Market A might receive 100 television GRPs a week; Market B, 150 a week; and Market C, 200 a week. Sales would then be measured to see how the different weights affected volume.

Still another way to test media weights in several markets would be to give each market a specified advertising weight for a limited period of time. Sales would be measured for that period, then a heavier weighting might be applied to each market equally or in different proportions and sales again measured. (For more details on test marketing, see Chapter 14.)

So test marketing strategy affects media planning in ways ranging from simple dissemination of advertising to special testing situations within all or portions of the test markets.

In summary, then, the marketing strategy plan will affect the media planner's operation in many ways. The media plan itself will grow out of a marketing plan. It is inconceivable for the media planner to operate without first having some kind of marketing strategy as a basis on which to select and use media. The ideal situation occurs when the marketing strategy plan is written and available for all personnel who work on a product or brand within the agency. The plan then serves as a unifying force and directs action toward a common goal.

Competitive Media Expenditure Analysis

Once the planner has scrutinized the marketing strategy plan to determine how media will be involved, it is time to consider the kinds of media and the way they are used by competition. Sometimes competition varies so much that the planner may have to sort out local and regional competitors as well as those on the national level. The planner's first job is to know just who the competitors are and, secondly, to what extent they affect sales.

There is little problem in finding such information if the advertiser or agency subscribes to Nielsen, SAMI, MRCA market data, or various other syndicated research sources. But there is quite a problem in discovering who competitors are when such research services are not purchased. Some information may be obtained from competitive media expenditure analysis, but products produced and sold locally may not be identified very well, especially if they do not advertise much. Other sources of information may be local media salespeople, media representatives, local media research departments, or the company's own sales staff.

In determining the effect of competitors' media plans and devising strategies to counter such effects, the key piece of information is the share of market held by the competitor compared with the advertiser's brand. Brands that are leaders or close behind may pose a threat. As far as media planning is concerned, the question is: "Should we use the same media competitors use, or make special efforts to use different media?" Another question is how much advertising to put into a market to counter competitors' advertising effects.

The answers to these and other questions about competitors depends to a great extent on the marketing objectives and an evaluation of what effect competitors may have in preventing the attainment of such objectives. Each situation may be different. Whether to use the same media competitors use may not be as important as answering the question "Which medium or combination of media best reaches the kind of prospects who are likely to buy my brand?" The media that best reach prospects for "my" brand may happen to be identical with the media used by competitors. But the media planner, while considering competitors, should not necessarily imitate them simply because they happen to have larger shares of markets.

Planners should try to assess weaknesses in competitors' media tactics. Perhaps a competitor is not using a medium properly, or has dissipated advertising money in too many media, or is missing an important segment of the market. These errors represent opportunities in media selection and use and should be exploited. The analysis of a competitor's activities and its effects on a brand is not done in order to copy its tactics, but rather to assess its strengths and weaknesses in light of the marketing objectives. Plans for attaining the objectives are not led by competitors, but are made on the basis of problem as well as opportunity situations.

In essence, then, the planner must know at least the following information about competitors before making plans:

- Which media are used? Which are most significant?
- How much is spent in each medium?
- In which markets are media concentrated?
- How much weight is placed in each market?
- Which issues, broadcasts, times are used? In other words, when do competitors use various media and how are they used?

We will see in the next section that the compilation of competitive media information is very much an inexact science.

Major Expenditure Data Sources

Media spending information can be purchased from regular reporting services, although they have limitations. They do not provide a perfect picture of competitive media expenditures because it is economically unfeasible to measure every dollar spent in every medium for every product. The task is simply too great. Expenditure analyses are therefore never quite complete. Furthermore, such analyses are not precise, because the dollars reported do not incorporate the discounts earned when each competitor purchased space or time. There may be large variations between what the syndicated services report and what competitors actually spent. Finally, competitive reporting companies often do not accurately break down spending allocations when two or three brands appear in a single ad. In other words, the entire cost of the ad may be credited to one of the three brands to the exclusion of the other two. The best way to assess the accuracy of competitive media use reports is to compare the findings of these reports to the actual media use for the product you have planned and placed in media.

These limitations do not render competitive media expenditure analyses invalid, but the data are not to be interpreted literally. Coupled with other marketing and media information, such data will help provide a more complete picture of a competitor's spending activities than would be possible otherwise.

Following is a brief description of the information provided by major media expenditure data sources. It should be noted that the data generally report expenditures of large national advertisers only; neither small national advertisers nor retail advertisers of any size are represented. Users of such data should be aware that often they may be missing significant information simply because it is not reported by any of the services. In such cases, it would be necessary to estimate spending.

Media Records (Expenditures in Newspapers). Media Records reports newspaper expenditures by large national advertisers in about 60 major markets of the United States. While not all daily newspapers are included, most of the larger ones are, and the data represent a good cross section of all daily newspapers throughout the country. Reports are published monthly, quarterly, and yearly.

Media Records shows both the number of dollars and the advertising linage purchased by each advertiser, broken into product classifications for each of the newspapers listed. Each city is listed separately and data for all major daily newspapers in the city are shown by the following classifications: (a) retail display advertising, (b) general display, (c) automotive display, (d) classified, and (e) total. The term *display* means all advertising using either pictures and/or text matter that appears in other than classified sections of the newspaper. Each of the classifications is subdivided into specific product classes. These product classes enable one to find which newspaper in a given market carried the most ad lines in a product class such as radio and television sets, women's clothes, food advertising, etc.

Section Two of Media Records is significant because it categorizes advertising expenditures, first by product class and individual brand name, and then by market and newspapers that carried the advertising in that market. It is possible to find a given product class such as soaps and detergents, and then find each brand of soap listed for which the advertiser spent money in the newspaper markets reported. The data are reported by number of lines and dollars of advertising that ran during the quarter reported.

Media Records combines all newspaper activity in its reports. Separate listings for each form (run-of-press, comics, supplements) are not provided. Additionally, the only newspapers listed are those that subscribe to the service. Therefore, it is difficult to determine the precise usage of newspapers by a given advertiser.

Leading National Advertisers Expenditure Analysis by Class, Company, and Brand. The Leading National Advertisers Company provides a report of advertising expenditures in six media: magazines, newspaper supplements, network television, spot television, network radio, and outdoor. What is most important about this report is that it shows expenditures by brand as well as company. Each competitor's brands can be identified and compared directly with the planner's brand. Like most other reporting services, however, it measures only leading national advertisers' brands. To further aid the planner, the data for product categories are summarized so that all brands that compete are listed together in a report titled: *Ad $ Summary*. Both *LNA Class/Brand $* and *Company/Brand $* samples are shown in Figures 4–2 and 4–3.

Leading National Advertisers Outdoor Advertising Expenditures reports expenditures in outdoor advertising by companies and brands in major markets of the country. Expenditures are broken down by posting and painted signs. Posting refers to sheets that are pasted on the boards in various locations throughout a given market. A sample of this report is shown in Figure 4–4.

Broadcast Advertisers Reports (BAR). Broadcast Advertisers Reports covers network and spot television and network radio expenditures. The spot television section, called "Barcume," reports expenditures by parent company, individual brands, and expenditures for each month, plus a cumulative compilation (listed as YTD, or year-to-date). One of BAR's most important services is listing the number of markets in which spot television advertising is purchased and listing individual markets by name (only the top 75 markets are listed). As a result, the planner can determine in which markets competitors are placing the most money and then estimate the value of each such market to the competitor's entire marketing plan.

A note of caution: BAR tabulates only one week of advertiser activity per month. Therfore, if an advertiser has activity scheduled only during a non-BAR report period, that advertiser will appear to have no activity running during the entire month. Conversely, an advertiser with only one week of activity running during the week BAR conducts its tabulations would be projected as having a full month's activity. A sample is shown in Figure 4–5.

Broadcast Advertisers Report also covers network television expenditures with data similar to the spot television section. However, for network television, expenditures by individual markets are not shown and, if a planner wants to know how much was spent in each market comprising a network lineup, he or she will have to estimate it. One important breakdown in the network data report shows expenditures by daytime and nighttime, in addition to breakdowns by networks. A sample page of network expenditures is shown in Figure 4–6.

FIGURE 4–2. Advertising Expenditures by Product Class (sample page)

LNA CLASS/BRAND YTD $ (000)

BRANDS BY CLASSIFICATION	CLASS	6-MEDIA TOTAL	MAGAZINES	NEWSPAPER SUPPLEMENTS	NETWORK TELEVISION	SPOT TELEVISION	NETWORK RADIO	OUTDOOR
F223 NON-CARBONATED SOFT DRINKS						CONTINUED		
DUFFYS INC								
SUNLIT BREAKFAST DRINK MIX	F223	6.6	--	--	--	6.6	--	--
FAIRMONT FOODS CO								
MIGHTY ORANGE DRINK	F223	51.9	--	--	--	51.9	--	--
FOREMOST-MCKESSON INC								
ALHAMBRA BOTTLED WATER	F223	248.1	--	--	--	248.1	--	--
SPARKLETTS BOTTLED DRINKING WATER	F223	889.7	--	--	--	889.7	--	--
GENERAL FOODS CORP								
COUNTRY TIME DRINK MIXES	F223	7,232.1	--	104.6	3,258.3	3,456.7	412.5	--
COUNTRY TIME DRINKS CANNED	F223	370.8	--	--	--	370.8	--	--
COUNTRY TIME DRINKS FROZEN CONCENTRATE	F223	326.7	--	--	--	326.7	--	--
COUNTRY TIME DRINKS FROZEN & POWDERED	F223	2.3	--	--	--	2.3	--	--
KOOL-AID	F223	15,975.3	68.8	--	11,236.3	4,670.2	--	--
*GLENWOOD-INGLEWOOD BOTTLED WATER	F223	37.5	--	--	--	37.5	--	--
*GREAT BEAR SPRING WATER	F223	6.3	--	--	--	6.3	--	--
GREAT WATERS OF FRANCE INC								
PERRIER MINERAL WATER	F223	575.9	146.1	15.2	--	414.6	--	--
*HINCKLEY & SCHMITT BOTTLED WATER	F223	15.9	--	--	--	15.9	--	--
IROQUOIS BRANDS LTD								
YOO-HOO CHOCOLATE DRINK	F223	511.1	--	--	--	511.1	--	--
LEE T G FOODS INC								
THIRSTY C FRUIT DRINK	F223	5.8	--	--	--	--	--	5.8
LEVER BROTHERS CO								
LIPTON CANNED LEMON TREE BEVERAGE	F223	464.0	--	--	--	464.0	--	--
*MINNEHAHA SPRING WATER	F223	4.5	--	--	--	4.5	--	--
*MOUNTAIN VALLEY MINERAL WATER	F223	.2	--	--	--	.2	--	--
NESTLE ENTERPRISES INC								
DEER PARK SPRING WATER	F223	124.9	--	--	--	124.9	--	--
NESTLES CHOCO CHILL DRINK MIX	F223	353.2	--	--	--	353.2	--	--
NORTHWEST INDUSTRIES INC								
ARROWHEAD PURITAS BOTTLED WATER	F223	517.6	--	--	--	517.6	--	--
PEPSICO INC								
FRITO-LAY SOFT DRINK MIXES	F223	451.3	--	--	--	451.3	--	--
PET INC								
PET COOLIE FRUIT DRINKS	F223	29.0	--	--	--	29.0	--	--
PET FRUIT DRINKS	F223	35.4	--	--	--	35.4	--	--
PILLSBURY CO								
PILLSBURYS FUNNY FACE DRINK MIXES	F223	579.5	--	--	331.3	248.2	--	--
SQUOZE LEMONADE MIX	F223	632.2	--	71.1	560.8	.3	--	--
RALSTON PURINA CO								
PAKA-PUNCH FRUIT DRINK	F223	.9	--	--	--	.9	--	--
REYNOLDS R J INDUSTRIES INC								
HAWAIIAN CANNED & FROZEN PUNCH	F223	5.0	--	--	--	--	--	5.0
HAWAIIAN CANNED PUNCH	F223	2,243.6	--	144.8	698.2	1,340.6	--	60.0
HAWAIIAN PUNCH POWDERED DRINK MIXES	F223	6,088.7	600.6	162.6	3,819.1	1,496.3	--	10.1
SARATOGA VICHY SPRING CO								
QUEVIC SPRING WATER	F223	6.2	--	--	--	6.2	--	--
SILVER SPRINGS WATER CO								
SILVER SPRINGS BOTTLED WATER	F223	1.3	--	--	--	1.3	--	--
*SLUSH PUPPY DRINK	F223	28.5	--	--	--	28.5	--	--
STALEY A E MFG CO								
BIG PITCHER LIQUID CONCENTRATE BEVERAGE	F223	44.6	--	--	--	44.6	--	--
STOKELY-VAN CAMP INC								
GATORADE NON CARBONATED DRINK	F223	1,204.7	--	--	640.5	549.0	--	15.2
GATORADE PREMIUM OFFER	F223	219.8	206.1	13.7	--	--	--	--
GATORADE REGULAR & CARBONATED	F223	47.7	--	--	--	47.7	--	--
SUPERIOR TEA & COFFEE CO								
KAYO FLAVORED DRINK MIXES	F223	19.8	--	--	--	19.8	--	--
TROPICANA PRODUCTS INC								
TROPICANA FRUIT DRINKS	F223	14.8	--	--	--	14.8	--	--
UNIVEST CORP								
GRANDMA GRAFS DRINK MIXES	F223	32.1	--	--	--	32.1	--	--
WELCH FOODS INC								
WELCHS POWDERED DRINK MIXES	F223	33.6	--	--	--	33.6	--	--
WOMETCO ENTERPRISES INC								
DEEP ROCK DISTILLED WATER	F223	36.6	--	--	--	36.6	--	--
WRIGLEY WILLIAM JR CO								
SWEET N LOW SOFT DRINK MIXES	F223	19.8	--	--	--	19.8	--	--
F223 TOTAL		51,163.9	1,428.7	656.8	25,558.2	22,989.4	412.5	118.3
F310 BEER								
ANHEUSER-BUSCH INC								
ANHEUSER-BUSCH GOLF CLASSIC	F310	30.2	30.2	--	--	--	--	--
ANHEUSER-BUSCH INC GENERAL PROMOTION	F310-B	137.7	--	--	--	137.7	--	--
ANHEUSER-BUSCH NATURAL LIGHT BEER	F310	6,807.4	--	--	4,738.5	1,131.6	386.1	551.2
BUDWEISER BEER	F310	16,472.7	556.9	--	12,108.6	2,792.2	776.6	238.4
BUDWEISER BEER MAIL ORDER PROMOTION	F310	56.3	56.3	--	--	--	--	--
BUSCH BAVARIAN BEER	F310	2,127.2	--	--	--	2,124.7	--	2.5
MICHELOB BEER	F310	7,050.6	888.8	--	5,615.5	216.8	329.5	--
ANSOR CORP								
SAN MIGUEL BEER	F310	52.1	48.6	--	--	--	--	3.5
ARMADA CORP								
STERLING BEER	CLASS	106.2	--	--	--	86.7	--	19.5
B S N CORP								
KRONENBOURG BEER	F310	273.7	103.7	--	--	170.0	--	--

*Company and Brand name are the same.

Source: Leading National Advertisers Company

FIGURE 4–3. Advertising Expenditures by Company (sample page)

LNA COMPANY/BRAND $ (000)

BRANDS BY COMPANY	CLASS	6-MEDIA TOTAL	MAGAZINES	NEWSPAPER SUPPLEMENTS	NETWORK TELEVISION	SPOT TELEVISION	NETWORK RADIO	OUTDOOR
REVLON INC	CONTINUED							
REVLON FORMULA 2 CREAMS & LOTIONS	D111	$ 197.5	$ --	$ --	$ 163.1	$ 34.4	$ --	$ --
REVLON LIPSTICK	D112	971.5	361.7	--	589.6	20.2	--	--
REVLON MAKE-UP	D114	520.1	--	--	391.0	129.1	--	--
REVLON MASCARA	D112	381.2	--	--	372.8	8.5	--	--
REVLON MILK PLUS 6 MOISTURIZING CREAMS & LOTIONS	D111	1,391.1	--	--	733.4	657.7	--	--
REVLON MILK PLUS 6 SHAMPOO/CONDITIONER	D142	1,225.9	--	--	638.3	587.6	--	--
REVLON MOON DROPS LIPSTICK	D112	808.9	160.3	--	648.6	--	--	--
REVLON MOON DROPS MOISTURE TREATMENTS	D111	895.2	895.2	--	--	--	--	--
REVLON MULTI-PRODUCT ADVERTISING	D116	1,869.4	320.5	--	559.9	989.0	--	--
REVLON NAIL POLISH	D115	292.1	--	--	285.8	6.3	--	--
REVLON NATURAL WONDER EYE MAKE-UP	D112	785.5	--	--	785.5	--	--	--
REVLON NATURAL WONDER LIPSTICK	D112	35.4	35.4	--	--	--	--	--
REVLON NATURAL WONDER MULTI-PRODUCT ADVERTISING	D116	653.2	532.7	--	--	120.5	--	--
REVLON NATURAL WONDER OIL-FREE MAKEUP	D114	717.3	--	--	637.2	80.1	--	--
REVLON PERFUMES	D113	3,931.1	806.9	14.9	1,997.3	1,109.9	--	2.1
REVLON REALISTIC CREME HAIR RELAXER	D141	22.3	22.3	--	--	--	--	--
REVLON REALISTIC SENSOR-PERM	D141	33.0	33.0	--	--	--	--	--
REVLON TOUCH & GLOW MAKE-UP	D114	1,237.5	435.8	--	798.5	3.2	--	--
REVLON ULTIMA II COSMETICS	D116	147.2	--	--	--	147.2	--	--
REVLON ULTIMA II CREAMS & LOTIONS	D111	228.5	210.4	16.4	--	1.7	--	--
REVLON ULTIMA II EYE MAKE-UP	D112	28.2	--	--	--	28.2	--	--
REVLON ULTIMA II MAKE-UP	D114	149.0	141.5	7.5	--	--	--	--
REVLON ULTIMA II MULTI-PRODUCT ADVERTISING	D116	105.7	98.2	7.5	--	--	--	--
REXALL DRUG CO		612.0	431.2	--	158.7	18.9	--	3.2
REXALL DRUG STORES	G603	161.9	--	--	158.7	--	--	3.2
REXALL VITAMINS	D215	450.1	431.2	--	--	18.9	--	--
REXCO CORP								
PERMABOND LIQUID ADHESIVE	H235	558.8	--	--	--	558.8	--	--
REXCRAFT								
REXCRAFT WEDDING INVITATIONS	B410	79.8	79.8	--	--	--	--	--
REXNORD INC		423.9	375.9	--	--	.4	47.6	--
REX FARM EQUIPMENT	T520	.4	--	--	--	.4	--	--
REXNORD INC GENERAL PROMOTION	B520-8	414.3	366.7	--	--	--	47.6	--
ZOOM HIGH PERFORMANCE PARTS	T154	9.2	9.2	--	--	--	--	--
REYNOLDS METALS CO		5,774.3	1,061.1	107.0	4,220.0	384.6	--	1.6
REYNOLDS ALUMINUM	B511	1,815.3	--	--	1,545.1	270.2	--	--
REYNOLDS ALUMINUM BUILDING PRODUCTS HOME	H512-5	100.0	89.0	--	--	10.1	--	--
REYNOLDS ALUMINUM RECYCLING CENTERS	B511	83.9	82.3	--	--	--	--	1.6
REYNOLDS BROILER BLOTTERS	H233	14.3	14.3	--	--	--	--	--
REYNOLDS BROWN-IN-BAG	H233	131.3	131.3	--	--	--	--	--
REYNOLDS METALS CO GENERAL PROMOTION	B511-8	337.0	331.9	--	--	5.1	--	--
REYNOLDS WRAP	H233	3,193.3	411.4	107.0	2,674.9	--	--	--
SHAKE-A-SCENT LITTER BOX DEODORANT	G532	99.2	--	--	--	99.2	--	--
REYNOLDS R J INDUSTRIES INC		94,812.0	43,185.8	18,221.6	4,517.3	3,749.5	--	25137.8
CAMEL CIGARETTES PREMIUM OFFER	G111	151.7	151.7	--	--	--	--	--
CAMEL FILTER CIGARETTES	G111	4,209.4	2,166.1	--	--	--	--	2043.3
CAMEL FILTER KING CIGARETTES	G111	1.8	--	--	--	--	--	1.8
CAMEL FILTER LONG CIGARETTES	G111	4.9	--	--	--	--	--	4.9
CAMEL FILTER LONG LIGHTS CIGARETTES	G111	1.7	--	--	--	--	--	1.7
CAMEL FILTERS GT ROAD RACING SERIES	G111	58.2	58.2	--	--	--	--	--
CAMEL LIGHTS FILTER CIGARETTES	G111	49.0	--	2.1	--	--	--	46.9
CHUN KING CANNED CHOW MEIN	F126	224.5	--	--	--	224.5	--	--
CHUN KING CHOW MEIN FROZEN & CANNED	F126	7.3	--	--	--	7.3	--	--
CHUN KING FOODS PREMIUM OFFER	F126	94.7	--	94.7	--	--	--	--
CHUN KING FROZEN CHOW MEIN	F126	457.8	--	--	--	457.8	--	--
CHUN KING FROZEN DINNERS	F126	2.6	--	--	--	2.6	--	--
CHUN KING FROZEN EGG ROLLS	F126	2.3	--	--	--	2.3	--	--
CHUN KING MIXES	F113	.4	--	--	--	.4	--	--
HAWAIIAN CANNED & FROZEN PUNCH	F223	5.0	--	--	--	--	--	5.0
HAWAIIAN CANNED PUNCH	F223	2,243.6	--	144.8	698.2	1,340.6	--	60.0
HAWAIIAN PUNCH POWDERED DRINK MIXES	F223	6,088.7	600.6	162.6	3,819.1	1,496.3	--	10.1
MORE 120S FILTER CIGARETTES REGULAR & MENTHOL	G111	6,197.7	3,305.3	1,438.7	--	--	--	1453.7
NOW REGULAR & MENTHOL FILTER CIGARETTES	G111	7,879.9	4,401.2	1,649.5	--	--	--	1829.2
PATIO FROZEN FOODS	F180	217.7	--	--	--	217.7	--	--
R J REYNOLDS INDUSTRIES INC CIGARETTES	G111	492.6	--	--	--	--	--	492.6
R J REYNOLDS INDUSTRIES INC DIVIDEND NOTICE	B156-8	7.5	7.5	--	--	--	--	--
R J REYNOLDS INDUSTRIES INC GENERAL PROMOTION	G111-8	7.1	--	--	--	--	--	7.1
REAL FILTER & MENTHOL CIGARETTES	G111	9,567.6	4,538.1	1,430.9	--	--	--	3598.6
SALEM LIGHTS MENTHOL FILTER CIGARETTES	G111	564.9	--	--	--	--	--	564.9
SALEM LIGHTS MENTHOL FILTER & FILTER LONG CIGARETTES	G111	5,807.5	3,294.5	2,457.4	--	--	--	55.6
SALEM LIGHTS MENTHOL FILTER & 100S CIGARETTES	G111	1,428.6	741.1	584.0	--	--	--	103.5
SALEM LONG LIGHTS MENTHOL FILTER CIGARETTES	G111	762.3	--	--	--	--	--	762.3
SALEM LONGS MENTHOL FILTERS	G111	1,943.0	825.6	403.4	--	--	--	714.0
SALEM MENTHOL FILTER CIGARETTES	G111	4,395.1	1,829.8	--	--	--	--	2565.3
SALEM MENTHOL FILTER KING CIGARETTES	G111	550.0	266.1	--	--	--	--	283.9
SALEM MENTHOL FILTER KINGS & 100S CIGARETTES	G111	2,869.4	2,111.3	758.1	--	--	--	--
SALEM MENTHOL LIGHTS 100S	G111	75.9	--	--	--	--	--	75.9
SALEM MENTHOL 100S CIGARETTES	G111	141.8	--	--	--	--	--	141.8
VANTAGE CIGARETTES MULTI-PRODUCT ADVERTISING	G111	5,296.2	3,523.9	1,772.3	--	--	--	--
VANTAGE FILTER CIGARETTES	G111	2,283.9	51.0	--	--	--	--	2232.9
VANTAGE FILTER & MENTHOL FILTER CIGARETTES	G111	292.1	245.4	--	--	--	--	46.7
VANTAGE LONGS FILTER CIGARETTES	G111	3,498.2	2,220.9	932.0	--	--	--	345.3
VANTAGE MENTHOL FILTER CIGARETTES	G111	9.2	--	--	--	--	--	9.2
VANTAGE 100S FILTER CIGARETTES	G111	1,479.1	856.3	545.4	--	--	--	77.4
	CONTINUED							

Source: Leading National Advertisers Company

FIGURE 4–4. LNA Outdoor Advertising Expenditures $(000)

PARENT COMPANY — BRAND — MARKET	CURRENT QUARTER			YEAR-TO-DATE		
	TOTAL	POSTING	PAINT	TOTAL	POSTING	PAINT
F330 LIQUOR	CONTINUED					
HIRAM WALKER-GOODERHAM & WORTS LTD				CONTINUED		
ROYAL CANADIAN WHISKY						
MICH DETROIT METRO MKT	42.8	32.2	10.6	110.6	81.4	29.2
FLINT METRO MARKET	2.0	– –	2.0	6.0	– –	6.0
GRAND RAPIDS METRO MKT	2.0	– –	2.0	6.0	– –	6.0
LANSING METRO MKT	2.0	2.0	– –	5.9	5.9	– –
TEX HOUSTON METRO MARKET	2.7	– –	2.7	11.7	– –	11.7
BRAND TOTAL	51.5	34.2	17.3	140.2	87.3	52.9
HIRAM WALKER-GOODERHAM & WORTS LTD						
TIA MARIA LIQUEUR						
CAL LOS ANGELES METRO MKT	18.9	– –	18.9	37.9	– –	37.9
HIRAM WALKER-GOODERHAM & WORTS LTD						
TWO FINGERS TEQUILA						
ARIZ PHOENIX METRO MKT	6.5	6.5	– –	17.1	17.1	– –
TUCSON METRO MKT	5.5	5.5	– –	9.5	9.5	– –
CAL LOS ANGELES METRO MKT	– –	– –	– –	105.2	95.2	10.0
SACRAMENTO METRO MKT	4.9	4.9	– –	16.5	16.5	– –
SAN DIEGO METRO MKT	– –	– –	– –	14.6	14.6	– –
SAN FRAN-OAKLND-SAN JO	25.2	21.9	3.3	78.2	68.7	9.5
COLO DENVER-BOULDER METRO M	6.5	6.5	– –	16.9	16.9	– –
FLA JACKSONVILLE METRO MKT	3.0	3.0	– –	3.0	3.0	– –
MIAMI METRO MARKET	8.3	8.3	– –	8.3	8.3	– –
NEV LAS VEGAS METRO MKT	.8	.8	– –	.8	.8	– –
RENO METRO MKT	.6	.6	– –	.6	.6	– –
TEX AMARILLO METRO MKT	.5	.5	– –	.5	.5	– –
AUSTIN TRADING AREA	1.6	1.6	– –	4.6	4.6	– –
DALLAS METRO MARKET	4.1	4.1	– –	10.9	10.9	– –
FT WORTH METRO MARKET	4.7	4.7	– –	13.1	13.1	– –
HOUSTON METRO MARKET	12.2	12.2	– –	31.6	31.6	– –
RIO GRANDE VALLEY DIST	.6	.6	– –	.6	.6	– –
BRAND TOTAL	85.0	81.7	3.3	332.0	312.5	19.5
HIRAM WALKER-GOODERHAM & WORTS LTD						
WALKERS DELUXE BOURBON WHISKEY						
MO ST LOUIS METRO MKT	.4	.4	– –	.4	.4	– –
HOOD RIVER DISTILLERS INC						
HOOD RIVER DISTILLERS						
ORE PORTLAND METRO MARKET	13.7	8.7	5.0	28.3	14.5	13.8
WASH SEATTLE-TACOMA METRO M	13.5	10.9	2.6	26.0	18.2	7.8
SPOKANE STD METRO MKT	– –	– –	– –	5.4	1.8	3.6
BRAND TOTAL	27.2	19.6	7.6	59.7	34.5	25.2
JACQUIN CHARLES ET CIE INC						
JACQUIN BRANDY						
MASS FALL RIVER MKT	– –	– –	– –	.6	.6	– –
LAWRENCE METRO MKT	– –	– –	– –	1.1	1.1	– –
PA ERIE METRO MARKET	.4	– –	.4	2.3	– –	2.3
HARRISBURG METRO MKT	– –	– –	– –	1.0	– –	1.0
LANCASTER METRO MKT	– –	– –	– –	1.0	– –	1.0
PHILADELPHIA & SO. JER	– –	– –	– –	16.5	– –	16.5
PITTSBURGH METRO MKT	– –	– –	– –	9.8	9.8	– –
WILLIAMSPORT METRO MKT	– –	– –	– –	.1	.1	– –
YORK METRO MKT	.5	– –	.5	1.5	– –	1.5
BRAND TOTAL	.9	– –	.9	33.9	11.6	22.3
JACQUIN CHARLES ET CIE INC						
JACQUIN CORDIALS						
N Y BUFFALO GREATER MARKET	1.1	1.1	– –	2.2	2.2	– –
JACQUIN CHARLES ET CIE INC						
JACQUIN GIN						
MD BALTIMORE MKT	– –	– –	– –	5.0	5.0	– –
PA HARRISBURG METRO MKT	1.5	1.5	– –	5.5	4.5	1.0
BRAND TOTAL	1.5	1.5	– –	10.5	9.5	1.0

FIGURE 4–4. (Continued)

PARENT COMPANY — BRAND — MARKET	CURRENT QUARTER			YEAR-TO-DATE		
	TOTAL	POSTING	PAINT	TOTAL	POSTING	PAINT
F330 LIQUOR	CONTINUED					
JACQUIN CHARLES ET CIE INC				CONTINUED		
JACQUIN PREMIER LIQUORS						
DEL WILMINGTON METRO MKT	- -	- -	- -	2.2	2.2	- -
D C WASHINGTON METRO MKT	2.3	2.3	- -	2.3	2.3	- -
MASS NEW BEDFORD MKT	- -	- -	- -	.8	.8	- -
PA ERIE METRO MARKET	- -	- -	- -	4.4	4.4	- -
WILLIAMSPORT METRO MKT	- -	- -	- -	2.6	2.6	- -
BRAND TOTAL	2.3	2.3	- -	12.3	12.3	- -
JACQUIN CHARLES ET CIE INC						
JACQUIN VODKA						
FLA JACKSONVILLE METRO MKT	.1	- -	.1	.1	- -	.1
PA ALLENTN-BETHLM-EASTN-P	2.7	2.7	- -	5.4	5.4	- -
ALTOONA METRO MKT	1.2	1.2	- -	1.6	1.6	- -
ERIE METRO MARKET	5.2	4.4	.8	9.6	8.8	.8
HARRISBURG METRO MKT	- -	- -	- -	1.0	- -	1.0
JOHNSTOWN METRO MARKET	1.0	1.0	- -	2.0	2.0	- -
LANCASTER METRO MKT	2.4	1.4	1.0	4.8	2.8	2.0
LAWRENCE & MERCER CNTY	.4	.4	- -	1.2	1.2	- -
PHILADELPHIA & SO. JER	1.2	- -	1.2	3.7	- -	3.7
PITTSBURGH METRO MKT	10.0	10.0	- -	19.9	19.9	- -
READING METRO MARKET	1.1	1.1	- -	2.2	2.2	- -
WILLIAMSPORT METRO MKT	1.7	1.7	- -	1.7	1.7	- -
YORK METRO MKT	.9	.9	- -	1.8	1.8	- -
BRAND TOTAL	27.9	24.8	3.1	55.0	47.4	7.6
JACQUIN CHARLES ET CIE INC						
JACQUIN WHISKEY						
PA ALTOONA METRO MKT	- -	- -	- -	1.8	1.8	- -
JOHNSTOWN METRO MARKET	- -	- -	- -	1.0	1.0	- -
PITTSBURGH METRO MKT	4.9	4.9	- -	14.9	14.9	- -
SCRANTON-WILKES-BARRE	2.8	2.8	- -	8.4	8.4	- -
BRAND TOTAL	7.7	7.7	- -	26.1	26.1	- -
KOBRAND CORP						
BEEFEATER GIN						
CAL LOS ANGELES METRO MKT	16.5	- -	16.5	72.2	23.8	48.4
SAN DIEGO METRO MKT	- -	- -	- -	3.6	3.6	- -
SAN FRAN-OAKLND-SAN JO	3.4	- -	3.4	18.5	8.7	9.8
COLO DENVER-BOULDER METRO M	2.6	- -	2.6	7.5	- -	7.5
FLA JACKSONVILLE METRO MKT	2.0	- -	2.0	5.7	- -	5.7
MIAMI METRO MARKET	3.9	- -	3.9	3.9	- -	3.9
TAMPA-ST. PETERSBURG M	6.3	- -	6.3	17.9	- -	17.9
MASS BOSTON GREATER METRO M	3.8	- -	3.8	11.1	- -	11.1
MICH DETROIT METRO MKT	12.2	- -	12.2	37.0	- -	37.0
MO ST LOUIS GREATER URBAN	3.1	- -	3.1	9.2	- -	9.2
NEV LAS VEGAS METRO MKT	6.0	- -	6.0	18.0	- -	18.0
N M ALBUQUERQUE STD METRO	1.1	- -	1.1	1.1	- -	1.1
N Y NEW YORK METRO MKT	2.3	- -	2.3	6.9	- -	6.9
OHIO CINCINNATI METRO MKT	2.5	- -	2.5	7.5	- -	7.5
CLEVELAND METRO MKT	6.6	- -	6.6	19.4	- -	19.4
COLUMBUS METRO MKT	2.3	- -	2.3	6.8	- -	6.8
ORE PORTLAND METRO MARKET	2.8	- -	2.8	2.8	- -	2.8
PA PHILADELPHIA & SO. JER	12.1	- -	12.1	35.1	- -	35.1
PITTSBURGH METRO MKT	3.0	- -	3.0	8.8	- -	8.8
TEX DALLAS METRO MARKET	3.6	- -	3.6	10.7	- -	10.7
WASH SEATTLE-TACOMA METRO M	2.6	- -	2.6	7.8	- -	7.8
BRAND TOTAL	98.7	- -	98.7	311.5	36.1	275.4
LIGGETT GROUP INC						
CAMPARI LIQUEUR						
CAL LOS ANGELES METRO MKT	- -	- -	- -	9.3	- -	9.3
LIGGETT GROUP INC						
CATTOS SCOTCH WHISKY						
CAL SAN FRAN-OAKLND-SAN JO	.9	- -	.9	.9	- -	.9
WIS MILWAUKEE GREATER MKT	- -	- -	- -	2.4	2.4	- -
BRAND TOTAL	.9	- -	.9	3.3	2.4	.9

Source: Leading National Advertisers Company

FIGURE 4–5. Barcume: Brand/Product Market Expenditures

BRAND/PRODUCT MARKET(S)	* ESTIMATED EXPENDITURES (000) JUL	AUG	SEP	QTR
************************************				
A111				
BLOUSES & SHIRTS				
************************************				
ARROW APPAREL-MENS SHIRTS				
CHARLESTON			8.1	8.1
DAYTON			31.6	31.6
DETROIT			.1	.1
TOTALS			39.8	39.8
HENRY GRETHEL APPRL-MENS SHIRTS				
BALTIMORE		6.4		6.4
CHICAGO			3.1	3.1
TOTALS		6.4	3.1	9.5
JONATHAN MARTIN APPRL-BLOUSES				
LOS ANGELES			.4	.4
NEW YORK		2.2		2.2
TOTALS		2.2	.4	2.6
MANHATTAN APPRL-MENS SHIRTS				
BALTIMORE		13.7		13.7
************************************				
A112				
COATS, SUITS, DRESSES, RAINWEAR & LOUNGING APP				
************************************				
BUSTER BROWN CHLDRNS CL				
NEW YORK		.1	.1	.2
GARANIMALS CHLDRNS APPRL				
ALTOONA	4.8	4.8		9.6
ATLANTA		17.3	2.8	20.1
BOSTON		36.2		36.2
BUFFALO		15.5		15.5
CHICAGO	6.5	32.2		38.7
CINCINNATI		9.8		9.8
CLEVELAND		18.0		18.0
COLUMBUS	10.1	8.0		18.1
DALLAS		19.1		19.1
DES MOINES		6.3		6.3
GREEN BAY		4.8		4.8
HARRISBURG	5.2	6.2		11.4
HARTFORD	16.1	16.8		32.9
HOUSTON		23.4		23.4
INDIANAPOLIS		11.8		11.8
KANSAS CITY		9.5		9.5
KNOXVILLE		6.9		6.9
LITTLE ROCK		5.3		5.3
LOS ANGELES	10.4	44.2		54.6
MEMPHIS		5.4		5.4
MILWAUKEE		9.2	1.3	10.5
MINNEAPOLIS		23.4		23.4
NASHVILLE	9.1	11.8		20.9
NEW YORK	10.8	72.7		83.5
OKLAHOMA CITY		7.0		7.0
PHILADELPHIA		35.2		35.2
PITTSBURGH		21.4		21.4
PORTLAND ORE		11.6		11.6

BRAND/PRODUCT MARKET(S)	* ESTIMATED EXPENDITURES (000) JUL	AUG	SEP	QTR
************************************				
BILL BLASS APPRL-VARIOUS JEANS				
ST LOUIS		23.1		23.1
BILL BLASS APPRL-WOMENS JEANS				
LOS ANGELES		17.1	4.4	21.5
SAN DIEGO		6.6		6.6
TOTALS		23.7	4.4	28.1
BILLY THE KID CHLD APRL				
OKLAHOMA CITY		6.4		6.4
BODY GLOVE WET SUITS				
LOS ANGELES			.5	.5
BON JOUR APPRL-CHILDRENS JEANS				
LOS ANGELES		.3	.5	.8
MINNEAPOLIS		1.1		1.1
NEW YORK			.3	.3
PHILADELPHIA		.5		.5
TOTALS		1.9	.8	2.7
BON JOUR APPRL CHILDRENS SPRTSWR				
ATLANTA		8.9	4.7	13.6
CHICAGO		16.4	10.9	27.3
DETROIT		1.1		1.1
HOUSTON		2.0		2.0
LOS ANGELES		7.5	5.4	12.9
MIAMI		4.9	.4	5.3
MINNEAPOLIS			17.5	17.5
NEW YORK		16.5	3.0	19.5
PHILADELPHIA			17.3	17.3
PHOENIX		4.2		4.2
SAN FRANCISCO		2.6		2.6
WASHINGTON		4.0	5.1	9.1
TOTALS		68.1	64.3	132.4
BON JOUR APPRL-MENS & WOMENS JEANS				
ATLANTA		11.5	2.8	14.3
BOSTON		8.4		8.4
TOTALS		19.9	2.8	22.7
BON JOUR APPRL-MENS SPORTSWEAR				
ATLANTA		1.5	8.8	10.3
BOSTON		9.1	16.7	25.8
CHICAGO		17.7	4.2	21.9
DALLAS		8.8		8.8
DETROIT		19.8		19.8
HOUSTON		5.3		5.3
LOS ANGELES		8.1	5.9	14.0
MIAMI		4.7	.9	5.6
MINNEAPOLIS		1.8	13.2	15.0
NEW YORK		11.5	15.8	27.3
PHILADELPHIA		9.8	8.3	18.1
PHOENIX		3.1		3.1
SAN FRANCISCO		4.8		4.8
WASHINGTON		1.3	2.6	3.9
TOTALS		107.3	76.4	183.7
BON JOUR APPRL-VARIOUS JEANS				
BOSTON		27.7		27.7
DALLAS		13.0		13.0

BRAND/PRODUCT MARKET(S)	* ESTIMATED EXPENDITURES (000) JUL	AUG	SEP	QTR
PHILADELPHIA			41.2	41.2
SALT LAKE CITY			5.6	5.6
SAN FRANCISCO		35.2		35.2
TAMPA		28.6		28.6
TOTALS		313.8	131.3	445.1
CALVIN KLEIN APPRL-WOMENS SPRTSWR				
CHICAGO		22.1	10.6	32.7
DALLAS		24.2		24.2
HOUSTON		2.4		2.4
LOS ANGELES		25.8	21.4	47.2
NEW YORK		33.2	30.8	64.0
PHILADELPHIA			12.4	12.4
SALT LAKE CITY			3.0	3.0
TAMPA		16.6		16.6
TOTALS		124.3	78.2	202.5
CARABINE APPRL-VARIOUS SPORTSWEAR				
NEW YORK		51.5	83.9	135.4
CAROLE LITTLE APPRL-WOMENS SPORTSWR				
CHICAGO		57.8	61.4	119.2
LOS ANGELES			64.4	64.4
NEW YORK		77.5	106.8	184.3
TOTALS		135.3	232.6	367.9
CHAMS APPRL-MENS SPORTSWEAR				
NEW YORK	1.0	.4	7.6	9.0
CHAPS BY RALPH LAUREN-MENS APPRL				
OKLAHOMA CITY			.8	.8
CHARDON APPRL-MEN&WOMEN JEANS				
BOSTON		17.9	6.8	24.7
CLEVELAND			.9	.9
DENVER	30.0			30.0
LOS ANGELES		64.3	14.3	78.6
MIAMI		1.5		1.5
NEW YORK		1.2		1.2
TOTALS	30.0	84.9	22.0	136.9
CHARDON APPRL-VAR SPORTSWEAR				
BALTIMORE		3.3		3.3
BOSTON		16.1	15.8	31.9
CHICAGO		50.7	4.3	55.0
CLEVELAND		9.0	.9	9.9
COLUMBUS		19.8		19.8
DAYTON		17.2		17.2
DETROIT		9.2		9.2
INDIANAPOLIS		7.7	2.2	9.9
MIAMI		2.5		2.5
NEW YORK		42.9	2.5	45.4
PHILADELPHIA		3.5	25.7	29.2
PITTSBURGH		11.8		11.8
SAN FRANCISCO			21.7	21.7
WASHINGTON		7.8	7.6	15.4
TOTALS		201.5	80.7	282.2
CHARDON APPRL-VARIOUS JEANS				
BALTIMORE		14.8		14.8
BOSTON		10.8	2.9	13.7
CHICAGO		1.2	1.3	2.5

(A portion of this page has been omitted.)

BRAND/PRODUCT MARKET(S)	JUL	AUG	SEP	QTR
BENNY HILL T-SHIRT OFFR				
MIAMI			6.3	6.3
BILL BLASS APPRL-MENS SPRTSWR				
NEW YORK			10.7	10.7

BRAND/PRODUCT MARKET(S)	JUL	AUG	SEP	QTR
CHICAGO		20.6	10.2	30.8
DALLAS		28.5		28.5
HOUSTON		61.8		61.8
LOS ANGELES		50.0	33.8	83.8
NEW YORK		89.1	40.5	129.6

BRAND/PRODUCT MARKET(S)	JUL	AUG	SEP	QTR
SEATTLE		3.4	2.9	6.3
SPOKANE		1.9		1.9
TOTALS		23.2	5.3	28.5

BARCUME - NATIONAL SPOT TV - THIRD QUARTER, 1981 BROADCAST ADVERTISERS REPORTS, INC.

FIGURE 4–6. Brand Expenditures by Daypart

CLASS CODE & PRODUCT CLASSIFICATION BRAND/PRODUCT	MO QTR YTD	TOTAL	DAYTIME	EARLY EVENING	NIGHT	LATE NIGHT	M K T S	NO. OF SPOTS IN MONTH	DAY	EVE	NITE	LATE	10	30	60
A111 BLOUSES & SHIRTS															
ARROW APPAREL-MENS SHIRTS	SEP	39.8	6.9	12.7	13.5	6.7	3	202	34	33	15	18		100	
	3RD QTR	39.8	6.9	12.7	13.5	6.7									
	YTD	995.3	206.3	313.8	118.6	356.6									
DAMON APPRL-MENS SHIRTS	YTD	12.7	1.2	.9	10.3	.3									
GARAN APPRL-SHIRTS	YTD	105.8	3.8	47.6	23.3	31.2									
GRAND SLAM APPRL-MENS SHIRTS	YTD	305.2	136.3	141.4	20.1	7.4									
HATHAWAY APPRL-MENS SHIRTS	YTD	1.2				1.2									
HENRY GRETHEL APPRL-MENS SHIRTS	AUG	6.4		3.1	3.3		1	24		50	50		100		
	SEP	3.1	.5			1.9	1	35	17	43	34	6	97		3
	3RD QTR/YTD	9.5	.5	3.6	3.3	1.9									
JONATHAN MARTIN APPRL-BLOUSES	AUG	2.2		3.1	.7		1	4	25	25	50			100	
	SEP	2.4	3.5	1.2				5	20	20	60			100	
	3RD QTR	2.6	3.6	1.2	1.4										
	YTD	5.5		.6	5.7	2.3									
LADY MANHATTAN APPRL-BLOUSES	YTD	122.7	14.2	39.9	5.7	62.9									
LEVI APPRL-MENS SHIRTS	YTD	5.7	5.7	.5		4.2									
MANHATTAN APPRL-MENS SHIRTS	AUG	13.7	.6		3.2	9.9	1	28	14	14	14	71		100	
	3RD QTR	15.8	.1		3.2	9.9									
	YTD				4.0	10.7									
VAN HEUSEN APPRL-MENS SHIRTS	YTD	215.7	6.5	4.6	39.7	164.9									
A111 CLASS TOTAL	AUG	22.3	6.9	13.4	13.2	8.6									
	SEP	43.3	8.3	15.7	13.9	8.5									
	3RD QTR	65.6													
	YTD	1785.1	370.5	554.6	226.4	643.6									
A112 COATS,SUITS,DRESSES,RAINWEAR & LOUNGING APP															
BUSTER BROWN CHLDRNS CL	AUG	.1					1	1	100					100	
	SEP	.2	.1	.2			1	2	100					100	
	3RD QTR	.4	.2	.4											
	YTD															
COAT TAIL MENS APPRL-SUITS&SPRTSCT	YTD	94.7	8.1	16.1	53.8	16.7									
COMFORT PDTS-OUTERWEAR	YTD	204.7	79.4	57.2	21.3	46.8									
	SEP	180.9	7.0	86.4	77.8	9.7									
	3RD QTR	950.2	46.7	489.1	232.1	182.3									
	YTD	2619.6	389.2	972.6	517.4	770.4									

(A portion of this page has been omitted.)

BARCUME - NATIONAL SPOT TV - THIRD QUARTER, 1981

BROADCAST ADVERTISERS REPORTS, INC.

Leading National Advertisers Magazine Analysis Service (compiled for the Publishers' Information Bureau—PIB). This reporting service shows expenditure data in consumer magazines for national advertisers. Released monthly, the data show expenditures for each month and cumulatively. There are seven different volumes of this report, as there are for each of the other Leading National Advertisers reports: apparel, business and financial, drugs and toiletries, food and beverages, general, homes and building, and transportation and agriculture.

In any one of these seven volumes, each company that purchased advertising is identified separately. (See Figure 4–7.) The magazines in which advertising space was purchased during a given month (or for previous months of the current year) are listed for each brand. Also listed are such data as the size of advertisements; cover; position, if applicable; and the use of color or bleed. A special edition of these reports contains data on expenditures in regional magazines. All expenditure information is based on the standard rate and does not include any discounts the advertiser might have earned.

Data for regional advertising expenditures also are reported on a monthly, quarterly, and yearly basis. Because there have been increased expenditures in regional edition advertising for some years now, it is also important to know to what extent competitors are concentrating their advertising efforts in certain areas of the country.

Gathering and Assembling the Data

The first of two major tasks involved in studying competitive expenditures is to gather and assemble the data. The second task is to analyze them.

What kinds of data should the media planner seek? The most obvious answer is to find the amount of money that each competitor spends annually in each medium. Such data provide a bird's-eye view of the competitor's media activities. To make such data more meaningful, the planner should analyze expenditures for individual brands, rather than total expenditures for a company. Because each brand is competing with others for a proportion of total market sales, specific expenditures by brands are most meaningful. In gathering expenditure data by brand, it is advisable to include the planner's brand as well as competitors' brands so that all are compared on the same basis.

Furthermore, in analyzing expenditure data, it is important not only to show dollars spent in each medium, but what percentage that comprises of each competitor's annual expenditures. (See Table 4–1.) The proportion of each competitor's total expenditures in each medium makes comparisons easier, though problems can occur in making comparisons on the basis of percentages when the bases differ widely. Ten percent of one brand's total budget spent in newspapers, for example,

TABLE 4–1. Competitive Media Expenditure Analysis for a Product Class

Brands	Magazines (%)	Supple- ments (%)	News- papers (%)	Network TV (%)	Spot TV (%)	Outdoor (%)	Totals (%)
A	9.8	12.8	50.3	19.8	—	7.3	100
B	36.7	11.5	43.1	8.7	—	—	100
C	0.5	5.9	47.8	45.3	—	0.5	100
D	5.4	2.9	5.9	80.6	5.2	—	100
E	0.5	—	9.6	20.2	69.6	—	100

may not be equivalent to a competitor's 10 percent spent in newspapers if the base of one was $3,000 and the base of the other, $3,000,000.

The study of annual expenditures is only one approach in analyzing competitors' marketing and media strategies. Another useful analysis may be made by comparing expenditures of a brand with its competitors on a market-by-market basis. This technique may be helpful in learning which markets were most important to competitors, and the analysis may serve as one basis for weighting media in a given market. It is easy to locate these markets in Media Records but difficult in LNA Network Television Service or LNA Magazine Analysis Service. It may be possible, however, to estimate which markets were used and the relative weights placed in these markets.

Still another kind of analysis may be made of the dollars spent in each medium by a brand and its competitors, correlated with the audience delivered for the dollars spent. This technique makes possible a quick analysis of the relative delivery effectiveness of competitors' media expenditures. Plans for a brand's reach and frequency often come from such an analysis.

Finally, it is important to learn how much was spent in each medium during each month of the year. Most brands have peak selling seasons and vary the weight of their advertising accordingly. This kind of analysis helps to establish timing and scheduling plans for the media selected later in the planning process.

Analyzing the Data

One worthwhile use of media expenditure figures is to examine spending by advertisers who lead in share-of-market. Those with smaller shares might want to learn which media, markets, and audiences are most important to the leaders. Sometimes it is possible to find that leading competitors ignore one or two media entirely. In such a case, it may be possible for those with lesser shares to preempt a medium for themselves. For example, all of the share leaders may emphasize network television. Then, a planner may select radio as a medium in which a brand could be very significant because no others are using radio. The

FIGURE 4–7. Leading National Advertisers Magazine Analysis Service

CUMULATIVE Pages	Dollars	JANUARY Space	Dollars	FEBRUARY Space	Dollars	MARCH Space	Dollars	APRIL Space	Dollars	MAY Space	Dollars	JUNE Space	Dollars
F330													
	F330	HIRAM WALKER-GOODERHAM & WORTS, LTD. (Hiram Walker, Inc., Detroit, Mich.), Walkerville, Ontario, Canada												
7.00	60,900	1 P4	7,000	2 C4	7,000	1 P4	7,000	1 P4	8,400				
										1 P4*s*	13,775		
						1 P4²s	6,098	1 P4*s*	5,390	1 P4³s	12,949	1 P4*s*	6,098
3.34	182,892			1 P4²s	6,098	1 P4³s	12,949	1 P4³s	13,775	1 P4⁵s	12,949	1 P4²s	12,949
1.45	95,105					1 P4s	14,915	1 P4s	14,915	1 P4s	14,915		
1.77	33,935					1 P4s	6,880	1 P4s	6,461	1 P4s	6,461		
						1 P4²s	20,301	1 P4²s	20,301				
2.97	170,159					1 P4*s*	20,301	1 P4*s*	20,301	1 P4*s*	7,795	1 P4³s	20,301
.96	81,782												
3.52	136,116									1 P4*s*	15,429		
				1 P4*s*	15,429	1 P4³s	15,429			1 P4⁵s	15,429		
21.01	760,889				28,527		103,873		103,318		92,025		39,348
	F330	HOUSE OF BANFI, Farmingdale, N. Y.											
.66	8.085							⅓ P	4,255				
.66	5,200												
1.65	11,620												
.33	1,800												
.33	2,750												
3.63	29,455												
1.60	13,140												
1.60	13,140												
5.23	42,595												
	F330	J & J DISTRIBUTING CO., Millburn, N. J.											
.32	13,776					1 P4s	1,722	1 P4s	1,722	1 P4s	1,722		
.32	16,240					1 P2s	2,030	1 P2s	2,030	1 P2s	2,030		
.64	30,016						3,752		3,752		3,752		
	F330	JACQUIN, CHARLES, eT CIE, INC., Philadelphia, Pa.											
1.60	13,140												
1.60	13,140												
	F330	KOBRAND CORP., New York, N. Y.											
.28	22,000												
2.00	17,848									1 P4B	8,707		
6.83	147,053	1 P4B¹	21,574					3 C4B³	21,574			CS4B²	43,148
2.00	38,526												
1.00	7,360												
4.00	57,192									1 P4	14,298		
2.00	30,800												
1.00	7,215												
4.50	76,819	1 P4B²	16,503							⅔ P4B¹	12,374	½ P4B²	9,074
1.00	21,942												
1.00	12,984												
1.50	28,693									3 C4B	18,136		
4.67	63,940					4 C4B	13,800			⅔ P4B	9,890	4 C4B	13,800
1.00	7,620												
										⅔ P4B²	7,280		
4.67	50,020									4 C4⁴	11,000	½ P4B²	5,635
										1 P4B¹	11,960		
12.00	146,395			1 P4B¹	11,960	1 P4B¹	11,960	1 P4B¹	11,960	4 C4B²	14,835	1 P4B⁴	11,960
6.27	296,771	1 P4B⁴s	17,561	1 P4B³s	17,561			1 P4B⁴	43,884			1 P4B2k	14,801
5.00	79.225					1 P4B²	15,496			1 P4B²	15,496	CS4B⁴	30,063
2.84	129,097											⅔ P4B	33,066
1.00	17,595					1 P4B	17,595						
1.00	10,495												
2.50	57,350									3 C4B	22,500		
4.67	70,554					1 P4B	14,718			⅔ P4B	10,197		
2.00	78.224												
2.00	18,113	1 P4B	7,763							4 C4B	10,350		
7.37	518,270	1 P4B⁴s	28,445	1 P4³s	28,445	1 P4B³k	33,373	1 P4B³k	33,373	⅔ P4B³	46,489	½ P4B³	36,702
1.00	30,383												
5.67	39,650									1 P4B	6,160	⅔ P4B	4,670
1.00	3,600												
91.77	2,085,734		91,846		57,966		106,942		110,791		219,672		202,919
2.00	40,830									4 C4¹	12,472		
8.00	91,648			1 P4³	10,845					1 P4⁵	10,845		
10.00	132,478				10,845						23,317		
101.77	2,218,212				68,811		106,942		110,791		242,989		202,919

FIGURE 4–7. (Continued)

Beer, Wine & Liquor—F300

MEDIA	JULY Space	Dollars	AUGUST Space	Dollars	SEPTEMBER Space	Dollars	OCTOBER Space	Dollars	NOVEMBER Space	Dollars	DECEMBER Space	Dollars
LIQUOR												
WALKER'S DELUXE BOURBON WHISKEY											$1,019,442	
Book Digest (182)							1 P4	10,500	1 P4	10,500	1 P4	10,500
Newsweek (420)							1 P4/s	3,925	1 P4/s	965	1 P4/s	965
Newsweek (420)			1 P4/s	6,098			1 P4/s	9,460	1 P43s	9,460	1 P43s	9,460
Newsweek (420)	1 P4/s	6,098	1 P45s	6,098	1 P4/s	9,460	1 P45s	3,925	1 P44s	3,925	1 P44s	3,925
Playboy (420)							1 P4s	17,702	1 P4s	16,329	1 P4s	16,329
Psychology Today (420)							1 P4s	4,711	1 P4s	4,711	1 P4s	4,711
Sports Illustrated (420)									1 P4/s	14,706	1 P4/s	14,706
Sports Illustrated (420)							1 P42s	14,706	1 P43s	2,035	1 P43s	14,706
Time (420)									1 P4/s	16,148		
Time (420)									1 P4/s	3,960	1 P4/s	1,350
Time (420)							1 P4/s	20,108	1 P43s	20,108	1 P43s	20,108
U.S.News&World Rep. (420)							1 P4/s	12,400				
U.S.News&World Rep. (420)							1 P43s	12,400	1 P4/s	12,400		
U.S.News&World Rep. (420)							1 P45s	12,400	1 P4/s	12,400	1 P42s	12,400
Total		6,098		12,196		9,460		122,237		127,647		109,160
CYNAR LIQUEUR											$24,470	
American Home (429)											1/3 P	3,830
Gourmet (429)									1/3 P	2,600	1/3 P	2,600
New Yorker (429)											1/3 P/	2,324
New Yorker (429)									1/3 P3	2,324	1/3 P2	2,324
New Yorker (429)									1/3 P/	2,324	1/3 P3	2,324
Town & Country (429)											1/3 P	1,800
Vogue (429)											1/3 P	2,750
Total										7,248		17,952
New York Times Mag. (850)											340 L/	3,285
New York Times Mag. (850)											340 L2	3,285
New York Times Mag. (850)									340 L4	3,285	340 L3	3,285
Total										3,285		9,855
Grand Total										10,533		27,807
LORD BARRY SCOTCH WHISKY											$10,740	
Sports Illustrated (420)									1 P/s	1,722		
Sports Illustrated (420)					1 P4s	1,722	1 P4s	1,722	1 P3s	1,722	1 P/s	1,722
Time (420)									1 P/s	2,030		
Time (420)					1 P2s	2,030	1 P/s	2,030	1 P3s	2,030	1 P/s	2,030
Total						3,752		3,752		7,504		3,752
DEVONSHIRE SCOTCH WHISKY												
New York Times Mag. (850)									340 L/	3,285		
New York Times Mag. (850)									340 L2	3,285		
New York Times Mag. (850)									340 L3	3,285	340 L/	3,285
Total										9,855		3,285
BEEFEATER GIN											$2,146,536	
Better Homes & Gar. (429)							1 P48k	11,000			1 P48k	11,000
Black Enterprise (396)											1 P48	9,141
Business Week (420)	1/2 P4B2	12,949	1/3 P3	4,660					1 P4B2	21,574	1 P4B2	21,574
Cosmopolitan (429)									1 P48	19,263	1 P48	19,263
Cue (429)											1 P48/	7,360
Ebony (680)					1 P4	14,298	1 P4	14,298			1 P4	14,298
Esquire (420)							1 P48	15,400			1 P48	15,400
Essence (420)											1 P48	7,215
Forbes (420)			1/3 P/	3,390					4 C4B2	18,975	1 P48/	16,503
Fortune (420)											1 P48	21,942
Golf (429)											1 P48	12,984
Golf Digest (420)	1/2 P4B	10,557										
Gourmet (429)							1 P4B	13,225			1 P48	13,225
Ms. (420)											1 P48	7,620
New York Magazine (420)												
New York Magazine (420)					1/2 P4B3	5,635			1 P48/	10,235	1 P4B2	10,235
New Yorker (429)												
New Yorker (429)	1 P4B4	11,960	1 P4B4	11,960	1 P4B3	11,960	1 P4B3	11,960	1 P4B2	11,960	1 P4B2	11,960
Newsweek (420)	CS4B4	87,768					1/2 P4B/	27,428	1 P4B4	43,884	1 P4B2	43,884
People Weekly (420)											1 P4B/	18,170
Playboy (420)			1/2 P4B	26,235			2/3 P4B	29,453			1 P48	40,343
Psychology Today (420)												
Ski (429)											1 P48	10,495
Smithsonian (420)	1/2 P4B	12,350									1 P48	22,500
Southern Living (420)	CS4B	29,436			1/2 P4B	8,844					1/2 P48	7,359
Sports Illustrated (420)							1 P4B2	39,112			1 P48/	39,112
Tennis (420)												
Time (420)	CS4B2	122,349			1 P4B3k	33,373	1 P4B4	61,174	1 P4B2k	33,373	1 P48/	61,174
U.S.News&World Rep. (420)											1 P48/	30,383
World Tennis (429)	4 C4B	8,250			1 P4B	6,160	4 C4B	8,250			1 P48	6,160
Yachting (420)					1 P4B	3,600						
Total		295,619		46,245		83,870		231,300		159,264		479,300
New York News Mag. (850)											1 P4/	19,915
New York News Mag. (850)											4 C42	20,915
New York Times Mag. (850)												
New York Times Mag. (850)	CS42	21,690			1 P4/	10,845	4 C45	13,346			1 P4/	11,605
Total		21,690				10,845		13,346				52,435
Grand Total		317,309		46,245		94,715		244,646		159,264		531,735

Source: Publishers Information Bureau, Inc.

planner should keep in mind, however, that if a competitor avoids a medium, there may be good reason to conclude that the medium is not appropriate for the product's advertising.

There are, of course, problems in analyzing media expenditure data. Most such data are incomplete, do not show any discounts earned in a medium, and cover only large advertisers. An additional problem is the age of the data. It is rare that any data are less than one month old, and, as a result, the nature of the data is historical rather than contemporary. The question arises whether such data have very much meaning, especially if a competitor is not currently using the same media in the same ways as in the past. Yet if a competitor uses media in a predictably consistent pattern, then additional data may be of little value. Probably the best use of an expenditure analysis is as part of an organized intelligence system including other kinds of marketing information to provide a clear picture of competitors' strategies. Although some advertising agencies tend to deprecate the use of expenditure analysis as not being worth the investment in money or time, most large agencies feel that it is valuable if used properly as an indication of spending strategy.

Probably the greatest danger in analyzing expenditure data may come from simply copying the leaders in a blind fashion. If a leading share competitor places 10 percent of its budget in Market A, then other competitors may follow the leader. But the followers' products and market strategies may not lend themselves to such weight in Market A. Furthermore, the share leader may establish its weight proportions for reasons quite different from those that followers ought to use.

An expenditure analysis is helpful as a means of knowing what competitors have done, but not necessarily as a means of knowing what to do as a result. These analyses may show, for example, that a competitor is test marketing a product, and this information may call for a revised market strategy to combat the situation. Intelligently used, expenditure data may be well worth the time and money invested.

Using Competitive Media Expenditure Analyses

Following is a list of uses of a competitive media expenditure analysis devised by the staff of *Media Decisions*.[3] It reviews the most important uses and values to be obtained by completing such an analysis:

1. The expenditure figures can show you the regionality and seasonality and how these marketing factors are changing for all competitive and potentially competitive brands.
2. The data can give you a fix on ad budget size and media mix market-by-market.

---

[3]*Media Decisions*, "Do You Know Your Competitive Brand Data?", August 1975, p. 60.

3. You can use the data to spot new product tests and to track new brand roll-outs.
4. You can infer from where the money is being spent how competitors view their target audiences, how they profile their brands, and where they seek to position themselves in your marketplace.
5. You can watch spending patterns of the opposition—TV flighting, radio station rotation, position practices in magazines, or day of week in newspapers.
6. Once you have complete knowledge of what your enemies are up to, you can make better decisions as where to meet them head-on and when to outflank them.
7. In new-product and line-extension planning, expenditure data are essential to estimate how much it will cost to get into a market, who's already there, and which competitive product types are growing fastest in the new product's market segment.

Sources of Marketing Data

Size and share of market for a brand and its competitors, and other information that comprise a situation analysis may be obtained from a number of syndicated research services. Other data may be obtained from periodicals, association reports, government, and media.

Major Data Services

The most widely used syndicated research services are those of the A. C. Nielsen Company, the Market Research Corporation of America (MRCA), Audits and Surveys, Inc., Selling Areas-Marketing, Inc. (SAMI), the W. R. Simmons Company, and Mediamark Research, Inc. Numerous other research companies also exist.

The A. C. Nielsen Company. Nielsen provides a national brand, store-audited service covering almost every product sold in food and drug stores. Each of these product categories is audited in a national sample of retail stores every 60 days. The service provides share-of-market data based on sales to consumers at the retail level, in addition to average retail prices, wholesale prices, inventory, out-of-stock, dealer support (displays, local advertising, and coupon redemption), and major media advertising. The sample data are then projected in order to obtain national and regional data. The figures are further broken down by county size, store type (chain and independent), brand, package size, and product type.

The method of making an audit is to count a store's inventory of a given product no matter where it is stored. Sales for a given period are found by subtracting the total stock on hand at the close of a period from the total available for sale at the beginning. Because only a sample of stores is audited, it becomes necessary to project average per-store sales to a national figure and to geographical regions, city-size groups, etc.

Market Research Corporation of America. MRCA maintains a consumer panel of 7,500 families who keep continuous diaries of their purchases. The panel members record food, grocery, and personal care items purchased during any given week and then mail their diaries to the company for tabulation. Diaries include quantities purchased, package sizes, prices paid, and the kind of retail outlet through which purchases were made. Other information includes effects of promotional activities such as coupons, one-cent sales, or combination sales of different products. Through such tabulations it is possible to learn the share of market for many different brands and varieties of food products.

Audits and Surveys. This service measures the national total market based on a sample of the client's product class distribution. The sample of stores to be audited is drawn only from the types of outlets in which the client has distribution. Information is provided on sales, inventory, distribution, out-of-stock, and the number of days stock is on hand. These data are projected to the total U. S. and the client's sales regions. Audit and Surveys telephones a flash report to the client at the close of the audit followed by a formal report two weeks later, compared to Nielsen's 45 to 60 days for reports to reach a client.

Mediamark Research, Inc., and W. R. Simmons. These companies provide marketing as well as media data on a regular basis. Each company reports how often products and/or brands are used so that a planner can identify heavy and light users demographically. In addition, each company reports how heavy and light users were exposed to either network television programs or national magazines. As a result, the planner can select media that not only have the largest audiences, but the largest audiences of heavy users of a given product or brand. Special studies are also available on a custom basis.

Other Sources of Data

The preceding sources of data provide specific and pertinent data for a situation analysis, but are relatively expensive. The cost may be too high for many small manufacturers or agencies, so it becomes necessary to find substitute sources of data. There are a number of relatively inexpensive sources, though they do not provide the same amount of detail, especially about competitors' sales and distribution practices. When the information is incomplete, assmptions will have to be made about the missing data. These assumptions, however, can often be checked by astute observers of the marketing action of both their own company and competitors. The following list, meanwhile, may be helpful in locating data for the situation analysis.

Sales Management Survey of Buying Power. Marketing and media planners often find the *Sales Management Survey of Buying Power* a convenient source of three kinds of data about markets:

1. population and household data for all major markets in the United States
2. income and spending statistics about markets
3. retail sales data by broad product classes. The classes reported are: (a) food sales, (b) eating and drinking places, (c) general merchandise, (d) apparel, (e) furniture and household appliances, (f) automotive, (g) gas stations, (h) lumber, building, and hardware, and (i) drugs.

No individual brand sales are shown, and there are no classifications of consumers other than by population and income. However, the periodical is convenient in locating and evaluating geographical markets by state, by Standard Metropolitan Statistical Area, by county, or by city. Furthermore, the three factors (population, income, and retail sales) have been combined into a multiple factor index number for each market that makes comparisons among markets easier. Convenient tables ranking markets by sales potential also facilitate comparisons by each of the nine retail product categories. A user trying to find and evaluate markets for a drug product, for example, will find a table that ranks markets from best to poorest on the basis of sales of drugs. *Sales Management Survey of Buying Power* is published annually.

Standard Rate and Data Service (SRDS). The Standard Rate and Data Service publishes media rate books for all major media. In its local media books (newspaper, spot radio, and spot television) are market data sections similar to those in the *Survey of Buying Power*. SRDS also shows geographical markets by state, Standard Metropolitan Statistical Areas, counties, and cities, but not in as much detail as the *Buying Power* book. Retail sales, too, are shown by seven different categories: (a) food, (b) drugs, (c) general merchandise, (d) apparel, (e) home furnishings, (f) automotive, and (g) service stations. Ranking tables are also provided, showing markets for the seven product types. Local media rate books are published monthly, and the market data are revised annually.

Editor and Publisher Market Guide. This annual publication contains geographical market data similar to that of the preceding two. Markets are also ranked by population, total income, total retail sales, total food sales, and by household income. The text also provides individual descriptions of markets.

Census Data. The U. S. Department of Commerce publishes many census analyses that are helpful in marketing planning. Most useful have been the Census of Business and Census of Population. But other census data, too numerous to list here, are available for special industries. The *Statistical Abstract*, published once a year, has been considered helpful as a quick source of data for media market planning.

Media Studies of Special Markets. Often local and national media conduct special market studies that may be quite helpful in learning about geographical as well as special markets. Although the purpose of these reports is to show a given medium in a favorable light, the researcher should not assume that all such studies are biased. Often a medium will sponsor a study that represents a significant contribution to the understanding of markets and media. Many times the only research available on a special market or medium is to be found in these studies.

Among the most widely used sources of market data and among the few that show brand share of markets are brand preference studies conducted by local newspapers and provided free of cost to agencies. Different newspapers use different names for these studies, but they are essentially home inventories of brands of many different kinds of products that have been recently purchased. The *Milwaukee Journal* has one of the most well-known of such studies and reports on brands of face soaps, coffees, packaged meats, and almost a hundred other items. The data are tabulated and the percentage of total sales that each brand has is computed so that, in effect, one may have a share of market for a given brand in that area. Since there are many such studies in existence, it is possible to get some idea of the relative share of market for a brand in various parts of the country by comparing data from a composite selection.

Unfortunately, most studies are conducted only once a year and some newspapers do not repeat their studies each year. Furthermore, there may be differences in the degree of control exercised in the collection and reporting of such data, so that it is difficult to know how precise the data are. Then, too, since the data are collected only once a year, there is no measure of total volume purchased, since an individual may just happen to have purchased a given brand only at the time the study was made.

There are a number of publications that offer market and media data on a regular basis. The more useful ones are: *Advertising Age, Marketing & Media Decisions, Marketing Communications, Adweek, Broadcasting, Editor & Publisher, Magazine,* and *Television/Radio Age*. Information can be obtained from the publications by either subscribing to them or by contacting their libraries to determine what studies were published in their past issues.

Associations. There are many trade associations that report market data for their members. In some cases, these data show sales by brands, but others tend to be rather general. Because there are so many different trade associations in the country, it is advisable to determine whether they can be of aid in compiling the situation analysis.

Miscellaneous Sources. There are yet other sources of data that are available at relatively low cost to the market/media planner. Federal, state, and local governments all produce various kinds of research that may be helpful. Federal data may be found by writing to the Government Printing Office in Washington, DC.

Chambers of Commerce, both national and local, may be helpful in finding the right kinds of data needed for marketing situation purposes. Obviously this kind of data will be rather general but may be useful for preliminary portions of the analysis.

Finally, for analysis of products and product values, both *Consumer Reports* (published by the Consumer Union of U.S., Inc.) and *Consumer Bulletin* (published by Consumer Research, Inc.) provide monthly and annual publications for a small cost. Both of these organizations put various brands of products through rigorous tests to determine quality and the best buy for the money. Not all brands or models are tested, but many of the most popular brands on the market are analyzed. Ordinarily, this kind of information is difficult to obtain except by special research services, so these two publications make the job of finding product values relatively easy.

In conclusion, then, the situation analysis is a very important document in the media planning area. To the extent that it is done thoroughly and with accuracy, it can help the media planner make more effective decisions by providing a complete picture of the marketing situation not only for the client's brand but for competitors.

QUESTIONS FOR DISCUSSION

1. Briefly explain the role of a marketing strategy plan in media planning.
2. Give some examples of marketing objectives and some related marketing strategies that could be used to attain each objective.
3. What is the difference between a marketing objective and the basic selling idea in a marketing strategy plan?
4. Why may it be advisable to place more dollars in markets where a brand has been selling well, rather than in a new or undeveloped market?
5. Why can't a manufacturer of cereals look at sales records and know how well the brand is selling at any local (retail) level?
6. Why may it not be a good idea for a national advertiser to select local markets in which to advertise only on the basis of shipments to those markets?

7. Should media planners use the same media that most of their competitors use? Briefly explain.
8. How can an advertiser "force" distribution sometimes in a market where its brand is not distributed?
9. In what ways does a sales promotion plan affect media planning?
10. Suppose that a planner feels that television is best for a given brand, but the creative people insist that an ad appear only in four colors in print. Whose judgment will probably be more significant?

SELECTED READINGS

Advertising Age, "Know Market Goals, Then Pick Media, AMC Exec Says," May 8, 1972, p. 32.

Advertising Age, "Bolte Tells of 12 Criteria to Check Marketing Approach," May 16, 1966, p. 98.

Blair, William, "Does Profile Matching Work?" *Media/Scope,* September 1965, pp. 82–86.

Bogart, Leo, "Relating Media Strategy to Sales," *Sales Management,* Nov. 1, 1971, p. 26.

Bruno, A. V., et al., "Media Approaches to Segmentation," *Journal of Advertising Research,* April 1973, pp. 35–42.

Chait, Lawrence, *Targeted Marketing,* Lawrence G. Chait & Co., Inc. 1965.

Colley, Russell H., *Defining Advertising Goals for Measured Advertising Results,* Association of National Advertisers, Inc., 1961

Garfinkel, Norton, "New Measurements of the Value of Marketing Targets and Media Vehicles." Speech delivered to the Advertising Research Foundation, 12th Annual Conference, 1966.

Greene, Jerome D., "Media Exposure as a Demographic," *Media/Scope,* November 1966, pp. 116–18.

"Guidelines for Advertising Media Management," *Journal of Small Business Management,* January 1978, pp. 34–40.

Honomichl, Jack J., "How Research Relates to the Marketing Process," in "The New World of Advertising," *Advertising Age,* Nov. 21, 1973, pp. 52+.

Joyce, Timothy, "Target Weighting Gives Boost to Consumer Studies," *Advertising Age,* July 15, 1974, p. 27.

Lodish, L. M., "Considering Competition in Media Planning," *Management Science,* February 1971, pp. 293–306.

"Media Market Planning." Speech given by Edward H. Meyers, reported in *Grey Matter,* Vol. 41, May 1970, Grey Advertising Agency.

Media/Scope, "How Media Strategy is Developed in the Marketing Concept," May 1960, pp. 45–48.

Ostrow, Joseph, "Let's Become Objective," *Media Decisions,* May 1972, p. 64.

Peckham, James O., "Can We Relate Advertising Dollars to Market Share Objectives?" Advertising Research Foundation, 12th Annual Conference, 1966, pp. 53–57.

Setar, John W., "How to Solve the Problem of Problem Markets," *Television Magazine,* September 1959, p. 56.

Sissors, Jack Z., "Matching Media With Markets," *Journal of Advertising Research,* October 1971, pp. 39–43.

Surmanek, Jim, "More to Media

Buying than Number Review," *Advertising Age*, May 21, 1979, pp. 64, 66.

Wolfe, Harry D., "The Dimensions of Media Audiences," in *Evaluating Media*, National Industrial Conference Board, Business Policy Study No. 121, 1966, pp. 31–41.

5
Who, Where, and When

Among the most important decisions that must be made early in the media planning process are:

1. To whom should we advertise?
2. Where, geographically, should we advertise?
3. When should we advertise?

Once made, these decisions will control other decisions. For example, if it has been agreed that advertising should be directed primarily to women aged 18 to 34, then media alternatives such as sports magazines or TV programs directed primarily to men would not be appropriate. (Obviously there are some exceptions—but not many.) To control later decisions, target decisions must be made early.

Sometimes the media planner makes these decisions alone, but more likely the process includes creative and marketing planners along with input from the client. It is most often a team process.

Answers to each of the three big questions rely most heavily on numerical analysis of marketing and media data, but they also involve judgment and subjective appraisal. Numbers that are evaluated literally may be subject to error. One must know where the numbers came from—how they were obtained or calculated. The best planners know the value of research methodology as well as how to analyze the numbers. The search for objectivity in planning requires both abilities.

In analyzing numerical data, there are three commonly used bases: raw numbers, percentages, and index numbers. Raw numbers are used least often because they are so large and because it is difficult to compare the raw numbers of one brand with those of another brand because each may have radically different bases. Percentages are a way to equalize the bases of numbers from two or more companies and thus are usually preferred over raw numbers. But for ease and quickness of seeing the relationships among many numbers, index numbers are preferred over the other two.

Using Index Numbers to Analyze Markets

As used most often in marketing and media analysis, an index number is a number that shows a relationship between two percentages or between two raw numbers. Generally index numbers are expressed as whole numbers, though they can be expressed as percentages. The value of an index number is that it relates population demographics to sales or product usage for many different demographic segments, enabling one to have a convenient common method for comparison. If the population segment is considered to be "average," then an index number for sales tells how much above or below average sales are, in absolute terms. An average index number is 100, while 125 is 25 percent above average, and 80 is 20 percent below average. An example of how index numbers may be used is shown in Tables 5–1 and 5–2.

Which demographic segments should be selected as target markets for media to reach? The usual answer is: Select those demographic segments with the largest volume of sales, or the largest number of users. In other words, advertise where the brand has a history of success. According to the traditional point of view, then, three age segments of homemakers in Table 5–1 might be the prime targets for soft margarine—those aged 25 to 34, 35 to 44, and 45 to 54. Obviously, income, occupation, education, and other demographic categories would also have to be checked before a final decision could be made.

However, there is another way to look at the data in Table 5–1, and that is to compare the percentage of usage in each age segment to the percentage of population in that segment. One could instead compare the

TABLE 5–1. Use of Soft Margarine by Age Segment

Age Segment	No. of Homemakers in U.S. (thousands)	U.S. Homemakers (%)	No. of Homemaker Users (thousands)	Homemaker Users (%)
18–24	9,565	13.1	3,204	14.9
25–34	16,151	22.1	5,238	24.4
35–44	11,812	16.2	3,582	16.7
45–54	12,028	16.5	3,457	16.1
55–64	10,687	14.7	2,990	13.9
65+	12,681	17.4	3,029	14.0
Total	72,924	100.0	21,500	100.0

Source: Simmons Market Research Bureau, 1978/79

raw numbers of usage and population distribution in each segment, but such comparisons are more difficult than those made using percentages.

When the percentage of usage is compared with the percentage of population distribution in each segment, an index number may be calculated to make the comparisons easier to analyze. The formula for calculating such numbers is as follows:

$$\text{Index number} = \frac{\text{\% of users in a demographic segment}}{\text{\% of population in the same segment}} \times 100$$

Using the formula to calculate index numbers for the data in Table 5–1 yields the index numbers in Table 5–2. The index numbers in Table 5–2 show how much the product is being used compared with the potential (or population proportion) for use in each age segment. An index number above 100, as seen in the 18 to 24, 25 to 34, and 35 to 44 age groups, indicates higher than average usage. Now one can see that the potential for usage has shifted a bit to younger aged segments. In this sense, index numbers more accurately indicate potential for usage or sales. One cannot easily see this kind of relationship, however, without first calculating the index numbers.

It may be helpful to think of index numbers as measures of central tendency, just as "averages" or "means" are in the statistical world. An average does not describe any one person in a group, only the group as a whole.

Likewise, an index number over 100 means that the usage of the product is proportionately greater in that segment than one that is average (100) or below average (any number below 100). Segments with index numbers over 100 do not necessarily have numerically more users in them than in other segments; they may only have proportionately more. Theoretically, the segment with the highest index number represents the best potential for usage. In analyzing marketing data, one should calculate index numbers for all demographic groups such as age, sex, income, occupation, and education. Combining the index numbers for all demographic groups will produce a market profile similar to the one shown in Figure 5–1.

TABLE 5–2. Calculating Index Numbers

Age Segment	Calculation	Index
18–24	14.9 ÷ 13.1	114
25–34	24.4 ÷ 22.1	110
35–44	16.7 ÷ 16.2	103
45–54	16.1 ÷ 16.5	97
55–64	13.9 ÷ 14.7	95
65+	14.0 ÷ 17.4	80

FIGURE 5–1. Profile of a Market

Classification with Index Numbers Above and Below Average

1+ years of college	141
Skilled workers	129
Retired + unemployed	117
D counties	115
East Central	112
Housewife aged 35–49	112
1–3 years of high school	111
Middle income	110
Children 6–17	110
Household head age 35–49	109
Any children	106
3–4 family size	106
West Central	105
C counties	105
A counties	100

97	1–2 family size
97	Housewife aged 50+
97	Professional and white collar
96	Northeast
96	South
96	5+ family size
96	Upper income
96	Household head under 35
94	No children
93	Pacific
91	Lower income
90	Housewife aged under 35
89	B counties
89	Children under 6
87	Graduated high school
75	Grade school education
72	Household head 65+
72	Unskilled

U.S. Average
100

Although the technique of calculating index numbers shown in Table 5–2 can be used, there is a simpler way of computing the numbers that is often preferred by planners. This method is shown in Table 5–3. Briefly stated, the method starts with the computation of the total number of users in a market. A percentage of the universe is then computed. This percentage indicates that of the total population, X percent are users. The number of users is compared with the number of individuals in each population segment and percentages are calculated. Finally, each of these segment percentages is divided by the total percentage of users. Note that the index numbers obtained by this method are identical to those obtained in Table 5–2.

TABLE 5–3. Another Method of Calculating Index Numbers

Step One: Find the total number of users compared with the total population in the market
as follows:
a. Total number of users in all segments: 21,500,000
b. Total number of homemakers in the U.S.: 72,924,000
c. Percentage of total homemakers that are users: 29.5%

Step Two: Find the percentage of users in each demographic segment (from Table 5–1):

18–24	3,204 ÷ 9,565	=	33.5%
25–34	5,238 ÷ 16,151	=	32.4
35–44	3,582 ÷ 11,812	=	30.3
45–54	3,457 ÷ 12,028	=	28.7
55–64	2,990 ÷ 10,687	=	28.0
65+	3,029 ÷ 12,681	=	23.9

Step Three: Divide each of the percentages in Step Two by the percentage in Step One:

18–24	33.5 ÷ 29.5	=	114 index
25–34	32.4 ÷ 29.5	=	110 index
35–44	30.3 ÷ 29.5	=	103 index
45–54	28.7 ÷ 29.5	=	97 index
55–64	28.0 ÷ 29.5	=	95 index
65+	23.9 ÷ 29.5	=	80 index

TABLE 5–4. An Example of Misleading Index Numbers

Age segment	Population in each segment (%)	Product usage in each segment (%)	Index
18–24	11.1	15.0	134
25–34	19.3	17.8	92
35–49	30.2	29.2	97
50+	39.4	38.0	96
Total	100.0	100.0	

A note of caution about using index numbers: One may be easily misled into believing that the demographic segment with the highest index number *always* represents the best potential. This is not true. Aside from the fact that one segment may have some other qualification that is of great marketing value, there is also the possibility that a segment with a high index number may have a low degree of product usage or sales or a low population size for that segment. If so, the segment with the highest index number may not represent the best potential for continued usage.

To illustrate, Table 5–4 shows marketing data for a fictitious brand, showing that, although the 18 to 24 age segment has the highest index number (134), it also has the lowest percentage of product usage and the lowest population percentage of any segment. It would not be very meaningful, therefore, to limit the selection of media to those reaching the 18 to 24 segment and ignore the other segments, especially since 85 percent of the usage is in the 25 and older segment.

One should first examine the volume of usage or sales in each demographic segment to determine whether the volume warrants inclusion as a media target. Only then will index numbers help locate good potential target segments.

Selecting Advertising Targets

The answer to the question: "To whom should we advertise?" implies that not everyone should be the target for advertising. Some individuals are unlikely to buy a given product or brand, while others are more likely to do so. The goal is to identify the targets—those who are most likely to buy. Targets will most likely be identified on the basis of one or more demographic characteristics of the market. Which demographic characteristics? Those typical of those who have purchased the product/brand in the past and those who resemble past purchasers in terms of age, income, occupation, education, etc. One source used frequently to gather demographic information is Simmons Market Research Bureau. (An example of Simmons' data is shown in Figure 5–2.) Custom-made research can also provide this kind of information, but it is usually quite expensive and time-consuming.

The planner must consider a number of factors in analyzing how consumers buy certain products. The first is to find those demographic segments that use the product most. Other considerations are: (a) whether any segment of product users ought to be singled out for special treatment, such as heavy users only, medium users, light users, or combinations; (b) whether users of the advertised brand differ from users of the product category in general; (c) whether the creative strategy positions the brand to appeal more to one demographic segment than another; and (d) whether some other kind of target identification, such as psychographics, should be used instead of or in addition to demographics.

Defining Target Audiences

The problem of defining target audiences primarily involves the use of demographic data, though other information may also be considered. The planner will want to know as precisely as possible which demographic segments of the market should be considered targets. There are usually many options from which to choose. Broad categories include age, sex, income, occupation, and education. These, however, can be broken down into more specific segments. The age category, for example, might be broken down into such segments as 18 to 24, 18 to 49, or 34 to 49. But age is only one way to define a target group. The planner might opt for an income segment such as upper or lower; or an education

FIGURE 5–2. Frozen Pizzas Usage by Female Homemakers

0282
P-20

FROZEN PIZZAS: USAGE
(FEMALE HOMEMAKERS)

0282
P-20

	TOTAL U.S. '000	ALL USERS A '000	B % DOWN	C % ACROSS	D INDX	HEAVY USERS A '000	B % DOWN	C % ACROSS	D INDX	MEDIUM USERS A '000	B % DOWN	C % ACROSS	D INDX	LIGHT USERS A '000	B % DOWN	C % ACROSS	D INDX
TOTAL FEMALE HOMEMAKERS	74975	37791	100.0	50.4	100												
18 - 24	9348	5006	13.2	53.6	106												
25 - 34	17130	9457	25.0	55.2	110												
35 - 44	12512	8132	21.5	65.0	129												
45 - 54	11866	6757	17.9	56.9	113												
55 - 64	10905	4780	12.6	43.8	87												
65 OR OLDER	13214	3659	9.7	27.7	55												
18 - 34	26478	14464	38.3	54.6	108												
18 - 49	44834	26204	69.3	58.4	116												
25 - 54	41508	24346	64.4	58.7	116												
35 - 49	18356	11741	31.1	64.0	127												
GRADUATED COLLEGE	9133	4389	11.6	48.1	95												
ATTENDED COLLEGE	11518	6223	16.5	54.0	107												
GRADUATED HIGH SCHOOL	30992	17290	45.8	55.8	111												
DID NOT GRADUATE HIGH SCHOOL	23333	9889	26.2	42.4	84												
EMPLOYED	36063	20449	54.1	56.7	112												
EMPLOYED FULL-TIME	27990	15680	41.5	56.0	111												
EMPLOYED PART-TIME	8073	4769	12.6	59.1	117												
NOT EMPLOYED	38912	17342	45.9	44.6	88												
PROFESSIONAL/MANAGER	9320	4941	13.1	53.0	105												
CLERICAL/SALES	14571	8718	23.1	59.8	119												
CRAFTSMEN/FOREMEN	731	*434	1.1	59.4	118												
OTHER EMPLOYED	11441	6356	16.8	55.6	110												
SINGLE	8476	3850	10.2	45.4	90												
MARRIED	49417	26761	70.8	54.2	107												
DIVORCED/SEPARATED/WIDOWED	17082	7180	19.0	42.0	83												
PARENTS	30584	19389	51.3	63.4	126												
WHITE	65754	33636	89.0	51.2	101												
BLACK	7875	3418	9.0	43.4	86												
OTHER	1346	*738	2.0	54.8	109												
NORTHEAST-CENSUS	16347	7822	20.7	47.8	95												
NORTH CENTRAL	18367	10889	28.8	59.3	118												
SOUTH	24634	12212	32.3	49.6	98												
WEST	15626	6868	18.2	44.0	87												
NORTHEAST-MKTG.	17609	8695	23.0	49.4	98												
EAST CENTRAL	11334	5821	15.4	51.4	102												
WEST CENTRAL	12967	7962	21.1	61.4	122												
SOUTH	20627	10088	26.7	48.9	97												
PACIFIC	12439	5225	13.8	42.0	83												
COUNTY SIZE A	28026	14211	37.6	50.7	101												
COUNTY SIZE B	21724	10812	28.6	49.8	99												
COUNTY SIZE C	13007	6318	16.7	48.6	96												
COUNTY SIZE D	12219	6450	17.1	52.8	105												
METRO CENTRAL CITY	23082	11491	30.4	49.8	99												
METRO SUBURBAN	31254	15726	41.6	50.3	100												
NON METRO	20639	10575	28.0	51.2	102												
HSHLD INC $35,000 OR MORE	8229	4486	11.9	54.5	108	991	12.9	12.0	118	1769	13.1	21.5	120	1726	10.4	21.0	95
$25,000 OR MORE	19918	11178	29.6	56.1	111	2630	34.2	13.2	129	3879	28.8	19.5	108	4668	28.1	23.4	106
$20,000 - $24,999	9366	5599	14.8	59.8	119	1080	14.1	11.5	113	1896	14.1	20.2	113	2623	15.8	28.0	126
$15,000 - $19,999	10045	5440	14.4	54.2	107	1008	13.1	10.0	98	2134	15.8	21.2	118	2298	13.8	22.9	103
$10,000 - $14,999	15094	7192	19.0	47.6	95	1454	18.9	9.6	94	2373	17.6	15.7	87	3364	20.2	22.3	101
$ 5,000 - $ 9,999	11542	5063	13.4	43.9	87	956	12.4	8.3	81	1883	14.0	16.3	91	2223	13.4	19.3	87
UNDER $5,000	9010	3320	8.8	36.8	73	*556	7.2	6.2	60	1320	9.8	14.7	81	1444	8.7	16.0	72
HOUSEHOLD OF 1 PERSON	11507	3858	10.2	33.5	67	*353	4.6	3.1	30	1194	8.9	10.4	58	2311	13.9	20.1	91
2 PEOPLE	25031	10648	28.2	42.5	84	1281	16.7	5.1	50	3507	26.0	14.0	78	5860	35.3	23.4	106
3 OR 4 PEOPLE	27025	16145	42.7	59.7	119	3501	45.6	13.0	126	6132	45.5	22.7	126	6512	39.2	24.1	109
5 OR MORE PEOPLE	11412	7140	18.9	62.6	124	2548	33.2	22.3	218	2654	19.7	23.3	129	1938	11.7	17.0	77
NO CHILD IN HSHLD	42501	17323	45.8	40.8	81	2197	28.6	5.2	50	5697	42.2	13.4	75	9429	56.7	22.2	100
CHILD(REN) UNDER 2 YRS	5834	3277	8.7	56.2	111	*523	6.8	9.0	87	1225	9.1	21.0	117	1529	9.2	26.2	118
2 - 5 YEARS	10959	6246	16.5	57.0	113	1434	18.7	13.1	128	2535	18.8	23.1	129	2277	13.7	20.8	94
6 - 11 YEARS	14546	8977	23.8	61.7	122	2439	31.7	16.8	164	3509	26.0	24.1	134	3029	18.2	20.8	94
12 - 17 YEARS	15977	10777	28.5	67.5	134	3593	46.8	22.5	219	3920	29.1	24.5	136	3264	19.6	20.4	92
RESIDENCE OWNED	50795	26347	69.7	51.9	103	5709	74.3	11.2	110	9243	68.5	18.2	101	11395	68.6	22.4	101
VALUE: $40,000 OR MORE	28371	15126	40.0	53.3	106	3006	39.1	10.6	103	5576	41.3	19.7	109	6544	39.4	23.1	104
VALUE: UNDER $40,000	22424	11221	29.7	50.0	99	2703	35.2	12.1	118	3667	27.2	16.4	91	4851	29.2	21.6	98

HOW TO READ THIS DATA

Top Row: There were an estimated 74,975,000 female homemakers in the U.S.

A – 37,791,000 homemakers used frozen pizza (within the last month)

B – Column A represents 100% of users

C – 50.4% of all homemakers used frozen pizza (37,791,000 ÷ 74,975,000 = 50.4%)

Second Row: There were an estimated 9,348,000 female homemakers who are aged 18–24 in the U.S.

A – 5,006,000 homemakers are frozen pizza users

B – 13.2% of all users are aged 18–24 (37,791,000 × 13.2% = 5,006,000)

C – 53.6% of all homemakers aged 18–24 are users (9,348,000 × 53.6% = 5,006,000)

D – the index of usage (users compared to the population base is 106 (53.6% ÷ 50.4% × 100 = 106)

Source: Simmons Market Research Bureau, Inc.

segment such as "attended college" as opposed to "high school grad-uate." Or the planner could combine segments from age, sex, income, and occupation. A caution, though—it becomes unwieldy to select too many demographic segments for target definition. Three or four seg-ments usually represent an optimum number for planning. If too many are selected, the planner may find media selection difficult because alter-native media vehicles must be compared on too many different bases. Using one segment, however, is usually too restrictive to result in good planning.

Another consideration in target definition is where the information comes from. There are at least three sources: the client's own past research; custom research, where a special study is designed and commissioned to delineate present and future users; and syndicated research studies such as those provided by the Simmons Market Research Bureau.

If possible, cross-tabulated demographic data should be used to determine precisely a target group. With cross tabulations the planner is able to define a target in multi-demographic terms, such as: men 18 to 34 in households with $20,000 or more income; or women 35 to 49 with a college education who have children under 18 living at home. The more precise the definition, the better. However, the more precise (or narrow) the target, the more unreliable are raw numbers insofar as the sample base in the research source is smaller.

Determining Product Usage Potential

In using market research data, the planner usually begins by studying usage habits for the product category of which the designated brand is a part. Examples of these categories may be food products such as instant coffee, automotive products such as tires, or drug products such as aspirin. Sometimes a product category may not be measured by Simmons, MRI, or other research services. In such a situation, the plan-ner may have to buy custom-made research or simply guess who the targets are.

Among the first steps in the analysis may be determining which targets to choose. Should the planner look for buyers, users, or influ-encers of buyers? Such decisions must come from research about who is the most influential person in the buying process. For example, the planner may have to decide whether to reach all adults, men only, women only, or female homemakers.

In making the analysis, the planner usually begins by studying both percentages and index numbers of all demographics for users of the product category, and then for the specific brand. The search will be for the demographic segments that have the highest percentages and index numbers. Table 5–5 shows part of such an analysis—brand usage by age.

Table 5–5 shows that the greatest usage is found in the 35 to 49 age

TABLE 5–5. Brand X—Incidence of Usage by Age

Age segment	U.S. population (%)	Users of brand (%)	Index
18–24	19	17	89
25–34	21	21	100
35–49	24	32	133
50–64	22	20	91
65+	14	10	71
Totals	100	100	100

TABLE 5–6. Brand X—Incidence of Usage by Age/Sex

	Age segment	U.S. population in each segment (%)	Users of brand (%)	Index
Adults	18–34	39.2	57.8	147
	35–49	24.0	20.5	85
	18–49	63.2	78.3	124
Men	18–34	19.1	30.2	158
	35–49	11.7	14.4	123
	18–49	30.8	44.6	145
Women	18–34	20.1	27.6	137
	35–49	12.3	6.1	50
	18–49	32.4	33.7	104

segment. It so happens that the same age segment also has the highest index number: 133. Examination of other data may show that the segment with the highest index number does not have the greatest degree of usage. In such a situation, the planner will have to decide whether to target advertising against the high index group, the high usage group, or both.

Another aspect to study in these data is whether the targets should be limited only to the 35 to 49 year age segment. Should the 25 to 34 year age segment be added, to broaden the age segment? Should yet another age segment be combined? Age segments that are too narrow will be difficult to reach; yet if they are too broad, they may be meaningless. If a strategy decision is made to use television later, it may be difficult to reach narrow groups because television is so much a mass medium. Decisions such as these require the experience and judgment gained by working with media planning over a period of time.

Some situations present a multi-faceted problem. Should the target be adults? Males or females? At which age level? Table 5–6 shows one way to analyze the data in such a situation. The table shows that the 18 to 34 age segment is clearly the one with the most potential (index 147), although, for men, the 35 to 49 segment (index 123) is not without merit. But the planner may well select the adults/18 to 34 category to reach two important targets at one time. In reading this table, however, it should be

TABLE 5–7. Brand X—Incidence of Sales by Age

Age segment	U.S. population in each segment (%)	Current sales (%)	Index
18–24	19	14	74
25–34	21	25	119
35–49	24	36	150
50–64	22	17	77
65+	14	8	57
Total	100	100	100

remembered that other marketing and/or media information might temper the decision about which segment to choose, so that some other targets would be selected.

After a usage study is made of the brand in question, another study may be made of actual sales volume by the same categories. The question to be answered here is: Are the segments who *use* the brand the same as the segments who *buy* the brand? These data may help narrow the decision. Here, too, the data should be examined for all demographic segments, not simply age, as illustrated in Table 5–7.

The search for a target audience, however, is not yet finished. A planner may also want to study purchasing influences. It is well known that wives or husbands, for example, have more or less influence in buying certain products, suggesting that advertising should be targeted to one or the other. But special research is needed to determine the relative influence of each.

Table 5–8 shows how the influence differs for three product categories. The data suggest that the target audience definition ought to take wives and husbands into consideration in varying degrees for different products. For purchases such as wine, both husbands and wives should be considered targets, while wives should be the primary target for dishwashing detergents and husbands for gasoline. This information should be added to demographic segment information to form a composite target picture.

Selecting Usage Groups

Another consideration in determining the target audience is whether to target one or more special-usage groups instead of the more general "all-user" category. The answer is more a matter of judgment than of following some formula. If the heavy-user segment is specially targeted, it may be difficult to reach because the segment members are so widely dispersed throughout the population. Research about the buying habits of a group, however, may be of help in target selection. For example, some product categories may have heavy users who tend to purchase lower-priced brands more often than premium-priced brands. Or, re-

TABLE 5–8. Purchasing Influences by Husbands and Wives for Three Product Categories

	Purchasers (%)		Direct Brand Influence (%)	
Category	Husbands	Wives	Husbands	Wives
Gasoline	58	42	70	30
Wine	48	52	54	46
Dishwashing detergents	20	80	10	90

TABLE 5–9. Demographic Data for the Dry Soup Mix Market

	Regular users (one or more packages per month)		Heavy users (two or more packages per month)	
	Demographic segment (%)	Index	Demographic segment (%)	Index
Total female homemakers	24.5	100	6.5	100
Age:				
18–24	20.5	84	6.1	94
25–34	23.7	97	5.6	86
35–44	26.8	109	6.9	106
45–54	31.0	127	9.3	143
55–64	27.5	112	6.2	95
65+	19.1	78	1.0	65
Household Income:				
Under $5,000	18.3	75	5.2	80
$5,000–$9,999	20.4	83	4.6	71
$10,000+	27.2	111	7.3	98
Household size:				
1–2 members	22.5	92	5.7	88
3–4 members	26.9	110	7.2	111
5+ members	25.3	103	7.2	111
Education:				
Grade school or less	17.7	72	5.0	77
High school (but not college)	27.5	112	7.6	117
College	28.5	116	6.5	100
County size:				
A	28.5	116	8.0	123
B	24.0	98	6.2	95
C	23.3	95	5.6	86
D	16.3	67	3.9	60

Source: Simmons Market Research Bureau 1978/79

search may show that light users tend to switch brands more often than other user groups. Sometimes, one or more groups may be more persuadable than others and therefore deserve special targeting. But when none of this guidance is available, the planner is likely to select the all-user category rather than any special group.

Table 5–9 is an analysis of the dry soup mix market showing how regular users differ demographically from heavy users. Although the demographics for the two groups are much the same, there are differences in the $10,000-plus income, the five or more household size, and the college segments.

Using Psychographic Analysis

The term *psychographic* is an adjective used to describe psychological characteristics of consumers. Psychographics are used to differentiate among prospects with the same demographic characteristics.

Psychographic descriptions of purchasers are sought because demographic descriptions do not discriminate well enough between consumers. For example, a janitor may be in the same income class as a college professor, but their lives and purchasing habits are likely to be vastly different. Two adults may have graduated from college, but their lifestyles could be radically different. Two men may be working in the same profession, but demographic analysis would not show that they tend to buy different kinds of products. Market researchers, therefore, have long felt that the best way to go beyond demographics is to use some kind of psychological description of consumers.

In the past, many different kinds of psychological descriptions were tried and discarded. Social class categorization was one of the first attempts at psychological-sociological discrimination, but it was only minimally helpful. Later researchers used findings from various psychological tests to help find better discriminators, but without success. Even intelligence quotients (IQs) were tried. In addition to the attempts of market researchers to find psychological discriminators, media publishers also sought a similar measure as a means of differentiating media audiences. *Better Homes & Gardens* conducted some well-known research in 1956 showing that the magazine's audience contained many *venturesome* persons—those who were first in a social group to try new products. Yet researchers were generally dissatisfied with most attempts to provide psychological descriptions of consumers.

More recently, a method of psychological analysis called *lifestyle research* has caught the attention of many marketing and media planners. Joseph T. Plummer, of the McCann-Erickson advertising agency, is one of the leaders in this research. Plummer describes lifestyle research as follows:

> Lifestyle is designed to answer questions about people in terms of their activities, interests, and opinions. It measures their activities in terms of how they spend their time in work and leisure; their interests in terms of what they place importance on in their immediate surroundings; their opinions in terms of their stance on social issues, institutions, and themselves; and finally, basic facts such as their age, sex, income, and where they live.[1]

---

[1]Plummer, Joseph T., "Life Style Patterns," *Journal of Broadcasting*, Winter, 1971-72, p. 79.

In order to find consumers' lifestyles, samples of individuals are selected and administered questionnaires which ask respondents to check such things as:

_____ I like gardening.
_____ I do not get enough sleep.
_____ I enjoy going to concerts.
_____ A news magazine is more interesting than a fiction maga-
zine.
_____ There should be a gun in every home.
_____ Instant coffee is more economical than ground coffee.
_____ I stay home most evenings.
_____ There is a lot of love in our family.[2]

These questions cover activities, opinions, and interests as well as media usage and preferences, and product and brand usage. Lifestyle analysis has shown that media audiences differ a great deal and can be used to predict who will prefer one medium over another.

Simmons Market Research Bureau also reports psychographic data as well as demographic research. To obtain a psychographic breakdown of users, Simmons asks each respondent to evaluate a list of 14 personality traits in terms of "how you would like to be." Then each respondent is asked to indicate from the same list "how you feel you are." Each of these 14 characteristics is cross tabulated for each product category, for heavy users (in those categories where usage rates are 10 percent or higher), for magazine audiences, and for demographics. Listed below are the 14 characteristics:

Trait	Meaning
Energetic	Usually energetic, active, and on-the-go
Courteous and cooperative	Always courteous, polite, and cooperative
Self-controlled	Cool-headed, even-tempered, and calm
Venturesome	Adventurous and willing to risk trying new things
Happy and outgoing	Cheerful, happy, and outgoing
Pragmatic	Practical, down-to-earth, and well-organized
Not anxious	Not worried or distressed
Influential	Able to persuade, convince, and influence others to accept your ideas
Benevolent	Always considerate, sympathetic, and kind
Not domineering	Not bossy, domineering, or stubborn
Inquisitive	Intellectually curious about others' opinions

_____

[2]Plummer, p. 81.

Self-confident	Self-assured and poised
Spontaneously decisive	Able to make decisions on the spur of the moment
Not egocentric	Not self-centered, egotistical, or conceited

One way in which such data may help planners in selecting target markets is to compare regular with heavy users, as in Table 5–10. The table shows some psychological differences between regular and heavy users of cigarettes. One might weigh this information subjectively with demographic information already obtained to get a more definitive picture of regular versus heavy users. Or one might evaluate media selected on the basis of demographic segments on the basis of their reach of desired psychographic segments in order to find which medium provides the best reach of both targets. The special needs of planners may also dictate other uses for psychographics.

Media planners who are looking for better target audience definitions will certainly find psychographic definitions radically different from demographics. But being different does not necessarily make psychographics better. The important question is: How useful are psychographic target definitions?

The answer is that psychographics can be useful in media planning when certain conditions are met. If a market has been identified demographically, yet there is reason to believe that the demographics do not segment the market precisely, then psychographic analysis may provide new dimensions of the target audience. If such new dimensions are found, however, it is important also to have available an analysis that shows which alternative media reach large numbers of the psychographic categories that are shown to be important for the given brand. This may be difficult, because syndicated research services such as Simmons provide only a limited analysis of psychographic categories. It may mean that the planner will require custom-made research in order to find which alternative media reach the required psychographic categories. If the data are available and if categories such as those provided by Simmons give

TABLE 5–10. Some Psychographic Differences Between Male Regular and Heavy Smokers

	Regular Smokers			Heavy Smokers		
	Index self image	Index ideal image	Total	Index self image	Index ideal image	Total
Traits	(Heavy smokers: 11+ packs a week)					
Energetic	96	101	197	144	88	232
Courteous & cooperative	97	112	209	119	169	288
Not anxious	127	106	233	156	50	206
Benevolent	98	89	187	181	113	294
Not domineering	96	105	201	75	50	125

Source: W. R. Simmons and Associates

the planner more insight about who the best target is, then psycho-graphics may play a large role in media selection.

After the data have been analyzed, the planner should have decided on one or more demographic and psychographic segments that will constitute the target audience. If the planner has access to a computer, it may be possible to have as many as three or four demographic segments all cross tabulated as a single target audience. An example of a cross-tabulated single target may include women 18 to 49 years of age, with household incomes of more than $25,000 a year, with high school or higher education levels, and with households of five or more people.

If such cross tabulation is not available, the planner will then have to take the top two or three mutually exclusive segments as targets and determine to what extent each is to be reached in the media plan. The reason for requiring mutually exclusive segments is to enable the planner to reach each segment separately, and then measure gross impressions delivered to each without confusion caused when part of one segment is also part of another. For example, women aged 18 to 49 is an exclusive segment. But once one adds the demographic segment "total women with incomes of more than $25,000 a year," there is bound to be some duplication. Some women will be earning less than $25,000 but still be in the 18 to 49 category, and some will be earning more than $25,000 who are not aged 18 to 49.

Only cross-tabulated data can bring the two segments together. Table 5–11 shows an example of cross tabulation.

TABLE 5–11. Cross Tabulation of User Demographics for a Product Category

| Total U.S. | (Adult female usage patterns) | | | |
	Average no. times used per week	Women in group (%)	Total usages per week (%)	Index of usage
Total U.S.	4.95	100	100	100
Household size 1–4; children 6–17 or none; B, C, D counties; college; $3,000+ income	6.54	6.2	8.2	132
Household size 1–4; children 6–17 or none; B, C, D counties; grade or high school; $8,000+ income	6.18	7.2	9.0	125
Same as above except income $3,000-$7,999	5.30	13.0	13.9	107
Household size 1–4; children 6–17 or none; income $3,000+; A counties	5.14	22.0	22.9	104
Household size 5+; high school or less	4.83	18.2	17.8	98
Household size 1–4; children 6–17 or none; income under $3,000	4.58	14.4	13.4	93
Household size 1–4; children under 6	4.27	13.1	11.2	86
Household size 5+; some college	3.03	5.9	3.6	61

Reprinted by permission of J. Walter Thompson Company

Where to Advertise

There are a number of answers to the question of where to advertise. The simplest, of course, is to advertise wherever the brand is distributed. Obviously, it is usually a waste of money to advertise in a geographical market where the brand is not distributed. Occasionally, however, the objective may be to "force" distribution by creating a demand for a brand through advertising, even though the brand is not distributed in the market. When the planner has this objective, it makes sense to advertise before distribution is available.

Beyond the obvious answer, however, is the question of whether it is better to advertise in geographical markets where sales for a given brand have been good, or where sales *have not* been good.

Some planners feel that to advertise where sales have been good is a good defensive strategy—one should protect what one has and also try to build on it. There is an additional aspect to this question. Have sales in the good markets been fully exploited? If not, why not spend more money there, rather than going to some other market where the risks would be greater? After all, many customers like the brand well enough to buy it repeatedly and their word-of-mouth influence may well prompt sales to people who have not purchased the brand in the past.

Choosing where to advertise is really a matter of risks. Despite the observation that "it is always good sense to fish where the fish are," is an advertiser missing productive new markets by placing most advertising in the best markets? Yet can the advertiser afford the risk of losing the best markets to sound out new, unknown markets? The so-called "defensive strategy" minimizes risks and maximizes potential.

Advertising in markets where a brand's sales are low is called an "offensive strategy" because success may require heavier advertising expenditures than previously used. Again, the risks must be carefully weighed. If competitors have been selling well in these markets, but the brand in question has not, the question is why. Is it due to poor distribution? Is it due to insufficient advertising expenditures in the market? Some other reason? Can these problems be corrected?

A planner selecting a market with a low-sales history should be able to answer the following question: Is there any evidence that increased advertising in this market will produce a corresponding increase in sales? This is a difficult, but necessary, question. Students in practice exercises often want to follow this approach because they believe that "advertising sells." But they usually cannot find any other strong reason for doing so except that competitors are selling well in the market. One must understand, however, that once a competitor becomes entrenched in a market with a good brand that meets the needs of consumers, there may be no reason for consumers to switch brands. In fact, it may be impossible to get them to switch brands, unless the new brand has some superior attribute that, if publicized, would cause consumers to switch.

The risks of trying to exploit such a market are great and the likelihood of success is, at best, indeterminable.

Finally, the greatest risk is to select new markets where neither the designated brand nor competitive brands have been exploited through advertising. These markets may have great sales potential, but may also be difficult places to sell a given product. It also might be assumed that if these markets really had great potential, competitors would have known about it too, and would have made efforts to exploit them. In any case, these markets constitute considerable risk.

Aside from these basic guides for market selection, there are other factors that should be taken into consideration. One of the foremost concerns selecting one or perhaps more markets in each of the client's sales territories. Almost all companies with nationally distributed products divide the country into sales territories, and these in turn may be subdivided into smaller groups. The names of such territories vary somewhat from company to company. Some use the terms "divisions and districts"; others use "regions and divisions" or other designations. No matter what they are called, it may be necessary to include at least one market in each of these divisions, depending on the needs of the company. The *weights* (or quantity of advertising used) in these areas may vary a great deal, however, so that the better markets receive more dollars of advertising than the poorer markets.

Thus, to answer the question of where to advertise, planners study distribution, sales records, or brand/product usage. Simmons provides data on usage, while Nielsen and other similar companies provide data on sales.

Classification of Geographical Areas

Sales should be analyzed by different geographical patterns, from the largest, i.e., regions of the country, to the smallest, i.e., neighborhoods, although the latter may not be possible because of the lack of research data. The idea behind geographical analysis at all levels is to learn precisely where prospects live. This serves as a guide in media selection. The following are the most commonly used geographical categories:

Regions
States
Counties
Metropolitan or nonmetropolitan
TV market delineation such as DMA (Designated Market
    Area), or ADI (Area of Dominant Influence)

In studying marketing and media research data, the analyst will find

TABLE 5–12. Comparison of Geographic Divisions

4As Media Audience Research Committee Divisions	Nielsen's Basic 10 Territories	Census Bureau's Nine Divisions	Census Bureau's Four Regions
1. North East	1. New England	1. New England	1. North East
2. North Central	2. Middle Atlantic	2. Middle Atlantic	2. North Central
3. South	3. Metro New York	3. South Atlantic	3. South
4. Pacific	4. East Central	4. East N. Central	4. Pacific
	5. Metro Chicago	5. West N. Central	
	6. West Central	6. East S. Central	
	7. South East	7. West S. Central	
	8. Metro Los Angeles	8. Mountain	
	9. South West	9. Pacific	
	10. Remaining Pacific		

a number of different methods used to divide the country geographically. The Census Bureau divides the country into four regions and nine divisions. The Media Audience Research Committee of the American Association of Advertising Agencies recommends that the country be divided into four areas. The A. C. Nielsen Company, however, uses a division consisting of 10 geographical territories, although it will divide the country in almost any way most suitable for a specific client. A comparison of these divisions is shown in Table 5–12. Figure 5–3 maps the states in Nielsen's ten territories.

What is a local market to a media planner? A *market* is a group of people living in a certain geographic area, who are likely to buy a given product or brand. But that definition is unsatisfactory for planners when it comes to determining the nature of a local market because there are many definitions, depending on the research company providing the data. Different research companies define markets differently to meet the needs of their users. A local retailer who advertises exclusively in newspapers in a given city may prefer to think of its market as the *retail trading zone*, which includes the central city and surrounding suburbs. But a national advertiser who uses all media may prefer that a market be defined in terms of the entire metropolitan area, and would use the Census Bureau's Metropolitan Statistical Area definition. Another manufacturer who uses television almost exclusively, however, may prefer to use Arbitron's Area of Dominant Influence. Each of these local market definitions is somewhat different.

As a result, it becomes important for the planner to know the various definitions of what constitutes a local market when planning media. Which is most suitable? There has been some agitation from media planners to standardize definitions, but without much success. Until standardization becomes acceptable, the differences should be clearly understood. The following list explains the most often-used definitions:

FIGURE 5–3. Nielsen Territories

Source: Reprinted by permission of the A. C. Nielsen Company

Area of Dominant Influence (ADI). All counties in which the home-market stations receive a preponderance of total viewing hours. This definition was conceived by Arbitron. The ground rules for the ADI allocations are relatively simple. Once the estimated total viewing hours for a county and the percentage of such estimated total for each station are known, Arbitron adds up the station percentages by market of origin. The market of origin having the largest total percentage is deemed by Arbitron to be the "dominant influence" in the county under consideration, and thus the county is allocated to that market for ADI purposes. The total number of ADI markets in the country may change from year to year as research on them is updated.

Designated Market Area (DMA). This definition, used by the A. C. Nielsen Company for a television market, includes counties in the metropolitan area of a market provided that at least one station in that area is estimated to have the largest average quarter-hour audience share from 9 a.m. to midnight, plus the remainder of counties in which this market's station are estimated to have the largest average quarter-hour share.

Metropolitan Statistical Area (MSA). The MSA has replaced the Standard Metropolitan Statistical Area definition used in the past. An MSA is a population area with a large nucleus at the center, and with adjacent areas that have a large degree of economic and social integration with the center. The MSAs will be classified on the basis of entire counties (except in New England) on the following basis:

Level A—population of 1,000,000 or more
Level B—population of 250,000 to 1,000,000
Level C—population of 100,000 to 250,000
Level D—population of less than 100,000

City Zone and Retail Trading Zone. These terms are used by newspapers in defining their markets. A *City Zone* represents the corporate city limits plus heavily populated areas adjoining a city in which the newspaper is sold, as designated by an agreement between the publisher and the Audit Bureau of Circulation. A *Retail Trading Zone* is an area beyond the City Zone from which retailers draw sufficient customers to warrant spending advertising dollars to reach them. This area is also determined by the agreement of the publisher and the Audit Bureau of Circulation.

Primary Market Area. This is another newspaper classification and covers the geographical area in which the newspaper provides primary editorial and advertising services. Decisions about which areas are to be included and the boundary lines are made by the Audit Bureau of Circulation in consultation with the publisher. Publishers who report their circulations by Primary Market Areas usually eliminate City and Retail Trading Zone circulation data.

Newspaper market definitions may also be made by counties in which coverage percentages are computed. Data show where newspapers have at least 50 percent coverage, 20 percent coverage, etc.

To illustrate how market definitions vary, even within one geographical market, a map of the city of Chicago and outlying areas is shown in Figure 5–4. It shows the ADI (with 20 counties in Illinois, Wisconsin, Indiana, and Michigan), the MSA (eight counties), and the Retail Trading Zone of one of the Chicago newspapers (with seven counties in Illinois and Indiana).

Sales Analysis

After sales volume information about a brand and its competitors has been gathered, it is possible to start making decisions about where to advertise. One approach is to select geographic markets on the basis of sales or market share produced in the past. In this situation the volume of past sales, rather than the index of potential sales, is the deciding factor. Without a doubt, the volume of sales produced by a geographic market in

FIGURE 5–4. ADI, MSA, and Retail Trading Zone of Chicago (by counties)

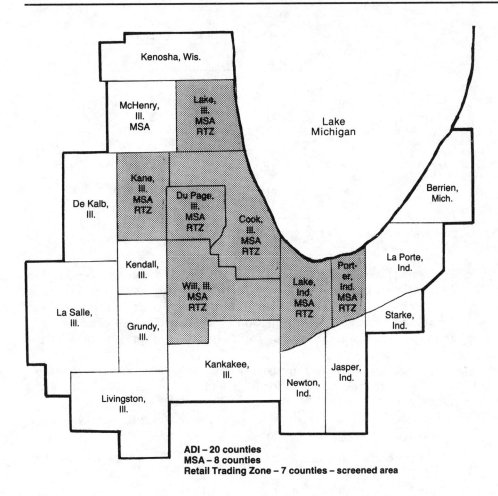

the past has to be the first consideration in making the selection. The question of whether to go to high-index potential markets depends to some extent on whether sales have been optimized in the existing high-volume markets. Perhaps an increase in advertising in current markets will result in an equivalent increase in sales.

Table 5–13 shows the sales of a company and its competitors reported on the basis of seven regions, plus three large metropolitan areas: New York, Chicago, and Los Angeles. In this table, index numbers were computed by comparing sales percentages for each brand with total industry sales by region.

TABLE 5–13. Sales of Brand X and Competitors—by Regions

| | Total industry sales | | | Brand X | | Brand Y | | Brand Z | |
| | U.S. House-holds (%) | Sales (%) | Index | Sales (%) | Index | Sales (%) | Index | Sales (%) | Index |
Region									
New England	5.8	3.4	59	3.5	103	3.5	103	2.4	71
New York	8.4	5.0	60	4.6	92	4.5	90	6.5	130
Middle Atlantic	11.4	10.8	94	11.0	102	10.1	94	12.9	119
East Central	15.8	17.6	111	19.5	111	16.8	95	18.3	104
West Central	14.0	16.0	115	17.5	109	16.2	101	16.4	103
Chicago	3.7	5.4	144	7.1	131	5.4	98	5.3	98
South East	15.7	13.3	85	13.1	98	12.1	91	14.0	105
South West	9.9	8.8	89	9.4	104	9.2	105	7.5	85
Los Angeles	5.1	7.0	138	4.7	67	9.1	130	5.8	83
Remaining Pacific	10.2	12.7	124	9.6	76	13.2	104	10.9	86
Total	100.0	100.0		100.0		100.0		100.0	

Source: Data provided by a major advertiser

Does Table 5–13 tell the planner precisely where to advertise? No, but it tells where the brand is doing well compared with competitors: in New England, East Central, West Central, Chicago, and the South West. Obtaining this kind of information is necessary before proceeding to more specific information that will help pinpoint markets in which to advertise.

Sales analysis by regions usually is followed by a county analysis that provides another dimension for the media planner in selecting media to reach markets.

To deal with county sizes conveniently, Nielsen uses an *A, B, C, D* classification system:

A counties—all counties belonging to the 25 largest metropolitan areas
B counties—all counties not included under A that have more
than 150,000 population
C counties—all counties not included in A and B that have more
than 35,000 population
D counties—all remaining counties.

Table 5–14 shows a sales breakdown by county size for liquid and powdered forms of a given product. For the total market, county size C has the best potential. The same is true for the liquid market segment with the addition that county size A also shows above average potential. But for the powdered market segment, C counties have the best potential. Once again, note the potential for sales shown by index numbers and the actual sales volume shown for the total market and its segments. In all

TABLE 5–14. Sales of Total Market and Segments—by County Size

County size	Population distribution	Total market sales (%)	Index	Powdered market segment sales (%)	Index	Liquid market segment sales (%)	Index
A	41.4	42.3	102	39.1	94	45.4	110
B	27.2	26.9	99	27.6	101	26.2	96
C	16.3	19.2	117	20.6	126	17.9	109
D	15.1	11.6	76	12.7	84	10.5	70
Total	100.0	100.0		100.0		100.0	

Source: Data supplied by a major advertiser

TABLE 5–15. Heavy and Light Users of Dishwashing Liquids

	Index			
	All users	Heavy users	Light users	Non-users
Metropolitan (central city)	98	78	106	116
Metropolitan (suburban)	99	98	103	85
Non-metropolitan	103	129	88	105

Source: Simmons Market Research Bureau, 1978/79

cases, county size A has the highest percentage of sales. Both volume and potential will have to be weighed before a decision is made.

Heavy User Data

While a geographic analysis may be a start in answering the question of where to advertise, some additional insight may be found through an examination of heavy user data. Often, a small percentage of heavy users account for the largest percentage of product usage. This is true for many product categories, but not for all.

Studying heavy users gives a different dimension of where the market is located. If the marketing strategy calls for heavy users, then their whereabouts becomes important. Table 5–15 shows that heavy users of liquid dishwashing detergents tend to be in nonmetropolitan areas, whereas light users are primarily within the metropolitan area.

The Brand Development Index (BDI)

One of the most useful tools available to a media planner in deciding where to advertise is the *Brand Development Index (BDI)*. The BDI is quite simple in structure, and calculated from data for each individual market in which the brand is sold according to the following formula:

$$BDI = \frac{\% \text{ of a brand's total U.S. sales in Market X}}{\% \text{ of total U.S. population in Market X}} \times 100$$

Here's an example of how the BDI would be calculated for a brand in Seattle:

$$\frac{\text{Sales of the brand in Seattle (\% of U.S.)}}{\text{Population in Seattle (\% of U.S.)}} \quad \frac{3.09\%}{1.23\%} \times 100 = 251$$

The BDI is an index number representing sales potential. It conforms to the same basic characteristics of index numbers discussed earlier. The larger the sales in a market relative to population percentage the higher the BDI in that market.

The Category Development Index (CDI)

The *Category Development Index (CDI)* is similar to the BDI except that it is based on the percentage of sales of a product category in a given market rather than a brand. The method of calculating the CDI is as follows:

$$\text{CDI} = \frac{\text{\% of a product category's total U.S. sales in Market X}}{\text{\% of total U.S. population in Market X}} \times 100$$

Example of the CDI in Seattle:

$$\frac{\text{Category sales in Seattle (\% of U.S.)}}{\text{Population in Seattle (\% of U.S.)}} \quad \frac{2.71}{1.23} \times 100 = 220$$

Both the BDI and CDI are useful in decision making. One tells the planner the relative strengths and weaknesses for the brand and the other, the relative strengths and weaknesses for the category. Any market where the brand is sold should have these indices calculated for it.

The following are the possible results (see Figure 5–5):

High BDI and high CDI. This kind of market usually represents good sales potential for both the brand and the category.

High BDI and low CDI. Here the category is not selling well, but the brand is. Probably a good market in which to advertise, but surely one to watch to see if the brand's sales decline in time.

Low BDI and high CDI. This kind of market shows potential for the category but demands that someone study the reason why the brand is not doing well here. Is it because of poor distribution? Not enough advertising dollars, GRPs, or reach in the market? To advertise in this market without knowing the answer would be a risk.

Low BDI and low CDI. This kind of market represents a risk for any brand. Here, too, a planner might want to know why the category doesn't sell well. Such a market would probably not be a good place to advertise under most circumstances.

FIGURE 5–5. BDI/CDI Relationships

	High BDI	Low BDI
High CDI	High share of market Good market potential	Low share of market Good market potential
Low CDI	High share of market Monitor for sales decline	Low share of market Poor market potential

In using the BDI–CDI data for each market in decision making, the planner has a number of ways to proceed. One is to set arbitrary parameters for each market. For example, a planner could decide that for a market to be selected it would have to meet at least one of the following requirements:

- It would have to have a BDI of 125 or higher.
- It would have to have a BDI at least 10 points higher than the CDI.
- It would have to have a certain percentage sales increase over a previous year in that market, and/or a sales volume of X dollars in the market.

Market selection on such a basis may seem arbitrary, but it could be based on the experience of a planner who, over a period of years, simply knows which market characteristics have been the most profitable.

Another method of selecting markets might be to weight the BDI and CDI to arrive at a single combined index. Before this weighting is done, however, a marketing strategy decision must be made to guide the media planner in the proper weighting of the two indices. A marketing strategy that calls for X dollars of advertising spending in direct proportion to sales (a basically defensive posture) requires that the BDI be used exclusively in allocating media expenditures to each market. At the other extreme, a marketing strategy that requires that brand advertising be allocated only on the basis of category development (a basically offensive posture that is generally used for new brands that have not developed a sales pattern) would force the media planner to use only the CDI in deciding spending by market. Any mixture of these two strategies requires a mixture of weights for the BDI and the CDI. For example, if the marketing strategy states that brand sales should be protected in all high sales areas, but that spending should be increased where category development is high and brand development is low, the planner might elect to weight the BDI 75 percent and the CDI 25 percent. The following illustrates how the calculation would be made in a typical market:

$$BDI = 165 \times .75 = 124$$
$$CDI = 140 \times .25 = 35$$
$$124 + 35 = 159 = \text{Weighted BDI/CDI}$$

All markets would be evaluated on the basis of a similar weighting and only those that reach a certain level would be selected. Weighting, however, may be a risky procedure unless the planner knows exactly what each weighting signifies. A safer procedure might be to weight the BDI and CDI 50 percent each and then combine them. Nevertheless, some kind of arbitrary decision would have to be made. The cut-off point might be set at 125. Any markets indexed at over 125 would be selected and any under 125 rejected, at least until experience dictates otherwise.

Using Buying Power Indices

There are times when an advertiser may not know its sales volume in each geographical market, possibly because the advertiser sells through distributors and wholesalers. While many manufacturers in the food, drug, and appliance fields know, from their own records, how large their sales are to wholesalers or distributors, they often do not know how well sales are going at the retail level. The factory is separated from the consumer by what is called the *pipeline* (composed of wholesalers and retailers). What happens at the consumer level is eventually reflected in activity at the factory, but the time lag can be exceedingly long. Sales to wholesalers may be high, but the wholesalers may have large inventories in their warehouses because the product hasn't been selling well at the retail level.

Furthermore, even if a manufacturer should eventually learn how consumer sales are going, this may not show how a brand's share of total sales compares to competitors'. The best that these advertisers can do is to examine the number of wholesale shipments into each market and prepare their media plans on such a basis. The weakness of this technique should be apparent, though, because the relative number of shipments into a given market may not be equivalent to the sales potential of that market. Lack of sales volume and share, market-by-market, handicaps the media planner in deciding where to place advertising. Nevertheless, many small advertisers simply cannot afford to purchase sales volume and share data from the syndicated research services. Shipments or sales potentials determined through other ways may then have to be used.

One source available to almost all advertisers and agencies is *Sales & Marketing Management's* "Survey of Buying Power," which can help determine the sales potential of geographic markets. The "Survey of Buying Power" is published annually and is available to anyone at a relatively low cost. The data are based on census measurements plus updated projections.

The survey uses a multiple factor index that is computed for every major metropolitan area in the country. A *factor* is a market quality that affects sales. Therefore, it is possible to examine the general sales poten-

TABLE 5–16. How a Buying Power Index Is Calculated

	Chicago Metro Area Share of total U.S. (%)	Weight		Total
Population	3.1927	× 2	=	6.3854
Retail sales	3.7180	× 3	=	11.1540
Effective buying income	3.7680	× 5	=	18.8400
Total		10		36.3794

$$\text{Buying power index:} \quad \frac{36.3794}{10} = 3.6379$$

Source: *Sales & Marketing Management*, "Survey of Buying Power," July 23, 1979

TABLE 5–17. Buying Power Indices of Five Selected Markets

City	Index
Denver	.7588
Milwaukee	.7012
Tampa-St. Petersburg	.6687
Indianapolis	.5783
Memphis	.3968

Source: *Sales & Marketing Management*, "Survey of Buying Power," July 23, 1979

tial of every geographical market. Generally, the more people there are in a market, the greater the sales potential; so population is a factor. Effective buying income based on total income after taxes (similar to disposable income), is another market factor. A third factor in the survey's index is total retail sales.

The three factors are arbitrarily weighted to indicate that some factors are more important than others in making sales. Population is weighted twice, total retail sales are weighted three times, and effective buying income is weighted five times. Table 5–16 shows how an index of buying power is calculated.

The indices described help the planner determine the relative value of each market. These values in turn may be used to determine budgets or media weights. On the other hand, the indices may be too general for certain kinds of products. Some specialized products may need additional or more specific marketing data. However, the information in the "Survey of Buying Power" may be used with data from other sources to provide a better and more selective index. An example could be the market for air conditioners. It would be possible to combine survey data with information on average maximum annual temperature and average annual humidity to create a special index number for each market. Furthermore, factors could be weighted in any way necessary to get a better perspective of the relative value of each market.

One can use the buying power indices for a quick evaluation of alternative geographic markets. As an example, Table 5–17 shows indices for five geographic markets.

The question of where to advertise is based on an analysis of sales and product usage or general sales potential, plus consideration of whatever marketing objectives must be met. The users of the buying power data will find that the index numbers are an easy way to compare a large number of categories. If raw numbers or percentages are needed, they are usually provided so that users need not make any further preliminary calculations.

Determining Cut-Off Points

In selecting markets for advertising, it is often difficult to judge at which point to drop markets at the bottom of the list. The place at which the list is divided into those markets that are selected from those rejected is called the *cut-off point*.

One way to establish a cut-off point is to select markets on the basis of some arbitrary number, usually in multiples of 10, 25, or 50. This is a widespread practice in industry. So whatever markets are listed as Number 51 or lower may be eliminated. Yet most media planners would agree that there isn't always much difference between the 50th market and the 51st market.

A more logical way to cut off is to determine how much weight (in terms of dollars) should be assigned to the best markets. Once these dollars have been allocated, then all remaining money may be distributed to the poorer markets based on a weighting system. Usually such weighting would be based on spending a minimum amount of money in a market. If a market's potential does not justify such an expenditure, then it may not be worthwhile to advertise. Weighting systems divide markets into groups titled A, B, C, etc. A markets might receive a given number of dollars of advertising, B markets receive somewhat less, and C markets receive much less.

At times a system of Gross Rating Points is used to determine how much money will be spent in a market. The money is allocated from the top of the list down, until it runs out, thereby automatically establishing the cut-off point.

In many cases, media planners and client representatives have, through experience, developed a minimum number of markets that must be on any list. Additional markets may be added if there is money left after allocating money to the basic list.

One of the problems in establishing cut-off points is that often a small number of markets account for a very large percentage of sales. For example, 25 markets might account for 75 percent of a brand's sales. But the next 25 largest markets might only account for 8 percent additional sales. Usually media planners prefer to have fewer markets, but have enough money to fully exploit the selected markets.

Often, too, marketing objectives affect the length of a list. For example, if an objective is "to protect the brand's share of market from inroads of competitors," then more money may have to be put into markets where competitors are trying to sell against the brand. Usually these are a brand's best markets, so the list may have to be reduced somewhat in order to allocate extra money at the top of the list.

The whole process of selecting markets and determining cut-off points is not the responsibility only of the media planner, but may be shared by the account executive and a client representative. In such cases, decisions are made by compromise as well as by logic. One media planner explained:

> This give and take process between the account executive, the client, and myself is often logical, but sometimes ludicrous. For example, I'll have both Rochester and Albany on my market list. The account man may take Albany off but leave Rochester in. But the client puts Albany back in and removes Rochester. Why? Well it could be that we can't afford both, or the client feels that he has to back a stronger sales force at Albany. But the whole process of selecting markets is an "editing" operation, in which we each edit the others' recommendations until a market list takes shape.[3]

In summary, market lists and cut-off points are established on the basis of subjective factors as well as objective criteria. The most important criteria are the sales goals and the money needed to attain them in each market. Experience, compromise, and some arbitrary factors also influence the process at various times. Other, more sophisticated methods of selecting markets to receive advertising are discussed in Chapter 6.

When to Advertise

Decisions about when to advertise depend on a number of important considerations such as (a) when sales are greatest or lowest, (b) budget constraints, (c) when competitors advertise, (d) the specific goals for the brand in question, (e) availability of the product, and (f) promotional requirements. Each of these points deserves individual discussion, though there is one point underlying them all: Advertise when people tend to buy the product in question, because it is difficult if not impossible to make them buy at any other time. Studying sales by product

---

[3]Personal conversation with an agency media planner.

category over a period of 20 or more years shows that buying takes place at fairly regular intervals and not capriciously. Therefore, it is important to learn when people tend to buy and to capitalize on these buying habits.

Analyzing Monthly Sales

The most important consideration in deciding when to advertise is to know when sales peaks occur for the product category compared with when sales peaks occur for the brand. Table 5–18 shows category sales indexed to brand sales by month. Sales for the category in question tend to be rather flat month by month, but the brand tends to have rather clear-cut highs and lows. Theoretically, the brand should advertise more heavily in those months when its sales have been higher.

However, the answer may not be quite so clear-cut. It may be that the category sells well in a particular month, while the brand does not. Thus the dilemma. Should the brand advertise more heavily in those months when the *category* is selling well or in the months when the *brand* is selling well? Usually, one would advertise more heavily in the months when the category is selling well. Although other considerations may require a change in this strategy, some planners use only category sales as their guide in planning.

Usually a monthly sales analysis for a product category will indicate a seasonal effect. Thus a planner should keep in mind the effect of certain seasons on sales in studying monthly sales records. Back-to-school or graduation months certainly affect the sales of certain kinds of products, as do Christmas or Easter. January and August have become the "white goods" months to sell bed linens, towels, and tablecloths. If a brand belongs to a category that is affected by seasons, then monthly sales should be more carefully studied so as not to miss an opportunity.

TABLE 5–18. Category and Brand Sales by Months

Month	Category Sales (%)	Brand Sales (%)	Index
January	8.5	6.9	59
February	7.7	6.5	85
March	8.5	8.2	96
April	8.2	7.5	91
May	8.5	8.9	105
June	8.2	8.9	109
July	8.5	9.4	110
August	8.5	10.3	121
September	8.2	6.8	83
October	8.5	8.8	103
November	8.2	7.6	93
December	8.5	10.2	120

Budget Constraints

Often the advertising budget is not large enough to permit year-round advertising. In such a situation, the planner will probably allocate the advertising dollars to the best selling months. Whether to maintain *continuity* (continuous advertising all year long) or *flights* (periodic advertising interspersed with no advertising) is dependent on other considerations that will be discussed later.

Competitive Activities

One consideration that is usually important in planning a media schedule is when competitors advertise. If their timing pattern is different than that of the overall category, then the planner will have to decide how important the difference is. Does it put the planner's own brand in a weaker position? If so, the planner may want to copy a competitor's timing. Most often, however, competitors tend to follow category sales patterns fairly closely.

Specific Goals for the Brand

At times a marketing or media objective is to react aggressively to competitive strategies. Perhaps such a strategy may be necessary to attain a market share increase. In such a situation, one might time heavy advertising to begin before most competitors start. As a result, a brand may achieve higher and quicker visibility before the normal buying season starts. Another specific goal may be to outspend competitors in some particular month. This may require withdrawing money allocated to the year-long advertising effort for the concentrated attack. Other marketing/media goals may also affect timing. New product introductions, for example, require a timing pattern of heavy initial advertising (first quarter of sales year) and relatively lighter weights later on.

Product Availability

In certain marketing situations, marketing demand outstrips a manufacturer's ability to supply the product. Even though a company may be building a new plant to keep up with demand, the added capacity may not be ready for some time. In such a case, the timing of advertising has to be related to production availability. Most often this occurs when new products are introduced, but it occasionally happens when there is a surge in sales for existing products.

Promotional Requirements

If an aggressive sales promotion campaign is planned for a brand preceding or during the brand's regular advertising campaign, this may affect timing. A cents-off deal, for example, may require an aggressive advertising campaign to announce the promotion.

QUESTIONS FOR DISCUSSION

1. Why are counties usually preferred to cities as a basis for analyzing markets?
2. If you knew that 11.1 percent of all housewives aged 18 to 24 had used a product within the last month, what other information would you need to compute an index number?
3. In searching for demographic target segments, is the demographic segment with the highest index number always the best target? Explain briefly.
4. What is the value of knowing a Brand Development Index number for a given market?
5. If 20 percent of the men who rented cars within the past year accounted for about 90 percent of all car rentals, should they be the only targets for advertising messages? Discuss.
6. In the *Sales & Marketing Management* "Survey of Buying Power" index, each factor is weighted differently. Briefly explain why.
7. How could the data from the *Sales & Marketing Management* "Survey of Buying Power" be used to create one's own index for outboard motors?
8. Percentages are easier to use than raw numbers in comparing sales or usage data for two brands. But why should the user pay special attention to the bases on which the two sets of figures were computed?
9. In studying sales or usage data, the planner will find that occasionally the research needed is not available. What does a planner do when necessary data are missing and the budget does not allow buying it?
10. Why might a manufacturer with national product distribution want to advertise only in the top 70 markets in the U.S.?

SELECTED READINGS

Advertising Age, "Newspaper Bureau Promotes Psychographics," Sept. 10, 1973, p. 6.

Committee on Research (Media Research Subcommittee) *Recommended Breakdowns for Consumer Media Data*, American Association of Advertising Agencies (revised), 1973.

Editor & Publisher, "Study Indicates Psychographic Data Are Weak Media Buying Tool," Sept. 8, 1973, pp. 8–9.

Garfinkle, Norton, "The Marketing Value of Media Audiences—How to Pinpoint Your Prime Prospects," Speech: ANA Workshop, July 19, 1965.

Maneloveg, Herbert, "Another Way to Look at Audience and Marketing Figures,"*Advertising Age*, April 13, 1964, pp. 95–96.

Media Decisions, "Is ADI the One?" November 1969, pp. 42–45.

Media Decisions, "How—Not Where," January 1968, p. 22.

Media Decisions, "What's the Competition Doing?" September 1973, p. 64ff.

Media Decisions, "How Nestlé Uses Psychographics," July 1973, pp. 68–71.

Media Decisions, "Beyond Demographics," February 1968, pp. 22–23.

Media Decisions, "The Campaign that Psychographics Built," April 1974, pp. 64ff

Media Decisions, "Timing," December 1978, p. 140.

Media/Scope, "What's a Market to a Media Planner?" June 1966, pp. 64–72.

Nelson, Alan R., "New Psychographics: Action-Creating Ideas, Not Lifeless Statistics," *Advertising Age*, June 28, 1971, pp. 1, 34.

Ostrow, Joseph, "Competitive Media Expenditure Analysis," *Media Decisions*, December 1971, p. 52.

Papazian, Edward, "Buzz Words Like Psychographics," *Media Decisions*, October 1973, pp. 14–16.

Papazian, Edward, "Media Targeting: Like Pinning the Tail on the Donkey," *Media Decisions*, November 1977, pp. 14–16.

Peterson, Robert A., "Psychographics and Media Exposure," *Journal of Advertising Research*, June 1972, pp. 17–20.

Plummer, Joseph T., "Life Style Patterns," *Journal of Broadcasting*, Winter 1971–72, pp. 78–89.

Sales Management, "New Ways to Measure Markets," Sept. 18, 1964, pp. 55–56.

Shiffman, Phil, "Psychographic Data Could Be the Base for Both Copy and Media," *Media Decisions*, August 1973, pp. 80–82.

Sissors, Jack Z., "What Is a Market?," *Journal of Marketing*, July 1966, pp. 17–21.

Sprague, Jeremy D., "Local Media Analysis Through Marketing Considerations," *Journal of Marketing Research*, January 1964, pp. 49–53.

Strong, Edward C., "The Spacing and Timing of Advertising," *Journal of Advertising Research*, December 1977, pp. 25–31.

Teel, J. E.; Bearden, W. O.; and Durand, R. M., "Psychographics of Radio and TV Audiences," *Journal of Advertising Research*, April 1979, pp. 53–56.

Tveter, Norman T., "What the Media Expert Gains from Studying Markets," *Media/Scope*, May 1964, pp. 94–100.

Van Bortel, F. J., "Applying What We Know About Marketing Segmentation," *Perspectives in Advertising Management*, Association of National Advertisers, April 1969, pp. 103–12.

Wells, William D., (ed.), *Life Style and Psychographics*, Chicago: American Marketing Association, 1974.

Wells, William D., "Psychographics: A Critical Review," *Journal of Marketing Research*, May 1975, pp. 196–213.

6

Weighting, Reach/Frequency, and Continuity

The preceding chapter discussed three major strategy decisions: target audiences, geographical market selection, and timing. These decisions must be made early in the planning process because they control other strategy decisions discussed in this chapter. This chapter contains a further discussion of geographical weighting, reach and frequency, and continuity versus flighting.

Geographical Weighting

Geographical weighting is the practice of giving extra consideration to one or more markets because they have more sales potential—because of location or demographics or other reasons—than other markets. A record of good sales and/or good potential for sales for both the product category and the brand being advertised may make one market more important than others. If all geographical markets had an equal record of sales and/or sales potential, then there would be no need to add extra advertising weight. But markets are rarely equal in value, so weighting is necessary.

There is another reason for weighting markets. Advertisers who buy national media usually find that the gross impressions delivered by a media plan do not match differences in local sales potentials. Market A may have good sales potential but receive relatively few impressions from national media, while Market B may have weak sales potential but receive many more impressions than required.

Table 6–1 illustrates the difference in Gross Rating Points delivered by a nighttime network TV schedule in different markets. As the table shows, the delivery of GRPs by a national medium such as network television is generally distributed unevenly among markets. If the delivery of these GRPs happened to match sales potential in each market closely, there would be no need for adjustment. Unfortunately, this rarely happens, so adjustments in advertising weight are required.

The final determination of the need for weighting is the wide variance in media costs—again, not necessarily in relation to sales potential. Therefore, a planner who allocates dollars on a proportional basis may be unable to buy as much advertising as required in the best markets because costs may be too high. On the other hand, one may be able to buy more impressions than needed in less expensive markets.

To illustrate the variation in media costs, Table 6–2 gives a cost-per-thousand analysis for several spot TV markets. The reader should recall that cost-per-thousand numbers reflect the relationship between target audiences delivered and the costs of media in delivering those targets. Table 6–2 shows that media costs-per-thousand for reaching women in various markets are not directly proportional to the size of each market. Smaller markets often have a higher CPM than larger markets to reach a given target audience.

Different Forms of Weighting

There are different techniques of weighting that will accomplish the same objectives. The simplest way, the *dollar allocation technique*, allocates pro-

TABLE 6–1. How Network Television Delivery of Gross Rating Points Varies by Market

	Night Network GRPs
National Average	100
New York	90
Miami	110
Detroit	110
Chicago	100
Denver	80
Los Angeles	80

TABLE 6–2. Cost-per-thousand Analysis

City	Spot TV CPM Women
New York	$2.36
Hartford	5.65
Chicago	3.41
San Francisco	3.78
Baltimore	8.16

portionately more money to good markets. Therefore, if Market A accounts for 10 percent of total sales, it receives 10 percent of the advertising budget. This technique, however, does not take varying media costs into consideration.

A second technique, *gross impression weighting*, does take varying media costs into consideration. It allocates the budget on the basis of gross impressions desired: Good markets are budgeted to receive more impressions and weaker markets, fewer.

Table 6–3 illustrates the differences between the first and second weighting techniques. The table shows that when dollars are allocated proportionately, gross impressions vary. But when gross impressions are allocated proportionately, dollars vary.

Why do these two techniques differ? Dollar allocation does *not* take media costs into consideration; therefore 10 percent of the available dollars buys more impressions in Market A than Market B, because cost-per-thousand is lower in Market A. So the dollar allocation technique leaves Market B with fewer gross impressions per year than Market A, even though sales potential is equal. To equalize the number of gross impressions in A and B, the planner will tend to favor gross impression allocation. Yet each technique has different values.

Dollar allocation tends to generate:

1. More impressions in cost-efficient markets. A cost-efficient market is one where the cost-per-thousand is relatively low.
2. Fewer impressions in inefficient markets or high cost-per-thousand markets.
3. The opportunity for good markets to develop their potential because more gross impressions are received in these markets, presumably generating more sales.
4. A slightly unbalanced advertising-to-sales ratio.

Gross impression allocation tends to generate:

1. Proportional communication pressure regardless of cost.
2. Balanced reach and frequency based on sales potential. This

TABLE 6–3. Differences in Weighting Methods

	Total Sales (%)	CPM	Dollar Weighting		Gross Impression Weighting	
			10% of Dollars	No. of Gross Impressions 10% Dollars Buy	10% of Impressions	Cost of 10% Impressions
Market A	10	$2.50	$100,000	40 million	32 million	$ 80,000
Market B	10	3.75	100,000	26 million	32 million	120,000
Total			$200,000	66 million	64 million	$200,000

Source: Ogilvy & Mather

means that the good markets get proportionately more reach and frequency than poor markets.

3. The opportunity for good markets to develop their potential because more gross impressions are received in these markets, presumably generating more sales.
4. A slightly unbalanced advertising-to-sales ratio.

In deciding which weighting technique to use, the planner has to consider which best meets the marketing objectives. In many instances, gross impression weighting is considered better because it is more directly related to communication goals. One of the main goals of media strategy planning is to reach large numbers of target audiences with a certain amount of repetition. Within a given budget, gross impression weighting accomplishes this goal best because it takes media costs into consideration. In the dollar allocation technique, costs may be directly proportional to sales, but audiences may not be reached often enough or in sufficiently large numbers.

Tables 6–4 and 6–5 provide another picture of the relationships of both processes. Table 6–4 shows again that when dollars are matched perfectly against sales percentage, gross impressions do not match (except in Market B). Table 6–5, on the other hand, shows that when gross impressions are matched perfectly against sales percentages, dollar costs do not match (again, except in Market B).

TABLE 6–4. How U.S. Dollar Allocation Matches Sales Distribution

Market	Sales (%)	Cost (thousands)	Dollar Allocation		
			Total Cost (%)	Gross Impressions that can be bought (millions)	Total Gross Impressions (%)
A	45	$ 675	45	343	48
B	30	450	30	214	30
C	15	225	15	93	13
D	10	150	10	64	9
Total U.S.	100	$1,500	100	714	100

Source: Ogilvy & Mather

TABLE 6–5. How Gross Impression Allocation Matches Sales Distribution

Market	Sales (%)	Gross Impressions Planned For (millions)	Total Gross Impressions (%)	Cost of Gross Impressions Planned (thousands)	Total Cost (%)
A	45	318	45	$ 637	42
B	30	212	30	444	30
C	15	106	15	251	17
D	10	71	10	168	11
Total	100	707	100	$1,500	100

Source: Ogilvy & Mather

Guidelines in Geographical Weighting

There is no one formula used to determine advertising weights applied in different geographic areas. Weighting decisions are usually a result of many factors. Using one or the other of the two techniques described earlier, a planner may weight advertising in geographic markets in many ways. The following guidelines comprise some of the more important considerations in weighting.

A general concept is to apply extra weight to markets where sales volume or market share is high. In a market-by-market analysis, a planner might look at the brand development index (BDI) and compare it with a category development index (CDI). At times, more weight is added to markets with high BDIs. More often, however, when a CDI is high and a BDI is low for a given market, additional weight may be added to bring the market up to its potential (as shown in the CDI).

Market potential, as a basis for weighting, may depend on any one, or perhaps all, of the following considerations:

1. Past history of each market's responsiveness to advertising. If a local market has not responded well to advertising in the past, then additional weight may not help.
2. History of profitability. While additional weighting in a local market may improve sales volume or market share, it may do so at an unprofitable level. There may be a point of diminishing returns relative to profit in adding extra weight to a market.
3. Pipeline problems. If distribution levels in a market are low, or difficult to increase, or there are other marketing channel problems, then these factors may influence the amount of extra weight to be applied.
4. Sales force input. Some companies use their salespeople as sources of marketing intelligence at the local level. Their information may affect the manner in which weighting is applied.
5. Local market idiosyncrasies. Some local markets may have problems in communication and/or selling that may not be true of other markets. One advertiser may find that an equal number of GRPs applied to both large and small markets usually produces greater awareness in smaller markets, regardless of other factors. If such idiosyncrasies exist, then they should be allowed for in the weighting decision.
6. Competitive noise levels. If competitors advertise heavily in a market, the net effect of the noise level may require heavier weight in that market.
7. Cost efficiency of advertising in the market. Additional weighting may cost too much or result in cost inefficiency.

Once these considerations are evaluated, the planner may want to decide on a course of action that could affect the final weighting. Does the advertiser want to defend strengths in good markets? Improve weaknesses in problem markets? Or develop opportunity markets? After this decision has been made and other factors considered, weighting decisions for local geographical areas can be made.

Case Studies 6–1, 6–2, and 6–3 are examples of how different advertisers have used weighting techniques.

CASE STUDY 6–1
Weighting Sales Branches on the Basis of Sales Potential

An advertiser who uses magazines almost exclusively has divided the country into 11 sales branches, with each branch composed of a number of counties.

In planning advertising weights, each sales force in each branch first estimates its dollar sales for the next year. These dollars then are converted into percentages of total sales for the entire country, which each branch is expected to deliver.

The circulations of all magazines in a media schedule for this company are broken down by counties to match the 11 sales branches. Weighting matches the number of dollars to be spent in each branch with sales potential percentages for that branch. The following example clarifies the process:

Branch	Sales Potential (% of total)	Advertising Expenditures in Magazines by Branches (%)
1	2.8	2.0
2	15.8	12.8
3	16.9	17.0
4	13.4	15.7
5	10.6	10.0
6	11.2	9.1
7	6.4	8.4
8	11.2	11.9
9	4.9	7.0
10	5.5	4.4
11	1.3	1.7
Total	100.0	100.0

Ideally, magazine weighting should follow sales potential weighting perfectly. Practically, however, this is difficult because of the manner in which advertising expenditures in magazines must be allocated. Magazine publishers do not charge for their space on the basis of cost-per-county-circulation delivered. Instead, they simply charge by the page—either nationally or regionally. The media planner must therefore take the national page cost and divide it by the proportion of its circulation that goes into any county. For example, if a page cost $50,000 and 0.67 percent of the magazine's national circulation went into County A, then $335 would be allocated to County A ($50,000 × .0067 = $335). When adding county costs of numerous magazines in a schedule, it is difficult to match cost percentages precisely with sales potential percentages. The only way to achieve a relatively close match is to purchase local (or city) magazines and/or newspaper supplements in addition to national and regional magazines.

CASE STUDY 6–2
Weighting Markets on the Basis of Minimum BDIs and CDIs

The previous chapter discussed how BDIs and CDIs are generally used in selecting target markets. These two evaluative statistics may also be used to weight markets on the basis of minimum standards.

In this method, sales goals are first set for each individual market. Then 5 percent of the budget is cut from each market and reallocated to problem and/or opportunity markets.

A problem market is one:
1. with at least 1 percent of brand sales
2. with a CDI and BDI less than 100
3. with an unfavorable sales trend.

An opportunity market is one:
1. with at least 1 percent of brand sales
2. with a CDI over 100, but BDI lower than CDI
3. with client's brand showing an unfavorable sales trend, but the product category doing well.
   (Note: When CDI is over 100, the category is doing well. A BDI under 100 usually indicates a brand is not doing well.)

The 5 percent that was cut from each market's budget is now distributed to both problem and opportunity markets. The idea underlying this practice is that problem markets may be strengthened by additional dollars, while opportunity markets need extra dollars to optimize potential. But at the same time, all markets were allocated *some* money based on potential.

Note: All markets will receive some advertising weight through the use of network television or national magazines. The weights discussed in this case are added to national weights.

CASE STUDY 6–3
Weighting Markets by Combining Quantitative and Qualitative Values for Each Market

This technique was used by an advertiser who purchased network TV to provide national coverage, and spot TV to weight the best markets. The value of each market was determined as follows:

Step 1. Calculate the cost index. The cost index is simply the average CPM for all spot TV markets in the country, related to the CPM for each individual market. If the average CPM for the country was $2.50 and it was $3.50 for Market A, then the cost index would be 140:

$$(\$3.50 \div \$2.50 = 140 \text{ cost index}).$$

Step 2. Calculate the CDI/CPM value for each market. If Market A had a CDI of 120, then the CDI/CPM value for each market would be 86:

$$(120 \div 140 = 86).$$

Market A now has less value than it had before because the CDI/CPM value is so low.

Step 3. Determine each market's responsiveness to advertising. This is primarily a qualitative judgment. If sales last year rose by more than 15 percent in a market, that market could be described as responsive. If sales rose between 3 percent and 15 percent, it might be described as somewhat responsive. If sales rose less than 3 percent, it might be described as not responsive. (An alternative method for making this decision is at the end of this section.)

Step 4. Assign extra weight on the basis of the following criteria:
> *Group A Markets* (Receive 50 percent more weight than average)
>> 1. CDIs are high
>> 2. CPMs are reasonable
>> 3. Network delivery is low
>> 4. Responsiveness to advertising was good in the past
>
> *Group B Markets* (Receive 25 percent more weight than average)
>> Combinations of those considerations above yield a lower number, but show that the market is important
>
> *Group C Markets* (No spot TV)
>> All other markets

The following example shows three sample markets assigned extra weight as described above:

Weighting on the Basis of CDI and CPM

Markets	Share of U.S. Population (%)	Industry Sales	Network TV Delivery	CDI	CDI/ Spot CPM	Sales Trend Last Yr. (%)	Weighting Used
Chicago	4.0	4.7	97	117	158	+19	A—add 50%
Seattle	1.2	1.8	85	150	117	+ 6	B—add 25%
Indianapolis	1.1	1.2	109	101	83	− 1	C—None

Note: Responsiveness to advertising could be determined differently. For example, an advertising-to-rates ratio figure could be calculated as follows: If sales in Market A were $1,450,000 and advertising in that market were $340,000, then the A/S ratio would be 0.235: (340 ÷ 1450 = 0.235).

Then an index of advertising to sales could be calculated whereby the A/S index for Market A was divided by the A/S index for the entire country. Example: 0.235 ÷ 0.405 = 0.58.

These indices could be added to the CPM average for each market and the CDI for each market to provide a multiple factor index as follows:

Market A

CDI/CPM Index:	86
CDI	120
A/Sales Index	58
Total	264

Average for Market A   88   (264 ÷ 3 = 88)

Population of Market A: 5 percent of total U.S. × 88 average index = 4.4 percent of the total allocation for Market A.

This technique could be used to allocate spot dollars proportionately throughout the country.

The three case studies indicate that different advertisers use different methods of weighting. No single method is used to the exclusion of all others. Each technique meets the needs of individual advertisers.

Analyzing Message Weight Distribution

Although geographical weighting may be used in planning current media strategy for a brand, it can also be a strategic base for future planning in combatting competitors. In this situation, one compares gross impressions delivered nationally against those by competitors for a given target. In reviewing an earlier media plan or one that has just been completed, it makes sense to check on the relationship of message weight delivery to market share, not only for the brand in question, but for competitors. The

TABLE 6–6. Message Weight Distribution for Nine Competitors

Brand	Share of Market (%)	Share of TV dollars (%)	Share of TV Messages to Women 18–39 (%)
A	35	25	19
B	26	25	28
C	17	16	16
D	8	8	12
E	7	4	6
F	4	3	6
G	3	2	4
H	Not avail.	14	8
I	Not avail.	3	1
Total	100	100	100

Source: Roth, Paul, "How to Plan Media," *Media Decisions,* 1976, p. 26

relationships that are revealed will help planners decide whether they have planned logically, or whether there are areas where they should increase or decrease the number and uses of vehicles.

Table 6–6 analyzes nine competitors and their message weight deliveries. The table shows that Brand A has 35 percent of the market but spends only 25 percent of the total TV dollars and has a relatively lower percentage of message delivery than Brand B.

The planner should ask, "Why?" Is Brand A inherently superior in quality to B? Does Brand A have better distribution? Better copy? Many questions can be asked about why Brand A's market share is so high compared with its message delivery. Most other brands show a high degree of consistency between market share and message share. Additional message weight analysis should be made of individual markets to see how they, too, relate to market share.

Reach and Frequency

As explained earlier, *reach* refers to how many people are exposed to a vehicle, while *frequency* refers to how often they are reached.

How Much Reach Is Necessary?

One of the most difficult decisions facing a media planner is setting the level of reach needed for a media plan. It is difficult because there is little hard evidence from research or experimentation that can provide the necessary direction. What is known about how much reach to use is the product of tradition, experience, common sense, and some research for a particular brand in certain market situations. But there is little evidence to prove that a given reach level is "correct" for a given marketing situation. Therefore the guidance provided here has of necessity to be general, and based on widely held beliefs. Even with all these qualifiers, there are some planners who may disagree.

It is generally held that high reach is necessary for new product introductions. The rationale is that few people know the name of a brand that is being introduced or what its value is. As many different people as possible ought to be informed; thus the need for high reach. But determining just how much reach is necessary is difficult.

Since the purpose of high reach is to generate awareness of the new brand, the reach level may be decided to some extent by the brand awareness level that is needed. Is the goal to make 65 percent of the targets aware of a brand name? Some people will need only one exposure to a vehicle to become aware of that brand. Others will need multiple exposures, so a certain level of frequency will be needed in addition to reach. Some planners might opt for a reach level higher than the brand awareness level desired, on the assumption that not everyone exposed to a vehicle will be exposed to the ad and the brand name. Others will want reach *and* frequency, which for planning purposes can be expressed in Gross Rating Points. Within a given number of Gross Rating Points, the reach and frequency levels can be juggled to bring either one to a required level. Some available research attempts to relate GRP levels to brand awareness levels. For example, one piece of research conducted by a well-known advertising agency found that about 2,000 GRPs a year produced a 70 percent brand awareness.

Sales promotion activities also need a high degree of reach because consumers need to be made aware when certain deals or promotional options are available. In planning media to advertise a cents-off deal, a high level of awareness is a requirement and, again, the precise amount of reach needed cannot be expressed.

One media planning strategy might be to set a reach level equal to or surpassing that of competitors who are deemed to be vulnerable to attack. Presumably these competitors have products that are not as good as the brand in question, or perhaps they are not advertising enough, or to the right targets. Setting a reach level equal to or higher than that of certain competitors offers a potential advantage to the planner, and it is a way to determine how much reach ought to be attained.

Another consideration in planning reach is the budget. No matter which media are chosen, a fixed budget size limits the amount of reach possible. All the planner has to do is to calculate the amount of target reach that each medium and vehicle will deliver, plus the amount of continuity desired, to set a reach level.

There is a media strategy that stretches media dollars and therefore also stretches reach. This strategy holds that by cutting ad unit sizes, more money will be available to buy new reach. (The same strategy can be used to buy more frequency.) If the planned ad unit is 30-second commercials or full-page ads, it could be cut to 10-second IDs or half-page ads. But there are two penalties for cutting unit sizes. First, the cost of smaller unit sizes usually is not exactly proportional to larger sizes—a 10-second ID costs 55 to 65 percent of a 30-second commercial; a half-page ad costs 55 to 65 percent of a full-page ad. Second, there is a possible loss in communication value from the smaller ad unit.

Probably the best level of reach is determined by looking at what levels were used previously. If a brand has successfully achieved certain marketing goals in the past with a given level of reach, this same level (or proportional adjustment) should probably be used again.

In essence, then, the amount of reach needed for a media plan is based more on judgment and experience than on research evidence. Since media plans almost always require a certain amount of frequency, the combination of reach and frequency can be calculated in terms of Gross Rating Points. But research on GRPs and communication effects is weak, and the GRP level is also a matter of judgment and experience.

How Much Frequency Is Necessary?

The question of how much frequency is necessary is probably the most pressing problem facing media planners. It is more important than learning how much reach or how many GRPs are necessary. A great deal of thinking and research has gone into this subject, although no clear-cut breakthroughs are yet apparent.

Frequency is needed whenever repetition of a message is necessary. Most planners feel that there are practical reasons for needing more than minimum amounts of frequency.

The first reason for needing frequency is that not everyone hears or sees an ad the first time it appears. Why? Because so many ads bombard a person each day that it is impossible for anyone to pay attention to all of them. Even if an individual has seen an ad many times, little or none of the information may have been absorbed by the person. Therefore, one goal of frequency is to surpass the *threshold*, the first few exposures, to the point where the audience member will absorb the message. Research has shown that there are indeed threshold levels, although it isn't known precisely whether the threshold is one, two, three, or more exposures.

In some cases, one exposure may be sufficient. Gus Priemer, advertising director of S. C. Johnson Company, has proved through test-market research on a new product that the first impression of an ad was remembered for a certain product/brand at a given time. As he explained:

> My own evidence strongly suggests that the first ad exposure actually *can* stimulate a large proportion of total *advertising response*, even when a product is using TV where the viewer is not in control of the communication vehicle.

> My TV evidence comes from some 35 first-exposure tests of commercials done for 16 new products prior to test marketing.
>
> For five of these products, viewers had already memorized the new brand name at significant levels (7 to 9 percent of those exposed to the test commercial). Almost one in four had clearly understood the new product promise of the testing brands . . .[1]

Priemer was not, however, generalizing about all products or all brands. He simply pointed out that there are different thresholds for different brands.

Frequency in media is not the same as frequency of ad exposure. In media planning, the frequency sought is vehicle exposure. But not everyone exposed to a vehicle also sees the ads in that vehicle. So, any frequency expressed as part of a media plan overstates the size of frequency of exposure to ads in the vehicles chosen. (Some refer to frequency as *opportunities to see*, which might be a more accurate term.) Since there is no syndicated research measurement of ad exposure, a planner must plan for more frequency than seems necessary; this creates a cushion of loss of exposure to account for audience members who see the vehicles, but don't see the ads of a given brand.

There has been a feeling in the industry for years that high frequency (or repetition) represents a strong form of persuasion in selling a product. The more frequently a persuasive message is heard or seen, the more likely the consumer is to see the merits of the advertised brand and be convinced to buy. At least, that is a widely held assumption. Additionally, the higher the frequency and the longer the advertising effort, the better the opportunity to reach a person when he or she is most ready to buy the product.

Some feel that every media planner should try to learn how many impressions (meaning frequency of exposure) a consumer needs before being persuaded to buy a given brand. This number is part of a cause-and-effect relationship. Planners assume that for every brand there exists a level of impressions that will directly affect sales. However, this level is probably somewhat different for every brand, and must be learned from experimental research. Test marketing experiments may have to be conducted, trying various frequency levels to learn which is the most productive. Such a research technique is one means of answering the question, how much frequency is necessary? The Advertising Research Foundation is working on a massive study to tackle this question.

Even those planners who view frequency as not necessarily a direct cause of sales see it as a necessary requirement for communicating with

---

[1]Priemer, Gus, "Are We Doing the Wrong Thing Right?" *Media Decisions*, May 1979, p. 64.

large numbers of disinterested consumers, or consumers who miss advertising because they are inundated by the noise level of all the competitive ads. Frequency, therefore, is a means of "getting through" to the consumer. The following quotation, from a hundred years ago, has often been cited as a generalization about how frequency affects communications, and eventually sales.

> The first time a man looks at an advertisement, he does not see it.
> The second time he does not notice it.
> The third time he is conscious of its existence.
> The fourth time he faintly remembers having seen it before.
> The fifth time he reads it.
> The sixth time he turns up his nose at it.
> The seventh time he reads it through and says, "Oh brother!"
> The eighth time he says, "Here's that confounded thing again!"
> The ninth time he wonders if it amounts to anything.
> The tenth time he thinks he will ask his neighbor if he has tried it.
> The eleventh time he wonders how the advertiser makes it pay.
> The twelfth time he thinks perhaps it may be worth something.
> The thirteenth time he thinks it must be a good thing.
> The fourteenth time he remembers that he has wanted such a thing for a long time.
> The fifteenth time he is tantalized because he cannot afford to buy it.
> The sixteenth time he thinks he will buy it some day.
> The seventeenth time he makes a memorandum of it.
> The eighteenth time he swears at his poverty.
> The nineteenth time he counts his money carefully.
> The twentieth time he sees it, he buys the article, or instructs his wife to do so.[2]

Many media planners believe that a plan should have a frequency level of at least four exposures a month. The thinking is that the first three exposures tend to be ignored, but the fourth is the threshold at which consumers begin to pay attention to the advertising message.

Other planners disagree. Some say that the frequency level must vary, because certain situations may require higher or lower levels. The uniqueness of the advertising message, for example, can affect frequency.

---

[2]Smith, Thomas, *Hints to Intending Advertisers* (London, 1885): quoted in Herbert E. Krugman, "An Application of Learning Theory to TV Copy Testing," *Public Opinion Quarterly*, vol. 26, 1962, pp. 626–34.

The more innovative and unusual it is, the more likely that consumers will notice it and pay attention to it. The converse is also true. A rather ordinary ad message might need many more than four exposures to be seen and remembered.

In all discussions on frequency levels, the planner must be aware that creative executions vary from brand to brand, and the creative element can argue for more or less frequency than the competition uses.

Another consideration affecting the frequency level is the perceived value of a brand compared with the values of competitors' brands. When a brand has an important and easily perceivable benefit not shared by competitors, then less frequency may be necessary. In other words, the brand has an easily exploited advantage over competitors. But when a brand is very much like all other brands in a product category, more frequency may be necessary for the message to be noticed or remembered.

The noise level in a product category also plays a role in deciding how much frequency is needed. If many similar brands are being advertised simultaneously, consumers may find it difficult to recall the message for any one brand amid the confusion caused by the noise level of competitors. On the other hand, when few competitors advertise, less frequency may be required.

Some planners feel that a frequency level should be based on the level of that used by a brand's most serious competitive threat. Or, the competitor who is the most vulnerable to a brand's promotional attack efforts should be singled out. The frequency level of that competitor should be equaled or surpassed, with the objective of gaining an advantage.

Media values may also be used in conjunction with Gross Rating Point planning to determine frequency (as well as reach) levels. Media value is simply the judgment that a given medium has been found, through experience, to be more effective for a brand and its creative message, thus justifying more frequency in that medium. The chief problem, however, in combining media evaluations and frequency levels is that of making too subjective an evaluation of each medium. Is daytime television always less than 35 percent as effective as primetime television? To say that it is *always* less effective is an unreasonable assumption. For certain brands, in certain marketing situations, at certain times, the 35 percent differential may be true—but it is dangerous to generalize. The method is a good one, however, when research evidence can be used to back up a generalization about media values.

Frequency levels in media plans therefore range quite a bit. When the threatening or vulnerable competitor technique is being used, frequency levels may go to as high as 15 average exposures a month. But these levels are not decided upon in a scientific manner in terms of a cause-and-effect relationship. Even when various frequency levels are tested in three or four local markets and one is found to be better than others, there is no guarantee that this level can be projected nationally. What is true in a test market may or may not be valid for every market. The experience of many national advertisers who have used test marketing for setting frequency levels varies from a few who have had excellent results to many who have had costly failures.

All of these considerations about where to set the frequency level are based primarily on common sense, and on unfortunately little research evidence. As a consequence, it is not surprising to find frequency levels being set somewhat arbitrarily, based on tradition plus common sense. In the future, the concepts and practices of *effective* reach and frequency may totally supplant present techniques.

One of the most important guidelines to remember in determining how much frequency is necessary is that vehicle frequency does not equal advertising frequency. The levels planned for media vehicles should not be confused with advertising frequency, which must also be planned.

Effective Reach

One of the most recent advances in media strategy decision making has been the development of a concept called *effective reach and frequency*. Since all reach comes with a certain degree of frequency, the term *effective* can apply to both terms under certain circumstances. The goal of planners who use this concept is to go beyond traditional reach and frequency measurements to a more sophisticated stage, that of considering to what extent their media plans communicate effectively.

The concept of effective reach was developed in 1976 by Alvin Achenbaum, now a principal of Canter, Achenbaum, Heekin, Inc., when he was at J. Walter Thompson agency. Others working on similar ideas at that time included Stanley Cantor and Jules Fine of Ogilvy & Mather, and Seymour Banks at Leo Burnett.[3]

Traditional reach and frequency data are based on exposure to media vehicles and may be assumed to be ineffective, because the data do not contain evidence that audience members either saw ads within the vehicles, remembered the contents of the ads, or were motivated to buy the advertised brands. In other words, *traditional reach measurements do not explain what communication effects media have.*

Effective reach and frequency, on the other hand, means that an audience member who was reached *has* been affected by the communication in some way. The person may have seen the ads within a vehicle, or remembered the essence of a message within a vehicle, or been motivated to buy the advertised brands. These are three possible measures of effec-

---

[3]Achenbaum, Alvin, "Feedback," *Journal of Advertising*, October 1978, p. 73.

FIGURE 6–1. Graph of Effective Reach

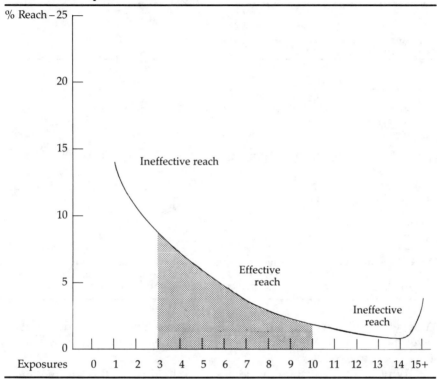

Source: J. Walter Thompson, *The Concept of Effective Reach*, Nov. 6, 1973, p. 6.
     The audience in the 3 to 10 exposure (shaded) areas would be the effective reach.
     Although the one exposure reach was 14.3%, the effective reach (3–10 exposures)
     would range from 9.4% to 2.2%, noncumulatively, or, 9.4% to 40.6%, cumulatively
     (9.4 plus 7.7 plus 6.2, etc. equals 40.6)

tiveness. At present, media experts tend to favor a concept of effectiveness based on recall of ads within vehicles.

There are differing views on how to implement the concept of effective reach or frequency. Figure 6–1 shows how one agency views the concept. The figure shows a reach curve drawn in a somewhat different manner than shown earlier. The earlier reach curves are called *cumulative curves* because they show how much additional reach occurs over time. The curve in this figure is an *incremental curve*, showing not accumulation but rather the percentage of a target audience added at *each* frequency level.

Effective reach is shown as a shaded portion of the curve area. Here's how to read the graph: At the zero exposure level, there is no reach because no one has seen the vehicles being used. But at exposure (or frequency) level one, 14.3 percent of the target audience has been reached.

TABLE 6–7. **Reaches at Various Frequency Levels**

(From Figure 6–1)

No. of Exposures (Frequency)	% Reached Noncumulative		% Reached Cumulative	
1	14.3		75.9	
2	11.6		61.6	
3	9.4		50.0	
4	7.7		40.6	
5	6.2	Sum:	32.9	
6	5.0	40.6	26.7	Effective
7	4.1	Effective	21.7	Reach
8	3.3	Reach	17.6	
9	2.7		14.3	
10	2.2		11.6	
11	1.8		9.4	
12	1.4		7.6	
13	1.2		6.2	
14	.9		5.0	
15+	4.1		4.1	

To read table: 14.3 percent of the audience was exposed to only one message; 11.6 percent to only two messages, etc.; 75.9 percent of the audience was exposed to one or more messages; 61.6 percent to two or more messages, etc.

At level two of frequency, another 11.6 percent has been reached. But at level three, effective reach begins and continues on until frequency level ten. (See Table 6–7.)

Why is reach considered *effective* from the three to the ten frequency levels? The answer lies in an effect that has occurred between these two levels. A number of experimental studies were performed on the recall of ads in various vehicles at various frequency levels to analyze at what levels of frequency the recall of advertising begins to rise dramatically, and at what point it either stops or declines. The three to ten frequency levels represent those points. The cumulative reaches that can be called effective, then, are from 35.3 percent to 66.5 percent, and represent reaches where communication of a plan is effective. Does this mean that all media plans should use effective frequency levels of *only* three to ten? No. Every brand may have a different range of effective reach and frequency, which must be discovered through experimentation.

The graph in Figure 6–1 shows that for every frequency level between three and ten there are effective reach levels that ought to be taken into account in planning. Whether one chooses a low or high reach within the effective reach range depends on how much money is available for the task, as well as on the reach and frequency goals that are part of a media plan's objectives. (Chapter 11 provides further discussion of effective reach and frequency.)

Case Study 6–4 illustrates how effective reach and frequency might be used in a media plan.

CASE STUDY 6–4
How Effective Reach Is Practiced by One Agency

Problem One. A planner has devised a media plan using 15 30-second spots in various markets generating the following reach and frequency:

Reach:	81 percent TV households
Frequency:	3.7
GRPs:	300 a month (primetime)

What is the effective reach of this plan?

Answer: Construct a frequency distribution and delineate 3 to 10 exposures as follows:

	Frequency	Reach		GRPs (Frequency × Reach)	
	1	14		14	
	2	15		30	
	3	14		42	
	4	12		48	
	5	10	Sum:	50	Sum:
Effective	6	7		42	
Reach	7	4	51	28	245
Range	8	2	Reach	16	GRPs
	9	1		9	
	10	1		10	
	11+	1		11 or more	

From this analysis, it can be seen that the *effective reach* is not 81 with a 3.7 frequency. It is 51 with an average of 4.8 frequency (245 ÷ 51 = 4.8).

Problem Two. If we double GRPs from 200 to 400 what is the effective reach advantage?

	GRPs	Reach	Frequency
Old way of making comparisons:			
Plan A	200	74	2.7
Plan B	400	88	4.5
Difference:	+100%	+19%	+67%
New way using effective reach*:			
Plan A	142	35	4.1
Plan B	319	60	5.3
Difference:	+123%	+71%	+29%

According to the *effective reach* concept, Plan B is 71 percent better than A (compared to only 19 percent better when making a comparison the old way).

*Effective reach is defined here as reach from 3 to 10 exposures.

Continuity, Flighting, and Pulsing

An important part of timing advertising is scheduling it so that it appears at the most propitious selling times. A major objective of scheduling is to control the pattern of times when advertising appears by plotting advertising timing on a yearly flow chart. There are three major methods of scheduling advertising, each with a somewhat different pattern, as shown below.

1. *Continuity* (sometimes called straight-through advertising)

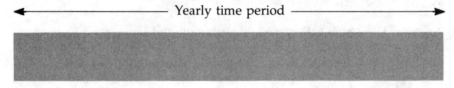

This pattern is continuous, although there may be small gaps of time, at regular intervals, when no advertising is done. One continuity pattern might be to run one ad every day for 365 days. Another continuity pattern might be one ad a week for 52 weeks. The time gaps show up in a pattern of dashes on a flow chart.

2. *Flighting*

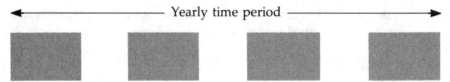

Flighting is an intermittent pattern where there are gaps of time when no advertising is done. If advertising were done once a month, this might be called flighting. Most often, however, flighting patterns are more irregular, with heavy concentrations of advertising at certain times interspersed with no advertising for considerable lengths of time.

3. *Pulsing*

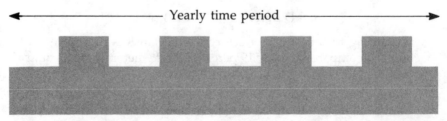

Pulsing is a form of flighting and continuity combined—where an advertiser buys continuous advertising throughout the year and "heavies up" at various propitious time periods. Pulsing is sometimes mistakenly called flighting, and when planners use either term (pulsing/flighting), they should be sure that everyone using these terms is using them correctly.

The media planner must decide, as part of the strategy, which pattern to use.

The first step in selecting a pattern is to examine purchasing patterns for the product category. Since most product categories have unique purchasing patterns, it is important to learn what they are before thinking about a scheduling pattern. An unusual example of a purchasing cycle is the market for Christmas trees. Trees are rarely purchased at any time of the year other than November or December. By the same token, typewriters are sold primarily during the spring, summer, and late fall as gifts or for back-to-school. While some typewriters may be sold throughout the year, under ordinary circumstances it would not be advisable to advertise at times other than the three heavy selling seasons. But for a product such as face soap that is purchased throughout the year, though with heavier consumption in the summer, the best scheduling plan might be pulsing (year-round advertising with "heavy-up" in the summer).

Continuity

Continuity is needed when an advertiser has a message that it does not want consumers to forget. Continuous advertising works as a reminder, keeping the message always before the consumer. That is one of the strongest arguments for continuity.

Another advantage of continuity is that the entire purchase cycle will be covered because there will be no gaping holes in time periods. This assures the planner that most of the customers are reached at all times, both when they will be purchasing and during times when they may not be buying.

Another reason for using continuity is that it makes it possible to take advantage of larger media discounts granted because so much advertising is purchased continuously. There may be cost efficiencies in such discounts, because the cost-per-target reached will tend to be lower than plans that do not contain such discounts. In addition, the advertiser may have an advantage in obtaining certain kinds of desirable positioning within media. Because the advertiser is buying a fairly large block of advertising, it may be easier to find the broadcast programs or times that are most favorable. There may also be positioning advantages in print where certain parts of the magazine or newspaper become more readily accessible to anyone who will buy a great deal of advertising over a long period of time.

Flighting

An advantage of flighting over continuity is that the advertiser may be able to meet competition better by placing advertising at the most favorable times relative to competition. Advertising can be concentrated in high sales potential times, either in broadcast time or print space. Advertising can be timed precisely to reach the best purchasing cycle time periods with little waste when buying is slow.

Ostensibly, flighting is used when there are budgeting limitations or sharp sales fluctuations. The advertiser buys ads only when sales are growing and drops out when sales trends are declining. This tends to save money.

Flighting also allows the planner to support advertising in one medium by using some other medium at the same time. If an advertiser plans to use television as the basic medium, then flighting allows concentration of radio and newspaper support at the same time.

Flighting also allows a series of ads and commercials to appear as a unified campaign rather than as a series of unrelated ads. By concentrating them at certain times of the year, the ads all appear to the consumer to be part of a single communication entity.

By concentrating advertising, an advertiser can sometimes catch competitors off guard and gain an advantage over them, especially if the competitors tend to use continuity rather than flighting in their strategy. The advantage is simply that the advertiser buys much heavier weight than competitors for a relatively short time.

But there are risks in flighting, too. The first is that so much advertising may be concentrated in one time period that the commercials could wear out before the flight is over. Great amounts of flighting in concentrated time periods tends to build high frequency.

A second drawback of flighting is that consumers might forget the essence of the advertising message between flights if too much time elapses between them. However, the effectiveness of advertising does not stop the moment advertising is stopped. There is some carry-over.

Finally, competitors may take advantage of the advertiser by placing heavy ad weights at precisely the time the advertiser is not advertising.

FIGURE 6–2. GRPs in Continuity vs. Flighting

Week No. ▶	1	2	3	4	5	6	7	8	9	10	11	12	13	14	15	16	
Continuity Pattern GRPs	40	40	40	40	40	40	40	40	40	40	40	40	40	40	40	40	Total 640
Flighting Pattern GRPs	80	80	80	80					80	80	80	80					Total 640

Source: Ogilvy & Mather

So during those times, competitors have an advantage over the advertiser.

Pulsing

Pulsing represents the best of both techniques; it is a mixture of continuity and flighting. All of the advantages of continuity and flighting are now possible, with none of the disadvantages. Pulsing is the safest of the three since it covers different marketing situations. Not all advertisers, however, would be advised to use pulsing. It best fits those product categories that are sold all year round, but have heavier concentrations of sales at intermittent periods.

Both continuity and flighting can develop the same reach and frequency over a long period of time (such as 16 weeks), as shown in Figure 6–2. However, there will be considerable differences of reach and frequency over the short run, as shown in Table 6–8. The table shows that, for a four-week period, the flighting pattern had a considerably larger reach than continuity had. The reason is the larger concentration of GRPs.

Relationships Among Reach, Frequency, Continuity, and Number of Markets

In planning strategy, there are usually four elements that are closely related: reach, frequency, continuity, and number of markets to be used. A person cannot plan for one of these elements without simultaneously considering the others, because of their close relationship. The relationship grows out of a fixed budget size, which means, in effect, that if any one of these elements is strongly emphasized, the others will, of necessity, suffer.

Each of these elements costs a considerable amount of money to attain. Reach, for example, usually means that advertising messages must be dispersed widely so that many different persons in the target

TABLE 6–8. Reach and Frequency of Continuity vs. Flighting

	Continuity	Flighting
Monthly GRPs	160	320
Reach	57	76
Frequency	2.8	4.2

Frequency Distribution No. times reached	Cumulative Reach	
	Continuity	Flighting
1	57.1	75.8
2	39.1	61.5
3	25.8	49.4
4 or more	15.7	39.0

Source: Ogilvy & Mather

audience will have an opportunity to see the messages. Generally, one single media vehicle, such as one television program or one magazine, will not deliver a high reach. Multiple vehicles are usually required, and the more that are purchased, the greater the cost. As the cost for reach goes up, the amount of money available for the other three elements becomes more limited.

The same holds true for continuity. If an advertiser wants to plan continuous advertising over 365 days, the cost will be relatively high, leaving minimal amounts of money for the other three elements. Often as much as six or more months of advertising must be sacrificed in order for the reach to attain a high enough level in the remaining six months.

Likewise, the number of individual markets in a plan, where national media may be used in conjunction with local media, clearly affects overall costs. Even if only local media are used, the same concept prevails. The more markets used, the higher the cost, and the less money available for the other elements.

Figure 6–3 shows to some extent what happens when a planner tries to manipulate the four elements within the constraints of a fixed budget. The figure shows some ways to vary the weights of reach, frequency, continuity, and number of markets. Other posssibilities, not shown, also exist. One part of a planner's job is to weight each of the four alternatives and decide which of the four needs more emphasis (usually at the expense of the others). Of course, if the budget size can be increased (unfortunately, it usually can't), then different emphases can be achieved. As a consequence of this dilemma, the planner needs some criteria for weighting the alternatives.

Weighting Alternatives

Reach and frequency are the two most important elements of a media plan. Because they occupy such an important position in a plan, they are usually considered before continuity or number of markets. When a media budget is very high, it may be possible to achieve both high reach *and* high frequency levels. But most often, the cost is too high to do both.

FIGURE 6–3. Some Different Strategies within Constraints of a Fixed Budget

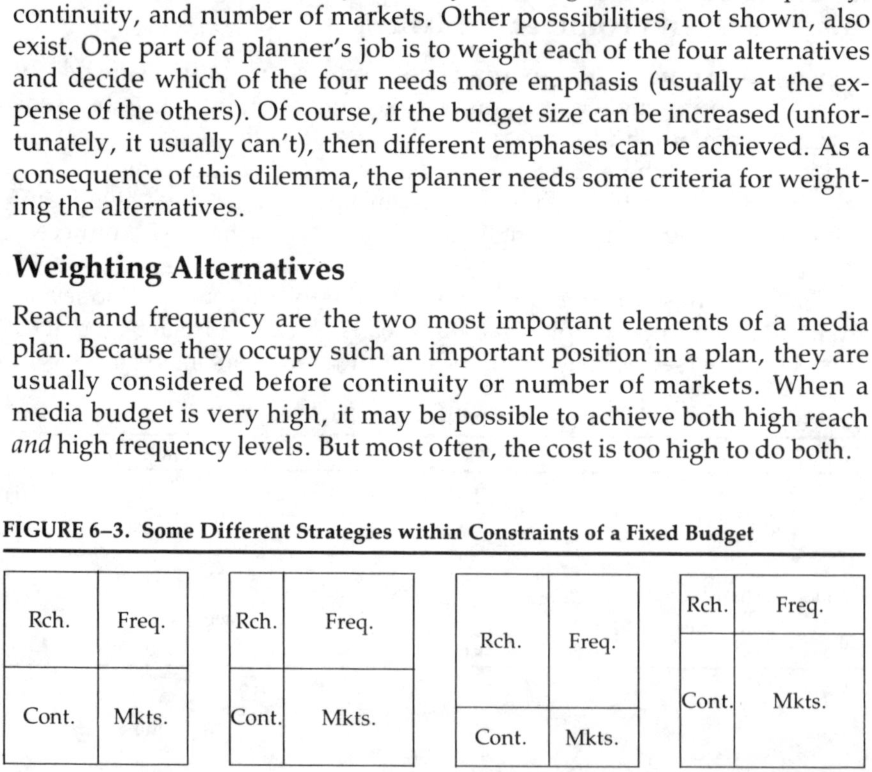

If high reach is planned, it will probably cause the frequency level to decline somewhat, because reach and frequency are inversely related. If, however, reach is very high (at the 90 percent level), then frequency can be increased by extra dollar expenditures because most of the money will go into building frequency and a very small increment will go to building reach. This is the natural consequence of trying to reach new persons who have not already been reached by some other vehicle.

Higher reach will be necessary when the media plan calls for building brand awareness at significant levels. If a brand awareness level is now at 25 percent and an objective is to raise it to 75 percent, then higher reach will probably be required, and frequency will be sacrificed. Also calling for higher reach is the announcement of various kinds of promotions such as cents-off deals, special coupon promotions, or refund offers. Such promotions need to build a great deal of awareness so that consumers will take advantage of the offer. Still another high-reach situation occurs when changes in the brand or changes in the creative strategy are important. Finally, more reach may be needed when it becomes necessary to meet or exceed competitive reach levels. One goal could be to steal customers from a competitor by showing them that the advertised brand better meets their needs, in which case enough reach might be needed to equal or better the competitor's reach.

More frequency, at the expense of reach, may be needed when the brand awareness levels are already high due to the cumulative effect of past advertising. At that point, more frequency may be needed to meet or surpass frequency levels of competitors. When the advertising noise level of all competitors is already high, then more frequency also may be needed to meet or surpass frequency levels of competitors. There are certain marketing situations where a minimum frequency threshold must be passed before consumers start paying attention to the message. The effectiveness of the media plan may be directly related to high frequency. Sometimes a frequency level from three to ten must be achieved for the campaign to be considered effective.

Although brand awareness may be a campaign or creative objective, it may be necessary to advertise in a pattern that matches the purchasing cycle of a product class. Some products are not sold to any great extent at certain times of the year. Calculators, for example, require heavy media usage in spring, early fall, and at Christmas time. Reach levels also will probably be high at those times. On the other hand, in the case of beer— sold all through the year with summer peaks—reach levels may have to be sacrificed at some times of the year in order to have enough money to cover the year and, at the same time, spend heavily during summer. When high reach is necessary, it is sometimes necessary to sacrifice continuity. In some situations, advertisers may drop out of advertising for as long as six months, allowing the product to keep selling at lower volume levels, in order to have sufficient money to advertise at high levels during peak volume seasons.

The fourth variable affecting the budget allocation is the number of markets to be used. There are two methods of arriving at this number. The older method consisted of creating national media plans where the number of markets would not be considered until after other strategies were decided. A newer technique starts with a market-by-market analysis and sets strategies for each market. Once communication goals are set for each market, then reach and frequency levels may be set after the number of markets has been decided. Another approach is to determine the number of markets and minimum communication goals simultaneously—meaning that reach and frequency levels and degree of continuity are also determined simultaneously.

Setting Priorities

An important step in weighting the four elements is that of setting priorities. A planner should do this early so that it will be easier to decide which of the four elements is most or least important. Priorities come from media objectives, and some objectives are obviously more important than others. If there is any doubt, then a planner must not only state the priorities, but also explain why one objective is more important than another and how much more important. Once the priorities are clear, then the allocation of a budget to the four variables should be relatively clear.

QUESTIONS FOR DISCUSSION

1. Briefly explain why a media planner for Brand X who intends to use only network television in the plan, should be concerned about sales potential on a market-by-market basis?
2. Which form of weighting—dollars or impressions—should be used to reach communication goals more easily?
3. What is meant by a threshold level of three impressions in a media plan?
4. Is the frequency of a media plan equivalent to advertising exposure frequency? Explain.
5. Suppose that an advertiser plans a month-long promotion of a brand of soap with three bars being sold for the price of two. Which would a media planner be most likely to adopt for his plan: reach or frequency? Explain.
6. How did one media executive arrive at an exposure level of three to ten to set effective reach levels?
7. Which will probably develop more reach: continuity or flighting? Explain.
8. Explain what a planner should do if the advertising budget is not large enough to reach the media objectives. (Assume that the planner cannot ask for more money.)

9. In what way can an advertiser's sales force contribute to the planning of geographic weighting in a media plan?
10. Suppose that we plan to run full-page ads in a media plan, but find that we need more reach. We cannot obtain more dollars to buy extra reach. What alternatives are available to possibly attain our reach goals?

SELECTED READINGS

Achenbaum, Alvin, "GRPs Can't Measure Effectiveness," *Media Decisions*, May 1977, pp. 64–65.

Adams, S. C., Britt, S. H., and Miller, A. S., "How Many Advertising Exposures Per Day?" *Journal of Advertising Research*, December 1972, pp. 3–9.

Advertising Age, "High Cost of Advertising Got You Down? Try ERPs," Nov. 7, 1977.

Geis, Robert H., and Jones, Richard P., *The Allocation of Advertising Funds: Put Your Money Where Sales Are*, Association of National Advertisers Media Workshop, Dec. 4, 1973, p. 14.

Haley, Russell I., "Sales Effects of Media Weights," *Journal of Advertising Research*, June 1978, p. 78.

Hill, Jack D., *Why Three Exposures May Not Be Enough*, Association of National Advertisers Workshop, Feb. 25, 1975, p. 9.

Kamen, Joseph M., "How to Get Higher Ratings and Sell Less," *Journal of Advertising Research*, April 1979, pp. 59–60.

Kingman, Merle, "Admen See Pulsing as Way to Beat Soaring TV Time Costs," *Advertising Age*, July 4, 1977.

Krugman, Herbert E., "Why Three Exposures May Be Enough," *Journal of Advertising Research*, December 1972, pp. 3–9.

Krugman, Herbert E., "Memory Without Recall, Exposure Without Perception," *Journal of Advertising Research*, August 1977, pp. 9–12.

Light, Larry, *Some New Ways of Allocating Media Dollars by Market*, Association of National Advertisers Advertising Research Workshop, New York, March 1977, p. 6.

Moran, William T., *Media Scheduling Patterns (When to Run, When to Stop and Flight)*, Association of National Advertisers Advertising Research Workshop, New York, March 1977, p. 10.

Naples, Michael, *Effective Frequency: The Relationship Between Frequency and Advertising Effectiveness*, New York: Association of National Advertisers, 1979.

Ostrow, Joseph W., "What Level Frequency?", *Advertising Age*, Nov. 9, 1981, p. S-4.

Papazian, Ed, "How Much Frequency Is Enough?" *Media Decisions*, May 1976, p. 12.

Shifman, Phil, "Frequency Not Reach," *Media Decisions*, August 1975, p. 86.

Staab, Walter, "Are You Making Media Plans? Watch for Geographic Skew," *Advertising Age*, March 24, 1975.

Stevenson, Robert L., "The Frequency of Newspaper Readership," *American Newspaper Publishers Association News Research Report*, Oct. 21, 1977.

7

Selecting Media Classes: Intermedia Comparisons

The two preceding chapters covered major strategy decisions comprising a part of the activities involved in media planning. This chapter and the next deal with the selection of media, covering decisions that usually follow strategy decisions. This chapter will discuss the selection of media classes—decisions on whether to use television, magazines, newspapers, or some other medium. Once media classes have been selected, then decisions about specific vehicles within classes will follow. (Vehicle choices are discussed in Chapter 8.)

To make decisions about media classes the planner must make *intermedia comparisons*—comparisons among different media. Comparisons among media vehicles in the same class, such as among magazines A, B, and C are called *intramedia* comparisons. It is obvious that intermedia comparisons should be made before intramedia comparisons.

The main problem is whether it is logically correct to make intermedia comparisons on a statistical basis. While it may be valid to compare media classes statistically in some cases, in most others it is not. The reason is that the numbers for one media class may not be comparable to another class. Comparisons of readers, viewers, and listeners may aptly be likened to the comparison of apples and oranges. The definition of a reader is so different from that of a viewer that comparisons of numbers may be misleading. For example, would it be correct to compare the cost-per-thousand viewers of a television program with a cost-per-thousand readers of a magazine? Only partially. If one vehicle delivers more audience at better cost efficiency than another in a different media class, the answer is correct to that point. But it is questionable whether a television commercial with its action and sound can be fairly compared with the static appearance of a four-color print advertisement. Yet the

TABLE 7–1. Differences Between Print and Broadcast Media

Print Media	Broadcast Media
Message must be read or seen	Message must be heard, read, or seen
Message can be read at the reader's convenience	Message is viewed/heard only when it is broadcast
Message does not interfere with editorial or entertainment content, although some articles are arranged in a format that does interrupt the reader	Message often interrupts editorial or entertainment content
A reader is defined as one who was exposed to the medium	A viewer is defined as one who has tuned in to the program
Messages can be reread as often as the reader wishes	Message appears only once and viewer has no idea when the same message will be rebroadcast
Generally, one pays full or partial attention to medium while reading or even scanning	It is possible to perform other tasks while program is on, so range of attention may be from none to full
Reader can search for products of interest	Viewer has little idea when a desired product will be advertised
Color fidelity is usually excellent	Color fidelity ranges from one extreme to another depending on the TV set
Medium can be read in almost any location	Viewing is limited by the size and portability of TV or radio set
Medium is sold in space units	Medium is sold in time units
Many production variables are possible, such as gatefolds, pop-ups, Day-Glo inks	Some kinds of production variables are possible such as split-screen, cartoons, stop-motion, cut-ins

planner must make such comparisons whenever it is necessary to choose between two different media classes. Table 7–1 shows some of the differences between print and broadcast media.

Review of Consumer Media

Following is a brief review of reasons for and against using major measured consumer media: newspapers, magazines, television, radio, supplements, direct mail, outdoor, transit, and cable TV. The pros and cons of using a medium often grow out of a planner's perceptions and impressions rather than from objective evidence. So there are some media experts who might take exception to the reasons and/or limitations stated here.

Newspapers—Reasons for Using

Sense of Immediacy. Readers tend to perceive newspapers as the most immediate medium on the market. Every day a newspaper contains something new and with the news come new advertisements. Newspapers may be thought of as having a *now* quality at all times. This quality is important when advertisers want to communicate something immediately. When manufacturers introduce new products to the market, they usually include newspapers as part of the media mix.

Local Emphasis. Almost all daily newspapers have a local quality that is important to advertisers. While advertisers may use a national medium such as network television, they may also want to use a medium with local impact. All selling is local and the newspaper helps emphasize this by advertising local merchants' names and addresses.

Flexibility. Newspapers are geographically flexible because they may be used nationally, regionally, and locally in a media plan. Even when a manufacturer's markets are widely scattered throughout the country, it is possible to reach them by using local newspapers.

Production flexibility allows copy to be changed easily and quickly. For example, some national advertisers want to have different prices for the same products in different markets. There are also special production techniques available. Perhaps an advertiser wants to include preprinted inserts in newspapers in certain geographical markets. These and other production alternatives are possible.

High-Fidelity Color. Through the use of Hi-Fi, Spectacolor, or other rotogravure-printed inserts, newspapers can compete favorably with magazines in given markets. Hi-Fi ads may be recognized by their wallpaper designs, while Spectacolor has a white margin border around the advertisement. Both are produced by rotogravure presses that print only on one side of the page. The paper is not cut into pages, however; it is rerolled and shipped to selected newspapers that print news on the back of the sheet and bind it into the regular newspaper edition for that day. The rotogravure printing gives the advertiser brilliant, life-like colors similar to those that enhance the brand's advertisement in magazines.

Mass Reach. Because newspapers are read by so many individuals in each market, total reach per market may include many individuals in each family. When a product's target audience includes mom, dad, and the children, then newspapers may be an ideal medium.

Catalog Value. A newspaper may serve as a catalog for consumers who are doing comparison shopping. Often consumers search their daily newspaper before they go shopping. The effect of such a search is that they are often presold before they walk into a store to buy the product. Some readers even cut out ads and bring them along as a reminder when shopping.

Ethnic Appeal. Although newspapers are considered a mass medium, they have the power to reach selective ethnic classes as well. If the local newspaper does not reach these markets, then an ethnic newspaper may do the job.

Newspapers—Limitations

Variation in R.O.P. (Run of Press or Run of Paper) Color and Black-and-White Quality. An advertiser buying advertisements printed in R.O.P. color may find great variations in color fidelity from market to market. This variance means that the message may be more effective in one market than in another even though all markets have the same value.

High Cost of Buying National Coverage. While newspapers are indeed a flexible medium, the cost of buying national coverage is very high and may be prohibitive for national advertisers with limited budgets.

National Advertising Rates Usually Higher than Local Rates. Most daily newspapers charge more for national advertising than they do for local. Of course, an advertiser who must advertise in a particular local market will pay the premium rate without question. What may aggravate the agency scheduling the advertising is that some newspapers will not grant them a 15 percent commission. Most do, however.

Small Pass-Along Audience. Newspapers are rarely passed along to other audiences as magazines are. This means that advertisements in yesterday's editions have a limited time value since relatively few other persons will see the newspaper after it is read by family members.

Magazines—Reasons for Using

Selectivity. Magazines are very successful in reaching certain kinds of selected audiences. There are an increasing number of magazines being started each year to meet the interests of special groups such as tennis or chess players, cooking enthusiasts, hobby fans, or those wanting to know more about investing in the stock market. In addition, some magazines have demographic editions such as a physicians' edition, a college students' edition, or one limited to those whose annual income is over $15,000. Finally, there are geographic editions that enable the planner to reach broad or narrow markets. This versatility and flexibility enable the planner to use magazines in many different ways.

Fine Color Reproduction. Many magazines are able to reproduce advertisements with excellent color fidelity. The necessity for fine color reproduction is obvious for certain kinds of product advertising such as food, clothes, and cars.

Long Life. Magazines usually have a long life, at least a week. But some last for more than a month and some for years. The effect of long life is that the advertiser can continue to build reach long after the present campaign has formally ended. While the product featured in the ads may even have been discontinued after a number of years, the effect on a person who reads an ad years after it originally ran is to build brand awareness for long periods of time. Reach built over long periods of time, however, may not help the planner attain short-range goals.

Pass-Along Audience. Magazines usually have pass-along audiences that increase the reach. The size of the pass-along audience varies, however, from magazine to magazine.

Controlled Circulation. Because magazines are able to locate and meet the needs of special interest groups, it is possible for many of them to have controlled circulation. In a controlled circulation arrangement, the publisher is able to identify a special group of targets, mostly by profession or occupation, and then send each of these individuals the magazine free of charge. The publisher then informs advertisers that a circulation audience of a certain size can be guaranteed. Most controlled circulation magazines are in the business field.

Magazines—Limitations

Early Closing Dates. Some magazines require advertisers to have their engravings for four-color ads in the printing plant as much as two and a half months before the cover date. The consequence is that the marketing, creative, and production work on the campaign must be completed so far ahead of publication date that the advertiser may lose the advantage of timeliness. It is even possible for a marketing situation to have changed by the time the ad appears in print.

Lack of Immediacy. With the exception of weekly news magazines, most magazines lack a sense of urgency and immediacy. In other words, readers may not even look at the latest issue of a given magazine until some time after it has reached their homes. Even news magazines do not have the sense of immediacy that newspapers have.

Slow Building of Reach. Because some readers do not turn to their magazines quickly, reach tends to build slowly in this medium. Some readers read a small portion of a magazine immediately and then continue at later dates and times, whenever convenient. Active people who are always on the go sometimes will scan through a number of issues at one time to catch up with their reading. At other times, they just ignore a number of issues and will read only the most current one.

Newspaper Supplements—Reasons for Using

Local Market Impact with a Magazine Format. Newspaper supplements offer the advertiser the advantage of being able to reach local markets with a format that closely resembles magazines. Therefore, many of the qualities of magazines are also qualities of the supplement. Most important, however, is the ability of the planner to reach many local markets with a magazine format.

Good Color Fidelity. Newspaper supplements are usually printed on rotogravure presses and therefore have high color fidelity.

Depth of Penetration. Whereas magazines usually would have limited penetration in any given market, supplements have high penetration. The reason is that magazines, because of their specialized natures, might have relatively small numbers of readers in any local market. But the supplement, distributed with newspapers, would naturally have access to large numbers of individuals for whom the editorial features are of general interest.

Broadened Coverage Area. One bonus of using supplements is that it is possible to reach some markets covered by newspapers that do not carry the supplement. This is possible because large metro area newspapers will often have extensive area coverage far beyond the Metropolitan Statistical Area. Consumers in these bonus markets may read their local newspapers on weekdays, but a large metro paper on Sunday.

Reach Prospects on Sunday Morning. When supplements are read, they will have little competition from other media, because Sunday mornings and afternoons typically offer freedom from other media. Many readers are more relaxed on Sundays and can spend more time reading than on other days.

High Readership. Since supplements have large penetration in individual markets, it is not surprising that they are widely read, especially by women. Working women especially tend to have the time to read this format, because it is available on Sunday, it is part of a newspaper, and because many features tend to cover women's interests.

Flexibility: Geographic and Production. It is obvious that supplements allow the planner to place advertising locally, regionally, or even nationally. But supplements also allow production flexibility such as the option of running a full-page ad in some markets, while at the same time running smaller ads in other markets.

Newspaper Supplements—Limitations

Early Closing Dates for Four-Color. Because supplements are printed by the rotogravure process, the material for ads must be in the printing plant as much as eight weeks before publication date. This timing is even earlier than that required for most magazines that are printed either by letterpress or offset process. Rotogravure is printed from copper cylinders that take an exceedingly long time to prepare. Furthermore, because it is so difficult to make corrections on rotogravure plates, greater care and time is taken in the preparation of the cylinders than is necessary for other printing processes.

Little Pass-Along or Secondary Readership. Because supplements come with weekend newspapers, they inherit some of the weaknesses of newspapers. One of these is that supplements rarely are passed along to others. They usually are thrown away after the family has read them. In addition, one rarely finds supplements in barber or beauty shops or doctors' or dentists' offices as one finds magazines.

Television—Reasons for Using

Sight and Sound for Dynamic Selling. Audio-visual demonstrations are one of the best teaching methods known. The combination of sight and sound gives the advertiser the benefit of a technique that comes closest to personal selling. Television selling is very dynamic. It is also one of the best methods of demonstrating the uses or advantages of a given product.

Flexibility. Network television offers broad national coverage, while spot television allows the planner to use markets in any number of combinations.

Reach of Both Selective and Mass Markets. Television may be used to attract both selective and mass markets through program selection. When professional football games are being broadcast, the audience is almost all male. Children's programming on Saturday mornings, or daytime television tends to reach selected audiences. On the other hand, some programming such as movies, comedies, or special events will attract audiences consisting of many different kinds and ages of people.

Cost Efficiency. Television can be very cost efficient at times. Daytime television, for example, usually has low costs-per-thousand as does fringe time. Though the overall costs are high, the audiences are large.

Television—Limitations

High Total Cost. The cost of commercial time can be beyond the means of some advertisers. The change from 60- to 30-second commercial lengths and even 10-second commercials reflects the advertiser's needs for lower total cost.

Short-Lived Messages. Although audio-visual messages may have the potential for high recall, the nature of television commercials is such that either viewers pay attention or they may miss the message. Therefore the commercial's life tends to be fleeting.

No Catalog Value. It is evident that viewers do not search for commercials when they are in the market for a product. While they pay greater attention to a commercial they happen to see for a product in which they are interested, they usually have little idea of the exact time such commercials will be broadcast.

Limited Availability of Good Programs and Time Slots. Since television is a widely used medium, there is a limit to the number of programs with large audience following or time slots that are available and desirable.

Radio—Reasons for Using

Reach of Special Kinds of Target Audiences. Radio is able to reach certain kinds of audiences very well. Through programming specialization where a radio station becomes known for its "sound," special kinds of audiences, such as men, women, teenagers, farmers, ethnic populations, blacks, the elderly and shut-ins are attracted. Many ethnic groups have programs dedicated to interests of their own such as the Greek, German, Italian, Mexican, or Polish. Religious groups, especially, have found radio to be an excellent communication medium.

A High Frequency Medium. Where a great deal of repetition is necessary, radio may be the ideal medium. The total cost is relatively low and there are usually many stations with time available to permit building a media plan with high frequency.

A Good Supporting Medium. Because of the low cost and good reach of special target markets, radio is often used as a supporting medium. Often when a plan uses print predominantly, radio can be added at low cost to bring sound into the plan.

Excellent for Mobile Populations. Since most Americans own and drive automobiles, radio becomes a means of reaching them while they are traveling. Many people drive long distances to and from work and the distances are getting longer as suburbs develop further from cities. Listening to the radio in what is known as "drive time" has become a diversion to help pass the long commuting time and is an excellent means of reaching commuters.

But commuters aren't the only ones who travel every day. Homemakers often take their cars to shopping centers that may be located far from their homes. They, too, will often turn on the radio to help pass the time while traveling. In fact, radio may be the last medium that homemakers are exposed to before they enter retail stores. Local retailers might very well carry on a campaign to communicate with these customers before they arrive at the stores.

Summertime Exposure. Related to general mobility is the fact that since so many people travel during the summer months, radio is an excellent medium to reach them while they are en route. This is disputed, however, by some experts who claim that radio tune-in is no higher in the summer than it is any other time. *When* listeners tune in, however, does change during the summer, especially among teenagers who are not in school during the day.

Flexibility. Radio, like television, may be used locally, regionally, or nationally. There are not too many production advantages to radio, however. Copy can be changed quickly, and added or eliminated from a program quickly, but radio is still not highly regarded for its great production flexibility except for very simple commercials.

Local Coverage Availability. Local radio is usually purchased because it reaches a given market very well. But radio signals may be carried far from the originating market into other geographical areas. This occurs at night when the "heavenside layer" (a natural atmospheric phenomenon) broadly disseminates signals far beyond the local market. For the national advertiser who is trying to build brand awareness in many different markets, this added feature may be perceived as a bonus when a planner buys local radio.

Radio—Limitations

Many Stations in Any One Market. In many large metropolitan markets, so many radio stations are vying for attention that only a relative few reach a substantial audience. If one wants to build large reach via radio, it will be necessary to buy more than one station and, in some areas, many stations. In New York City, there are 29 AM and FM stations and another 34 in the greater metropolitan area. In Chicago, there are 26 stations in the city and another 19 in the greater metro area. And the numbers are constantly changing. Another consequence of the large number of stations available is the fragmentation of audiences caused by specialized programming. On the one hand, specialized programs do waste few exposures because the program structure is not attractive to everyone. But on the other hand, they may fractionalize the audience too much for an advertiser who wants a mass—not class—audience.

Fleeting Messages. Like television, but even more so, radio messages are fleeting and may be missed or forgotten if only partially heard.

Direct Mail (Direct Response)—Reasons for Using

Very Selective. Direct mail is the most selective of all media, provided that the names and addresses of a target audience are known, and the list is up-to-date and complete. When such a list is available, there may be minimal waste, so the advertiser pays only for targets that are reached.

Response to Advertising Is Easy to Check. It is relatively easy to learn whether a direct mail piece was effective. One simply counts the number of responses to an offer. The number of inquiries from direct mail may or may not be related to sales, but inquiries from direct mailings do constitute one form of measurement. Often alternative copy treatments are sent out by direct mail and the most effective one is easily checked. Chapter 11 raises the question of how to measure the response function of media. Although it is very difficult to measure response functions in most other media, the same cannot be said of direct mail.

A Personal Medium. Direct mail can be a personal medium when it bears a consumer's name and address. Most advertising is very impersonal because, in most media, it is impossible to address anyone by name. Direct mail, using specific names and addresses, comes closest to overcoming this problem. Of course, not all recipients of direct mail pieces appreciate advertisers calling them familiarly by name. But many people do appreciate seeing their names in print, and may pay more attention to the offer as a result.

Geographic and Production Flexibility. Direct mail is probably the easiest of all media to tailor precisely to the geographic marketing needs of an advertiser. The beauty of this flexibility is that direct mail can be adjusted to very small markets (as few as needed), and also can be adjusted to as large an area as needed.

The medium is also flexible in terms of production. Almost any size and kind of paper and any kind of ink or special printing technique is possible. Advertisers with special creative problems may turn to direct mail because it is so versatile. Samples of a product can be mailed with ads; special die cuts can be made; special kinds of foldings and special kinds of packaging are available only in this medium.

Long Life for Certain Mailings. Consumers tend to keep catalogs for long periods of time. Some educational materials also share this quality. If the educational matter has value, such as a chart showing how to administer first aid, or a booklet on how to eliminate stains on clothing, it may be retained for long periods of time.

Possible Savings When Direct Mail Is Inserted with Bills. No special envelope, special addressing, or extra postage is necessary when direct mail advertising is sent along with bills. The bills have to be sent anyway, so the addition of a direct advertisement may not even cost extra postage. Printing costs, however, must be borne. Even when the total weight of the advertising enclosed with a bill is greater than the bill alone, there may still be substantial savings because there are no extra envelope and addressing costs. The addition of the advertising may increase the total cost only slightly.

Direct Mail—Limitations

Possible Expense. There are two situations, at least, where direct mail is very expensive, perhaps more so than any other medium—when a production technique requires the use of very heavy enameled or other expensive papers or when some unusual method of engraving, artwork, or printing is used, or when very large mailings are made that cannot take advantage of bulk mailing privileges. It is unlikely that postage rates in the future will decline, and these high costs will continue to affect direct mail usage.

Inaccurate and Incomplete Lists. Without an accurate and complete mailing list, direct mail cannot do its best. In this era when so many individuals move from one place to another, it may be too difficult or expensive to keep lists up-to-date or develop new ones. In the past, it was possible to buy large mass mailings at low cost and not be concerned about the accuracy of the list. But today's high postage and production costs require that accurate and complete lists be used.

Variance in Delivery Dates. Although a large mailing may be delivered to the post office at one time, the pieces may be delivered to various individuals at widely different times. If time is not of the essence in the marketing objectives, then the lag doesn't matter. But timing of an advertising message is often critical and the direct mail user cannot control it very well. Compared with other media, direct mail comes off second best in respect to timing. When ads are placed in newspapers, they are printed on the day requested. When broadcast commercials are purchased, they are delivered not only on the day, but the hour requested. In comparison, direct mail delivery dates are unpredictable.

Outdoor—Reasons for Using

Wide Coverage of Local Markets. Outdoor advertising is able to build large local coverage of the mobile population in many markets in a 30-day period. However, this coverage does not represent reading of the messages, only exposure to them.

High Frequency. Billboards also have high frequency in reaching the mobile population of a market. It is in this area that billboards may be strongest. While the differences in reach of a 100 versus a 50 showing are not great, the frequency levels are quite different.

Largest Size Print Ad Available. Size is a powerful attraction. Outdoor allows the advertiser to buy the largest size print ad available. The use of attractive color printing plus dramatic lighting and, at times, moving portions, all offer the advertiser great attention-getting power.

Geographic Flexibility. Outdoor may be used locally, regionally, and nationally. Even within any given market, it is possible to add emphasis wherever desired. Movable billboards enable an advertiser to concentrate messages in many places, or to increase the potential for exposure.

High Summertime Visibility. Media plans often will include billboards in the summer, because they increase the visibility of a brand name at a time when many people are traveling. Warmer weather encourages people to take to their cars, and it is possible to reach them through billboards and other outdoor signs.

Around-the-Clock Exposure. Because many billboards on main thorough-fares are lighted, anyone passing a any time of day or night can see the messages. As long as there is a mobile population, there is an opportunity for exposures.

Good for Simple Copy Theme and Package Identification. When the message is relatively short and simple and the package is distinctive, outdoor can be an excellent way to attract attention and build frequency for the message. Building brand awareness is a strength of the medium.

Outdoor—Limitations

Limited to Simple Messages. The best use of outdoor is for a simple message; complex or long messages do not work very well. This restriction means that the medium cannot be used in precisely the same manner as other print media.

High Outdoor Reach Does Not Necessarily Mean High Recall of Messages. Though outdoor may provide high reach, and sometimes good recall of ad messages, it is not necessarily true that high reach means high recall. The creativity of the message is an important criterion in assessing the ability of the message to be recalled. But because of the nature of this medium, people may often look at billboards and be unable to recall what they saw.

A Relatively High Cost Medium. Although the cost-per-thousand is low, outdoor is a relatively high cost medium when compared to some other media. For a 100-showing nationally, the cost is more than a million dollars for a month. Considering that outdoor is a medium often in the background, that it requires very short messages, and that drivers' interests are primarily focused on the road ahead, this cost may be prohibitive for many advertisers.

Transit Media—Reasons for Using

Transit media involve interior and exterior displays on mass transit vehicles, and terminal and station platform displays.

Transit Provides Mass Coverage of a Metropolitan Area. When an advertiser wants to reach individuals in the heart of a market, then mass transit advertising may be desirable. It is primarily a vehicle for reaching adults either on their way to, or returning from, work. But its reach is extensive.

High Frequency. Since this medium takes advantage of normal travel patterns that are duplicated many days throughout the year, there is an opportunity for a great deal of repetition of message delivery.

Relative Efficiency. Based on potential exposures, this medium can deliver large numbers of individuals at low unit costs.

Flexibility. An advertiser can select transportation vehicles in which to place ads that reach certain kinds of demographically defined groups. The advertiser does not have to select all mass transit systems, only those that are known to have large numbers of targets.

Opportunity to Position Messages to Consumers on the Way to Their Points of Purchase. Local advertisers can buy messages that reach consumers on their way to their places of purchases. Therefore, it is possible that, for some consumers, the transit ads will be the last medium they are exposed to before making a purchase.

Transit Media—Limitations

Limited Message Space. Most often, large or complex messages cannot be disseminated in this medium because there is not enough space available to carry such messages.

High Competition from Other Media and Personal Activities. Transit is not an intrusive medium—it competes for attention with other things such as the attractiveness of scenery, the nature of the transit vehicle, or other people. The person who travels to and from work on the same transportation vehicle may be tired, bored, or interested in some other media vehicle. For exterior displays, something of extra creative pulling power is often necessary to attract attention, a requirement that may be difficult to achieve.

Cable Television—Reasons for Using

In 1980, cable television had about 20 percent national penetration of U.S. television homes. As of this writing, nearly one third of homes have cable. Cable television is generally transmitted via a community antenna in a local market that sends programming to individual homes via cables connected to the main station. Individuals must pay for this service.

Good for Reaching Homes That Have Difficulty Picking Up Local Stations. Cable provides a planner with an opportunity to add to an existing schedule television viewers who for different reasons cannot pick up signals from local stations. At present, this number is relatively small, but it is expected to grow.

Provides Some Reach for Special Pay Programming. Some cable operators have the ability to provide movies and special events, such as sports, for an extra charge to cable subscribers. This could provide a substantial audience, depending on the interest in the programming being broadcast.

Specialized Programming Allows Advertisers to Reach Selective Audiences. Most cable operators offer their subscribers specialized programming, not available on broadcast stations. Many of these programs appeal to a small, and therefore selective, audience, based on demographics or lifestyles.

Low Out-of-Pocket Costs. Because cable is very localized and audiences are proportionately small in number, the cost to advertise is relatively low, on either a per commercial or total continuous campaign basis.

Availability of Unusual Commercial Lengths. Cable operators allow the use of shorter or longer commercial units than broadcast stations.

Cable Television—Limitations

Weak in Major Markets. At present, cable is weak in large markets. New York City has only about 10 percent penetration; Chicago only about 4 percent. San Diego, however, has 37 percent. Smaller markets do much better as a rule. Austin, Texas, has 39 percent and Columbus, Ohio, has 25 percent penetration.

High Cost-Per-Thousand. The advertising rates are relatively high at the same time that audiences tend to be relatively low.

Unavailability of Audience Demographic Measurements. Present measurements cover households only. Some other demographic measurements have been made at times, but not on a continuing basis, and not for most of the cable market.

Programming on Cable Tends to Duplicate That Provided by Networks and Local Stations. Although local cable operators have a great opportunity to create truly innovative programming that will pull specialized audiences to their stations, that hasn't happened to any great extent. Cable programming so far tends to resemble that offered by free television broadcasting. This may change in the future, as more homes sign up for cable.

Intermedia Comparisons for Nonmeasured Media

Almost every medium in existence has some qualities that are useful for one or another advertiser. There are times when nonmeasured media are useful. A nonmeasured medium is one that is not measured regularly to find precisely who is exposed to it. Such media include: car cards, telephone book advertising pages, theater or concert program advertising pages, and others. A planner who wants to use such media may have to rely on much more subjective judgments about audience sizes and/or demographics, especially when comparing nonmeasured to measured media.

Sometimes nonmeasured media will conduct research that may help the media planner in making intermedia comparisons. Unfortunately most such research is suspected of being biased in favor of the company that pays for it, because it has a vested interest in the outcome. As a result, it is difficult to make intermedia comparisons even on a subjective basis for nonmeasured media except in simple, obvious areas.

Recall Scores

One way to approach the dilemma of noncomparable measuring techniques for intermedia comparisons is to use response functions as a criterion of effectiveness. If it could be shown that an ad in one medium generates more recall than an ad in another medium, then one might assume that the medium with the higher recall is better. However, the ad or ads used for comparative purposes cannot be indiscriminately chosen. Nor can average recall of many ads be used in measuring recall of one medium versus another. The reason is that some products or brands may be inherently more interesting than others and therefore generate higher recall scores.

To prevent such bias, the same ad is usually measured in two different media. As a result, researchers hope that any variation in the recall scores is due to the effect of the medium rather than the ad. While this procedure attempts to solve the problem, it still is questionable whether dual measurement represents a valid means of intermedia comparisons.

The reason is much the same as mentioned earlier: When comparing print and broadcast, the differences in each medium are like comparing apples and oranges. If a cola product were being tested on television and a similar ad were tested in a print medium, it would be difficult, if not impossible, to keep the copy and creative elements constant. A commercial for a cola drink usually features an announcer's voice, whether on or off camera. Most of the time the message features action, rather than still scenes. Then, too, the audience sees it on many different-sized television screens, some in black and white, and some in color.

If a similar cola ad were placed in print, the size of the ad would probably be constant from magazine to magazine, and there would be no sound of a well-known personality's voice and no music. Furthermore, if the print ad were placed in a magazine, there would be competition for attention from other ads, while the television program in which the commercial was placed would have no competition for attention at the same time.

Therefore, any results of recall measurements could not be considered unbiased. Any one of the variables exclusive to the ad in a given medium could account for the greater or lesser recall scores. While such techniques may be helpful for other purposes, they may not be entirely valid for use in intermedia comparisons.

Often a media class such as magazines will spend a great deal of money to prove that it is better than some other medium. While the results are interesting, they cannot be considered valid for intermedia comparative purposes because of the vested interest problem.

The Media Mix

In planning strategy, the planner may decide to use a single medium or a number of media. When more than one medium is used, the result is called a *media mix*, meaning that the plan mixes a number of media classes to reach certain target audiences. A major question for the planner is whether to use a single medium or a mix. Is one strategy better than another?

Generally, a planner uses a media mix because a single medium such as television cannot reach the target market in sufficient numbers to attain a media objective. When a planner does not define the target market narrowly, the targets represent such a broad spectrum of consumers that the only way to reach them is through multiple vehicles. Most planners narrow the definition of targets to reach *only* those with the best potential. Another situation that might call for a media mix strategy occurs when a planner has segmented targets into primary and secondary groups, each of which are about equal in importance.

A question that a media planner ought to raise when trying to decide whether to use a media mix is: what part of the market *cannot* be reached with a single medium? Generally, vehicles within one media class can reach a substantial part of a market, perhaps 90 percent. The percent of the market not covered may not be worth the extra cost of employing an additional medium. If 20 percent of the population accounts for 80 percent of product consumption, and this 20 percent is within the reach of a single medium, it may be inefficient to try to reach more with additional, but different, media. *Inefficiency* means that the additional media have substantially higher costs-per-thousand than the original medium.

John J. Meskill, senior vice president and director of media at Warwick, Welsh & Miller, Inc., has pointed out another consideration in the media mix question: There are times when a medium covers a market, but heavy users are only lightly exposed to the medium.[1] Generally, it is assumed that it is better to reach heavy users who are heavily exposed to a given medium under consideration.

When to Use a Media Mix

Following are some important reasons for using a media mix:

1. To extend the reach of a media plan. By doing so, the plan adds prospects not exposed by using a single medium.
2. To flatten the distribution of frequency so that there is a more even distribution of those who are exposed to a medium.
3. To add gross impressions, assuming, of course, that the second or third medium is cost efficient.
4. To reinforce the message—or help audience members remember the message by using different kinds of stimuli.
5. To reach different kinds of audiences, perhaps differentiated by lifestyle as well as demographics.
6. To provide unique advantages in stressing different benefits based on the different characteristics of each medium.
7. To allow different creative executions to be implemented.

Meskill, however, felt that the idea of using a media mix ought to be challenged more often than it has been, and that many times one medium will do the job.

---

[1]Meskill, John J., "The Media Mix," *4A Media Letter*, January 1979, pp. 1–2.

QUESTIONS FOR DISCUSSION

1. Explain whether it is valid to compare a cost-per-thousand for a commercial on radio with a cost-per-thousand for an ad in a magazine.
2. What are the general advantages of a print medium vs. a broadcast medium and vice versa?
3. Briefly explain the two kinds of flexibility that may be important in media planning.
4. Explain the reasons why cable television may not be a good medium in which to place advertising now. Also explain why, in the future, it may be an excellent medium for advertising.
5. What is the most important reason for a publisher choosing to have controlled, rather than paid, circulation for a magazine?
6. What advantages does a Sunday supplement have over a magazine and vice versa?
7. Why might a media buyer who wants to build very high frequency choose radio rather than television for a media plan?
8. If a planner wants a high level of brand visibility during the summer months, which medium is the likely choice?
9. Which medium is probably the most selective of all in reaching very selective target markets? What conditions must be met, however, before this medium can be called most selective?
10. If a motorist passes any outdoor billboard, is he or she covered by that showing for the month? Briefly explain.

SELECTED READINGS

Audits and Surveys, "Study of Advertising Communications," *Look Magazine*, Cowles Publishing Company, 1962.

Editor & Publisher, "CBS-TV Claims Newspaper Ad Reading Time is Under 6 Seconds," Sept. 5, 1970, pp. 9–10.

Forkan, James P., "Tele-Research Gives TV an Edge over Magazines in Latest Effectiveness Fight," *Advertising Age*, May 29, 1972, p. 6.

Goldstrom, Donald G., *How a Change in Media Mix Paid Off for Armstrong*, ANA Media Workshop, New York, Dec. 4, 1973, p. 8.

Grass, Robert C., *Corporate Image Advertising: Print vs. Television*, ANA Advertising Research Workshop, New York, March 15, 1977, p. 15.

Greenberg, A., "Point-of-View: Intermedia Comparisons," *Journal of Advertising Research*, October 1972, pp. 47–49.

Grudin/Appel/Haley Research Corporation, "Advertising Recall in *Life* vs. Television," *Life Magazine*, 1970.

Kanner, Bernice, "TV vs. Print Study Finds Readers More Attentive," *Advertising Age*, Aug. 7, 1978, p. 2.

Keshin, Mort, "Apples and Oranges Revisited," *Media/Scope*, June 1966, pp. 12–14.

Kinley, Daniel L., "Inter-media Comparisons," *Media/Scope*, September 1959, p. 28.

Krugman, Dean, "Cable Television and Advertising: An Assessment," *Journal of Advertising*, Fall 1978, pp. 4–8.

Life, "A Six-Step Inter-Media Comparison," Spring 1971.

Lodish, L. M., "Exposure Interactions Among Media Schedules," *Journal of Advertising Research,*, April 1973, pp. 31–34.

Maneloveg, Herbert, "Television Isn't Alone in Commercial Clutter—Magazines, Newspapers Have It Too," *Advertising Age*, Oct. 11, 1971, p. 47.

Media Decisions, "The Clutter Crisis," December 1971, pp. 40ff.

Media Decisions, "Update on Cable TV: Big Impact, Weak Numbers," January 1979, pp. 62–63.

Media/Scope "No Simple Solution to Comparison of Media," March 1959, pp. 54–63.

Meskill, John J., "The Media Mix," *4A Media Letter*, January 1979, pp. 1–2.

Newsweek, *Eyes-On, A Comparison of Television Commercial Audience with Magazine Page Audience*, Audits & Surveys, New York, 1978.

Orenstein, Frank, "When People Want to Know, Where Do They Go To Find Out?" *Media/Scope*, October 1967, pp. 61–68.

Roper Organization, *What People Think of Television and Other Mass Media 1959–1972*, Television Information Office, May 1973.

Shiffman, Phil, "Comparability—It's Still a Very Important Question," *Media Decisions*, December 1978, pp. 94–96.

Surmanek, Jim, "Spot vs. Network TV," *Media Decisions*, October 1978, pp. 78ff.

8

Evaluating and Selecting Media Vehicles

After selecting media classes, the media planner is ready to select media vehicles within classes. To some extent, previous strategy decisions will spell out criteria for this selection. These criteria grow out of an evaluation of relative media values. The discussion in this chapter covers the most important considerations.

Determining Media Values

An elementary principle for selecting media stated in Chapter 1 was to select those vehicles that reach a large number of targets at a cost-efficient price. While this principle seems to suggest that this is all there is to the selection process, nothing could be further from the truth. A more advanced principle is to determine the full extent of each vehicle's value in terms of the desired criteria *and then* select from among those that best meet the criteria. Some of these criteria may be measured quantitatively and the numerical values of various criteria can be combined into a single number. Others are qualitative, and it is more difficult to assign numerical weights to these. But both should be considered in the selection process. Table 8–1 lists the most important objective and subjective criteria usually considered in magazine selection.

Target Reach and Cost Efficiency

The most important criterion in determining media values is a combination of two principles: (1) finding vehicles that reach a large number

191

TABLE 8–1. Criteria for Determining Media Values

Primary objective criteria
  a. Delivery of demographic targets
  b. Cost efficiency of delivered targets
  c. Delivery of product-class user targets
  d. Delivery of strategic targets
  e. Delivery of psychographic targets

Secondary objective criteria
  a. Primary vs. pass-along readers
  b. Editorial features/content related to brand's image
  c. Special editions/issues/sections in print
  d. Media imperatives
  e. Color reproduction
  f. Circulation trends in print vehicles
  g. Geographic flexibility
  h. Production flexibility
  i. Positioning opportunities within print vehicles

Subjective (or qualitative) criteria
  a. Writing tone
  b. Reader respect
  c. Leadership in media class
  d. Believability

of targets, and (2) selecting from among these only those with the lowest cost-per-thousand. The logic of using these two criteria in combination should be obvious. Advertising and marketing today are directed to certain demographic targets. Assuming that these targets can be identified precisely, it follows that media vehicles should be selected to reach the largest number of targets efficiently.

It should be noted, however, that the decisions to select or reject alternative vehicles do not always rest *only* on finding vehicles that reach large numbers of targets. Another variable in the decision process occurs when a given media strategy calls for high frequency. When frequency is needed, vehicles with less reach (and more duplication) may be preferred. Because reach and frequency levels are inversely related, the selection process may result in sacrificing some reach for more frequency. However, most planners have minimum levels of reach below which they will not go even to attain high frequency. For example, reach may not be allowed to go below 50 percent of a target base, such as women aged 18 to 34.

Some media planners tend to use the two criteria of high reach and low cost almost exclusively to define media values. Others, however, see that the selection process requires much more input on what constitutes value. Shown in Table 8–2 are four print vehicles compared on the basis of target delivery and cost-per-thousand. In the table it is obvious that the vehicle that delivers the largest number of prospects (targets) also has the lowest cost-per-thousand. Such is not always the situation, however.

TABLE 8–2. Comparison of Four Print Vehicles on Targets Delivered and Cost-per-thousand

Vehicle	Cost per insertion	Targets delivered men 18–49 (thousands)	Coverage (%)	Cost-per-thousand
A	$54,849	13,992	31.8	$ 3.92
B	25,641	2,772	6.3	9.25
C	10,696	484	1.1	22.10
D	15,382	3,344	7.6	4.60

Note that the term *coverage* as used in this context is sometimes called *selectivity percentage*. Both terms mean essentially the same thing, but one advertising agency may prefer to use one term rather than the other.

If computer capability is available, it is possible to cross tabulate demographic segments to make composite analyses. For example, a computer makes it possible to find the best media vehicles to deliver women, aged 18 to 49, with over $25,000 annual income, who live in households of five or more persons.

Occasionally, a planner will find that the vehicles that deliver demographic targets most efficiently do not deliver the most users efficiently. When that situation occurs, the planner will have to decide whether demographic targets or users are the more valuable criterion. The planner may also compromise and select vehicles that deliver both kinds of targets.

Strategic Impressions

In evaluating alternative media vehicles, it may be necessary to reach different targets in certain proportions. In other words, a planner evaluating media vehicles in terms of ability to deliver certain kinds of targets does not want these targets delivered in a capricious pattern. If, for example, the planner felt that most advertising messages ought to go to women aged 18 to 49 and a much smaller number ought to go to men aged 18 to 49, then the desired proportions for each should be determined and appropriate vehicles selected to deliver these proportions. If the planner wants 60 percent women and 40 percent men, it would not be logically sound to have the delivery total reversed (40 percent women and 60 percent men).

To decide on the relative proportions, a planner studies product usage and demographic data, then uses judgment to arrive at the desired proportions. If women are the primary decision makers in the purchase of a product, then they should be allotted a larger percentage than men.

In selecting media, then, the planner tries to select vehicles whose audiences are divided in roughly the same proportions as the desired target audience. Because media vehicles may not deliver audience seg-

TABLE 8–3. Impressions Delivered by a Simulated Schedule

	(Goal: 75% women, 25% men) Gross impressions delivered by each vehicle		
	Men	Women	Total
Magazine A	1,500	15,000	16,500
Magazine B	1,500	14,000	15,500
Network TV Program C	5,540	7,000	12,540
Network TV Program D	4,000	9,000	13,000
Total Gross Impressions	12,540	45,000	57,540
Percent Total Impressions	21.8%	78.2%	100%

ments in precisely the same percentages that the planner feels desirable, the division of gross impressions may not be precise, but approximate. For example, if the planner decides that women aged 35 to 49 should constitute 70 percent of targets delivered and women aged 18 to 34, 30 percent, then either a 65 percent/35 percent split or a 75 percent/25 percent split might be acceptable.

Table 8–3 shows strategic impressions from a media plan that delivers targets close to the proportions of 75 percent women and 25 percent men, aged 18 to 49. In studying Table 8–3, one should remember that the desired division of impressions was 75 percent/25 percent. But because of the difficulty of finding media vehicles with precisely the desired proportions, those vehicles that come close are usually accepted as satisfactory, as long as the impression proportions are not equal, or reversed.

The planner should also keep in mind that the same type of vehicle need not be used consistently in order to deliver the desired division of impressions. In Table 8–3, for example, all four media vehicles provide audiences that are concentrated among women (women account for the majority of adult delivery for each vehicle). A combination of male-oriented vehicles and female-oriented vehicles, combined possibly with dual audience vehicles, could also produce a net effect that divides total impressions according to objectives.

Other Media Values

Secondary Audiences

Secondary (or pass-along) audiences also must be considered in evaluating media vehicles. Since the primary audiences have a regular opportunity to see a given magazine and secondary audiences do not, then primary audiences should be more valuable to the media planner. "A Study of Printed Advertising Rating Methods" (PARM), conducted by the Advertising Research Foundation and Alfred Politz, Inc., found that

TABLE 8–4. Recall of Ads Using Starch and Gallup-Robinson

Type of Audience	Recall using Starch (%)	Recall using Gallup-Robinson (%)
Primary	20.0	3.2
Out-of-home pass-along	17.9	2.5

Source: Advertising Research Foundation and Alfred Politz Research, Inc., *A Study of Printed Advertising Rating Methods,* Vol. III, N.Y., 1956

TABLE 8–5. Percent of Respondents Who Were Able to Recall Advertisements

Type of Audience	Verified Recall Average (%)
Subscribers (primary)	27.4
Nonsubscribers (secondary)	17.8

Source: Roth, Paul, "Why We Discount Out-of-Homes by 50%," *Media/Scope*, March 1967, p. 64

primary readers were more valuable than secondary readers—not necessarily because they had a better opportunity to see the magazine, but because they paid more attention to advertisements than did secondary readers. Furthermore, the PARM study showed that, for the Gallup-Robinson (Aided Recall) Measuring Technique, fewer of the out-of-home pass-along readers were able to recall ads than other secondary readers. Table 8–4 shows some of the findings that support the conclusion that primary readers are more valuable than secondary readers. Although there were differences between Starch and Gallup-Robinson, each method found less recall among pass-along audiences than primary audiences. Audits and Surveys Research Company also conducted a study for *Look* magazine and found the differences between primary and secondary audience recall as shown in Table 8–5. Here again, fewer secondary readers were able to recall ads than were primary readers.

These research studies provide some clues about the value of secondary, pass-along audiences. If the secondary audiences are deemed less valuable, then it seems reasonable to discount them in some way. But few media planners would ignore them entirely.

Dr. Seymour Marshak, manager of advertising and distribution research of the Ford Motor Company, felt that simply discounting the secondary audience was not correct.[1] Instead it would be better to determine the value of a secondary reader on the basis of how important that individual was in the target audience and then determine what oppor-

---

[1]Marshak, Seymour, "Forum Question: Generally Speaking, What Value Do You Place on the Secondary or Pass-along Reader?" *Media/Scope*, February 1970, p. 26.

tunities he or she had to see a given advertisement in a given medium. For example, secondary readers may be even more important than primary readers when they receive only one or two exposure opportunities compared to primary readers who might receive over 20 opportunities. This assumes that high frequencies (or many exposure opportunities) are not automatically good media strategy. Each marketing/media situation may be different. Foremost in this kind of evaluation is the assumption that secondary readers are the most important target audiences and have to be reached if the advertising message is to have the proper effect.

One method that could be used for discounting the pass-along secondary audience is simply to cut their numbers in half. If Medium A has a 37,000,000 total audience of which 75 percent is primary and 25 percent is secondary (out-of-home) readers, then the latter is discounted 50 percent.

Table 8–6 shows an example that first treats the secondary audience at full value and then at a 50 percent discounted value. The example is based on the total audience. Typically, media planners discount only the demographic group that comprises the target audience such as men aged 18 to 34, or women who graduated from high school, etc.

Marshak cites examples of two different ways to determine the value of a pass-along reader:

1. The product is advertised in only one medium. The secondary reader has a regular source for obtaining the medium and he is a member of the target group. His value should be equal to the value of a primary reader.
2. The product . . . is advertised in many small circulation magazines (e.g. camping and fishing magazines plus others). The secondary reader, by chance, sees the ad for a product in medium Z while waiting in a pizza parlor. The reader has already seen, or had the opportunity to see, the ad in 20 other media. The value of this 21st exposure within a short time period may be very low.[2]

Marshak, therefore, feels that the value of the secondary audience depends on a number of things: (1) whether it is possible to reach the target audience entirely through primary readers; (2) the relative importance of targets where, perhaps, one demographic group may be as much as three times as important as some other demographic target; and (3) whether the planner needs some other measurement on which to base a decision.

In conclusion then, there seems to be good evidence for not using secondary audience data at full value. The method of discounting the secondary audience should be based on logic and research evidence rather than on subjective judgment alone.

---

[2]Ibid.

TABLE 8–6. Two Bases for Analyzing the Audiences of Magazine A

Full Value Basis	Number (millions)	Out-of-Home Audience Discounted 50% Basis	Number (millions)
Primary audience	27.75	Primary audience	27.75
Out-of-home audience	9.25	Out-of-home audience	4.63
Total audience	37.00	Total audience	32.38

TABLE 8–7. Index of Editorial Environments for Salad Dressings

Magazine	4-color food pages	Food photo-graphs	Number of recipes	Editorial lines dealing with salads	Average of four scores
Better Homes & Gardens	127	255	107	135	156
Good Housekeeping	138	56	89	192	119
Woman's Day	84	29	212	108	108
Sunset	12	165	102	121	100
Family Circle	136	83	105	59	96
Ladies Home Journal	115	85	81	51	83
McCall's	104	70	57	53	71
American Home	86	56	48	81	68

Source: Kaatz, Ronald B., *Dr. (un)Strangeperson, or, How I Learned to Stop Worrying (About Some Numbers) and Love My Magazine Plans!* Paper presented to the American Academy of Advertising Convention, April 1975, Knoxville, Tennessee.

Editorial Environment

It is conceivable that vehicles that reach targets efficiently may not be well-suited to an advertiser's messages because the editorial environments of the vehicles under consideration are incompatible with the ad message. This concept is related to the need for psychographic data to fit demographic data discussed earlier. Two college graduates may be the same age and in the same income class, but lead radically different lives. Similarly, two media vehicles can reach the same demographic targets with about the same cost efficiency, but each may feature editorial material of interest to different kinds of readers. This difference may be important in determining a media vehicle's advertising value.

An example might occur when an advertiser for salad dressings is considering eight potential vehicles, each of which may reach the demographic targets fairly well. But the editorial environments may differ widely, as Table 8–7 shows. The editorial environment criteria in the table are: number of food pages printed in four colors, number of food photographs, number of recipes, and number of editorial lines dealing with salads. These criteria were arbitrarily selected by the planner, so others could be substituted or added to provide a composite evaluation of the media alternatives. If this evaluation is combined with criteria of target reach and cost efficiency, a better approach to evaluating media

TABLE 8–8. Some Demographic Editions of Magazines

Publication	Name of Edition	Target
Better Homes & Gardens	Super Spot	Upper income homes
Fortune	Manufacturing	Manufacturers
McCall's	V.I.P./ZIP	Upper income homes
Nation's Business	Industry	Top management in industry
Nation's Business	Leadership	Members—Chamber of Commerce
Newsweek	College Student	College students
Newsweek	Women	Women
Time	Student/Educator	Students & educators
Time	B	Business executives
Time	Doctors	Doctors
Time	T	Top management
Sports Illustrated	Homeowners	Homeowners
U.S. News & World Report	Blue Chip	Top management
Playboy	Military	Military

may be found. Based on the criteria shown, the data show that *Better Homes & Gardens* was found to be the best vehicle.

The only problem with this kind of evaluation is that the planner must have someone available to do the research, because it is not always readily available for every product class. Such research can be very expensive and time-consuming to collect. Furthermore, the research would have to be repeated year after year to determine whether or not any changes in editorial policies were taking place.

Special Opportunities in Magazines

Media planners who want to reach special or limited markets may find that magazines can be adapted to meet their needs. This is because special demographic or geographic editions have been devised by some media for just that purpose. Table 8–8 lists some of the demographic breaks that are available in major consumer and business magazines.

In addition to offering special demographic and geographic break-outs, most magazines offer two-way (and in some cases even four-way) copy splits. *Reader's Digest*, for example, can distribute special copy to one out of every four subscribers across the nation through the use of zip coding and computers. This trend toward increased flexibility and specialization is expected to continue.

Media Imperatives

A planner considering media vehicle alternatives must be aware that although some vehicles reach target audiences very well, the data on reach can sometimes hide important facts. For example, the planner may find that television best reaches a given target audience, but those reached

TABLE 8–9. General Findings of Media Imperatives

Group	Population (%)	Magazine Reading (%)	Television Viewing (%)
Heavy Mag/Light TV	33	47	16
Heavy TV/Light Mag	39	20	57
Dual (Heavy TV/Heavy Mag)	15	29	23
Neither (Light TV/Light Mag)	13	4	4
Total	100	100	100

Source: Ogilvy & Mather

may be light television viewers and heavy magazine readers. In other words, reach figures do not indicate the degree of exposure to a given medium. *Media imperatives* is a form of research that provides information on the degree of exposure to television and magazines.

Television imperatives show that some targets are heavy television viewers and light magazine readers, while *magazine imperatives* show that some persons are heavy magazine readers and light television viewers. In addition, media imperatives can also show dual audiences (or heavily exposed individuals in both media, and lightly exposed individuals in both media).

So media imperatives is a means of comparing magazines and television based on the degree of exposure to each medium. It also shows how much of various product categories are purchased by the four groups measured. Table 8–9 provides a general analysis of heavy versus light exposure to magazines and television on the basis of the media imperative's data:

A study of media imperatives, then, may motivate a planner to shift spending into or away from either television or magazines. The data do not answer all questions, but add another quantitative dimension to help solve the selection problem, as well as the problem of allocating money.

Position Alternatives

Some print vehicles offer advertisers selected positions, which, if accepted, may turn out to be advantageous in reaching the targets with more impact. Sometimes premium rates are charged for position, but other times, the cost may be relatively low. So the planner may consider the availability of favored positions as a factor in weighing one vehicle against another. Those that offer selected positions may be a better buy than those that do not.

Advertising Clutter and Product Protection

In both television and print media, it is possible to measure the amount of clutter that occurs. Presumably, the medium that reaches the maximum number of targets at the best cost efficiency, and at the same time, is the least cluttered, would be the most desirable. There are, however, exceptions to this assumption. For example, in certain magazine classes, such as fashion and shelter, readers look for many ads and they buy the magazine to shop through advertising. On the other hand, if all competitors are in the same magazine, and there are also many other ads in the magazine, it may be questionable whether that vehicle is the most desirable for a specific advertiser. Brands with a clearcut competitive advantage over other brands should prosper when placed in close proximity to competitors. Other brands, perceived as less desirable, may suffer from such competition. Generally, clutter is undesirable and product protection is something to be sought. This means keeping competitive ads within the vehicle at a reasonable distance from the advertised brand.

In evaluating the effect of clutter in a print medium, one should consider the Starch studies that show that the readership of the average advertisement in a magazine declines as the number of ads in the vehicle increases.

In television and radio, product protection is often felt to be a necessity, without question.

Circulation Trends

An objective measurement of a medium's value is the trend of circulation over a period of at least a year or two. Because advertising is sometimes planned more than a year ahead of time, media planners might want to study the latest Audit Bureau of Circulation (ABC) circulation figures for the last 12 to 24 months to see what has been happening. If a magazine under consideration has shown a decline, it may be dropped from the list. On the other hand, magazines with increasing circulation trends may be considered valuable.

New Product Editorial Features

Some magazines are known for their editorial features on new products. It is assumed, therefore, that readers know this and when they want to learn about the existence of new products they turn to such a magazine in preference to another magazine.

Advertising Copy Checking

Some media have a reputation for examining the veracity of all advertising copy and claims and annually reject many dollars of advertising. They publicize this fact regularly. The assumption here is that readers, knowing of this practice, will prefer to read ads in such a vehicle in preference to others that do not publicize their censorship efforts. *Good*

Housekeeping, many newspapers, and network television organizations are some that check copy carefully.

Response to Coupons, Information, or Recipes

Measurements of the number of audience members who send in coupons or ask for information or recipes may constitute a qualitative measure that could help a planner differentiate one magazine from another. This information, however, is not public for all magazines and may be difficult, if not impossible, to obtain. In situations where an advertiser runs the same ad in more than one magazine, it is sometimes possible to learn which magazine pulled best.

Available Discounts

Sometimes the value of a medium is directly affected by the nature of the discounts that it offers. If a number of ads are planned for a calendar year in several vehicles that are otherwise about equal, that vehicle offering a substantial discount may represent the best value of all. However, it would seem obvious that discounts rank relatively low on the scale of various criteria. Target reach and target cost efficiency, for example, are more important than discounts. Likewise, the vehicle with the larger number of product users is usually more important than the vehicle with a large discount potential.

Flexibility

Two kinds of flexibility can affect media value. One is the degree to which a medium can be used to reach geographically superior markets precisely, while at the same time avoiding relatively weak markets. Generally, local media such as newspapers, spot radio, spot television, and outdoor are considered flexible media in the geographic sense. Magazines have some flexibility with their regional and local market issues. But often there may not be a local edition for a market that the planner deems necessary, or the regional editions do not cover an advertiser's sales divisions with much precision. A media vehicle that has the potential for geographical flexibility may be more valuable than one that is not flexible.

A second kind of flexibility concerns the ability of the medium to make quick changes in copy. This is a production flexibility. There could be many reasons why an advertiser might need to change an advertising message quickly. In some media, this is a relatively easy job; in others, it is not. Black and white ads in print media can usually be changed quite easily and quickly in many vehicles. When a print ad is to be printed in four colors, however, it becomes more difficult to make changes because it may be necessary to remake four-color engravings. Generally, print media printed by letterpress are easier to change than those printed by offset. Rotogravure-printed media are the most difficult to change, especially if the printing cylinders have already been prepared and are ready for printing. In broadcast, it is easier to change live commercials than film commercials, and it is easier to change videotaped commercials than filmed ones. So production flexibility may be a consideration in determining media value if changes in the advertising message are contemplated.

Color Quality

In print media, color quality can be important in determining media values. The problem of color quality is twofold. On the one hand there is the problem of simply achieving the color quality of the original artwork planned for an advertisement. Some publications may find it difficult to attain this quality because of the kinds of ink and paper they use. A second problem concerns the maintenance of consistent color quality during the entire press run. Printing presses running at high speeds sometimes wear out printing plates because of the friction of metal on paper, thereby allowing certain colors to print heavier or lighter than required. The planner should know the printing abilities of the publishing organization. Some vehicles have a distinct production control advantage over others.

The Qualitative Values of Media

As stated earlier, media selection is based mostly on the ability of specific media vehicles to reach precise target audiences with high cost efficiency and little waste. Some other considerations in planning might be the total cost of the medium plus the reach and frequency to be generated. Before a final decision for or against any medium is made, however, the planner may want to consider the qualitative values of each medium and how important they are for the plan.

What Is a Qualitative Value?

A qualitative value of a medium is some characteristic of that medium that would enhance the chances that an advertising message carried within it will be effective. It is based on the assumption that media are not simply passive carriers of advertisements; they are active carriers. A media vehicle is an environment with a personality of its own that may rub off on its advertisements and make them more effective in disseminating their messages. Social Research, Inc., defined this environment as follows:

Think of a magazine as similar to a geographic location, a neighborhood, or a section of town. There are certain meanings that are generally associated with the location, and these meanings usually are known and taken for granted by most people living in the community. When an advertiser buys a lot in that location, it automatically buys whatever connotations the neighborhood carries. The building erected on this site (or the ad placed in this magazine) is responded to in terms of its own merits. But the edifice is also thought of in connection with its location, and this will either add to or detract from the impression the building makes.[3]

A medium's environment, therefore, may represent a qualitative value that could affect each advertisement carried within it. William Weilbacher, former vice president of Dancer, Fitzgerald, Sample, defined a qualitative value in a more specific way as follows:

> . . . Qualitative media value is the total increment to advertising message effect contributed by the medium or media vehicle. This qualitative medium value includes such individual contributors . . . as the special characteristics of the audience attracted to the medium or vehicle, and whatever personality characteristics are attributed to it by its audience members.

> Implicit in this usage of the term qualitative value is the notion, that, beyond individual and definable source . . . such as demographic and attitudinal characteristics, the medium may also contribute completely undefined, even unanticipated, values to the advertising process. . . .[4]

Weilbacher warned, however, that his concept of a qualitative value did not include such general media characteristics as the image and prestige of each medium because these, although easily measured, did not necessarily add to advertising effectiveness. He preferred to deal with qualitative values that specifically affect individual advertisements.

Weilbacher's warning, however, focuses attention on the kinds of problems planners face in using the concept of qualitative values in media planning. Because it is so easy to measure the image of a magazine, it is often done. One way to measure the image is to compile a list of adjectives that could describe a magazine and ask respondents in a study which best represents the medium being studied. Such adjectives might include: interesting, learned, dynamic, timely, modern, alert, etc. Then

---

[3]Social Research, Inc., *Advertising Impact and Business Magazines,* Chicago, 1959, p. ii.

[4]Weilbacher, W. M., "The Qualitative Value of Advertising Media," *Journal of Advertising Research,* December 1960, p. 14.

FIGURE 8–1. Graphic Profile of a Magazine's Image

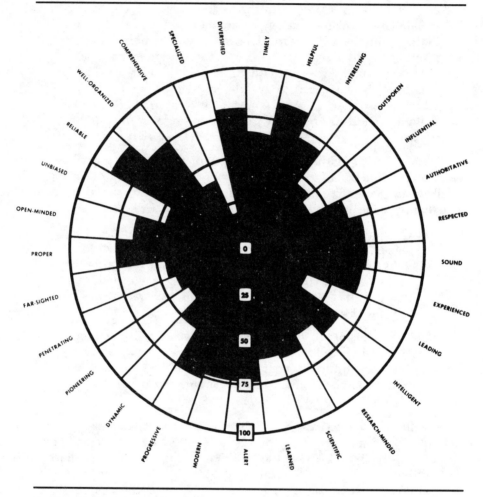

Reprinted by permission of the Marsteller Co., Inc.

the findings may be presented in a graphic form as shown in Figure 8–1. Shown in boxes are the percentages of respondents who felt that the adjective in question best described the magazine.

The problem with studies of magazine images is: What does one do with the results? Because one magazine has a different and presumably better image than another magazine, does this have anything to do with advertising effectiveness? There is very little evidence to suggest such a relationship. Therefore image studies, though a form of determining a qualitative value, have little importance in media planning.

TABLE 8–10. Some Findings from the Politz Study

Respondents who:	McCall's (%)	Life/Look (%)
1. Were familiar with the brand:		
a. With no exposure	16.3	15.0
b. With one exposure	20.6	18.2
2. Believed claims found in ads:		
a. With no exposure	17.0	16.5
b. With one exposure	19.4	17.8
3. Considered advertised brand to be one of the "very highest quality":		
a. With no exposure	17.6	17.8
b. With one exposure	21.4	18.8
4. Were interested in buying the brand:		
a. With no exposure	10.3	10.1
b. With one exposure	13.2	11.6

Source: Politz, Alfred, and *McCall's*, "A Measurement of Advertising Effectiveness," November 1962, p. 11

Measuring Qualitative Values

The kind of research needed to prove that media have qualitative values is that which tests the effectiveness of the same advertisement in two or more media. If all variables are held constant, then differences in reactions to the same advertisements may be due to qualitative values.

Alfred Politz studied responses by women to 12 advertisements appearing in *McCall's* against responses to the same 12 advertisements placed in *Life* and *Look* magazines. In order to isolate the qualitative media effects of each vehicle, he first solicited responses from his sample with no exposure to the ads to determine what respondents knew about the brands without having seen the ads.

Then he exposed the ads to the respondents in all three magazines, after which he measured responses again. Any differences between no exposure and one exposure were attributed to the qualitative differences of the medium as they affected readership of ads within them.[5] Shown in Table 8–10 are some of Politz's findings. Not only were there differences in responses with no exposure between *McCall's* and *Life/Look*, but there were greater differences after one exposure between the two magazine measurements. Presumably these differences were the effect of the magazine.

Using Qualitative Values

Notwithstanding Politz's and others' research on qualitative values, there is still little consensus about the matter. The tendency in most advertising

---

[5]Politz, Alfred, and *McCall's*, "A Measurement of Advertising Effectiveness," November 1962, p. 11.

agencies is to rely very little on such evidence of qualitative values in media planning. When they do use qualitative values, they are apt to prepare the following kind of statement for their plans: "We feel that Medium A reflects greater authority and prestige than other media and therefore recommend that we purchase X number of ads in it."

Other terms that are used in the same manner are: impact, mood, believability, atmosphere, excitement, and leadership. In addition, print media are sometimes judged on the following qualitative values:

Reputation of media for attracting ads of only the highest quality products. It is assumed, therefore, that readers knowing this fact will be more favorably inclined toward products and brands advertised in these media than they would for products and brands advertised in other media.

Reading days. How many days, totally, are alternative magazines read? If a magazine is opened at any time on a given day, this constitutes a reading-day. If, for example, there is evidence that magazine A is read more total days than magazines B, C, D, and E, (all under consideration) then the planner has one more qualitative reason to select A. More reading days represent more opportunities to see ads.

Reading time. In a similar manner, it is possible to measure the total or average number of hours spent reading magazines. These measurements may indicate that the magazine with the largest number of reading hours is more attractive than others. It may be assumed that audience members have more opportunities to see ads if they spend more time reading.

Page openings. It is possible to measure the number of pages opened in alternative magazines. A technique in which a tiny spot of glue is applied to pages containing ads may be used. Respondents may be given specially glued magazines on a given day. On the next day (or two) the interviewer may return and pick up the special copies. The number of pages pulled open are then counted. Another variation of page-opening measurements is simply to count page traffic on all ad pages. Using a "recognition measuring technique" researchers count the number of pages where any ads on the page were noted by audience members who comprise a sample. Page traffic data is a measure of the net potential audience size of a magazine and may play a role in the final selection decision.

The above list is by no means complete, but it does show how media planners might use the qualitative values of various media in planning.

Probably the most misused of all media qualitative value terms is that of "impact." Print media executives often claim their magazine has more impact than other magazines. If they mean that an ad in their magazine will sell more of the product than an ad in any other magazine, this cannot be proved and is, therefore, conjecture on the part of the executives. It is generally not possible to determine the effect of a media vehicle and an advertisement on sales.

Conceivably, there could be a careful testing program conducted for one advertiser, with strict controls, to prove that more people recalled a given ad in one magazine than in any other. But recall and sales are quite different. How can one prove that it wasn't the price, the packaging, the distribution, or the sales promotion that sold the product? Some vehicles are better than others, but not on the basis of impact, which is too vague a concept to be used in media planning. Only when a clear-cut cause-and-effect relationship can be established for the brand and the vehicle on sales can the concept of impact be used.

Qualitative rationales for selecting media have a place in planning procedures. But there are some reasonable guidelines that ought to be kept in mind if they are used:

1. Qualitative, or subjective, rationales should never be a total replacement for quantitative substantiation.
2. Qualitative considerations should be used *after* quantitative analysis has been made and thereby modify numerical relationships.
3. If possible, more than one person should contribute to making the subjective analysis in order to reduce the possibility of individual bias.
4. Media sponsored research concerning qualitative values such as high impact, "liked most," etc., should be considered suspect. Much of this kind of research tends to be highly promotional rather than objective. It is very difficult to transfer the findings from one medium to another.

In conclusion then, qualitative values of media do exist, but they can't be used as the main criteria in media planning. They are simply not objective enough to be used alone for decision making. Perhaps ways will be found in the future to prove that one medium indeed has more impact than others, but at present it cannot be proved. Experts can only agree that media are not passive carriers of ads. They do have qualitative values, and some can be used for planning purposes.

Ad Positions Within Media

Assuming that media vehicles have been selected, the budget allocated, and a schedule worked out, theoretically media planning could end at this point.

Practically, however, questions are often asked by planners themselves and others interested in media: Is there nothing else that can be done to help in the advertising communication process? Are reach and frequency all there is? The problem is to find ways for the media planner to go beyond delivery and not only get vehicles exposed, but get ads within those vehicles exposed, and, finally, get the ads read.

To a great extent, this last responsibility belongs to the creative people: planners, writers, and art directors who have special talents for getting advertising communication "through" to the reader. The copy people, for example, can write scintillating headlines and meaningful words. The art director can devise fascinating layouts. The creative people can ask for four-color ads, bleed pages, reverse printing, gatefold-size ads, two-page spreads; or they can print ads on unusual stock such as acetate or aluminum foil, or use unusual inks such as day-glo or perfumed inks. These are but a few of the many options open to the creative personnel in getting ads noticed and read.

What, then, can media planners do to help the situation? The answer is that they can ask for certain positions within media that are felt to be better than other positions. Hard evidence that one position is better than another, however, is subject to questions that have kept position strategy from playing a more important role than it has.

Problems of Positioning Research

There are a number of media positions that seem better than others. For example, the fourth cover of a magazine is generally conceded to be the best place in a magazine for an ad. In fact, research shows the fourth cover to be one of the best positions. But many media experts question such research. For a fourth cover position, there is some logic, even without research, to suggest that it is a valuable position. But for other media positions, there is not much agreement among experts. The research tends to be weak, and therefore inconclusive.

Perhaps the foremost problem of position research is that it is difficult to separate measurements of position from copy effects. Most research techniques that are used to establish the effects of position are really a mixture of copy and position. In some research studies, another dimension, that of size, is added. Then, too, averaging data for position effects that contain widely varying degrees of copy effectiveness may not truly represent the effects of position because averaging tends to be unduly affected by extreme copy effect scores. Some media experts question whether there is any copy measuring device that is totally valid. But assuming that most are valid, there is still no way, through present-day measurements, to know the effect of position alone.

A solution would be to design experiments where the ad copy is held constant and the only variable is position. Because the same ads would be measured in different positions in different media vehicles, then the effects of position alone could be found. However, there still is dissatisfaction with much research that is devised to measure position because it is not carefully controlled to eliminate bias. Research designs are often poor or nonexistent. Samples are often nonrandom and selected haphazardly. Questionnaire design and interviewing controls are not always the best. As a result, much position research is suspect.

Some Position Effects

The following is a brief summary of position effects that some media planners accept. The reader is cautioned about accepting them as valid evidence. They are presented to show a sample of the kinds of positions that *may* affect the communication power of advertisements placed in vehicles.

Position in Magazines. (a) Fourth cover positions are usually considered better than any inside positions if Starch Adnorm data are used as a guide; (b) second cover and page one positions are about equal and are the next best to fourth cover positions; (c) front of the magazine positions (from page 2 to about page 20) are the next best positions; (d) righthand pages are somewhat better than lefthand pages, with some exceptions. Keep in mind that these are generalities based on the research findings across many different magazines. Specific magazines, which might have uncommon editorial layouts, might produce different readership patterns.

Position in Newspapers. (a) Ads near the front are considered better than those near the back, but the differences are small; (b) there is no significant difference between righthand and lefthand pages; (c) inside a newspaper section is better than the last page of the section; (d) there is little difference between ads above or below the fold; (e) editorial environment affects the readership of ads (ads for male products prove better on sports pages and ads for female products do better on women's pages); (f) preprint stuffers, while they cost about 4.6 times as much as ROP color, do about 3.8 times better in responses.[6]

Position in Television. (a) Attention to programs is greatest during late fringe and poorest in early fringe times; (b) mysteries, spy adventure programs, and movies do a little better than varieties and western programs in recall of messages; (c) daytime is about 50 percent to 80 percent as good as nighttime recall; (d) a 30-second commercial has about 60

---

[6]Jain, Charman L., "Newspaper Advertising: Preprint vs. R.O.P.," *Journal of Advertising Research*, August 1973, p. 32.

percent to 75 percent the recall value of a 60-second commercial; (e) high-rated programs have higher attention levels than low-rated programs; (f) in-program commercials do better in recall than between-program commercials.

Cost Considerations

A major consideration in deciding whether to use a special position in a vehicle is the premium cost. Some positions may not be worth the extra cost. Even if it seems to be worth the cost, it may be difficult to support a decision one way or the other because the research is questionable.

QUESTIONS FOR DISCUSSION

1. In planning media strategy, why does it make a difference whether a print vehicle reaches its audience slowly or quickly?
2. How important should the cost-per-thousand evaluation of vehicles be in comparison to other selection criteria?
3. Why do some media planners believe that the primary audience is more important than the secondary audience of print vehicles?
4. Explain how product protection is given to ads in a print vehicle. In a broadcast vehicle.
5. What kinds of marketing situations would require a media plan to have good geographic flexibility?
6. What is the value of having special demographic editions of print vehicles?
7. If a vehicle charges more for a special position, is it worth the extra cost? Discuss.
8. Suppose salespeople for a given publication point out that their vehicle has a better image than competitors. Is this fact alone enough to make a difference in the decision to buy or not buy that vehicle?
9. How does one decide what proportions of strategic impressions are needed for an effective media plan?
10. Why isn't editorial environment used more often as a criterion in making vehicle selections?

SELECTED READINGS

Carter, David, "Newspaper Advertising Readership: Thick vs. Thin Issues," *Journal of Advertising Research*, September 1968, pp. 39–42.

Frankel, Lester R., and Solov, Bernard M., "Does Recall of an Advertisement Depend on Its Position in the Magazine?" *Journal of Advertising Research*, December 1962, pp. 28–32.

Graphic Communication Weekly, "Study Shows Reader Conflicts," March 12, 1968, p. 13.

Jain, Charman L., "Newspaper Advertising: Preprint vs. R.O.P." *Journal of Advertising Research*, August 1973, pp. 30–32.

Joyce, Timothy, "Target Weighting Gives Boost to Consumer Studies," *Advertising Age*, July 15, 1974, p. 27.

Marder, Eric, "How Good is the Editorial Interest Method of Measuring Magazine Audiences?" *Journal of Advertising Research*, March 1967, pp. 2–6.

Maneloveg, Herbert, "The Total Audience Concept for Magazines—Good if Understood," *Advertising Age*, Oct. 14, 1963, pp. 84–85.

Marsteller, Rickard, Gebhardt and Reed, Inc., *Qualitative Media Measurements*, Chicago, 1959.

Media Decisions, "How Ayer Applies Weights to Media Plans," September 1972, p. 48.

Media Decisions, "When JWT Picks Magazines, Numbers Aren't Everything," June 1975, pp. 65–69.

Media/Scope, "Position in Broadcast Advertising," No. 1, August 1962, p. 50; No. 2, September 1962, p. 41; No. 3, October 1962, p. 48; No. 4, November 1962, p. 46.

Media/Scope, "Timing in Broadcast Advertising," September 1962, p. 46.

Media/Scope, "How Important is Position in Consumer Magazine Advertising?" June 1964, pp. 52–57.

Media/Scope "Forum Question: Generally Speaking, What Value Do You Place on Secondary or Pass-along Readers?" February 1970, p. 26.

Newspaper Advertising Bureau, Inc., and The *Minneapolis Star and Tribune* (Facts), *The Influence of Position, Size, Color, Creativity on Newspaper Advertising Readership*, 1972.

Ostrow, Joseph, "Some Problems in Profile Matching," *Media Decisions*, November 1972, pp. 72–74.

Papazian, Ed, "Qualitative Comparisons—a Necessary Ingredient in the Planning Process," *Media Decisions*, January 1979, pp. 16–18.

Rice, Roger, and Severance, Dick, "Who's Winning the War of Imperatives?", *Media Decisions*, December 1978, pp. 64–65.

Roth, Paul, "How to Plan Media," *Media Decisions*, 1974.

Roth, Paul, "Why We Discount Out-of-Home by 50%," *Media/Scope*, March 1967, pp. 63–68.

Roth, Paul, "What is the Value of the Pass-along Audience?" *Media/Scope*, November 1963, pp. 84–87.

Shiffman, Phil, "Special Significance of Newsstand Sales Data on Magazines," *Media Decisions*, July 1973, p. 82.

Starch, Daniel, "Do Inside Positions Differ in Readership?" *Media/Scope*, February 1962, pp. 44–46.

Starch, Daniel, "Is Preferred Position Worth It?" *Printers Ink*, Aug. 25, 1961, pp. 43–44.

Swan, Carroll J., "In Magazines—Selectivity Within Within," *Media/Scope*, July 1968, p. 33.

Weilbacher, William, "The Qualitative Values of Advertising Media," *Journal of Advertising Research*, December 1960, pp. 12–17.

Wheatley, John J., "Influence of Commercial's Length and Position," *Journal of Marketing Research*, May 1968, pp. 199–202.

Wiener, Norman, "What's Wrong with Newsstand Distribution of Magazines?" *Advertising Age*, Oct. 16, 1972, pp. 59–60.

9
Putting a Media Plan Together: The Mechanics

The last four chapters have dealt at length with the important decisions that go into media planning. This chapter explains how to pull these elements together into a document, the *media plan*. The chapter analyzes the writing of media objectives and strategies, as well as the organization of the media plan.

Organizing the Plan of Action

It is possible, and often probable, that media planning is done in such a way as to end with a series of decisions only remotely related to each other or to the original problem. One might find, for example, that media were selected on the basis of cost-per-thousand for target audiences reached, while neglecting the reach or frequency that resulted. Or, the media selected might have little to do with the marketing objectives. Or, a series of media decisions might represent a loosely organized plan of action. Sometimes, media are selected first, and then scheduled. Following this, a strategy may be devised. Such practices are inefficient.

It is important, therefore, for a planner to organize media planning in such a way as to be logical and efficient. The goals should be as follows:

1. All media decisions should be based on marketing objectives and strategies. The goal of the planner is to select and use media to help attain some one objective or to carry out the overall strategy.
2. The first step in media planning should be to create media objectives, whose purpose is to implement the marketing objectives and strategy.

3. Media strategy should be created after the objectives have
been written. It should consist of a series of broadly conceived
decisions directly aimed at fulfilling specific media objectives.
The reason media strategy should represent broad (or general) media decisions is that it is logical to proceed from the
general to the specific. Thus, the strategy should serve as the
basis for the next step in planning: tactics or implementation,
which in turn leads to media buying.

Table 9–1 presents the relationship between the various general
steps in media planning. Table 9–2 summarizes some of the most important variables that may be manipulated in planning, and Table 9–3 shows
some of the marketing objectives and strategies that may affect media
variables.

TABLE 9–1. Steps in Media Planning

The following shows the logical progression of steps in developing a media strategy and plan:

1. Marketing Objectives	2. Marketing Strategies	3. Media Objectives	4. Media Strategies	5. (Tactics) Decisions Implementing Strategies	6. Media Buying
A number of marketing goals for a given brand. Presumably they are based on best opportunities for sales or solving other marketing problems	A number of broadly conceived marketing decisions, organized into a unified plan of action aimed at attaining marketing objectives	A number of media goals, all related in some way to helping attain marketing objectives, or related to marketing strategy	A number of broadly conceived media decisions, organized into a unified plan of action aimed at attaining media goals	A number of very specific decisions that implement the media strategy. In many in- stances, these decisions serve as a basis for media buying	Actual purchasing decisions involving the selection and use of media
		Examples			
Goal: to increase brand share of market by 5 percent over last year, nationally	Concentrate on stealing customers from competitors by using ads that show ways in which our brand is better than theirs	Goal: plan media selections so as to deliver at least 80 percent of both our and competitors' target markets. (Targets are defined demo- graphically)	Frequency goal: 4.5. Use network TV, day and late fringe, spot TV in top 30 markets. Use: 30s. Buy 600 GRPs in spot markets.	Eliminate newspapers, spot radio, spot TV, and billboards from consid- eration. Use network TV or magazines. Find which gives 80 percent net reach of targets at lowest CPM	Make pur- chase of best alternative media accord- ing to the specifications laid down in strategy and tactical plans, and according to any other specifications (such as creative requirements)

Determining Media Objectives

The best way to plan media is to decide what goals are most important and then to find ways to achieve them. *Media objectives*, the group of goals designed to enable marketing goals to be met, serve the purpose of helping planners decide where they want to go, while the media strategy serves as the means of getting there.

TABLE 9–2. Variables That May Be Manipulated in Media Planning

1. *Constraint variables*
   a. Budget size
   b. Creative strategy
   c. Nature of the product
   d. Nature of the brand
   e. Past use of media
   f. Competitive uses of media
   g. Competitive spending in media

2. *Media plan objective variables*
   a. Reach (or market coverage) needed
   b. Frequency needed
   c. Continuity patterns needed

3. *Media strategy variables*
   a. Strategy concept variables:
      Concentration
      Media dominance
      Flighting
   b. Levels of reach needed
   c. Levels of frequency needed

   d. Weighting proportions:
      By geographical markets
      By demographic targets
      By heavy-user targets
      By season
      By Gross Rating Point levels
   e. Schedule length
   f. Schedule patterning
   g. Cost efficiency standards
   h. Discounts
   i. Allocation of budget to media or markets or both
   j. Number of ads or commercials to be run
   k. Number of different media to be used
   l. Number of different markets to be used

4. *Other variables*
   a. Size of ads or lengths of commercials
   b. Kind of sponsorship in broadcast media
   c. Use of qualitative factors
   d. Availability of media units

TABLE 9–3. Some Marketing Variables That Affect Media Strategy Variables

1. *Introduction of new products*
   a. Roll-out patterns
   b. Key market patterns
   c. Broad-scale national introductions

2. *Increasing market share requirements*
   a. Steal from competitors
   b. Get present users to consume more
   c. Expand the entire market

3. *Changes needed in brand image*
   a. Requiring new creative strategy
   b. Requiring new timing strategy

4. *Changes in corporate image*
   a. Requiring new creative strategy
   b. Requiring new timing strategy

5. *Changes in brand positioning*
   a. Requiring new creative strategy

6. *Reductions in the advertising budget caused by*
   a. Attempts to increase profits
   b. Attempts to cut losses
   c. Production problems of all kinds

7. *Increases in the advertising budget caused by*
   a. Movement into new markets
   b. New product introductions
   c. Need for any changes in communication

8. *Changes in sales promotion strategy*
   a. New relationship between sales promotion and advertising
   b. New or different sales promotion techniques required

9. *Test marketing situations*
   a. Testing various budget levels in different markets (same media)
   b. Testing various budget levels in different markets (different media)

10. *Changes in the life cycle of a product: growth, maturation, decline*

11. *Meeting competitive marketing strategies head on*

Because media objectives are not ends in themselves, but are aimed at implementing either marketing objectives or strategies, it is necessary to study both marketing antecedents. But it may not be obvious how such a study can lead to media objectives, nor is it possible to find an easy-to-use formula for creating media objectives. Perhaps the best direction that could be given to a media planner who wants to create objectives would be to first answer the following question as thoughtfully as possible: "In what ways can I use media to help implement either a marketing objective or strategy?"

The answer to this question must come from a thorough knowledge of media, research, and marketing, plus good judgment. Furthermore, there may not be one answer to the question, but a number of alternatives, each of which may be important to a greater or lesser degree. If, for example, one of the marketing objectives is to introduce a new brand of soap to a market, then a number of alternative media objectives might be considered.

1. Use media that reach heavy users of soap.
2. Use media that other soap manufacturers have used most often in the past (assuming, of course, that such media will reach heavy soap users).
3. Spend at least as much money in the same media as the manufacturer of the number one brand in market share does.
4. Try to reach as much, or more, of the market as the manufacturer who has the number one brand share.

Which should become *media* objectives? The answer may depend on what the other marketing objectives are, the relative importance of each, and what marketing strategy has been devised. After such considerations, perhaps one or all may be adopted as media objectives.

Sometimes, however, media objectives are based on marketing strategy rather than marketing objectives. If, for example, the objective is to introduce a new brand to the market, and the marketing strategy is to use a roll-out pattern of introduction, then the media objective would specify the geographical areas where media would first be used. Sometimes a roll-out pattern might be limited to the states in the northeastern United States, and only after the brand is selling well would it be introduced gradually to adjacent western states. Media objectives could clearly indicate which states should receive media and when such media might be used.

It is not possible to explain precisely how media objectives should be created. Instead, the idea of a "relationship" between media objectives and marketing objectives or strategy should serve as a guide in planning.

Budget Constraints

Even though the relationship of marketing-to-media objectives is clear, a number of constraints often temper the planner's decision. The size of the budget, if known ahead of time, is one such constraint.

Many times, the marketing budget is set before any media planning has taken place. In such a situation, the media objectives will have to be written with that constraint in mind.

On the other hand, if no budget is available, then media objectives may well serve as a guide to setting a budget, at least as far as the cost of time or space is concerned. Once planners have a general idea of their goals, they are in a position to estimate what it will cost to achieve them. Sometimes, a budget cannot be set at the media objectives stage, but must wait until the strategy has been worked out. In such cases, media objectives may have to be rewritten later to accommodate the size of the budget. Perhaps a series of marketing/media priorities may have to be set so that the planner achieves those goals that are most presssing, while secondary goals may have to wait for another day. The size of the budget may be recommended by a media planner, but it may be reduced by the client after examining marketing/media objectives and strategy.

Creative Constraints

Creative strategy can be a constraint in setting media objectives. The role of creative strategy in planning media was discussed earlier. Suffice it to say that a media planner should first study creative strategy before writing objectives.

Reach and Frequency

When planners select media they are, in effect, choosing those that will deliver a given number of target audiences. Delivery, however, is nothing more than potential exposures. Because all research data represent measurements taken in the past, the data therefore represent only "estimates of exposures." The future may be somewhat different.

But the number of estimated exposures contracted for in a media plan may be patterned in such a way as to maximize either reach or frequency, or to attain effective reach and frequency. Media objectives should be set so as to obtain whichever goal is sought. Brown, Lessler, and Weilbacher called this pattern the "message basket."[1] They meant that, without clear-cut, deliberate planning, all of the potential exposures

---

[1]Brown, Lyndon O.; Lessler, Richard S.; and Weilbacher, William M.; *Advertising Media*, Ronald Press, New York, 1957, p. 118.

planned may produce only a confused basket of numbers, some of which may even represent contradictory goals. Therefore, media objectives should be written in such a way as to bring control and order out of chaos in the basket.

More explicitly, media objectives should state whether reach or frequency is to be the goal, and explain why each is or is not needed. In addition, the levels of reach and frequency should become objectives. Here, too, an explanation is needed to justify, logically, why any given level is desired.

Continuity

It should be apparent that media objectives will affect the kinds of strategies that later evolve. One important goal that will affect the timing of advertising during weeks and months of a year is continuity. *Continuity*, as previously described, is the consistency of advertising placement. Like reach and frequency, continuity may result in many contradictory patterns of placement if not controlled.

One placement pattern for example, may consist of advertising appearing every day of the year, while another pattern may be limited to placing ads once a month. Which is better? The answer is relative. What are the brand marketing goals and strategy? Do they require a given pattern? Does the creative strategy require a different pattern? For example, if the creative strategy includes a very complex message in television commercials, will audiences be able to grasp the meaning if the commercials are shown once a month? Will a pattern of frequent showings be required?

Therefore media goals will have to be based, at least to some extent, on continuity.

Market Coverage Levels

Coverage (or reach) levels desired should be stated in the media objectives, if possible. As it was previously defined, *coverage* is the percentage of a target market that a combination of all media will reach. It is important to set that level carefully, keeping in mind how much coverage is needed to attain a given marketing or media objective.

It is also a good practice to explain why a given level of coverage is required. In other words, if a media plan is supposed to deliver 75 percent of the market, the planner ought to be able to explain, reasonably, why 75 percent was chosen. Why not 65 percent or 85 percent? Budget limitations, frequency, and marketing objectives probably constitute the main considerations in determining coverage levels. A coverage level gives the market/media planner a given number of potential consumers, many of whom, it is hoped, will be turned into buyers through exposure to the advertising message.

Media Targets

To whom will advertisements be directed—users, persons who influence users, or both? The more specific a planner is in identifying targets by demographic or other means, the easier it will be to find media that will reach those targets. Most media targets are defined demographically. Occasionally, some other description such as psychographics (the psychological descriptions of targets) is used. The goal, however, is to be as specific as possible, because a vague description may mean exposures wasted on individuals who would never buy a given product or brand under any circumstances. Once media targets have been specified, then all subsequent decisions can be checked to see whether the correct targets are being reached by the media selected.

Media objectives usually also include a statement indicating where targets are located geographically. Sometimes this information is stated in the strategy portion, rather than the objectives portion, of the plan.

Cost Efficiency

Cost-per-thousand maximum levels may or may not be a part of media objectives. Usually, cost-per-thousand targets are needed to discriminate between media. In past years, when media planning was often based on large audience figures (sometimes called *box-car figures*) representing crudely identified media audiences, maximum cost-per-thousand levels were usually stated in media objectives. For example, one media objective might have been written to warn buyers not to buy any medium that had a cost-per-thousand over $5 for total audiences. But at the present, and most likely in the future, maximum levels of cost-per-thousand may be meaningless, because cost-efficiency formulas are now used mostly to help discriminate between the ability of various media to deliver prospects at the lowest unit cost. But even the lowest CPM among all alternatives may be high.

Examples of Media Objectives

The actual practice of writing media objectives often results in statements that are mixtures of both objectives and strategy. The probable reason for this is that there are too few objectives, so both objectives and strategy are planned about the same time. Often there is little difference between the two.

The following are examples of media objectives (with some strategy statements intermixed) taken from various advertising agency media plans.

Media Objectives from Plan A. Television will continue to be X's primary medium because of its ability to provide efficiently:

1. Audience: the desired woman, or heavy user, recognizing the role of women as the decision maker regarding X type of food.
2. Effectiveness: demonstration of X's palatability, via sight, sound, and motion.
3. Schedule and pressure variation—based on need for:
   a. Continuity: year-round support that can reasonably be expected to reach a significant number of established customers on a regular basis.
   b. Impact: heavy pressure during certain flight periods affording the brand the opportunity to reach a large audience with a frequency substantially above the continuity level, the purpose being to help stimulate new trial.
   c. Flexibility: to capitalize on geographic variation in existing market potential and to support major promotions.

Media Objectives from Plan B. Based on the outline of the problem, the specific objectives of the media plan are:

1. To reach large families with special emphasis on the housewife, who is usually the chief purchasing agent.
2. To concentrate the greatest weight of advertising in urban areas where prepared foods traditionally have greater sales and where new ideas normally gain quicker acceptance.
3. To provide advertising continuity and a fairly consistent level of impressions throughout the year except for extra weight during the announcement period.
4. To deliver advertising impressions over the entire country in direct relation to food store sales.
5. To use media that will help to strengthen the copy strategy and put major emphasis on convenience, ease of preparation, taste, and economy.
6. To attain the greatest possible frequency of advertising impressions consistent with the need for broad coverage and the demands of the copy plan.

Since, as we have pointed out, the regional strategy normally stems from the national plan, we will outline first the campaign that is proposed for phase II when full national distribution will have been attained.

Media Objectives from Plan C.

1. Coverage of all homemakers, with special emphasis on those in larger urban markets, in middle and lower-middle income groups, and in larger families.

2. Maximum frequency, within budgetary limits, to match the relatively frequent pattern of purchase in this category.
3. Adequate time or space for a complete, thorough, multi-season sales message.
4. The opportunity to punctuate a continuous level of coverage with two crescendos of special weight, one in the summer in the south and one in the winter in the north.
5. Maximum efficiency for every advertising dollar spent—to combat higher competitive per-pound expenditures by buying more impressions per dollar than competition.
6. A corollary requirement, if it can be realized, is dominance of advertising weight in Brand X's markets to appear more important than any competitor.
7. To reach housewives as close as possible to mealtimes; early morning, noon, and dinnertime.

Determining Media Strategies

A strategy is a series of actions, usually planned far ahead of time, to accomplish specific and stated goals. Whenever there are alternative ways of accomplishing a goal, then there is the need for a strategy. In media planning, there are many opportunities to use strategy, and inevitably a problem arises in trying to find a way to know, objectively, which course of action will be optimal. The mental process of weighing media strategy alternatives, however, presents a formidable task because there are many alternatives to think about at any one time. While thinking about audience sizes, a planner must, at the very same time, be thinking about cost efficiencies, availabilities of media units, discounts that could change the whole plan, the effect of competitors, the creative strategy and execution, the amount of money that is available, and the time available to accomplish objectives—and this is only a partial list.

Generally, no single strategy comprises a media plan. Instead, there are a number of strategies, with varying priorities, that constitute the essence of a plan. There may be a weighting strategy, a spending strategy, a reach and frequency strategy, and so forth. Each strategy should be clearly stated and defended. Usually, strategy statements are organized so that the most important strategies come first.

Although a selected strategy may represent the best of all alternatives, the net total of a number of strategies to be included in a single plan may not represent a unified or coordinated plan. A unified plan is an objective of good strategy planning. Perhaps the term "orchestrated" better describes how all media actions work together for the attainment of media and marketing goals. Contradictory or incomplete actions have no place in good strategy.

It is important to place media strategies into a frame of reference so that one can see what position each occupies relative to other parts of a plan. Strategies are neither the beginning, nor the end, of planning. Media objectives precede them, and media selections usually follow them. Selection decisions are sometimes called the "tactics" of a plan.

How is strategy judged? The answer is that, eventually, the strategy will be evaluated on what happens as a result of the planning. Someone will have to answer a question such as: "Were the marketing and media objectives attained as a direct result of the strategy or in spite of the strategy?" Such questions really comprise a post-evaluation, however, and they are far removed from the immediate problem of evaluating strategy in the short run.

There are several ways to evaluate strategy *before* a plan is implemented. One way is to determine the risks of doing or not doing something. This requires subjective judgment plus the experience of having tried various strategies and finding them not worth the risk. Another evaluation technique is a weighing of economy of effort and time. If a strategy takes too much effort, or is too time-consuming to execute, it may not be worthwhile. If it costs more than the budget provides, then a question arises: Can one be sure that the extra money is worth the risk?

Another method of evaluation is based on estimating the probabilities of success. Unfortunately, beginners have no way of knowing whether a plan will succeed, especially if the marketing situation is unique or new. But there may be strong clues. One clue is the experience of others in an organization who have created plans or know of plans that are similar and have succeeded. Another clue may be found in published reports of competitors' strategies that have succeeded. The planner will have to determine whether their experience is directly translatable to the present situation.

Sometimes marketing and/or media consultants may have to be hired to provide expert opinion of whether a strategy will work. At other times testing and experimenting may be necessary to provide the answer. In addition, journals of marketing and advertising often provide information and/or theories that can be adapted to fit the needs of a given situation.

Finally, however, there is no substitute for good reasoning and logic. Even if the evidence is not available, the planner can make assumptions about how the marketing/media environment is operating. But the better planners go beyond making assumptions. They first attempt to check the validity of their assumptions by keen observation of what happens after a strategy has been tried to determine whether or not it has been successful and whether the assumptions were valid. Secondly, good planners are always challenging their own assumptions and changing them if necessary, as time progresses.

Once strategies have been devised, it is the responsibility of planners to prove that the media choices are the best of all alternatives. Planners should be able to defend their decisions with as much evidence as possible, plus good judgment. For a continuation of this discussion on judging the adequacy of a strategy, the reader is directed to Chapter 11, which concerns response functions.

Considerations in Strategy Planning

The first consideration in planning media strategy is to take a close look at the entire marketing/media situation, with special attention to competitors' marketing and media strategies. Perhaps one of the first steps should be to answer the question: "To what extent do I copy competitors' media strategies?" At times in planning media strategy, there may be the temptation simply to implement media objectives without first considering the strategies of competitors. But such temptations should be subdued by the realization that no brand exists in a vacuum, so strategy will have to be based, in some part, on what competitors are doing.

The Competitive Situation

What should the planner look for in considering competitors? Perhaps the most important consideration is market-share position. What rank does the brand in question have in the market? If a brand has the greatest share, then it deserves special study. Does it have the best product in its class? Is its distribution outstanding, its creative efforts in advertising superior, or its selection and use of media better than others? The final answer may grow out of a combination of these and other considerations. In any case, brands with smaller shares cannot ignore the leader if they intend to make inroads against competitors' shares. If the leaders tend to limit their media choices to spot and network television, then brands below the leaders must take this fact into consideration in planning their media strategies. One of the most important questions relating to competitors' media selections may have to be: "Should I fight it out with competitors in the media they use, or shall I seek media they don't use?"

The answer to this question depends on how much money a brand has budgeted to fight competitors. If a brand has a much smaller budget than its competitors, then its advertising may be lost among that of competitors who can buy much more advertising. But even if a brand has about the same budget as that of a leading competitor, another strategy consideration arises. It is possible that the brand in question is perceptively superior to the competitor's brand. Is it possible to demonstrate its superiority in advertisements? If so, the brand may not require as much money as its competitor because its superior qualities are so obvious.

Advertisements may not have to work so hard to communicate essential information. Perhaps there may even be word-of-mouth advertising.

Still another consideration is whether a brand's advertising targets are the same as its competitors'. If the targets are different, then strategy can be worked out using media different from that of competitors. If, however, a brand's targets are identical to competitors', then the brand's planner may have to use the same or similar media.

Finally, in considering competitors' strategies, it may be necessary to determine whether competitors are using their media effectively. If they are not, then even though a brand may have a smaller budget, it may succeed in the same media. For example, if a brand reaches the correct targets, but with not enough frequency to be optimally effective, another brand may use the same media more effectively if it can match or surpass its competitor's frequency.

The Effect of Media Budgets

The size of the budget, as mentioned earlier, gives the planner a frame of reference regarding what can be done to attain a media objective. Media planners know what it costs to buy a low- or high-impact level in 25 or 150 markets for spot television, or for a lineup of 200 stations on network television. They know about how much it takes to buy a full-page ad and 100 GRPs in the top 60 markets, or 100 GRPs in outdoor billboards in 50 markets. The number of dollars available affects the choice of media and the depth of impact needed.

What strategies are available when there are insufficient funds to attain media objectives? There are at least four different courses of action, and possibly more.

1. Marketing objectives may have to be changed toward more modest and realizable goals for the amount of money allotted.
2. A series of priorities may have to be set up in which the greater part of the budget will have to be allocated to the most pressing priorities. Minor priorities will have to be ignored until more money is available.
3. It may be possible to obtain large discounts from media, which will spread a small amount of money farther. This might be done by limiting advertising to one medium. In addition, the flighting strategy could be used to spread a small amount of money over a longer period of time.
4. Finally, the client may be advised not to advertise until there is enough money. The media planner is often responsible for giving this advice. If the agency proceeds to buy media with a budget that is known to be inadequate, the client may later blame the agency for poor advertising performance.

Attempting to attain objectives with an inadequate budget is like fighting a war without enough troops, ammunition, or troop carriers. A high degree of realism is necessary to make a plan work.

Flexibility Needs

One factor that can affect the strategies and objectives of a media plan is the need for flexibility. It is often necessary to change media at the last minute because the marketing situation has changed or because new opportunities in different media become available. But this isn't possible unless care has been taken to select media that are flexible. Generally, local media such as newspapers, spot radio, and spot television are flexible because they can be purchased in many different ways and at different times. For example, spot television may be purchased nationally, regionally, or locally. Furthermore, it can be purchased in very small amounts (such as two or three spots a week), or it may be possible to buy the large volumes of time needed for a saturation campaign within a given market. Then too, spot television often can be cancelled at short notice, and sometimes reinstated (if there are time slots available).

Flexibility is needed most when the marketing situation is liable to change, requiring subsequent changes in media selection or use. Media selection for some large-budgeted products such as automobiles, however, may achieve flexibility in different ways. Instead of limiting themselves to local media, such advertisers can buy network television time or national magazine space in what is called an *umbrella pattern*: Through these two classes of media they reach a national audience, but they achieve flexibility through additional purchases of local media where they can make changes easily and relatively inexpensively. In most cases, however, advertisers cannot afford to buy both national and spot media and must limit themselves to those that are the most flexible.

Authority and Prestige

Authority and prestige are qualitative aspects of media that are difficult to measure but which, experts feel, have some effect on audiences' awareness or perception of advertising. Some media such as *The New Yorker* or *Fortune* are felt to have considerable amounts of both qualities, but because research in this area is so meager it isn't known precisely just how these, or other media, affect audience reaction to advertisements. That research has not been able satisfactorily to measure prestige, however, does not mean prestige is not a factor. While authority and prestige may not be the most important factors in media planning, they often become quite significant in helping the planner make a decision about two or more media vehicles that are very much alike.

Seasonal Impact on Media Effectiveness

In considering whether to use a medium, one might also look at how it performs during all seasons of the year. Summer months, for example, are a problem when planners use television because so many people are out-of-doors or on vacation and may miss advertising. Winter months, on the other hand, may not be as effective for outdoor advertising. Newspaper and magazine reading, too, may vary to some extent during the summer months. Furthermore, there may be differences in the year-round effectiveness of local media. In some parts of the country, where there are extreme hot or cold temperatures, reading habits as well as viewing or listening habits may affect local media effectiveness. So, in planning media, the degree to which media effectiveness fluctuates during key selling seasons becomes an important consideration.

Assembling Elements of a Plan

What information belongs in a media plan, and in how much detail? Where do various kinds of information belong? These questions can best be answered by using checklists that serve as the planner's reference. The checklists that follow will help one understand what belongs in a media plan and where it should appear. The first is a subject checklist that simply calls attention to the contents of a plan. The second is an operational checklist showing how to proceed in the actual planning process. Chapter 10 is devoted to the presentation of an actual media plan prepared by a professional in a large advertising agency. This plan is a concrete example showing how the contents appear and explaining what has been done and/or why. The explanations appear in the form of notations after each major section.

Before preparing a media plan, planners must have a broad perspective of what they are trying to accomplish. A plan is more than a list of media selected and a schedule sheet. It is really part of the solution to a marketing problem: that part that will be solved through the selection and use of media. It is more than a listing of actions to be taken, but also a proof that the planner has made the best of all possible decisions, given the constraints of a budget, a creative strategy, and a brand whose qualities have been perceived by consumers to such an extent that the brand now occupies a given position in the marketplace.

It is first necessary to make sure that all important information, whether numerical data or text, is presented so as to show how the planner intends to use media to solve the problem(s). The reader of a plan should not have to ask too many questions about what is recommended or why. Second, each piece of information must be presented within an organizational framework that represents a logical progression from the most important decisions to the least important. Third, the document must be organized in such a way that it is easy to read and understand. This may require the use of subheads in appropriate places, plus the careful heading of all tables, charts, graphics, or whatever else is presented. Sources and dates of research should be presented.

Some advertising agencies place most of the statistical details in an appendix, while others place data in a logical position next to text. This is probably a matter of individual preference. It is also a good idea to provide a summary to give the busy executive a quick overview of decisions. The details can follow.

While there is no one form for presenting media plans, there are similarities among all well-presented plans. The main goal is always that of achieving good communication, which will lead to good decision making.

CHECKLIST 9–1. Media Planning Subject Checklist

The following checklist shows the major considerations in planning media. It is a means of checking to see that everything of importance is included.

I. Marketing Objectives
   A. Restatement of the marketing objectives in media terms
   B. If plan is for a new product, differentiation between introductory and sustaining periods. Duration of each
   C. Relative need for reach, frequency, impact, continuity (including seasonal aspects)
   D. Broad indication of how media strategy and creative strategy support each other
      1. Are copy considerations necessary in media planning, such as need for sound, motion, demonstration, color?
      2. Will "word pictures" be enough?
      3. Is the story emotional or rational?
      4. Is the story complicated? Is there a need for space and time to tell the story? Will short messages be sufficient? Or, is some combination of short and long better?
   E. Brief indication of how merchandising and promotion strategy and media strategy support each other
   F. The consumer profile
      1. For the product class
      2. For the brand
   G. The profile of the brand's target audience
   H. Is the media strategy flexible, in terms of markets, timing, or ability to switch from medium to medium on short notice?

II. Media Summary
   A. Summary of proposed budgeting by media for the company's fiscal year
      1. By product
      2. By major company division
      3. By sales districts
   B. Where appropriate, differences with preceding year, with reasons for differences
   C. Sales objectives
   D. Media investment per unit of sales
      (For C and D, show for past year and for projected year. Sales projections should be reasonably conservative, so that there is a reasonable chance that they will be met and probably exceeded.)
   E. Reasons, in broad terms, for major media recommendations. How do major elements in the media plan meet the specified media objectives?
   F. Is it possible to test media program in each major medium or market area?

    G. Merchandising support that might be expected of media

    H. Does the media program have any marks of originality, inventiveness, ingenuity?

III. Stand-by Plan

    A. What should be done, if during the year:

        1. Sales expectations are not being met. How should plans be changed or reduced?

        2. Sales expectations are being exceeded. How should advantage be taken of this situation?

        3. A major competitor takes some serious anticipated action, such as introduction of a new and improved product, with certain predictable results.

IV. Media History

    A. Media history over at least the past five years, showing comparison with sales trends

        1. By product

        2. For competition

    B. Information on media tests previously conducted

        1. Nature of tests

        2. Products

        3. Places

        4. Dollars invested, actual and per thousand population. Indicate regular media used during that period

        5. Results

V. Commentary for Subject Brands

    A. For each medium logically a candidate for brand advertising:

        1. Advantages for subject product (document as necessary)

        2. Disadvantages (document)

    B. Indication as to how chosen media contribute to attainment of objectives, and where each falls short (document)

    C. How composite media mix meets brand objectives (document)

    D. For major rejected media, the reasons for rejection (document)

VI. Media Specifics

    A. Business publications

        1. Editorial

        2. Circulation

        3. Total market potential

        4. Advertiser acceptance

        5. Space cost

        6. Services available to advertisers

    B. Consumer magazines

        1. Audience buying potential

        2. Advertiser acceptance

        3. Space cost

        4. Services available to advertisers

        5. Editorial

        6. Circulation and audience

        7. Audience composition—characteristics

    C. Direct mail

        1. Source of names

        2. Set-up of list

        3. Filing method

        4. Maintaining accuracy

    D. Newspapers

        1. Market and economic factors

        2. Circulation

        3. Reader characteristics

        4. Editorial

        5. Advertiser acceptance

        6. Newspaper services available

E. Outdoor advertising
1. The outdoor plant
    a. Distribution and coverage, visibility of showing, traffic and circulation, rates and costs, etc.
    b. Type of panels: 24-sheet, junior panels, painted bulletins, rotary plan, lighting, embellishments
2. The market
    a. Size of market, economic factors, special market characteristics
F. Point-of-purchase
1. Marketing factors
2. Planning, including materials to be used
3. Merchandising and distribution
4. Technical considerations and finding the right producer
G. Radio
1. The market—area, size, economic factors, special market characteristics
2. The station—coverage, audience characteristics, programming and ratings, station identification, policies, facilities, time cost, advertiser acceptance, station services available
H. Television (network)
1. Day vs. night
2. Program ownership vs. participation
3. Children vs. teens vs. adults
4. Type of program: drama, comedy, documentary, etc.
5. Time period
    a. Sets in use
    b. Seasonal variation
    c. Lead-in and lead-out program
    d. Competitive programs
    e. Cost-per-thousand
    f. Length of commitment
6. Details (by season where appropriate)
    a. Period of sponsorship
    b. Name of program, if known
    c. Number of commercials per week
    d. Expected ratings (household, adult male, adult female, etc.)
    e. Expected cost-per-thousand
    f. Expected reach, frequency
    g. Expected net coverage of a given schedule over a four-week period
7. Market lists
    a. Markets covered and not covered
    b. If necessary, markets where coverage is expected to be weak, because of delayed broadcasts or other reasons
    c. Necessity of supplemental coverage
    d. Whether markets over a certain size are covered by originating market or from outside

I. Television (spot)
1. The market
    a. Market area and size
    b. Economic factors
    c. Special market characteristics
2. The station
    a. Coverage/audience characteristics
    b. Programming and ratings
    c. Station identification, policies, facilities
    d. Time cost
    e. Advertiser acceptance
    f. Station services available
J. Transit advertising

    1. The market—size, economic factors, special characteristics
    2. The medium—circulation and traffic, audience characteristics, the system, advertiser acceptance, operating procedures and policies, reproduction of car cards and posters
  K. General considerations in respect to media
    1. Investments by market in each medium
    2. Cost-per-thousand for estimated noters, or thousand exposures, or thousand households reached, or other measure appropriate to the medium
    3. Conversion of medium's audience into units of consumption of advertised product and medium's cost per unit of product
    4. Relationship of proposed schedule to audience objectives
    5. Use of local media—what coverage is also obtained from national media
    6. Competitive advertising—budgets and media used

CHECKLIST 9–2. Media Planning Operational Checklist

Some elements in the subject checklist often are not pertinent for a given media plan. The *operational* checklist shows what is most likely to be required for a typical media plan and in about what order items should appear.

  I. Marketing Objectives and Strategies that Relate to Media
These are usually summarized rather than being presented in detail. Presumably, they already have been explained in detail in another document, the marketing strategy plan.

  II. Copy Strategy Statements and How Media Will Support or Relate to Them
A copy strategy is not always a part of a media plan. If there is any special reason for including it, such as to clarify decisions of media selected, or media used in a certain way, then it belongs here.

  III. A Summary of the Entire Plan
This section allows an executive a quick overview of what actions are recommended so that the full scope of the plan is visible. Often the details occupy so many pages that it is difficult to get an overview of the plan easily.

  IV. Media Objectives
    A. A clear statment of each objective is necessary, using enough words to make them meaningful
    B. Statements should show precisely how media objectives relate to marketing objectives and/or strategies
    C. Objectives should cover the following topics as a minimum:
      1. Specification of target audiences (in demographics and psychographics if pertinent)
      2. Budget available and any restrictions on its use
      3. Reach and frequency needed
      4. Effective reach levels needed
      5. Continuity needed
      6. Pattern of monthly and yearly continuity
      7. Special geographic weighting needed
      8. Merchandisability of media if necessary
      9. Flexibility needed
      10. Degree to which media will have to support promotions
      11. Creative strategy implications
    D. A rationale for decisions must be included

  V. Media Strategy
    A. Each strategy must be stated clearly
    B. Each strategy should be related to one (or more) media objectives
    C. Why certain other obvious strategies were *not* used should be explained
    D. Strategies should include (as a minimum):

1. Media classes selected (e.g., network television, or magazines)
2. Strategy for allocating the budget to geographic areas (roll-out vs. national introduction; spot only or national plus spot heavy-up)
3. Allocation of budget to media classes (dollars and percentages of total)
4. Allocation of budget by months and/or quarters of year; introductory vs. sustaining period strategy
5. Reach and frequency levels desired by months and/or quarters of the year
6. Effective reach and frequency levels per typical month
7. Size of the primary and secondary target markets
8. Weighting of strategic targets
9. Geographical weighting requirements that must be used
10. Cost-per-thousand standards, if required
11. Explanations of why a strategy is different from previous ones
12. Specifications of the size of media units to be used (30- or 60-second commercials; full or fractional pages)
13. Criteria to be used for selecting or scheduling media (need for flighting)
14. Relationship of strategy to that of competitors, with special emphasis on certain key brands that must be dealt with specifically
15. A rationale for each strategy statement

VI. Media Plan Details (and Documentation)
   A. A statement of criteria for determining media values
   B. Proof that vehicles selected are the best of all alternatives (using media value criteria) and for the budget (data plus words)
   C. Data showing net reach and frequency for targets reached by a combination of all vehicles, including frequency distributions
   D. Data showing gross impressions for a combination of all vehicles, especially for target audiences
   E. Cost-per-thousand shown for all vehicles selected or considered
   F. Cost summary tables showing each vehicle, number of times used per month, cost-per-insertion, and total cost-per-month
   G. Yearly cost summary
   H. Yearly flow chart (or schedule) showing vehicles, weeks of insertions, reaches, frequencies, and costs per month for the year
   I. Any other data that will help buyers implement the plan

VII. Overview
   A. Is the plan well organized? Is it easy to find specific information desired?
   B. Are topics delineated with appropriate headings?
   C. Are all tables of data headed properly so as to explain precisely what the data are about?
   D. Is there a Table of Contents with page numbers?
   E. Is there a review of key marketing objectives and/or strategies?
   F. If data are voluminous, have some been relegated to a special documentary section?
   G. Are there any weaknesses in the logic or reasoning of the plan?

The Media Flow Chart (or Schedule)

Special consideration ought to be given to the flow chart (also called a schedule sheet) of a media plan. A *flow chart* is a graphic presentation of all major actions that comprise a media plan. It is presented in notation form (or a form of shorthand) enabling the planner to place a great deal of information in a small amount of space.

The most important purpose of a flow chart is to provide everyone involved—the planner, the media buyer, the account executive, the client—with a bird's-eye view of the entire plan of action. Elsewhere in the plan are myriads of details explaining what actions are to be taken and why, but the flow chart places all actions in a single, easy-to-see frame of reference showing the flow of media purchases throughout the year. Some planners refer to this flow as a *pattern* of media delivery. The pattern is clearly discernible and makes it relatively easy to compare one part with another.

It is important, then, to make this flow chart understandable and not to omit anything that is essential to this bird's-eye view. For example, it would overly complicate a flow chart to list the number of targets reached in raw numbers, but it is imperative to show the reach and frequency in percentages. It is not necessary to show the dollars spent in media each week of the year, but it is imperative to show how much will be spent by each month or quarter of the year. If quarterly figures are not important, then monthly figures should be shown.

Essentials of a Flow Chart

Although different advertising agencies may organize their flow charts differently, there are some basic elements that are essential to all:

1. The name of the brand and the year the plan covers should be at the top.
2. All months of the year should be aligned across the top of the page, usually placed horizontally on the page so that more space will be available. Some media planners prepare their flow charts on large sheets of paper and reduce them photographically to an 8½"x 11" size so that they can be assimilated easily in a bound document.
   a. The month that is shown first is usually the first of the fiscal, or financial, year. Some companies have fiscal years that begin with months other than January. At times, the first month listed may be the month in which the first media vehicles are to be bought. This is purely a matter of judgment.
   b. The months may be divided by quarters if the planning is done on a quarterly basis. If not, each of the months is listed next to each other across a page.
3. Each week of the year should be given a separate column under each month. Months with five weeks should contain five columns instead of four. It is debatable whether or not

each week should be numbered from 1 to 52, or numbered on the basis of the first day of each week. Some media plans do not show any week numbers.

4. The left side of the page should contain media information.
   a. Each medium class used (by daypart if pertinent).
   b. Length of commercial or size of page and color. (Example: 30-second commercial, or ½ page/four color)
   c. If spot television is used, each market group should be shown, and the number of markets in each group. (This number will refer to a market list that appears elsewhere in a plan.)
   d. If market groups receive different GRPs, this fact should be listed at the left or in a prominent place.
   e. A row labeled reach, and one underneath labeled frequency, should appear somewhere, often placed at the left side, bottom. If Gross Rating Points are important, then this information should appear below reach and frequency rows. If different geographic areas are to receive varying weights, then each area should be listed with a row underneath for reach, another for frequency, and another for Gross Rating Points (if important).
   f. At the bottom there usually is a row showing media expenditures by month and/or quarter of the year. At the extreme right side, these should be summed.
   g. At the very bottom, percentages of total media expenditures are usually shown by month and/or quarter with a 100 percent total at the extreme right.
5. Each week of advertising should be blocked-in. Some agencies eliminate all the column lines from their flow chart, so their flow charts would show the number of weeks of advertising as a rectangle. Inside the rectangle should be the number of GRPs to be used per average week. The length of the rectangle should cover the number of weeks of advertising required. Some planners place a small numeral above the rectangle to show how many weeks of advertising will occur. Such a numeral is not needed if the length of time covers the entire year.

The reader should study Figures 9–1, 9–2, and 9–3 for examples of different kinds of flow charts prepared for different kinds of media plans. No matter which format is used, it should contain all the essential details. Above all, it should be easy to read and understand without the use of excessive explanatory symbols or other notations.

FIGURE 9–1. A Sample Media Plan Flow Chart for Television

	January				February				March				April				May				June				July				August				September				October				November				December		
29	5	12	19	26	2	9	16	23	2	9	16	23	30	6	13	20	27	4	11	18	25	1	8	15	22	29	6	13	20	27	3	10	17	24	31	7	14	21	28	5	12	19	26	2	9	16	23	30	7	14	21

Network Television

Day

25 Women
18–49
GRPs/wk
24 Weeks

Cost: $1,323.6

Late Fringe

43 Women
18–49
GRPs/wk
24 Weeks

Cost: $4,281.3

TOTAL
COST: $5,604.8

FIGURE 9–2. A Sample Media Plan Flow Chart for Magazines

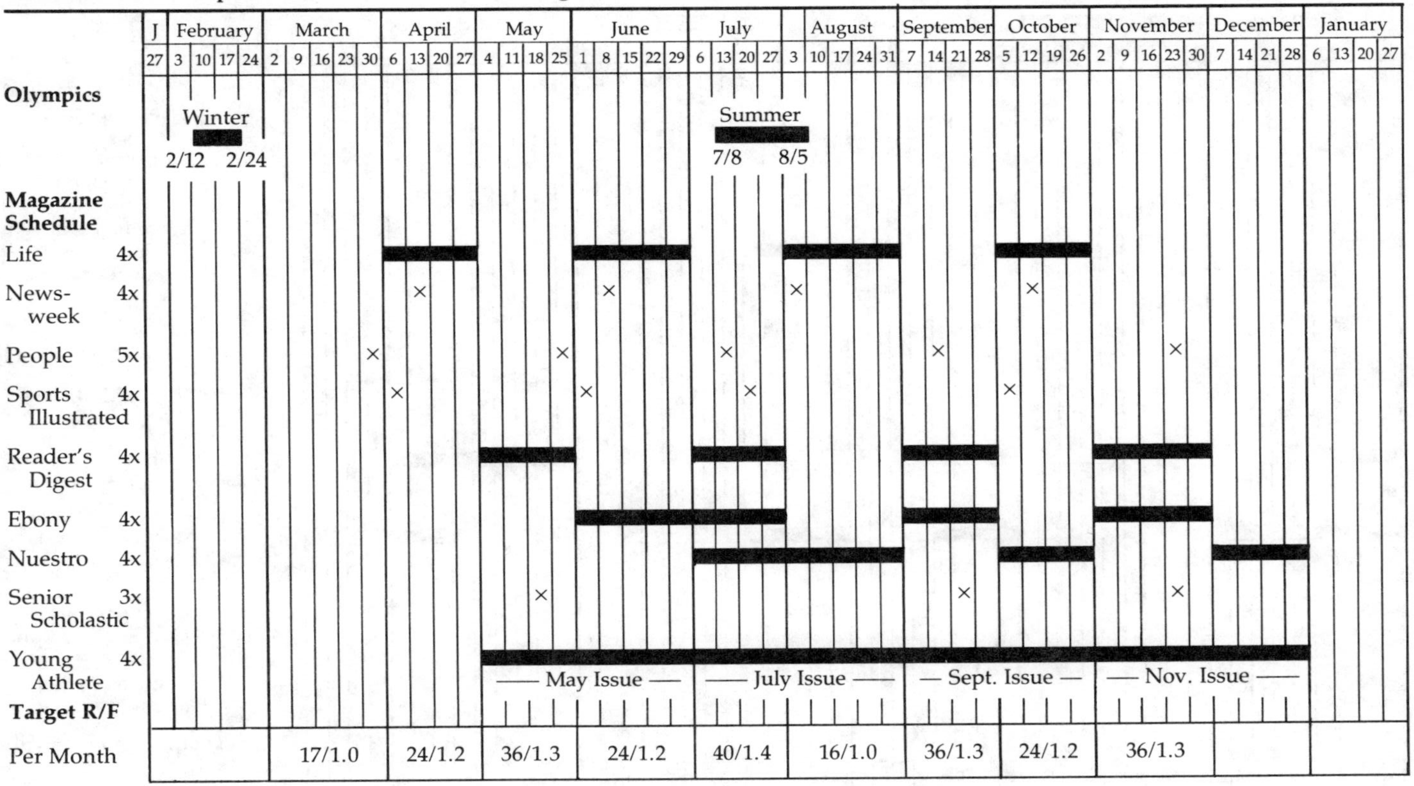

Total Year: 75/4.2

*Adults 18–49 with household income $15,000+

FIGURE 9–3. A Sample Media Plan Flow Chart for Specialized Publications

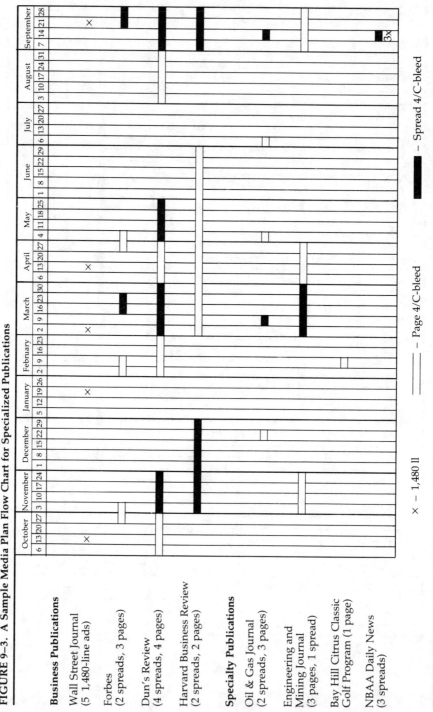

QUESTIONS FOR DISCUSSION

1. Briefly explain why it is so important to relate marketing objectives and strategies to media objectives.
2. What are the consequences of writing very short, general statements of objectives vs. detailed, specific objectives?
3. Briefly explain the difference between a media objective and a strategy.
4. It is widely believed that not all media objectives and strategies are of equal importance. How should a planner take these inequalities into consideration and note them in the plan?
5. What strategies might be used when there are insufficient funds available to meet media objectives?
6. Why do many media planners prepare alternative media plans to show a client, if their first plan is presumed to be the best of all alternatives?
7. In preparing a flow chart, which month should be listed first on the chart (usually placed to the extreme left)? Why?

SELECTED READINGS

Advertising Age, "Pulsing Schedules of Ads an Effective Technique," Oct. 20, 1969, p. 270.

Frankel, Lester R., "Where Does Effective Exposure End and Irritation Begin?" *Media/Scope*, November 1957, pp. 40–41.

Gomer, Frank J., "Problems in Media Planning and How to Solve Them," *Media/Scope*, October 1963, pp. 49–73.

Greene, Jerome, "Using Media Research to Help Build and Appraise the Media Plan," *Perspectives in Advertising Management*, Association of National Advertisers, Inc., April 1969, pp. 173–77.

Jones, Richard P., "Building and Appraising the Media Strategy," *Perspectives in Advertising Management*, Association of National Advertisers, Inc., April 1969, pp. 185–95.

Kanner, Bernard, "Building and Appraising the Media Strategy," *Media/Scope*, September 1965, pp. 157–65.

Krugman, Herbert, "What Makes Advertising Effective?" *Harvard Business Review*, March–April 1975, pp. 96–103.

Maneloveg, Herbert, "How Media Men Buy Media—Six Factors for a Good Plan," in "The New World of Advertising," *Advertising Age*, Nov. 21, 1973, p. 62.

McCann-Erickson, *A Point of View on Advertising Strategy, White Paper I*, October 1972.

Media Decisions, "Why Reach for Frequency?" June 1969, pp. 36–37.

Media Decisions, "The Name-Callers," April 1973, p. 66.

Ochs, Malcolm B., "The Fight for Awareness," *Media/Scope*, July 1966, pp. 58–61.

Papazian, Edward, "Bottom Up Planning," *Media Decisions*, August 1978, pp. 16–18.

Papazian, Edward, "Structuring Media Plans for Maximum Effect," *Media Decisions*, March 1974, pp. 12–14.

Papazian, Edward, "Creative Media —A Time and Place for Everything," *Media Decisions*, March 1973, p. 12.

Ray, Michael; Sawyer, A. G.; and Strong, E. C., "Frequency Effects Revisited," *Journal of Advertising Research*, February 1971, pp. 14–20.

Roth, Paul, *How to Plan Media*.

Surmanek, James, "Let Reps In On Media Planning," *Advertising Age*, Sept. 11, 1978, p. 78.

Vedder, Blair, "An Outline for Media Plans," *Media/Scope*, August 1961, pp. 69–71.

Vedder, Blair, "Smart Media Buying Begins with a Plan," *Media/Scope*, October 1960, pp. 49–56.

10
An Annotated Media Plan

This chapter is intended to help readers visualize a media plan as created by a professional planner in a large advertising agency. It is assumed by this time that the reader will know the concepts and terminology used in planning and therefore be able to easily follow and understand the plan. Because this plan was made for a brand product in a highly competitive market, a number of changes were made in it to keep certain proprietary information confidential: the brand is called X, the product category is not identified, and certain pieces of information have been eliminated, such as a creative strategy statement. This plan was implemented in the mid-1970s, a time when costs and cost efficiency data shown were significantly lower than they are now.

All other essentials are included and explained in annotated remarks immediately following each section. The plan has been divided into more sections than the original plan contained, but these parts should help the reader more easily understand the underlying thinking that went into the planning. In addition, each notation has been coded with a circled number which refers back to the same circled number in the plan.

① PART 1
Brand X Media Plan (Next Year) Summary

② **A**. TASK
    1. Maintain the current strength of Brand X franchise

③ **B**. AVAILABLE FUNDS

Total advertising budget	$4,100,000
Less production	380,000
Working media budget	$3,720,000

④ **C**. MEDIA PLAN
    1. Objectives

   a. Direct advertising toward current users
   b. Maintain current share
   c. Encourage ongoing use of the brand

⑤   2. Strategy
   a. Direct impressions toward all women proportionate to their
      Brand X volume contribution, with emphasis on the primary
      targets: women aged 35-plus living in $15,000-plus house-
      holds, in A counties.
   b. Allocate media dollars in proportion to current Brand X sales
      volume by market, while maintaining competitive levels in
      high-volume Brand X areas.
   c. Achieve at least a 75 reach with an average frequency of five
      among total women in key areas. Concomitantly, seek a reach
      of 50 among women exposed at least three times within any
      given four weeks of advertising.
   d. Distribute advertising pressure according to quarterly volume
      contribution.
   e. Maintain financial and geographic flexibility.
   f. Provide continuous support within the quarterly investment
      allocation once the reach/frequency goals are met.
   g. Employ media vehicles that are compatible with the copy
      requirements and overall brand image.

⑥   3. Plan

	Dollars	Percent
Day Network TV	$1,026,100	27.6
Late Network TV	1,048,600	28.2
Fringe Spot TV	1,645,300	44.2
TOTAL	$3,720,000	100.0

⑦ D. DELIVERY
   1. Demographics—Slightly underdeliver upper income category as
      a result of concentrating in television.
   2. Geographics—Overspend spot TV markets by 11 percent in order
      to maintain competitive posture in key franchise areas.
   3. National Effort—Network television represents 56 percent of
      total media budget.
   4. Reach/Frequency—Delivery achieves goal in key markets.
   5. Allocation Requirements—Generally follows the quarterly sales
      volume.

⑧ E. TASK ACCOMPLISHMENT
   1. The plan accomplishes the task of providing support to maintain
      current franchise of the brand.
   2. Minor deviations from demographic and geographic targets
      result from optimizing total plan delivery.

Notes on Part 1—Summary

(Circled numbers refer to same circled numbers in plan)

① This summary is a quick overview of the entire plan. In a typical media plan, the exact year would appear in place of the phrase "next year."

② This states one important marketing objective: to maintain the current strength of the Brand X franchise. The term *franchise* is not used here to mean a franchising business, such as McDonald's hamburgers. Rather, it means "the brand's usage or financial position in the marketplace."

③ The available funds statement breaks down the budget into media and production costs. Production costs can be estimated before media costs, if the creative strategy has been devised and the numbers of broadcast commercials and print ads have been spelled out. It should also be noted that the budget is one of the most significant constraints on media objectives and strategy and therefore must be discussed early in the planning process.

④ ⑤ Objectives and strategies have been reduced to simple declarative statements here. Later on, however, more will be said about each.

④ It is important to note the nature of objectives. User demographics have been spelled out earlier. Although it usually is a part of marketing objectives, market share here is listed as a media objective, which is acceptable. Likewise, the encouragement of ongoing use of the brand (item C1c) is related to creative objectives and therefore might appear in a different place in other media plans.

⑤ Strategies C2a to C2g are very specific and cover parts of the recommended media strategy.

⑤ **C2a.** Media targets are identified first. Two kinds of targets are to be reached: one target is broadly based and consists of all women. A second target consists of those demographic segments that have greater sales potential because they purchase more. They will be given special treatment.

⑤ **C2b.** While the targets in C2a were based on personal demographics, this category considers geographic demographics. The identification of both kinds of targets is usually necessary for media planning. Advertising impressions are to be delivered proportionately to sales potential in each area.

⑤ **C2c.** Reach and frequency requirements in key market areas are spelled out here. A 75 reach and a five average frequency are to be attained. Although the planner did not specify the time period for such reach and frequency, it is presumed to be for a four-week period. The planner did specify an effective reach goal in a four-week period of 50 with a frequency of three or more. It is important to remember that this reach is for women targets only.

⑤ **C2d.** This is an allocation strategy and explains that the budget is to be proportionately distributed according to the volume of sales made in each quarter of a year. If the first quarter of the year accounts for 27 percent of sales, it would receive about 27 percent of the advertising budget.

⑤ **C2e.** The need for flexibility influences the strategy. Although reasons for wanting it are not given, presumably flexibility is needed to make quick media changes if sales opportunities or problems develop. Competitors' activities often cause a company to make changes in media plans after the plan has been devised. When the plan is flexible, it can be changed easily.

⑤ **C2g.** Some media vehicles may not be suitable for a given copy strategy, even though they have a large number of targets in their audience. The brand image must be suitable to the media selected.

⑥ This is an expenditure analysis in both raw dollars and percentages. Media plans must show expenditures in both forms to enable easy analysis.

⑦ **D1.** Delivery analysis explains how well the plan's statistical data prove that the plan reaches the objectives set out for it. For example, D1 explains that the plan will slightly underdeliver upper-income targets. Slight underdelivery is not considered to be an error.

⑦ **D2.** It also points out that the budget will be overspent by 11 percent in spot TV markets and why.

⑦ **D3.** Network television accounts for 56 percent of the media budget.

⑦ **D4. D5.** Reach and frequency are attained as planned, and expenditures follow sales volume by quarters, also as planned.

⑧ This is an evaluation statement based on judgment. It explains that the plan accomplishes the tasks set for it and why there are minor deviations. It is important to note that the planner tries to anticipate questions and answer them before they can be asked.

PART 2
Marketing and Copy Background

⑨ **A.** OVERVIEW

For the preceding year, Brand X had a severe business decline. Brand performance showed loss of momentum and was characterized by market share erosion, volume misses, and weakened distribution.

⑩ **B.** OBJECTIVE

Stabilize the franchise in key marketing areas.

National share and volume objectives:

Share: 6.0
Volume: 3,606

⑪ **C**. MARKETING STRATEGY
  1. Allocate marketing funds according to the brand's consumption.
  2. Continue to place heavy emphasis on promotion, especially consumer.
  3. Implement a program of case rates designed to put Brand X back in the feature cycle.

⑫ **D**. COPY STRATEGY
  (Omitted for reasons of confidentiality)

Notes on Part 2—Marketing and Copy Background

⑨ This is a brief overview of the marketing situation of Brand X for the past three years. Its market share was declining, its sales volume was not reaching goals set for it, and the number of stores distributing the product was declining.

⑩ This is a marketing objective in terms of market share and sales volume. The number 3,606 refers to millions of units sold.

⑪ Marketing strategies are stated here. Strategies Cl and C2 are obvious. Marketing strategy C3 is to build distribution and is to be accomplished by giving retailers a higher mark-up on cases purchased as an incentive for stocking the brand.

⑫ The copy strategy has been omitted here because it would have revealed the name of the brand. But the categories in the copy strategy may be stated. They were: copy objective, definition of prime prospects, competitive stance, key benefits, support, copy tone, and manner of presentation.

PART 3
Marketing Objective/Rationale

⑬ Objective: Direct advertising toward current users to capitalize on current strengths.
Rationale: The goal is to maintain share and encourage ongoing use of the brand.

  Next year is expected to be a year of intense competitive pressure when Brand A (Brand X's main competitor) dominates the product category with its key selling features and Brand B dominates consumer promotion activity.

  At this time, no product improvements for Brand X are planned for next year.

Notes on Part 3—Marketing Objective/Rationale

⑬ The main objective is to retain present users. Ordinarily, such an objective is listed as a creative responsibility or perhaps a marketing responsibility. Essentially, all that media can do to keep present customers is to deliver the message to the correct targets with a certain amount of repetition. However, because media do at least play some role in helping attain this objective, it may be considered appropriate here.

Another media objective is to capitalize on current strengths. The above comment applies here as well. Media cannot capitalize on current strengths, but copy can.

The reader, therefore, has to recognize that the planner from this particular advertising agency is not following the recommendations of writing objectives as presented in this text. His objectives are communication-oriented, and as such they are copy objectives rather than media objectives.

⑭ PART 4
Media Strategy/Rationale

⑮ Part 4A—Prospect Definition

Direct impressions toward all women proportionate to their Brand X volume contribution, with emphasis on the primary Brand X targets.

Primary targets are women with the following characteristics:
1. Age 35-plus
2. In $15,000-plus households
3. Living in A Counties

Demographic details are provided in Table 10–1.

Notes on Part 4—Media Strategy/Rationale

⑭ This part of the plan consists of strategy details and rationale, much of it fairly obvious statistical data.

Notes on Part 4A—Prospect Definition.

⑮ This definition first apeared in the summary ⑤ but is spelled out in greater detail here. There are two bases for selecting media targets (prospects): (1) the volume of Brand X that was purchased (as shown in percentages in ⑲), and (2) the index numbers that relate volume-usage to population distribution by demographics (as shown in ⑳).

⑯ The source of statistical data is at the bottom of Table 10–1.

TABLE 10–1. ⑰ **Demographic Targets**

		⑱ U.S. Women (%)	⑲ Brand X Volume (%)	⑳ Index
Total Women		100.0	100.0	100
Age: Total		100.0	100.0	100
	18–24	18.0	13.9	77
	25–34	20.4	17.9	88
	35–49	23.0	21.3	93
	50-plus	38.6	46.9	122
Non-Working		56.6	60.4	107
	18–24	8.4	6.0	71
	25–34	10.4	9.7	93
	35–49	11.1	11.0	99
	50-plus	26.7	33.7	126
Working		43.4	39.6	91
	18–24	9.6	7.9	82
	25–34	10.0	8.2	82
	35–49	11.9	10.3	87
	50-plus	11.9	13.2	111
Household Income	Under $8,000	38.1	28.6	75
	$8,000–$14,999	34.5	33.0	96
	$15,000-plus	27.4	38.4	140
Household Size	1–2	39.9	38.0	95
	3–4	35.8	37.7	105
	5-plus	24.3	24.3	100
County Size	A	40.9	51.0	125
	B	26.2	24.1	92
	C	19.4	17.3	89
	D	13.5	7.6	56

⑯ Source: MRCA Demographic Analysis

⑰ ⑱ ⑲ ⑳ A study of demographic usage and index numbers shows some interesting data. The largest index of users is for women, aged 50-plus, with income of $15,000-plus, who live in A counties. Why, then, did the planner select women aged 35-plus instead of only those aged 50-plus? The reason is that the target market would have been too small (only 38.6 percent of U. S. women are age 50 or over). By increasing the primary target segment to all women over 35, the population base has now been increased to 61.6 percent (23.0 + 38.6 = 61.6 percent) and brand volume to 68.2 percent. Why also were *all* women considered a target? It is probable that the client wanted a very broad target rather than a narrow one, and all Brand X users are to be reached, even though there are proportionately fewer Brand X users in the younger demographic segments.

㉑ Part 4B—Media Allocation

Allocate media dollars in accordance with the current Brand X sales volume of each market.

The media budgets of the individual markets will be prorated to the estimated volume contribution of each area. However, in the interest of strengthening the Brand X franchise in key markets and also recognizing the competitive spending environment, additional weight will be placed in the following areas. To the degree affordable, the following minimum spending versus Competitor A will be sought:

Eastern Region	85%
Detroit District	85%
Chicago District	65%
Los Angeles District	65%

Table 10–2 shows in detail the geographic targets based on Brand X volume.

TABLE 10–2. ㉒ Geographic Targets

	㉓ U.S. Women (%)	㉔ Brand X Volume (%)	㉕ Brand X Development Index (BDI)
Eastern Region			
Boston	5.28	6.60	125
New York	9.42	13.04	138
Philadelphia	7.75	13.34	172
Syracuse	3.38	5.91	175
Youngstown	4.78	6.55	137
Total Eastern	30.61	45.44	148
Southern Region			
Charlotte	5.55	3.83	69
Atlanta	4.03	3.24	80
Jacksonville	3.89	3.08	79
Detroit	4.76	8.52	179
Cincinnati	5.44	4.42	81
Total Southern	23.67	23.09	98
Central Region			
Chicago	6.44	5.35	83
St. Louis	3.57	2.91	82
Memphis	4.65	2.89	62
Kansas City	3.92	2.46	63
Dallas	6.46	3.60	56
Total Central	25.04	17.21	69
Western Region			
Minneapolis	4.15	2.01	48
Denver	2.40	1.30	54
Portland	2.77	1.80	65
San Francisco	4.01	2.67	67
Los Angeles	7.35	6.48	88
Total Western	20.68	14.26	69
Total U.S.	100.00	100.00	100

Source: A. C. Nielsen Company

Notes on Part 4B—Media Allocation

㉑ This part of the media plan deals with strategies for weighting advertising by geographical area. The main strategy is to allocate the media budget proportionately to the sales volume contributed by each of four sales regions: eastern, central, southern, and western.

However, another part of the strategy is to add extra weight in those geographical markets that have done best in sales. A study of ㉕ shows that all markets in the Eastern Region have indices over 100 and therefore are among the best in the country. Detroit also has an index over 100. Chicago and Los Angeles do not have exceptionally high index numbers but do have large volumes of sales as shown in ㉔. The planner, therefore, wants to add extra weight in these key markets. The goal is to add 85 percent more dollars than Competitor A in the Eastern Region and Detroit and 65 percent more in Chicago and Los Angeles. Although the planner does not show competitors' media expenditures, it is assumed that estimates are available. Also note that the extra spending depends on "the degree affordable." This means that the extra money can be spent if it is available after other priorities have been met.

㉒ ㉓ ㉔ ㉕ These figures show sales volume and Brand Development Indices. Such data provide the basis for the decisions in ㉑.

Part 4C—Communication Goals

㉖ **A**. Total Reach/Average Frequency
Provide at least 75 reach with an average frequency of 5 among total women in the key areas.

B. Effective Reach
Concomitantly, seek a four-week reach goal of 50 among women who have been exposed at least three times.

	Four-Week Reach/Frequency Goals
Total Reach/Average Frequency	75/5.0
Effective Reach	50/3+

㉗ **C**. Distribute Advertising Pressure According to Quarterly Volume Contribution.

Quarter	Volume (%)
April–June	24
July–September	23
October–December	26
January–March	27
TOTAL	100

㉘ **D**. Maintain Flexibility

It is recommended that all media activity be scheduled to run at the same time and that a substantial portion of the budget be placed in flexible media so the Brand can quickly react to:

1. Competitive activity
2. Key promotional events

㉙ **E**. Continuous Support Within the Quarterly Investment Allocation Will Be Sought Once the Reach/Frequency Goals Are Achieved.

Continuous advertising is desirable for the following reasons: (a) there is sufficient evidence of advertising recall erosion among consumers during non-advertising periods; (b) the daily traffic in stores includes Brand X purchases; (c) pressure against competition should be maintained. Therefore, as soon as reach/frequency goals are achieved, advertising periods will be extended within the boundaries of the quarterly investment allocation. A total of 36 weeks of advertising has been set as the minimum.

㉚ **F**. Employ Media Vehicles That Are Compatible with the Copy Requirements and Overall Brand Image.

A balance of highly efficient and effective media will be sought to ensure the most desirable combination of copy and media.

Notes on Part 4C—Communication Goals

㉖ Communication goals are listed in A as reach/frequency and effective reach.

The use of the term "communication goals" tells the reader how the planner perceives reach and frequency. Both serve as controllers of message distribution: reach controls dispersion, while frequency controls the degree of repetition.

The reader should note that a reach of 75 and a frequency of 5 is for total women, in certain parts of the country only. It is for women in the key marketing areas mentioned in Part 4B—the Media Allocation Section. The levels of 75 and 5 have been arrived at on the basis of experience and judgment.

The *effective* reach and frequency is different: 50 and 3. These levels come from an analysis of a frequency distribution (see ㊲). The reader should note that an effective frequency of three is based on a judgment about the specific needs of Brand X. So the reach percentages at a three frequency were determined (from the frequency distribution) to be 50.

㉗ Quarterly distribution of sales volume is shown. Media planners use sales volume data by month or by quarter of the year in making budget allocation decisions. Most planners use both.

㉘ The need for flexibility is explained here. Flexible media are usually local media such as spot television, spot radio, newspapers—media which can be purchased or cancelled quickly.

㉙ This part of the strategy discusses the use of continuity in relation to reach and frequency *per quarter*. The planner sets reach and frequency as a higher priority than continuity. But once the reach and frequency levels have been reached, good continuity should be attained within a 36-week period. The flow chart located at ㊱ shows a flighting pattern of continuity in which there are five time periods in which a hiatus occurs, not counting the weeks before advertising starts and after it ends. These are brief, two-week hiatuses. So the pattern of continuity is fairly extensive within the 36-week period, from May to the middle of March the following year.

㉚ The requirement for the kinds of vehicles to be selected in the plan is clear: Use only those that best convey the copy and the brand image.

㉛ PART 5
Description of Media Plan

㉜ The next fiscal year, the Brand X media plan will use television as the sole medium for the following reasons:

1. The intrusive nature of the medium makes it the most effective vehicle for communicating the Brand X message.
2. It is highly efficient in reaching the target audience.
3. On judgment, at the current budget level, concentrating efforts on the primary medium should maximize the effectiveness of communication.

㉝ Daytime network television will provide the base upon which other national and local media efforts will be structured. This medium is the most efficient vehicle for reaching a broad national base of adult women.

㉞ Late night network television will be used to extend reach nationally and increase the delivery of women in the higher income category ($15,000-plus).

㉟ Fringe spot television will be implemented to align media to targets and, tactically, to furnish additional support for Brand X's markets against competitive pressures.

Both network and spot television will be scheduled to run at the same time in order to maximize advertising pressure.

Notes on Part 5—Description of Media Plan

㉛ ㉜ ㉝ ㉞ ㉟ The description of the media plan consists of statements about which classes of media and kinds of vehicles should be selected and the rationale for selecting each. Essentially, television—network and spot—is recommended with network being restricted to daytime and late night (fringe time).

PART 6
Recommended Plan

Part 6A—Flow Chart

The major recommendations of the media plan are summarized in a yearlong flow chart, as shown in Figure 10–1.

Notes on Part 6A—Flow Chart

⊛ Note carefully how this flow chart has been arranged. It is the source of a great deal of important information. These are its key components:

1. The year has been divided into 52 weekly segments, which in turn have been divided into quarters, with the first fiscal quarter (April–June) coming first. This first fiscal quarter could start in January or any other month, depending upon the client's fiscal year.

2. The vehicles to be used are shown at the left, followed by the length of commericials. These are listed as :30, meaning 30-second commercials. The third listing of vehicles in the left hand column is a combination of early and late fringe television. Immediately underneath are specific delivery goals of 45.8% of all U. S. women and 62.2% of target women (aged 35-plus). These are not reach goals. They are gross impression goals.

3. Next on the left, geographical targets have been divided into key markets and the remainder of the U. S. Then key target markets are indicated: total women and women with incomes of $15,000-plus a year.

4. The dollar expenditure per quarter is listed at the bottom for each category of vehicles used, and at the very bottom a percentage of the total is shown.

5. Advertising is shown by number of consecutive weeks followed by the number of Women Gross Rating Points (WGRP). The number of weeks during each flight is shown. For example, Day network (:30's) starts in the last week of April and continues for nine weeks in the June quarter plus one week in the September quarter. Then there are two more four-week schedules in the September quarter, and so on. The number of weeks per month is shown on the top of each rectangle as follows: 9, 1, 4, 4, 5, 4, 5, 4.

6. In the category of reach and frequency levels, note that the designation for total women in the June quarter is shown as

FIGURE 10–1. ㊱ Recommended Plan—Flow Chart

Television	June Quarter			September Quarter			December Quarter			March Quarter			Total Year
	Apr.	May	June	July	Aug.	Sept.	Oct.	Nov.	Dec.	Jan.	Feb.	Mar.	
		9			4		5		4	5		4	
Day Network :30		35 WGRP/Wk.			35 W		35 WGRP/Wk.		35 W	35 W		35 W	
Late Network :30		14 WGRP/Wk.			14 W	14 W	25 W		25 W	25 W		25 W	
Combination Fringe :30 45.8% U.S. Women 62.2% Target		54 WGRP/Wk.			54 W	54 W	65 W		65 W	65 W		65 W	
Reach/Frequency Spot Area													
Total Women		81/5.1			81/5.1			84/5.9			85/5.8		
3+		53			53			59			60		
$15M+		77/4.5			75/4.3			80/5.3			80/5.2		
3+		47			44			53			52		
Remainder U.S.													
Total Women		57/3.4			57/3.5			61/3.8			63/3.7		
3+		27			27			32			33		
$15M+		51/2.9			51/2.8			56/3.5			56/3.4		
3+		21			21			27			27		
Day Network		$257.2			$231.1			$ 284.9			$252.9		$1,026.
Late Network		191.6			176.4			392.2			288.4		1,048.
Comb. Fringe		373.3			373.3			449.3			449.4		1,645.
Total		$822.1			$780.8			$1,126.4			$990.7		$3,720.
Percent		22.1%			21.0%			30.3%			26.6%		100.0%

81/5.1 (81 reach and 5.1 frequency for total women). Reach of women with $15,000-plus income is shown in the same manner (77/4.5). But the designation for 3+, referring to effective reach, comes from frequency distributions where the effective reach is 53 for total women for the average four weeks in the first quarter for spot area and 27 for the remainder of the U. S. See next section.

Part 6B—Frequency Distribution Analysis

Going beyond the summary flow chart, the media planner has also provided a frequency distribution analysis (see Tables 10–3 and 10–4) that breaks down the reach and frequency, and total exposures, among all women in the selected spot TV markets and secondarily in the remainder of the United States.

Notes on Part 6B—Frequency Distribution Analysis

㊲ ㊳ These are frequency distributions for determining effective reach. Since effective frequency is felt to be three or more impressions, the corresponding reaches are shown by quarter for the spot area ㊲ and the remainder of the U. S. ㊳. The data come from computer analysis of television programs and time periods that were selected.

Note also that the weekly Women Gross Rating Points are shown at the bottom. This comes from the planner's desired GRP levels as shown in the bars on the flow chart.

㊴ PART 7
Gross Impression Analysis

Gross impression analysis, as detailed in Table 10–5, shows the duplicated weight of advertising to each target audience member.

Notes on Part 7—Gross Impression Analysis

㊴While the frequency distribution analysis shown in Part 6B gives the client an idea about how many different target members were reached an average number of times, gross impression analysis enables everyone to see whether or not advertising is distributed to these various targets in the correct proportions. Some planners may be inclined to call such data strategic impression analysis, implying that the distribution of impressions is not haphazard, but rather part of the strategy.

㊵ ㊶ ㊷ ㊸ The numbers shown in these columns are the duplicated impressions delivered by the various media. They are calculated by multiplying the average ratings for the vehicles by the audience base

TABLE 10–3. ㊲ Total Women Frequency Distribution Analysis–Spot Area

	June Qtr. May	Sept. Qtr. Sept.	Dec. Qtr. Oct.	Mar. Qtr. Jan.
Reach/Frequency	81.1/5.1	81.0/5.1	84.3/5.9	84.7/5.8
No. of Exposures				
1+	81.1	81.0	84.3	84.7
2+	65.8	65.7	70.8	71.1
3+	53.2	53.2	59.2	59.5
4+	43.0	42.9	49.5	49.5
5+	34.6	34.6	41.2	41.1
6+	27.8	27.8	34.2	34.0
7+	22.3	22.3	28.4	28.0
8+	17.8	17.8	23.5	23.0
9+	14.1	14.2	18.8	18.0
10+	11.2	11.2	15.9	15.4
11+	8.9	8.9	13.1	12.6
12+	7.0	7.0	10.7	10.2
Weekly Women Gross Rating Points				
Day Network	35	35	35	35
Late Network	14	14	25	25
Spot TV	54	54	65	65
Total	103	103	125	125

TABLE 10–4. ㊳ Total Women Frequency Distribution Analysis–Remainder U.S.

	June Qtr. May	Sept. Qtr. Sept.	Dec. Qtr. Oct.	Mar. Qtr. Jan.
Reach/Frequency	56.8/3.4	56.5/3.5	61.4/3.8	62.6/3.7
No. of Exposures				
1+	56.8	56.5	61.4	62.6
2+	38.5	38.5	43.5	44.4
3+	27.3	27.4	32.0	32.5
4+	19.7	19.8	23.9	24.2
5+	14.3	14.5	18.0	18.1
6+	11.5	10.7	13.6	13.5
7+	7.6	7.8	10.3	10.2
8+	5.5	5.7	7.8	7.6
9+	4.0	4.2	5.9	5.7
10+	2.9	3.1	4.4	4.2
11+	2.1	2.2	3.3	3.1
12+	1.5	1.6	2.5	2.3
Weekly Women Rating Points				
Day Network	35	35	35	35
Late Network	14	14	25	25
Total	49	49	60	60

times the number of commercials telecast during the plan, or simply by multiplying the annual GRP's by the audience universe.

㊹ This column indicates the strategic impression proportions. For ex-

TABLE 10–5. Gross Impression Breakdown (thousands)

	㊵ Day Network	㊶ Late Network	㊷ Fringe Spot	㊸ Plan Total	㊹ % of Plan	㊺ % of Target	㊻ Index
Total Women	929,464	531,122	722,917	2,183,503	100.0	100.0	—
Age							
18–24	156,150	86,573	108,438	351,161	16.0	13.9	115
25–34	177,528	104,631	137,354	419,513	19.2	17.9	107
35–49	198,905	142,872	170,608	512,385	23.5	21.3	110
50+	396,881	197,046	306,517	900,444	41.3	46.9	88
Household Income							
Under $8,000	448,002	195,984	261,696	905,682	41.5	28.6	145
$8,000–14,999	310,441	198,108	234,225	742,774	34.0	33.0	103
$15,000+	171,021	137,029	226,996	535,046	24.5	38.4	64
Household Size							
1–2	370,856	215,104	329,650	915,610	41.9	38.0	110
3–4	340,184	182,175	166,271	688,630	31.5	37.7	84
5+	218,424	133,843	226,996	579,263	26.6	24.3	109
County Size							
A	308,582	246,972	471,342	1,026,896	47.0	51.0	92
B	276,980	151,370	153,981	582,331	26.7	24.1	111
C	187,752	72,764	78,798	339,314	15.5	17.3	90
D	156,150	60,016	18,796	234,962	10.8	7.6	142

ample, women aged 18 to 24 are to receive 16.0 percent of total impressions for the age category, and households with incomes under $8,000 a year are to receive 41.5 percent of all impressions for that income level.

㊺ This column, however, shows what proportion of impressions these demographic segments actually received.

㊻ This is simply an index relating targets to delivery. For example, in the category of women aged 18 to 24, the index is calculated as follows: 16.0 ÷ 13.9 × 100 = 115, or 15 points higher than the goal.

A careful investigation of the impression analysis reveals that the percent of delivery for the three key target groups (women aged 35+, in households with $15,000+ income, and in A counties) is slightly less than desired. As shown in Part 8 of the plan, the planner opted to purchase more impressions overall (through the purchase of daytime network) than to purchase fewer impressions but in the desired proportions. Also see Part 9 of the Media Plan.

㊼ PART 8
Media Rationale

㊽ **A.** Daytime Network Television :30s

Daytime network television at a level of 35 WGRPs per week will be scheduled for 36 weeks beginning in April of next year.

1. It delivers the Brand X target audience more efficiently than other television dayparts.

	Television Efficiency Comparison (:30)			
	Daytime Network	Prime Network	Late Night Network	Combined Fringe
Total Women	$1.20	$ 2.71	$2.26	$2.32
Women 35+	1.87	4.18	6.19	3.99
Women $15,000+	6.56	10.44	8.50	7.63

2. It furnishes efficient national coverage while supporting the Brand X high-development areas. At comparable rating levels, the cost of daytime network is 1 percent less than day spot and delivers 34 percent more audience than using spot in the top 60 U. S. markets.

	:30 Cost	U.S. Women (%)
Day Spot		
10 WGRPs Top 60 Markets	$8,592 (100)	73 (100)
Daytime Network		
10 WGRPs	8,501 (99)	98 (134)

3. Daytime television offers the greatest concentration of women viewers compared with the other television dayparts.

		Women Audience Composition					
	% U.S. Adults	Daytime (%)	Index	Prime Time (%)	Index	Late Night (%)	Index
Total Women	52	81	(156)	57	(110)	56	(108)

In addition on an equal dollar basis, daytime television furnishes the greatest absolute number of the Brand X target audience members.

	Women Delivery (Equal Dollars)					
	Daytime		Prime Time		Late Night	
	(Millions)	Index	(Millions)	Index	(Millions)	Index
Total Women	43.4	100	18.6	43	24.9	57
Women 35+	27.8	100	12.1	44	9.1	33
Women $15,000+	8.0	100	4.8	60	6.6	83
Women in A Counties	14.4	100	7.1	49	11.7	81

4. Thirty-five Women Gross Rating Points weekly are judged to be a desirable level of daytime network for Brand X. That level provides adequate women delivery nationally and also serves as a strong base upon which to build other national and local advertising efforts.

	Total Women
Reach	42
Average Frequency	3.2

⁴⁹ **B**. Late Night Network :30s

Late night network television will be implemented for 36 weeks at a level of 14 WGRPs per week for the first two quarters of the fiscal year. This will provide one announcement a week on each of the three networks. For the balance of the year, 25 WGRPs weekly will be used in recognition of the brand's quarterly volume contribution.

1. Late night network extends the reach nationally among the $15,000-plus household income group.

2. Late night television usage is not affected by seasonal variations as much as other dayparts. This gives the daypart excellent reach opportunities even during the summer months.

Index of Homes Using TV

	Average	Spring	Summer	Fall	Winter
Daytime	100	96	96	100	107
Prime Time	100	95	89	107	111
Early Evening	100	92	85	110	113
Late Evening	100	100	100	96	104

⁵⁰ **C**. Combined Fringe/Spot Television :30s

A combination of one-third early and two-thirds late fringe will be implemented at varying levels for 36 weeks in 32 Brand X markets.

1. This permits the opportunity to align the allocation of expenditures in accordance with the anticipated business opportunities in these markets.

2. The use of this medium further increases advertising pressure in key markets.

3. The flexibility of spot TV allows quick reaction to competitive activity.

4. Spot television improves the delivery of the Brand X target audience in A counties.

Total Audience Delivery

	Day Net	Prime Net	Late Night Net	Spot TV
A Counties	33.2%	38.1%	47.0%	65.3%
Index	100	115	142	197

Notes on Part 8—Media Rationale

ⓐ This is an explanation (or rationale) for the decisions about which media are recommended.

ⓐ   Note that 35 Women Gross Rating Points (WGRPs) were chosen for daytime network television. Why 35 and not more or less? The answer is based on the planner's judgment that with a given budget and with the given goals, 35 WGRPs a week for 36 weeks are adequate, as explained in A4 of the plan.

A1. This section shows relative cost-per-thousand for the three key targets for alternative television classes. The plan consists of daytime network and a combination of late night and fringe network times. But the cost-per-thousand figures also show primetime and late night television alone as alternatives. The latter two alternatives are shown to be fairly efficient in reaching some targets, but on balance, the selected alternatives are better.

A2. The planner is trying to show in this paragraph that another alternative to daytime network TV might be considered. Is this alternative better? The planner proves that daytime network TV, when compared to an alternative of daytime spot TV in 60 markets, would deliver more targets at a lower cost. The method employed was to take 10 WGRPs in each alternative, cost them out, and see which delivered the most women. The proof is that daytime network TV both costs less and delivers 34 percent more women (100 vs. 134 index numbers).

A3. The purpose of this section is to compare deliveries of primetime and late night television with daytime network television in reaching target groups. Index numbers for daytime are all 100, while alternatives are shown to be less capable of reaching targets (with index numbers less than 100).

ⓐ This explains why late night network television was selected.

ⓐ This explains why a combined early and late fringe pattern for spot television was recommended.

ⓐ PART 9
Comparison of Plan with Strategy

This section explains how the proposed media plan meets the designated strategy and objectives. Table 10–6 outlines this comparison in detail.

Notes on Part 9—Comparison of Plan with Strategy

ⓐ This part of the plan explains how the plan as outlined achieves the objectives set for it. The strategies are listed at the left and the proof

TABLE 10–6. Comparison of Plan with Strategy

Strategy	Plan
⑤② 1. Concentrate impression delivery among the primary Brand X demographic targets.	1. The recommended plan furnishes the best delivery among the target audience (women 35-plus, living in A counties) than alternative plans investigated.

	Total U.S. Women (%)	Target (%)	Index	Impressions (%)	Indices Women	Target
Age						
18–24	18.0	13.9	77	16.0	89	115
25–34	20.4	17.9	88	19.2	95	107
35–49	23.0	21.3	93	23.5	102	110
50-plus	38.6	46.9	122	41.3	107	88
Household Income						
Under $8,000	38.1	28.6	75	41.5	109	145
$8,000–$15,000	34.5	33.0	96	34.0	99	103
$15,000-plus	27.4	38.4	140	24.5	89	64
Household Size						
1–2	39.9	38.0	95	41.9	105	110
3–4	35.8	37.7	105	31.5	88	84
5-plus	24.3	24.3	100	26.6	109	109
County Size						
A	40.9	51.0	125	47.0	115	92
B	26.2	24.1	92	26.7	102	111
C	19.4	17.3	89	15.5	80	90
D	13.5	7.6	56	10.8	80	142

In terms of absolute impressions delivered, the recommended plan furnishes about 10 percent more impressions than Alternative III delivers (day net, prime net, fringe spot plan).

Women	Recommended (thousands)	Prime Net Alternate (thousands)	Index
35-plus	1,412.8	1,318.9	107
$15,000-plus	535.0	481.3	111
A Counties	1,026.9	932.4	110

2. Allocate dollars according to current Brand X sales volume while trying to stimulate development in high volume areas.

	U.S. Women (%)	Volume (%)	Index
Primary Markets	45.76	62.16	136
Remainder U.S.	54.24	37.84	70
Total U.S.	100.00	100.00	100

2. The recommended plan provides a 111 index of investment among the primary Brand X markets.

Investment (%)	Index (Vol. = 100)
69.06	111
30.94	82
100.00	100

3. Provide at least a 75 reach with an average frequency of 5 among total women in key areas. Concomitantly, seek a reach goal of 50 among women who have been exposed at least three times.

	R/F Goals
Total Reach/Frequency	75/5.0
Frequency Distribution	50/3+

3. The reach/frequency goals were achieved in the key areas that provide Brand X with 62 percent of its volume.

	Volume (%)	Low	High
Key Markets	62		
Reach/Frequency		81/5.1	85/5.8
Frequency Distribution		53/3+	52/3+
Remainder U.S.	38		
Reach/Frequency		57/3.4	63/3.7
Frequency Distribution		27/3+	33/3+

4. Distribute advertising pressure according to quarterly volume contribution.

Quarter	Contribution
June	24
September	23
December	26
March	27
	100

4. The plan follows the contribution pattern.

Quarter	Contribution
June	22
September	21
December	30
March	27
	100

5. Flexibility should be maintained.

5. The plan is sufficiently flexible to permit a reallocation of funds from one geographic area to another or from one quarter to another. About 45 percent of the budget is invested in spot TV.

6. Provide as many weeks of activity as affordable within the quarterly investment allocation once the reach/frequency goals are met.

6. The plan provides for 36 weeks of activity in flights ranging from four to ten weeks in length with short (2 weeks) durations of non-advertising periods after an initial hiatus of four weeks.

7. Employ media vehicles that are highly compatible with the copy requirements and overall brand image.

7. The plan uses television exclusively, capitalizing on the effectiveness of the medium in communicating the taste appeal of the product.

that the strategies were fulfilled is shown at the right in statistical form. For example, look at women aged 50-plus. The plan delivers 41.3 percent of its impressions to women 50 years and older. This is less than desired as shown by the index of 88 to the target (41.3 ÷ 46.9) but more than needed to concentrate among older women in the population (41.3 ÷ 38.6).

㊾ Note that at the end of the demographic analysis of delivery there is a statement about a plan titled Alternative III. Alternative III was one of three media plan alternatives devised for the client to provide other options in media strategy. The manner in which these options are compared is through gross impression analysis. In ㊾ the planner points out to the client that the recommended plan (Alternative I) delivered about 10 percent more gross impressions than Alternative III, which consisted of a strategy of day network television, prime network, and fringe spot. The big difference between Alternatives I and III was the use of late night network in I and prime network in III. Alternatives II and III were omitted from this text, since much of both plans consisted of similar kinds of data and strategies as Alternative I.

㊾ PART 10
Spot Television: Market Selection Methodology

As stated in the strategy sections, media dollars are to be allocated to current Brand X sales volume by market while maintaining competitive levels in high-volume areas. The allocation of delivery to each market is on a dollar basis, following the philosophy of spending in those areas where business is best.

The dollar allocation is based on the brand's total budget, not just the spot television budget. By using the total budget (national and local), the contribution made in each local TV market by network television is included in the allocation.

The market selection procedure employs a computer system that allocates media budgets to each TV market based on a target percentage. Adding all of the targets for all markets in the U. S. equals 100 percent. The target is obtained by weighting various factors in each market: sales, Nielsen county size consumption indices, and population. Once the targets are obtained, the computer system then calculates delivery of the network television portion of the media plan as well as the amount of money to be spent in spot television.

The following explains how markets were selected to receive spot TV and how much spot TV is to be used in each market.

    1. District sales are put into the computer. Example: Boston District sales = 6.6% of total U. S. sales.

2. Nielsen county size consumption indices are put into the computer (note that each Sales District has a different consumption index):

A Counties	128
B Counties	128
C Counties	150
D Counties	150

3. Each market's total women population by county size is weighted by (multiplied by) the brand's regional Nielsen county size consumption index:

Example: Boston TV Market

	Population (thousands)	Index	Weighted Population (thousands)
A Counties	1,195.4	128	1,530.1
B Counties	434.4	128	556.0
C Counties	215.9	150	323.9
D Counties	23.3	150	35.0
Total	1,869.0		2,445.0

4. The weighted women populations are totaled by District and each market is assigned a percentage of the District total. These percentages are then applied to the appropriate District sales volume contribution of each market:

Boston District

Market	Weighted Women Population (thousands)	% of Total	% of Sales Target*
Bangor	159.1	3.17	0.20
Boston	2,445.0	48.79	3.22
Hartford	896.9	17.89	1.18
Portland	401.1	8.00	0.53
Presque Isle	43.5	.87	0.06
Providence	770.0	15.38	1.02
Springfield	295.6	5.90	0.39
Total	5,012.1	100.00	6.60

*Obtained by multiplying the percentage of weighted women population in each market by the District sales percentage total of 6.6%.

5. In order to concentrate dollars in the most productive markets, a judgment was made to eliminate from spot television consideration any market that had less than 0.35 percent of U. S. sales. In the Boston District, two markets (Bangor and Presque Isle) were eliminated.

6. Network television expenditures are allocated to each TV market based on the local rating point delivery of the network programs that will be purchased. Total network dollars and specific day-parts have already been determined.

(Note: As discussed in Chapter 6, a national medium such as network television does not produce the same level of Gross Rating Points in each market. To allocate network TV dollars to each market, therefore, local GRP delivery of programs must be obtained. Local GRPs are then multiplied by a local market's population to yield impressions. Impressions are multiplied by the national cost-per-thousand of network TV, which results in the prorated local market dollar allocation of network TV. These calculations can be done by hand. For this media plan, the computer system automatically makes all these calculations.)

	Network Budget	% of Total TV Budget
Boston TV Market	$ 41,717	1.12
Total Network Budget	$2,074,700	
Total TV Budget	$3,720,000	100.0

Note that the network delivery in the Boston TV market comprises 1.12 percent of the total TV budget of $3,720,000. An additional 2.1 percent investment is required to align the expenditures with the target of 3.22 percent of the total budget.

7. Supplementary spot television weight is added as required to align total market expenditures with market targets.

Boston TV Market

	Dollars	% of Total TV Budget
Network TV	$ 41,717	1.12
Spot TV	78,067	2.10
Total	$119,784	3.22

8. Insofar as markets with less than 0.35 percent of sales contribution were eliminated from spot television consideration, the total spot TV budget of $1,645,300 was not completely allocated. The remaining spot TV budget is therefore re-allocated proportionately to each selected TV market based on the target percentage. This results in an increase of spot TV expenditures in each market.

Boston TV Market

	Dollars	% of Total TV Budget
Network TV	$ 41,717	1.12
Spot TV	83,343	2.24
Total	$125,060	3.36

9. Spot TV dollars are converted to Gross Rating Points per week by using individual market cost per rating point data. It had been predetermined to schedule a minimum of 36 weeks of activity with spot television:

Boston Market

Spot TV Budget	$83,343.00
Cost per GRP	61.67
Total Affordable GRPs	1,351
Weekly GRPs (for 36 weeks)	38

10. Adjustments in spending were made after the initial computer calculations to recognize both competitive pressures and minimum GRP levels:

a. It was decided, in light of competitive pressures and the brand's development, to further increase support in spot TV markets in the Chicago and Los Angeles districts.

b. Four markets—Hartford, Johnstown, San Diego, and Phoenix—were scheduled to receive less than a minimum amount of weekly GRPs (over 36 weeks). Rather than construct a separate spot TV market group for these four markets (with less than 36 weeks of activity), it was decided to increase spending in these areas until a full 36 weeks of activity was affordable.

Table 10–7 shows the spot TV market list for Brand X that shows GRP delivery for network TV and spot TV, as well as the dollar allocation to each TV market.

⑭ PART 11
Spot Television: Buying Strategy

Target audience	Primary—women aged 35-plus
	Secondary—total women
	Others—$15,000-plus household income
	A counties
Fringe Mix	$\frac{1}{3}$ early fringe
	$\frac{2}{3}$ late fringe
Buying Goal	Spend to budget
Spot TV Objectives	Spot television is being implemented to align impressions in accordance with the anticipated business opportunities in these markets. Spot TV is also being used to extend reach among the brand's target audience in key markets.

In general, high-rated shows with an above average concentration of women aged 35-plus are the most desirable. Implicit in high-rated shows are

TABLE 10–7. Spot TV Market List—Brand X

District/DMA	Pop. (%)	Tgt. (%)	BDI	Day Net.	Late Net.	Spot TV	Total
					36 Week Average WGRP/Week		
Boston							
Boston	2.61	3.22	123	32	10	38	80
Hartford/N.H.	.95	1.18	125	32	12	25	69
Portland	.39	.53	132	39	12	72	123
Providence	.83	1.02	123	35	20	41	96
Spgfld./Holyoke	.32	.39	123	39	8	38	85
Total Markets	5.10	6.34	124	33	12	39	84
Total District	5.28	6.60	125				
New York	9.42	13.04	138	32	20	69	121
Syracuse							
Alb./Sch./Troy	.60	1.10	182	32	14	75	121
Buffalo	.89	1.58	178	35	18	53	106
Burlington	.25	.37	149	46	10	59	115
Rochester	.44	.77	175	35	20	62	117
Syracuse	.60	1.10	183	35	10	67	112
Total Markets	2.78	4.92	177	35	15	63	113
Total District	3.38	5.91	175				
Philadelphia							
Baltimore	1.12	1.91	170	32	8	52	92
Harr./Lanc./York	.60	1.03	172	32	18	60	110
Philadelphia	3.47	5.91	171	39	18	71	128
Washington, D.C.	1.86	3.22	174	28	8	91	127
Wilkes-Barre	.62	1.09	176	46	22	85	153
Total Markets	7.67	13.16	172	35	14	73	122
Total District	7.75	13.34	172				
Youngstown							
Cleveland	2.01	2.82	140	35	14	63	112
Johnstown	.52	.41	79	49	18	25	92
Pittsburgh	1.67	2.30	138	42	22	49	113
Youngstown	.33	.46	139	35	20	44	99
Total Markets	4.53	5.99	132	39	18	52	109
Total District	4.78	6.55	137				
Detroit							
Detroit	2.33	4.35	187	35	14	78	127
Flint	.56	.95	171	42	14	102	158
Ft. Wayne	.29	.48	170	35	16	55	106
Grand Rapids	.64	1.11	174	39	10	60	109
Lansing	.26	.46	176	39	8	43	90
Toledo	.48	.83	173	46	28	64	138
Total Markets	4.56	8.18	179	38	15	73	126
Total District	4.76	8.52	179				
Chicago							
Chicago	4.07	3.48	86	32	32	51	115
South Bend	.37	.43	117	39	18	104	161
Milwaukee	.90	.69	77	32	26	31	89
Total Markets	5.34	4.60	86	32	30	51	113
Total District	6.44	5.35	83				
Los Angeles							
Los Angeles	4.98	4.81	97	25	18	47	90
San Diego	.67	.57	86	21	10	25	56
Phoenix	.71	.55	78	28	12	25	65
Total Markets	6.36	5.93	93	25	16	42	83
Total District	7.35	6.48	88				
Total Key Markets	45.76	62.16	136	33	18	59	110
Total Key Districts	49.16	65.79	134				
Rem. U.S. Key Markets	54.24	37.84	70	37	22	—	59
Rem. U.S. Key Districts	50.84	34.21	61				
Balance U.S.	100.0	100.0	100	35	20	—	—

Budget				Dollars	Index
Day Network	Late Network	Spot TV	Total	(%)	= 100
$ 23,827	$ 17,890	$ 83,343	$125,060	3.36	100
8,732	7,561	33,573	49,866	1.34	114
4,319	2,695	13,706	20,720	.56	105
8,209	9,752	21,629	39,590	1.07	105
3,448	1,573	10,149	15,170	.41	105
$ 48,535	39,471	162,400	250,406	6.74	107
50,996	40,234	162,400	253,630	6.82	103
84,335	116,744	307,748	508,557	13.69	105
5,921	5,411	31,588	42,920	1.16	105
9,245	9,647	42,528	61,420	1.66	105
2,504	1,237	10,689	14,430	.39	105
4,453	5,097	20,050	29,600	.80	105
5,582	3,272	34,066	42,920	1.16	105
27,705	24,664	138,921	191,290	5.17	105
35,185	31,269	138,921	205,375	5.55	94
10,353	5,872	58,145	74,370	2.01	105
5,643	6,186	28,131	39,960	1.08	105
37,483	36,575	155,712	229,770	6.21	105
15,104	9,438	100,518	125,060	3.38	105
8,086	8,210	25,884	42,180	1.14	105
76,669	66,281	368,390	511,340	13.82	105
77,173	66,837	368,390	512,400	13.85	104
19,650	16,086	73,784	109,520	2.96	105
5,623	4,017	7,123	16,763	.45	110
19,506	20,774	49,260	89,540	2.42	105
3,232	3,995	10,533	17,760	.48	105
48,011	44,872	140,700	233,583	6.31	105
51,243	48,917	140,700	240,860	6.47	99
23,436	20,804	124,850	169,090	4.57	105
6,311	4,404	26,285	37,000	1.00	105
2,812	2,601	13,087	18,500	.50	105
7,306	4,089	31,895	43,290	1.17	105
2,719	1,364	13,677	17,760	.48	105
5,931	7,571	18,688	32,190	.87	105
48,515	40,833	228,482	317,830	8.59	105
51,490	42,442	228,482	322,414	8.71	102
36,263	75,310	98,185	209,758	5.67	163
3,345	3,126	19,425	25,896	.70	163
8,838	13,199	19,852	41,434	1.12	163
47,991	91,635	137,462	277,088	7.49	163
60,376	106,862	137,462	304,700	8.24	154
36,498	52,966	117,852	207,316	5.58	117
4,361	3,890	24,283	32,534	.87	153
5,151	4,646	19,332	29,129	.78	142
46,010	61,502	161,467	268,979	7.23	122
53,983	67,216	161,467	282,666	7.60	117
427,771	486,002	1,645,300	2,559,073	69.06	111
464,781	520,521	1,645,300	2,630,602	70.93	108
598,329	562,598	—	1,160,927	30.94	82
561,319	528,079	—	1,089,398	29.07	85
$1,026,100	$1,048,600	$1,645,300	$3,720,000	100.00	100

higher than average levels of attentiveness. In addition, in-show positions are preferable to those during the break.

The ⅓ early, ⅔ late dispersion of WGRPs is designed to place additional pressure among upper income women who are available in late fringe. It is also an attempt to capitalize on the higher attentiveness levels generated during late fringe. This dispersion, however, is directional and should not be construed as being inflexible.

Notes on Parts 10 and 11—Spot Television Market Selection and Buying Strategy

⑤③ Whenever a media plan calls for the use of spot television, there must be some statement explaining how the markets that are part of the spot plan are to be selected. There are many ways to make market selections. The criteria for this plan are listed here.

⑤④ When the media plan has been approved, it will be necessary for the spot television buyer to buy spots as the plan recommends. To make the buyer's job easier, specific criteria for buying have been listed here.

A Final Note

Some readers may wonder why the names of individual television programs were not mentioned in this plan. The reason is that the selection of individual programs is part of the buying strategy. The buying strategy is always to select those programs which best fulfill the demographic profile stated in the media objectives. The plan shown on the preceding pages clearly specifies the kind and the number of television programs that need to be selected. After the plan has been approved, buying will begin through negotiation with network and spot time sales representatives.

11

Response Functions
of Reach and Frequency

One of the most difficult problems facing a media planner is that of proving the effectiveness of a given plan. At present, a plan culminates in a given estimated reach and frequency of target audiences. The problem is to know what to do or how to go beyond reach and frequency goals. Alec M. Lee, director of operations research for Trans-Canada Air Lines, aptly pointed out that there is nothing wrong with using reach and frequency to determine an optimum media schedule if the levels of reach and frequency that will attain a specific marketing objective are known.[1] But they are not known. They are intuitive estimates based on very little objective evidence.

At present, the quality of a media plan is judged subjectively, based on answers to a number of questions, such as:

- Has the plan clearly defined the target audiences?
- Has it selected media vehicles that best reach those targets with good cost efficiency?
- Are the vehicles appropriate to the product and the message?
- Are the reach level and the average frequency level appropriate for the specified budget and copy considerations?
- Is the schedule matched to the best sales or communication opportunities?
- Does the plan help achieve the marketing objectives?

If the answers are all affirmative, then the plan may be judged effec-

---

[1]Lee, Alec M., "The Search for Decision Rules for Optimal Media Scheduling," *Advertising Research Foundation 8th Annual Conference Proceedings*, October 1962, p. 28.

tive. The answers, however, are based to some extent on marketing and media data analysis, and to a greater extent on the personal experience and subjective judgment of an individual (or advisory group). But there is little that can be judged on empirical evidence before the plan is implemented. It is not clear at all that the plan is really effective because there are no effectiveness criteria other than logic or experience. Reach levels cannot be a criterion because there is no evidence that any given reach accomplishes a specific business objective. Frequency levels cannot be used as a criterion because there is too little evidence that they accomplish either a communication or marketing objective. In fact, there has been no way to parse out the contribution of media vehicles selected, from the results of an advertising campaign. Perhaps the best that can be said about a plan is that, according to present-day practices in widespread use in sophisticated advertising agencies and the state of knowledge about media planning, it represents what *appears* to be a good plan.

But media theoreticians have been thinking about and discussing this subject for a long time. What they consider to be most appropriate is a measurement of consumer response to a media plan. After all, a media plan is a combination of individual decisions. Without knowing the results of these decisions, it would be difficult to judge their adequacy. Therefore, the wisdom of a media plan should depend on what happens as a result of its proper implementation. If the results are observable, and many of the results are, then they should be measurable.

The results are often called response functions to indicate that they are responses to media vehicle stimuli. A *response function* is an effect on target audience members caused by an association those individuals make between media vehicles and ads in those vehicles. Sales effects also could be considered a response function, but this term is rarely used because it is difficult to determine advertising's contribution to sales. In other words, people do things as a result of having been stimulated by advertisements presented in a certain media form (television, magazines, etc.). While it may seem desirable to measure the results of media stimuli alone, the effects of copy must also be considered. Presumably then, the same ad placed in two different media vehicles should have somewhat different degrees of response. Combination copy and media effects are recommended rather than media effects alone, because the latter is too difficult to observe and, consequently, too difficult to measure.

In discussing response functions, it may be advisable to divide them into at least two classes. One kind of response is the result of a mechanical association between an individual and a vehicle such as happens when a person receives a magazine through the mail. He or she may unwrap it, lay it on a table, and perhaps never read it because of the press of other activities. This association is purely mechanical because it involves little interaction. On the other hand, if a person opens the magazine and thumbs through it, that, too, is a mechanical interaction, but one of a higher level. If the person should stop while thumbing through and look at an ad or two, then an even higher level of mechanical response has occurred, called *advertising page exposure*. This is defined as the act of opening a spread of facing pages wide enough to glance at the advertising.

But a different kind of response is one that is psychological. If a person opens a magazine, sees a given ad, and, upon being questioned by an interviewer, remembers having seen that ad, then the response is psychological because the advertisement communicated something that was remembered. There are other kinds of psychological responses that might be measured, such as the kind of buying behavior that results from reading an ad.

At present, most media planning is based on a very low level of mechanical response called *vehicle exposure*—whether an audience target has a chance to be exposed to the vehicle. One often hears statements, not necessarily correct, that the media plan that delivers the most target exposures is best. Such a statement is an oversimplification.

The purpose of this chapter is to examine the concept of response functions and how they may be used in media planning evaluation. The objective is to discuss some of the more widely recommended response functions and help the reader see whether any of them can accomplish the goals discussed earlier.

The reader should clearly understand that no single measurement of response exists in the industry by which media plans can be evaluated. This chapter will identify some of the response techniques employed by various firms or individuals within the advertising field. Knowledge of the various techniques, their strengths and weaknesses, should aid in understanding how media planning criteria, beyond reach and frequency, may sometimes serve as a basis for making recommendations.

Frequency Effects as the Ultimate Response Function

A growing number of media experts in this country have turned their attention to the effects of media frequency as the most valuable of all response functions. These experts have been impressed by research findings that show there are positive effects on consumers as a result of various frequency levels. This research came about because two different groups of advertising researchers were looking for answers to two different, though related, problems. Although the research was done for different reasons, ultimately the findings of both kinds of research were helpful to each group.

The first kind of research dealt with an older advertising problem, namely: how many times must a consumer see (or hear) an advertisement for it to have some effect? This is related to how consumers learn advertising messages. Frequency could affect not only the ability of audience members to recall ads, but to be motivated to switch brands, to change attitudes, or to buy a given brand.

The second kind of research is more recent. It was aimed at answering a media planning problem, namely: how much frequency is optimal in a media plan? Frequency for many years has been considered to be the average number of vehicle exposures, or opportunities to see a vehicle, that a media plan delivers. Planners have always known that the frequency in a media plan represented only potential, not actual, exposure to advertisements. So the effect of advertising frequency was not foremost in the minds of planners who initiated this kind of research.

What happened was that each kind of research contributed something of value to both groups of researchers. Both learned that response functions were the product of at least two elements: vehicle *and* advertising frequency. Although it seems obvious that one cannot have advertising frequency without vehicle frequency, most research centered on advertising frequency and its relationship to responses of various kinds. More recently, attempts have been made to relate vehicle frequency directly to responses (assuming, of course, that advertising frequency must play some role in the response function).

Frequency effects, then, are a response function of great importance. So high is the prevailing interest in research studies that show the effects of various frequency levels that Michael J. Naples, former director of market research at Lever Brothers, and now president of the Advertising Research Foundation, has assembled the major research findings on frequency into a book entitled *Effective Frequency: The Relationship Between Frequency and Advertising Effectiveness*.[2]

Naples' Conclusions About Effective Frequency

Michael Naples' work on frequency has a two-fold value: (1) he provided a service to the industry by collecting and reporting on significant theories and research studies, and (2) after studying this material, he formed conclusions about its value for media planning. Although media strategists do not necessarily agree with all of his conclusions, they are valuable because they represent the first published synthesis of varying kinds of research. Briefly, his conclusions are:

1. One exposure of an advertisement to a target consumer group (within a purchase cycle) has little or no effect.

---

[2]Naples, Michael J., *Effective Frequency: The Relationship Between Frequency and Advertising Effectiveness*, Association of National Advertisers, 1979, pp. 63–79.

2. Because one exposure is usually ineffective, the main thrust of media planning should be on emphasizing frequency rather than reach.

3. Most of the research studies suggested that two exposures within a purchase cycle is an effective threshold level.

4. Three exposures within a purchase cycle, however, is felt to be optimal.

5. After three exposures within a purchasing cycle, advertising becomes more effective as frequency is increased, but at a decreasing rate. If this were drawn on a graph, it would appear as a convex curve rising from a zero point.

6. Wearout of an advertising campaign is not caused by too much frequency *per se*. It is caused by copy and content problems.

7. Generally, small and less well-known brands will benefit most by increased frequency. Larger and well-known brands may or may not be helped by increasing frequency "depending on how close they are to advertising saturation levels."

8. Different dayparts on television are affected by different frequency levels. A similar idea applies to thin vs. thick magazines, with the thinner ones having better response effects than the thicker ones.

9. Frequency responses are affected by the amount of money an advertiser spends as a percentage of the product category total. Those brands with the greatest proportion of exposures within their categories should also gain great effect when frequency is increased.

10. The responses due to increased frequency are not affected by different media. What is true for one medium is true for others.

11. Each brand may require a different level of frequency of exposure. One cannot generalize from a given brand's experiences to some other brand. Specialized research is required to find the unique frequency level for a brand.

12. Two brands spending the same amount of money for advertising may have different responses to their frequencies.

A Discussion of Naples' Conclusions

Not everyone agrees with all of Naples' conclusions.

The concept of threshold. One area in which there is no general agreement is the concept of a threshold. A *threshold* has been previously defined as the number of impressions below which the response to advertisements is relatively low—that is, nothing much is happening as a result of advertising. After the threshold has been passed, there is a dramatic rise in response to advertising.

There are a number of problems, however, that confront media planners who want to use the threshold concept. The first is that it is necessary to know whether the threshold being discussed is an advertising or a media vehicle effect. Much of the research on thresholds has centered on advertising effects. (This problem will be discussed again later in this chapter.) Suffice it to say at this point that a planner should know which threshold he or she wants to consider. Perhaps it is both.

The second problem is that there is some question about how many exposures constitute a threshold. Naples pointed out that two are acceptable, but that three are optimal. Other media planners disagree. One in particular, Gus Priemer, advertising director of S. C. Johnson Company, argues that at times, one exposure is all that is needed. He came to this conclusion by studying research on new product introductions. Of course, he did not generalize to all products and brands.[3]

Colin McDonald, in a study of the short-term effect of advertising, found that a two-exposure level was significant in motivating an experimental sample of homemakers to switch brands.[4] On the other hand, the DuPont Study, which used television to measure learning 24 hours after exposures, found that two or three exposures were ideal.[5]

Another expert in this area, Herbert Krugman, director of public relations at the General Electric Company, advocates no more than three exposures.[6] Some researchers call Krugman's concept the "three-hit method," a colloquialism for three exposures. The idea is that it is a waste of time and money to buy more than three advertising exposures. Krugman has suggested that a consumer receiving the first impression of an ad asks only "what is it?" that is being advertised. At the second exposure, the consumer knows what the brand is and its name, and asks "what of it?" In other words, the consumer wants to know what the brand's benefits are. At the third exposure, the consumer either makes a decision to buy or puts the ad message out of mind until a later date when ready to buy the product class being advertised. According to Krugman, most people stop paying much attention to a specific brand's advertising at the second exposure if they are not in the market for the product. So advertising works best when the consumer is interested in buying. Frequency levels may not need to be high until consumers are ready to buy.

There seems to be a great deal of logic about the idea of a threshold level, and there is also much to be said for Krugman's concept that con-

---

[3]Priemer, Gus, "Are We Doing the Wrong Thing Right?" *Media Decisions*, May 1979, p. 64.

[4]McDonald, Colin, "What Is the Short-Term Effect of Advertising?" in Naples, *Effective Frequency*, p. 94.

[5]Naples, *Effective Frequency*, p. 48.

[6]Naples, *Effective Frequency*, pp. 24, 25.

sumers tend not to pay attention to advertising until they are in the market for the product. There are occasions, however, when consumers pay a great deal of attention to a brand's advertising, even though they may have no intention of buying immediately. This may occur when an ad message is inherently interesting apart from the product.

Threshold levels may vary considerably. Conceivably an advertising campaign with a strikingly innovative message may require only one impression to produce significant responses. A dull creative effort, on the other hand, may require more than three exposures to be effective. A dynamic market may also affect the threshold level. When there is a strong demand for a product category, all competing brands may need only a one- or two-exposure level to achieve effective response. An example might be the advertising of snow blowers during a period of heavy snowstorms. Other factors, too, may affect the threshold level such as:

1. The degree of product advantage that one brand has over its competitors.
2. The cumulative effect of all past advertising on consumers (such as Coca-Cola has).
3. The noise level of a product category, which may be so high that the threshold level also must be high.

Frequency responses ought to be based on a product's purchase cycle. Naples did not recommend that all media planning be based on a product's purchasing cycle; he concluded only that the research on responses to frequency was based on purchasing cycles. Erwin Ephron and Jack Hill, two media experts, have both advocated a change from traditional media planning time periods to the purchasing cycles of brands.[7,8]

If the purchasing cycle basis is used in media planning, reach and frequency should be calculated for time periods of as little as one day to as long as one or more years, depending on how often a person purchases a particular product. The inherent problem in using a purchasing cycle for this purpose, however, is that the time span between purchases might be similar for all people, but the actual time of purchase may vary considerably from one person to the next. If, for example, a product is purchased once a month, one person might buy the product the first day of the month, while another buys it in the middle of the month. Therefore, it behooves the advertiser to schedule advertising continuously in order to have advertising exposure immediately prior to the day that a given person will make a purchase.

[7]Ephron, Erwin, from Media Decisions Paris Seminar, "The U.S. Advertiser: No Longer a Silent Media Partner," *Media Decisions*, 1978, pp. 146–47.

[8]Hill, Jack D., *How to Measure Television Commercial Effectiveness*, Association of National Advertisers, New York, February 25–26, 1975, p. 7.

Perhaps greater attention to products' purchasing cycles will occur in future media planning, but there is no movement in the industry to change. The four-week reach and frequency schedule will probably remain standard for the time being.

Point of Diminishing Returns. Is there a point of diminishing returns in response to increased frequency levels? In 1965, Jacobvits and Appel found that as frequency increased, so did responses until a point was reached where responses began to decline.[9] If this response pattern were drawn on a graph, it would appear much like an inverted U. A consequence of such a finding might be that once a given frequency level has been reached, any additional frequency would be detrimental to advertising effectiveness.

In 1968 Robert C. Grass of DuPont found through research that there were satiation effects on attention and learning levels as a result of increased advertising frequency. After two or three exposures, attention and learning seemed to decline.[10] On the other hand, Grass also found that favorable attitudes toward a company developed because of advertising frequency, and there were no satiation effects.

Some studies did not find points of diminishing returns, while others did. Today there are commonly accepted ranges of frequency effectiveness. The range may extend from two to seven impressions, three to ten impressions, or some other range. Many media experts consider effective reach and frequency beyond ten to be inefficient, suggesting that they believe there *is* a point of diminishing returns. There is a need to have more precise information on this subject than is currently available. Planners may want to keep an open mind about whether there is or is not such a turning point in advertising frequency.

Media Vehicle Exposure vs. Advertisement Exposure. Probably the most controversial part of the effective frequency concept is that of equating vehicle frequency with advertising frequency. There is no one-to-one relationship between the two. Almost all media experts believe that vehicle frequency represents an opportunity-to-see. The number of opportunities-to-see that a media vehicle (or group of vehicles in a media plan) develops does not guarantee any exposure to ads, as it is easily possible for audience members to read a newspaper or magazine without looking at any of the ads. For radio and television, it is likewise known that sometimes audience members will walk out of the room when commercials come on. Perhaps the best known research studies on the dif-

---

[9]Naples, *Effective Frequency*, p. 19.
[10]Grass, Robert C., and Wallace, Wallace H., "Satiation Effects of TV Commercials," *Journal of Advertising Research*, September 1969, pp. 3–8.

TABLE 11–1. Differences Between Homes Tuned-in, Viewing, Exposed, and Recalling Commercial Content in St. Louis and Chicago

	St. Louis Index	Chicago Index
Homes tuned in to program	100	100
Homemakers viewing program	59	50
Viewers possibly exposed to commercial	36	38
Viewers recalling content of commercial	16	20

Source: Gomer, Frank G., and Vedder, Blair B., "Another Look Beyond the TV Ratings," A.N.A. Television Advertising Workshop, New York, June 17, 1964.

ferences between vehicle and advertising exposure were done by the Foote, Cone & Belding and Needham, Louis & Brorby agencies in 1962 and 1963.

As Table 11–1 shows, the number possibly exposed is considerably fewer than the number who viewed the program, and the recall level is even less than that, for both Chicago and St. Louis. If the "possibly exposed" group is considered the equivalent of "exposed" (and there is no reason to disagree with that assumption), then there is strong evidence that vehicle and audience frequency are very different.

The effective frequency concept for media planners relates most importantly to this point: How much media vehicle frequency is necessary to achieve the advertising exposure frequencies found in most of the research studies? Radio and television ratings and magazine audience exposures represent only exposures to vehicles. To go beyond vehicle frequency, we need research that either relates vehicle frequency to advertising frequency, or directly shows the effects of vehicle exposure frequency to a given response. Some research studies have tried to do the latter, but more research is obviously needed.

Howard Kamin, media director of the Richard K. Manoff agency, believes he has a technique for bridging the gap.[11] Using the "three-hit" theory of Krugman, his technique involves estimating the probability of audience members being exposed to exactly three exposures (or hits). He does this by plotting the exposure probabilities of a normal distribution curve on a graph relating the percent of probability of three exposures against media vehicle frequency levels. He points out that doing this is "an independent event and can be described using a binomial formula."

As a base for this estimating, he uses the research findings from Burke measurements, where it was found that 25 percent of an audience can recall the content of a commercial when asked 24 hours later. Figure 11–1 shows the curve plotted on a graph. At the height of the normal

---

[11]Kamin, Howard, "Advertising Reach and Frequency," *Journal of Advertising Research*, February 1978, pp.23–24.

**FIGURE 11–1. Estimated Probability of Being Exposed and Able to Recall
Three Commercials at Various Frequency Levels**

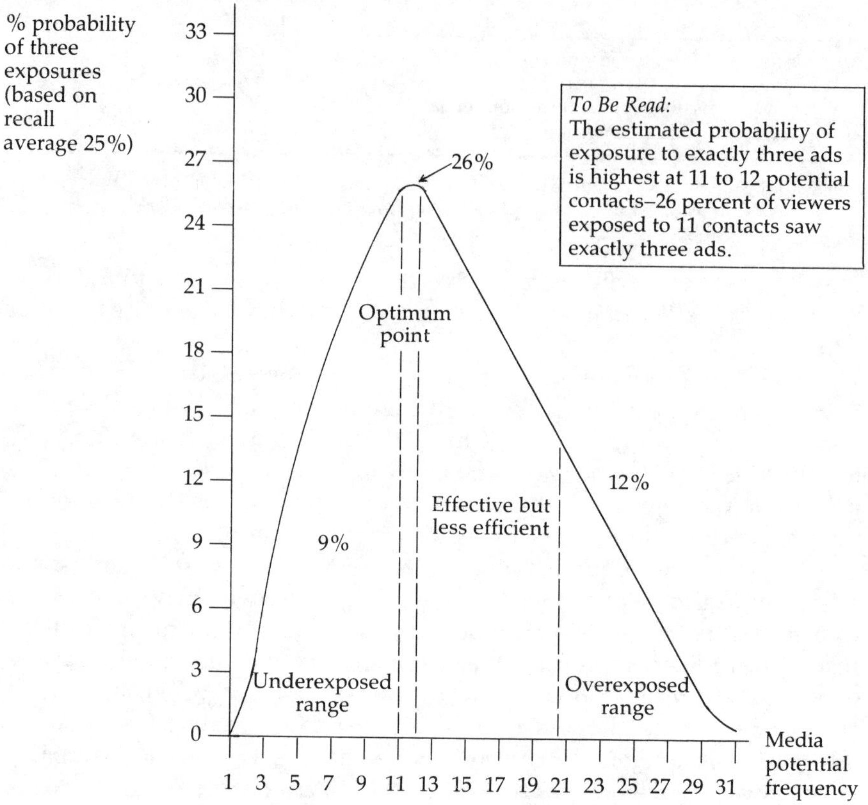

Source: Kamin, Howard, "Advertising Reach and Frequency," *Journal of Advertising
Research*, February 1978, pp. 23–24.

distribution curve, 26 percent of the viewers saw exactly three ads. The
frequency level at that point was 11 to 12 vehicle exposures. The range of
vehicle exposures was from 5 to 20, which means that at fewer than 5
exposures there was little probability of audience members receiving
communication from the commercials, while at more than 20 there was
more frequency than needed for the three-exposure goal. Exposures over
20 were wasted.

Keep in mind that vehicle exposure and advertising exposure are two
different things. It is safe to assume that advertising exposure is usually
much less than vehicle exposure. Again, more research is needed to show
the best relationship.

In conclusion then, the concept of effective frequency offers a media planner much information about how much frequency to use in planning. But it does not provide immediate answers to everyday problems. At present the concept is most helpful in providing some considerations not previously proved that can have a bearing on the frequency level of a given media plan. But it will not provide specific answers, as some believers in the concept are apt to hold.

Reach as a Response Function

Meanwhile, is there no interest in *reach* as a response function? The answer is that there have been no research studies of importance directly related to this problem. Of course, the concept of effective reach is an outgrowth of effective frequency research. Naples concluded that reach is not as important as frequency, but media planners are cautioned to place reach in proper perspective to frequency. Both are important in media planning. The planner should not ask whether to emphasize reach *or* frequency, but rather to aim for reach *with* frequency. Reach is a media strategy, while frequency is not only a media strategy, but an advertising communication strategy as well.

Some media planners want to go beyond effective frequency to a concept they call *impact*. Under the effective frequency concept, there is a range of frequency that is considered to be effective, such as three to ten exposures, or two to seven exposures. *Impact*, however, may be defined as giving a quality to the effective range, by an estimated number of responses; it is the extent to which the medium and ad affect their audience. Case Study 11–1 gives an example.

Other Kinds of Response Functions

Advertising Recognition

Measurements of individuals who remember having seen ads in magazines or newspapers have been used as response functions from time to time. The measuring technique is very simple. A respondent is first *qualified* to be questioned further, which means that the respondent, when shown the cover of a magazine, claims to remember having looked inside it. If the respondent is qualified, then the interviewer opens each page with a full-page or half-page ad on it and asks the respondent whether he or she saw a specific ad. Affirmative answers are considered as "noting" or "recognizing" the ad. Recognition scores are tabulated for each ad in a magazine. The same ads can be measured in many different magazines, thus providing a rough measurement of a vehicle's ability to generate recognition levels.

CASE STUDY 11–1
Using the Effective Frequency Concept to
Determine the Impact of Alternative Media Plans

The following is a practical example of how effective frequency might be used to judge the impact of three alternative media plans. Impact is defined as providing the largest number of responses to advertising at various frequency levels.

1. Reach, frequency, and target GRPs of three media plans:

	Monthly GRPs	Reach	Frequency
Daytime only plan	296	52	5.7
Nighttime only plan	142	71	2.0
Day + magazine plan	296	80	3.7

2. Subjective judgments are made about effectiveness of three media:

Daytime network TV	65 index of value
Nighttime network TV	100 index of value
Women's magazines	50 index of value

3. GRPs are multiplied by index of values:

Daytime plan $296 \times .65 = 192$ net delivery

Nighttime plan $142 \times 1.00 = 142$ net delivery

Day   (157 GRPs) $157 \times .65 = 102$ net delivery $\left.\right\}$ Total: 172
Magazine (139 GRPs) $139 \times .50 = 70$ net delivery

4. Gross reach and frequency are converted to net delivery:

Example: Daytime network TV

Gross Delivery			Net Delivery		
GRPs	Reach	Frequency	GRPs	Reach	Frequency
296	52	5.7	192	48	4.0

Effective frequency has been determined to be from 2 to 7 exposures. Therefore, a frequency distribution has been given an index of effective response for every frequency level. These indices are subjectively made here, but they could be objectively measured in test marketing situations.

5. Subjective judgments about indices of responses:

Frequency levels	Index of Response
From 1 to 3 exposures	50
From 4 to 7 exposures	100
From 8-plus exposures	100

A frequency distribution (from computer analysis) is now performed to show percentage of net delivery reach for each frequency level. These reaches are multiplied by the index of responses.

6. Frequency distribution × Index of Responses:

Example: Daytime network TV

Frequency Levels	Net Reach	×	Index of Responses	=	Net Impact
1 to 3 exp.	28.8%	×	50	=	14.4
4 to 7 exp.	11.8	×	100	=	11.8
8+ exp.	7.2	×	100	=	7.2
Totals	47.8%				33.4

7. Now, all net impacts for three alternatives are calculated:

Media Plan Alternative	Net Impact	Original Gross Reach	Frequency
Daytime plan	33	52	5.7
Nighttime plan	39	71	2.0
Day + magazine plan	39	80	3.7

8. Results:

1. The nighttime plan and the day plus magazine plan are equivalent in impact. This was not evident by studying reach and frequency alone.

2. The daytime plan is clearly the one with less impact potential.

3. The most critical points in these analyses were the subjective judgments of media values, and index of responses.

   These judgments can be improved by taking a consensus vote and averaging scores of a number of media experts within an organization. Or, they can be measured objectively through test marketing where variable weights can be determined.

4. Although this technique seems somewhat arbitrary, especially in the value judgments that have to be made, such judgments are usually made in media planning outside the confines of the data. In other words, data is collected on reach and frequency, cost-per-thousand, etc., but eventually someone has to make judgments about their values. This technique formalizes the judgment process.

Source: Jules Fine, *Sex and Sanity in Media Planning*, A.N.A., March 21, 1979.

Theoretically, recognition scores should represent evidence that a certain percentage of individuals was affected by the vehicle and the ads in it. If one vehicle has a higher average number of recognition scores than another, it may be a better vehicle. Alfred Politz called recognition scores a measurement of a magazine's *efficiency*, or performance in attracting readers to ads.[12]

Practically, however, media planners do not accept recognition scores as measurements of response functions without some reservations. These reservations are:

1. Many readers are confused about where they saw a given ad. There is no reason for them to remember that they saw an ad in one magazine, or that they saw the same ad in two different magazines. This confusion affects the validity of comparing media by using the recognition technique.

2. Whenever bogus ads are inserted in magazines that are to be measured by this technique, there are always a number of individuals who claim they remember having seen those ads. This is an unusual response and casts doubt on the validity of the measuring technique. One would think that respondents would be able to remember that they did not see the bogus ads, which had never been printed in any magazine. Perhaps respondents want to empathize with interviewers and claim they read more than they really did.

3. There is no way to prove that respondents really did see the ads they claim to have seen. How can a researcher know whether a respondent is telling the truth, especially when respondents are shown each ad directly? Is it not possible that some people who saw few or no ads do not want to admit their actions? Since there is no penalty for misrepresentation, then it is possible that some recognitions are not correct.

4. Recognition measurements do not seem to be based on memory. In a study conducted by the Advertising Research Foundation, called Printed Advertising Rating Methods (the PARM Study), recognition scores did not drop when the same respondents were measured after an interval of time, as shown in Table 11–2. Most experts felt that recognition scores should have declined because there had to be some loss of memory over time.

5. There is some question about what the technique really mea-

---

[12]Politz, Alfred, "What Is Essential to Know from Magazine Media Research?" *Media/Scope*, April 1959, p. 40.

TABLE 11–2. Recognition Scores After Various Lapses of Time

Interviewing dates	Recognition scores
May 13 to 15	19.5
May 16 to 19	18.8
May 20 to 22	18.6
May 23 to 25	20.7

Source: Lucas, Darrell B., "The ABC's of ARF's PARM," *The Journal of Marketing*, July 1960, p. 15.

sures. To say that it measures recognition is not satisfactory to many who might use it for media evaluation.

6. Appel and Blum found that, using this technique, there were more false responses when people were very interested in the product types being advertised, or when a product had a high market share compared with similar products. They also found that some persons have a greater tendency than others to claim noting or recognizing ads regardless of whether they really did see the ads.[13]

In conclusion, then, recognition technique measurements have varying degrees of acceptability among media planners and should only be used when one understands the data limitations.

Other Response-Function Alternatives

A number of other possible measurements can be used as response functions. None of them, however, has been found completely satisfactory, for one reason or another. Media traffic scores, for example, have been proposed as a response function. In radio or television, traffic could be measured by the number of homes using television or radio during a specific daypart. In print media, page traffic scores could be used. A *page traffic score* indicates the number of individuals who looked at anything on a given page. The problem with these scores is that they are too general to be useful. They represent the size of the potential, rather than the actual, audience. If the H.U.T. from 7:00 to 7:30 p.m. were 60 percent, that would in no way indicate the size of audience for any given program that was broadcast at that time. Conceivably, there could be great variation in audience sizes for the programs.

Another possible response function could be coupon returns or inquiries generated as a result of ads in print media. But this measurement has minimal application because there is no guaranteed relationship between returns and sales. Furthermore, there are many individuals who

---

[13]Appel, Valentine, and Blum, Milton L., "Ad Recognition and Respondent Set," *Journal of Advertising Research*, June 1961, p. 14.

do not return coupons and yet eventually do buy the product. Finally, there are some individuals who return coupons, not because they are interested in the product, but because they want to receive something in return through the mail, whatever the offer may be.

Still another possibility that has been seriously considered is measurement of attitude change caused by the combination of ads in media. If it could be shown that an ad in one medium produced more attitude change than the same ad in another medium, then this could constitute a response function for comparing alternative media. However, the entire area of attitude change is subject to so many questions with no valid answers that the measurements are not considered viable.

Some of the unanswered questions are: Does attitude change precede or follow behavior change? If behavior changes, is it due to attitude alone, or attitude and other variables that are difficult to control? Is it possible for consumers to have strongly negative attitudes and still purchase a brand regularly? Is it also possible for consumers to have strongly positive attitudes and yet not buy a given brand under any circumstances? Questions such as these have kept attitude change measurements from being accepted as a response function. Most important, however, is the fact that no one knows the contribution of a media vehicle to attitude change.

Finally, other mechanical kinds of response functions have been proposed and rejected for various reasons. Some of these methods have even been used to a limited extent, but not as a major method of evaluating media alternatives. They are: attention levels paid to media, time spent reading, amount of editorial material read, and a relatively new one—brain-wave measurements.

Attention level measurements play a minor role in media plan evaluation since they have been limited to measurements of television program audiences. They cannot be used in measuring magazines. On the other hand, Simmons has been able to measure the amount of a given magazine that was read. But no measure is applicable to both broadcast and print media. Validation of attention levels, too, is very difficult. As William R. Simmons noted:

> You can sit and talk to people, but you can't always tell whether they're paying attention or not. It is almost a self-evaluation type of question. You almost have to read a person's mind to really know whether they are literally paying attention . . . . This sort of measure is not easily susceptible to any kind of clearcut test. [14]

Time spent reading or viewing is also a response function that has

---

[14]Media/Scope, ''Roundtable on 1968 Simmons,'' March 1968, p. 46.

been measured from time to time, but it is not powerful enough to be used as an evaluation technique in media planning.

Finally, brain-wave measurements have been recently tested, but it is much too early to tell whether or not they will be valuable as a response function. Much more research is needed to tell whether the technique can discriminate adequately for various kinds of media.

In conclusion, then, the use of communication response functions is a potentially good method of evaluating alternative media plans. The effective frequency concept coupled, perhaps, with some kind of impact measurement represents the ultimate in practical methods of evaluating media plans. But it is too soon to say with finality that the answers are known. Communication response functions represent a big step beyond vehicle reach and frequency. Needed now are refinements to the response function concept. If it should be possible to make brand sales a response function, then even better methods may become available for evaluating media plans.

QUESTIONS FOR DISCUSSION

1. Explain how one can judge the effectiveness of a media plan before it has been implemented.
2. Why aren't sales used as a response function for media?
3. Since response functions represent the contribution of an advertisement and a media vehicle, how can one know how much of the function is attributable to each?
4. In measuring recognition of ads in magazines, what should one expect of results if the same sample of respondents is measured at two periods of time (six weeks apart) for the same magazines?
5. Why aren't advertising frequency and vehicle frequency the same? Explain the differences of each as it relates to finding an optimum frequency level.
6. What is a threshold? At what frequency levels do thresholds usually occur?
7. Explain Krugman's "three-hit" concept.

SELECTED READINGS

Appel, Valentine, and Weiss, Tabor, "Sense and Non-sense in Attitude Change Copy Testing," *Advertising Research Foundation 19th Annual Conference Proceedings*, 1973, pp. 54–58.

Audience Concepts Committee, *Toward Better Media Comparisons*, Advertising Research Foundation, 1961.

Banks, Seymour, "The Need for New Multi-Dimensional Measurements of Media," *Advertising Research Foundation 5th Annual Conference Proceedings*, September 1959, pp. 39–42.

Banks, Seymour, "Media Performance vs. Copy Performance," *Media/Scope*, August 1961, pp. 53–56.

Broadbent, S. R., and Segnit, S.,

"Response Functions in Media Planning," *The Thomson Medals and Awards for Advertising Research*, London, 1967, pp. 35–86.

Caffyn, J. M., *Qualitative Aspects of Reader Data*, Institute of Practitioners in Advertising, London, April 1964.

Clunies-Ross, C. W., "The Practical and Theoretical Problems and Effects of Introducing Explicit Theories of Response Functions into Media Planning," *Thomson Medals and Awards for Advertising Research*, London, 1967, pp. 125–30.

Dodge, Sherwood, "What Readership Studies Really Measure," *Media/Scope*, February 1961, pp. 44–49.

Dodge, Sherwood, "Dodge and Simmons Debate Recognition and Exposure," *Media/Scope*, May 1961, p. 51.

Dodge, Sherwood, "Comments on the Current Scene in Copy Research," *Perspectives in Advertising Management*, Association of National Advertisers, Inc., April 1969, pp. 206–19.

Eliasberg, Jay, "ARF Media Comparisons Report Supported by CBS TV Network," *Media/Scope*, August 1961, pp. 58–61.

Fuchs, Douglas A., "Two Source Effects in Magazine Advertising," *Journal of Marketing Research*, August 1964, pp. 59–62.

Gerhold, Paul E., "Predicted Advertising Yield ARF Proposes an Outline of How Advertising Works," *Advertising Research Foundation, 15th Annual Conference Proceedings*, October 1969, pp. 46–50.

Gomer, Frank J., and Vedder, Blair G., "Another Look Beyond the TV Ratings," from Association of National Advertisers Television Advertising Workshop Paper, June 1964, pp. 1–24.

Grass, Robert C., "Satiation Effects of Advertising," *Advertising Research Foundation 14th Annual Conference Proceedings*, October 1968, pp. 20–28.

King, Charles W., and Summers, John O., "Attitudes and Media Exposure," *Journal of Advertising Research*, February 1971, p. 26.

Krugman, Herbert E., "Answering Some Unanswered Questions in Measuring Advertising Effectiveness," *Advertising Research Foundation 12th Annual Conference Proceedings*, October 1966, pp. 18–23.

Krugman, Herbert E., "The Measurement of Advertising Involvement," *The Public Opinion Quarterly*, Winter 1966–67, pp. 583–96.

Krugman, Herbert E., "Brain Wave Measures of Media Involvement," *Journal of Advertising Research*, February 1971, pp. 3–10.

Lee, Alec M., "The Search for Decision Rules for Optimal Media Scheduling," *Advertising Research Foundation 8th Annual Conference Proceedings*, October 1962, pp. 25–29.

McConnell, J. Douglas, "Do Media Vary in Effectiveness?" *Journal of Advertising Research*, October 1970, pp. 19–22.

Media/Scope, "Roundtable on 1968 Simmons," March 1968, p. 45.

Media/Scope, "New Measures of Attitude Change," October 1967, pp. 127–130.

Media Decisions, "Beyond Demographics," February 1968, pp. 19–26.

Orenstein, Frank, "The Ad and the Market: Some First Results," *Advertising Research Foundation 14th Annual Conference Proceedings*, October 1968, pp. 10–13.

Philadelphia Inquirer and Research,

Inc., of Ohio, *Exposure/Ratings of Measuring Newspaper Readership, Philadelphia Inquirer,* 1962.

Politz, Alfred, "Media Performance vs. Copy Performance," *Media/Scope,* November 1960, pp. 61–63.

Politz, Alfred, "What Is Essential to Know from Magazine Research?" *Media/Scope,* April 1959, pp. 39–44.

Rothman, L. J., "The Role of Response Functions: A Discussion and an Alternative," *Thomson Medals and Awards for Advertising Research,* London, 1967, pp. 89–122.

Simmons, W. R., & Associates, Inc., *Commercial Impact Study for Golden West Broadcasters,* 1973.

Stanton, Frank, "A State of the Art Appraisal of Advertising Research Measurements," *Perspectives in Advertising Management,* April 1969, pp. 238–45.

Vitt, Sam B., "Editorial Environment" *Hidden Media Values or Going Beyond the Numbers,* Papers from the 1964 American Association of Advertising Agencies Meeting, pp. 17–28.

12

Media Costs and Buying Problems

One of the major tasks of a media planner is to match markets with the best media for reaching those markets at the most favorable cost to the client. Earlier chapters have discussed how markets are defined in terms of people and their product consumption, geographic distribution, and demographic characteristics. Those chapters also noted that individuals are exposed to media in varying degrees. For example, full-time home-makers are more likely to watch daytime television shows and read women's service magazines than are teenagers or working men and women. On the other hand, men are more likely than women to read sports magazines.

Each of these media alternatives has a different cost. The final media plan emerging from the marketing strategy should effectively maximize the delivery of the designated marketing target in the most cost-efficient manner. Therefore, the media planner must be familiar not only with market definition but also must be fully versed in how people utilize various media. In some cases, the cost of media varies with supply and demand, as is the case with television time. Other media, such as magazines and newspapers, tend to remain fairly constant in cost, thereby providing a high degree of predictability as planners develop costs for the media plan.

The costs that go into the final media plan are always in a state of flux. Estimating such costs is as much an art as a science and depends heavily on the experience and professionalism of the media planner and the media buyer. If a plan is based on costs that are way out of line with marketplace realities, it can result in faulty media plan delivery. For example, if a planner estimates that 100 Gross Rating Points of primetime television can be purchased for $200,000, and the actual cost of that time is $300,000, the deliverability of the plan is seriously impaired. The client can then justifiably question the value of that media plan as well as the competence of the planner.

Estimating media costs is a complex task. In addition, different media have different problems connected with the buying process. This chapter will identify the importance of the planner's involvement in the media buying process and explain why it requires familiarity with both the cost of media and the problems associated with purchasing different media types.

Some Considerations in Planning and Buying

The value of a media plan is related to how well it delivers the designated marketing targets at the lowest cost with the least amount of waste. The criteria for determining how well the plan accomplishes its mission are related to such concepts as reach, frequency, and target market impressions delivered. The gross number of target market impressions, coupled with the reach and frequency associated with those impressions within the designated budget, form the nucleus of an effective media plan. The media planner must go through a calculated process of matching the cost of various media alternatives with the delivery of the plan to arrive at the optimal relationship between cost and delivery.

For example, the cost-per-thousand of women 18 and over for daytime network television is currently about $2.77 (:30 basis) while the cost-per-thousand for the same audience segment in nighttime network is approximately $6.97. Therefore, in terms of total impressions, daytime network will deliver 2½ times more impressions to women 18 and over than will nighttime network. However, for a $5,000,000 budget over a one-year period of time allocated to 30-second commercials, it is estimated that the reach for nighttime would be 2 percent more than the same budget in daytime, though the frequency would be lower, as is illustrated in Table 12–1.

Two ways most often used to analyze media costs are to calculate cost-per-thousand on the basis of either gross impressions or net reach. Whichever method is used, the cost efficiency of media delivery is important. It may be found that the medium with the largest reach or the most gross impressions is not necessarily the best buy because its cost efficiency is so low. Table 12–2 shows a rough comparison of alternative media deliveries and cost efficiencies.

An examination of the table shows that different coverage levels are achieved by different media vehicles, with certain cost-per-thousand implications. The media planner's task is to fully combine a familiarity with media costs and delivery dynamics with the goals of the marketing plan

TABLE 12–1. Average Four-Week Delivery Estimated for a $5,000,000 Budget

	Night Network	Day Network
Commercial unit	30 seconds	30 seconds
Total affordable GRPs:		
Households	1,128	2,584
Women	838	2,146
Average four-week GRPs:		
Households	87	199
Women	64	165
Average four-week R & F:		
Households	57/1.5	55/3.6
Women	45/1.4	44/3.7

TABLE 12–2. Alternative Media—Cost and Delivery

Medium	Advertising Unit	National Equivalent Cost (000)	Women 18+			Men 18+		
			Number (000)	U.S. (%)	CPM	Number (000)	U.S. (%)	CPM
Night Network	:30	$78.8	11,300	13.3	$6.97	8,950	11.8	$8.80
Day Network	:30	11.4	4,120	4.9	2.77	1,110	1.5	10.27
Sports Network	:30	53.5	4,140	4.9	12.92	7,960	10.5	6.72
Late Night Network	:30	16.7	2,580	3.0	6.47	2,050	2.7	8.15
Early Network News	:30	34.2	7,510	8.9	4.55	5,800	7.6	5.90
General Magazines (11 magazine avg.)	1P 4-C	48.1	13,963	16.5	3.44	10,768	14.2	4.47
Women's Magazines (7 magazine avg.)	1P 4-C	48.9	19,922	23.6	2.45	3,959	5.2	12.34
Newspapers	Full Page B/W	1,250.0	45,310	53.5	27.59	45,310	59.5	27.59
Network Radio	:60	2.4	1,067	1.3	2.25	1,067	1.4	2.25
Outdoor Poster	#100 showing	103.6	41,128	48.5	2.52	53,424	70.2	1.94

Sources: A. C. Nielsen, Cost Per 1,000 Report, October 1981
　　　　Standard Rate & Data, August 1981
　　　　Newspaper Advertising Bureau
　　　　Radio Advertising Bureau
　　　　Institute of Outdoor Advertising
　　　　Simmons Market Research Bureau, 1980
　　　　MRI, Fall 1981

to reach designated audiences. The planner must be careful to employ correct media cost assumptions in the development of the plan. Table 12–2 shows that, if inappropriate cost assumptions are used in estimating the costs of daytime network versus women's service magazines, it

TABLE 12–3. Media Cost and Cost-per-Thousand Trends Indexed to 1970

	Primetime Network TV		Daytime Network TV		Consumer Magazines		Newspapers		Network Radio	
	Unit Cost	CPM	Unit Cost	CPM	Unit Cost	CPM	Unit Cost	CPM	Unit Cost	CPM
1970	100	100	100	100	100	100	100	100	100	100
1971	96	93	94	89	100	101	104	104	111	99
1972	109	99	98	84	97	100	107	107	117	89
1973	124	111	113	95	97	99	114	112	119	89
1974	137	120	121	105	102	103	130	130	117	89
1975	147	122	140	110	107	111	144	147	123	90
1976	160	133	163	137	110	113	159	161	129	99
1977	203	167	204	177	119	123	173	175	148	108
1978	228	187	227	191	130	135	190	190	159	116
1979	256	205	247	200	140	146	205	205	171	123
1980	300	232	279	222	156	162	226	224	195	129
1981	324	249	296	231	173	179	248	243	207	135

Source: *Marketing & Media Decisions,* August 1981

would be possible to include one media type in the plan to the exclusion of the other.

There are several ways media planners can help ensure correct and current media cost estimates. It should be noted that although we refer to media planners here, it is common for many companies to have media buyers, professionals trained in purchasing, make these decisions.

First, the planner must maintain close contact with media market-place cost mechanisms. For example, pricing for print media such as magazines, newspapers, and newspaper preprints tends to be related to the cost of producing the product. As paper, ink, and wage costs increase, magazine and newspaper publishers will pass these costs on to the reader, to some degree, and to the advertiser. Generally speaking, magazine costs have tended to grow at a relatively modest annual rate compared with broadcast, as shown in Table 12–3.

Conversely, broadcast media costs, particularly television, are importantly influenced not so much by the cost of the product as by the law of supply and demand. The media planner assesses supply and demand in broadcast by maintaining constant contact with broadcast suppliers, that is, the network and television station representatives. These contacts give the planner a feel for what is transpiring in the market and thus enable the forecasting of changes (upward or downward) in broadcast pricing.

Second, intelligent media planners will include media buyers in the development of media cost estimates. Many agencies and advertisers employ media buying specialists whose sole responsibility is the purchase of media. Such media buyers are in regular contact with the media suppliers with whom they do business on behalf of the agency/client. During the course of the numerous media buyer/seller transactions, the buyer acquires a familiarity with what is occurring in the marketplace. Such familiarity can assist the media planner in forecasting media price changes. Media buyers are expected to maintain good media supplier relations to facilitate this flow of information. Media planners should make it a point to maintain close communications with the media buyers so as to tap this source of media cost information.

Third, agencies develop expertise in estimating media cost changes based on the agency's total experience. Over a period of time, the agency can compile media cost information in various markets, or nationally, by generalizing from various specific buying experiences. It is not necessary to breach security within an agency in order to develop this information. Generalized experience is one of the reasons many agencies have gone to buying media by market as opposed to buying by brand. The individual responsible for buying an individual market (or markets) is intimately acquainted with the media cost picture in those areas.

Once the media plan has been implemented and the schedules completed, the media planner should examine how closely the media cost estimates compare with actual costs. By conducting such a post-buy analysis, the planner can sharpen the capability to forecast costs by reviewing what went into the original estimates. Such trial-and-error devices assist the media professional in developing the personal art of media cost forecasting. Major variations between cost estimates and actual plan delivery cost may uncover flaws in understanding or thinking, or may be the consequence of significant media marketplace cost changes that could not have been anticipated. In any event, the media planner, in checking back over the implemented plan, should consider the exercise an important learning experience.

A Discussion of Media Costs

Table 12–4 shows national media expenditures by major consumer media types for 1980. The chart identifies the major media to which national advertisers direct their dollars. Note that television and magazines comprise nearly 27 percent of national expenditures. The magnitude and complexity of planning and buying these media require close attention to cost implications.

Within these broad media types, there are numerous alternatives available with which the media planner must be acquainted. In addition to understanding general media cost relationships, for example between television and magazines, the professional media planner must be familiar with costs of network versus spot, and the different availabilities

TABLE 12–4. National Media Expenditures (1980)

Medium	Dollars Spent (thousands)	Portion of Total (%)
Total	54,750	100.0
Newspapers	15,615	28.5
Magazines		
Total	3,225	5.9
Weeklies	1,440	2.6
Monthlies	990	1.8
Women's	795	1.5
Television		
Total	11,330	20.7
Network	5,105	9.3
Spot	3,260	6.0
Local	2,965	5.4
Radio		
Total	3,690	6.7
Network	185	0.3
Spot	750	1.4
Local	2,755	5.0
Farm Publications	135	0.3
Direct Mail	7,655	14.0
Business Papers	1,695	3.1
Outdoor	610	1.1
Miscellaneous	10,795	19.7

Source: *Advertising Age*, January 5, 1981

within the general broadcast medium as well as the changes over time—a complex and difficult assignment, but a necessary one.

Television Costs

Table 12–4 showed that television expenditures accounted for 20.7 percent of total advertising dollars spent in 1980. Most of the television investment was for consumer goods and services. However, there has been a growing use of the medium by industrial and business-related advertisers. In view of the magnitude of the investment in television, a media planning professional must be fully conversant with all phases of the medium. The major characteristic of television, insofar as media costs are concerned, relates to the "perishability" of the inventory. Generally speaking, there is a fixed amount of television time available for sale. Unlike a magazine or newspaper that can expand or contract the number of advertising pages available for sale in any given issue, a commercial minute that is unsold can never be recovered. The sellers of television time must contend with this perishability concept in selling the medium.

Although marketplace pricing conditions prevail at any given point of time, these prices are subject to change as advertisers' demand for that time strengthens and weakens. The stronger the demand and the earlier

FIGURE 12–1. Daypart Programming Available for Network Use

6	7	8	9	10	11	12	1	2	3	4	5	6	7	8	9	10	11	12	1	2
AM						PM												AM		

| LOCAL | Network | LOCAL | Network Daytime Programs | LOCAL | NETWORK | LOCAL | Network Primetime Programs | LOCAL | Network Late Night Progs. | LOCAL |

the sale in relationship to the program air date, the more likely that pricing will be higher. Less advertising demand close to air date can create lower pricing, assuming inventory availability. These interrelated conditions of perishability, demand, and inventory create a dynamic marketplace. The buyer of television time must, therefore, be alert to these changes by maintaining close contact with the marketplace.

Under the broad heading of television, there are basically two subcategories, national network and local spot.

Network Television. Certain parts of the broadcast day are programmed by the three national networks, the American Broadcasting Company, the Columbia Broadcasting System, and the National Broadcasting Company. Figure 12–1 illustrates the dayparts when network programming is usually made available to *affiliates* (the individual stations that comprise a network lineup). The number of stations serviced by a given network can vary from 150 to 225, depending on the strength of the network programming available. The networks sell commercial time to advertisers to run within specific programs. These programs can appear throughout various parts of the day—for example, daytime network series, primetime network, or late night (post-primetime) segment.

Primetime (8:00 pm to 11:00 pm EST), because of the high H.U.T. (homes using television), generally provides the highest ratings. This time period tends to deliver a family audience with high reach levels of most viewing segments. Media costs for primetime are generally the highest per commercial minute of all network time segments available for sale. The cost for 30 seconds in primetime, as indicated in Table 12–2, can be in the area of $79,000 (or higher for certain programs). Individual program costs will vary depending on rating level and the amount of inventory available for sale. As discussed earlier, the less inventory, generally, the higher the cost.

Daytime network (10:00 am to 4:30 pm EST) is generally the least costly of the network dayparts. An average cost for 30 seconds will be somewhere in the vicinity of $11,400 with an average household rating of approximately 6.7. This results in an extremely efficient cost-per-thousand delivery of homes and women.

Late night (11:30 pm to conclusion EST) network programming tends to vary from network to network and over time. This time period is generally programmed with talk shows, movies, and different types of entertainment including drama, rock concerts, and comedy. Pricing for this time period, since fewer sets are in use than during primetime, tends to be about $16,700 for 30 seconds with an average household rating of 6.4. Although the rating levels for late night are comparable to daytime, there is a dual audience (both men and women) included in late night that is not generally the case in daytime. Thus, pricing for that dual audience tends to be somewhat higher than daytime.

Most network programming on weekends is in the sports and children's areas. Sports programming, for the most part, is the domain of the male-oriented advertiser. Such products as beer, male grooming aids, investment counseling, and automobiles are heavily represented on weekend sports programming. In general, there is a limited amount of broadscale sports programming compared with other network program time. Therefore, pricing tends to be relatively high on a cost-per-thousand basis for the higher interest sporting events. However, the value of identifying with a major high-interest sports event has distinct rub-off effects on brands associated with such programming.

Children's programs, often referred to as "kid TV," are the primary fare on Saturday mornings. Nearly all of this programming is cartoons, but there has been a slow shift over the years to include live-action shows, especially in the action/adventure area. The predominant audience is children, and the advertising, therefore, is highly child-oriented. Cereal, toy/game, and candy advertisers concentrate a significant portion of their advertising budget in kid TV.

The diversity of programming provided by the networks ranges from the all-family interest generated in primetime to highly selective shows of interest to perhaps relatively few households. Such diversity provides the media planner with rich opportunities for reaching broad national markets with programming aimed specifically to target market interests. Costs for such programming will change as marketplace demand changes so that the media planner must be ever alert to the buying implications of the programming selected for inclusion in the media plan.

Local Stations. Announcements can be purchased on local television stations, which can either be affiliated with a network and carry network programming at certain times of the day or they can be independent stations, which means they do not have any network affiliation and thus must program the entire day on their own.

Costs for local announcements vary from market to market based on audience delivered. Generally speaking, the costs for scheduling announcements in markets like New York, Los Angeles, and Chicago are higher than for smaller markets because of the amount of circulation delivered by these stations. Time is made available for sale, whether network-affiliated or independent, across almost the entire daypart. Even within daypart programming by the networks, such as primetime, there are certain segments of time set aside for local sale, which means it is possible for a local advertiser, for example in Chicago, to purchase a 30-second announcement (if available) in a network-originated program, or between programs at the station break.

Since independent stations program for the entire day, there are numerous opportunities for the advertiser to select specific dayparts and programming to reach the target audience. In addition to adjacencies next to and, at times, within network programming, commercial time can be selected in what is termed *fringe time*. Generally speaking, the fringe dayparts and the programming contained therein might look something like the following:

Sample Schedule

Station	Local Time (EST)	Program
A	6:00 pm–6:30 pm	Local news
	6:30 pm–7:00 pm	Local news
	11:00 pm–11:30 pm	Local news
	11:30 pm–Conclusion	Movie
B	5:00 pm–5:30 pm	"I Dream of Jeannie"
	5:30 pm–6:00 pm	"Bewitched"
	6:30 pm–7:00 pm	"Andy Griffith"
	10:30 pm–Conclusion	Local Movie

Pricing for dayparts and specific programs within dayparts will again vary based on audience delivery and availability of commercial time. It is difficult to generalize about pricing relationships between dayparts, stations within a market, and between markets because of the diversity associated with purchasing local announcements. However, in general, spot television is a highly cost-efficient media vehicle for reaching specialized geographic markets. Such geographic selectivity enables the advertiser to concentrate dollars in markets representing the greatest sales potential.

Magazine Costs

The two major print advertising categories are magazines and newspapers. Advertising pricing for print space tends to be somewhat more stable than for broadcast media since magazines and newspapers can adjust upward or downward the number of pages they print on an issue-to-issue basis. Thus the cost of printing is somewhat variable in contrast to the fixed commitment of television and its resultant commercial time perishability. Newspapers and magazines generally issue rate cards that cover future costs with a high degree of certainty. A media planner constructing a plan for a year in advance can be relatively assured that these costs will change little, if at all, during the course of the year.

There is considerable diversity within the broad category of magazines. Some of the categories include the following:

General Interest (Dual Audience). Such publications as the *Reader's Digest*, *TV Guide*, and perhaps to some degree *Time* and *Newsweek* are viewed as general interest magazines in view of the diverse audiences they reach. Their editorial content by nature does not exclude any potential reading group. Along with the large circulation delivered by these publications goes a commensurately high cost-per-page.

	Cost per 4-Color Page	Circulation (thousands)
Reader's Digest	$89,600	17,750
TV Guide	76,000	18,300
Time	76,960	4,250
Newsweek	57,780	2,950
People	34,800	2,350

Women's Service Magazines. More editorially selective publications, such as *Ladies' Home Journal, McCall's, Good Housekeeping, Family Circle, Woman's Day,* and *Redbook* gear their interest primarily to women. The editorial content of these publications is designed to be informative and entertaining. However, male readership, as a percentage of total readership, is not very high compared with the general interest magazines. Following are sample costs for these selected magazines.

	Cost per 4-Color Page	Circulation (thousands)
Ladies' Home Journal	$50,200	5,500
McCall's	56,400	6,200
Good Housekeeping	52,745	5,000
Family Circle	52,800	6,900
Woman's Day	62,320	7,300
Redbook	43,900	4,300

Home Magazines. Other magazines segment their editorial target in a different way, namely by environmental considerations such as the home. Such magazines as *Better Homes & Gardens* speak to the interests and concerns of homeowners. By editorial nature, these magazines tend to be adult and dual audience oriented. Here again, selectivity of editorial content as well as audience gives the advertiser an opportunity to position a commercial message in a highly compatible environment. The costs for some of these magazines are as follows:

	Cost per 4-Color Page	Circulation (thousands)
Better Homes & Gardens	$68,195	8,000
House & Garden	23,330	1,000
House Beautiful	18,140	800
1001 Decorating Ideas	14,875	1,100
Sunset	19,736	1,250
Southern Living	26,820	1,900

Categorization of these magazines is somewhat arbitrary. One could argue that *Better Homes & Gardens* is a general interest publication based on the duality of the readership. In the final analysis, categorization is not nearly so important as the quantity and quality of the readership, compatibility of editorial with the sales message, and the cost of running the insertion—all of which must be taken into account by the media planner. A cost delivery relationship, however, is a good starting point in categorizing magazines from which to select those that then can be qualified based on the editorial content within which the message will appear.

Newspaper Costs

At the beginning of 1982, there were 1,745 daily newspapers in the United States, in addition to 7,600 weekly newspapers. Newspapers provide the distinct benefits of flexibility in adjusting efforts from market to market, quick closing dates, strong local market coverage, and individual market identification. As with other media, newspapers are also highly diverse in the ways they can be bought and the advertising units available for sale. The major categories include the following:

ROP (Run of Paper). ROP advertising can be purchased in virtually any size unit from full page down to just a few lines in both black and white and color. Generally speaking, color costs about 40 percent more than black and white.

Supplements. Preprinted newspaper distributed supplements can be purchased either on a syndicated basis (*Parade, Family Weekly*) or on an independent basis such as the *Chicago Tribune Magazine Section*. Preprinted supplements provide all the benefits of newspapers in today's market coverage with four-color magazine-type reproduction when desirable. Costs for independent supplements vary from market to market. Cost and circulation levels for the syndicated supplements are as follows:

	Cost per 4-Color Page	Circulation (thousands)
Parade	$180,495	22,069
Family Weekly	96,225	12,350

Custom Inserts. In addition to ROP and preprinted magazine supplements, newspapers provide space for other preprints such as Spectacolor, Hi-Fi, and hard stock inserts. Spectacolor and Hi-Fi are high-fidelity rotogravure advertisements printed on glossy stock (as compared with typical newspaper stock). Spectacolor is printed in register: the advertisement conforms to the page size. Hi-Fi is printed like wallpaper, and cut randomly before insertion in the newspaper. The advertisements created for Hi-Fi, therefore, usually have a repeated pattern so no matter where the paper is cut, the essential ingredients in the advertisement will be on the page inserted into the newspaper. Not all newspapers have the capability of running Spectacolor and Hi-Fi; at present, Spectacolor can be run in newspapers covering 42 percent of U.S. households, while Hi-Fi's total coverage potential is 97 percent. Costs for these custom-tailored inserts must include production charges, since the advertiser provides these preprints directly. Here again, costs must be determined on a newspaper-by-newspaper basis, but it is well for the planner to know of their availability.

Radio Costs

Radio is offered both on a national network and individual local market spot basis.

Network Radio. Network radio programming available for advertiser sale includes news, music, sports, and drama. There are currently nine radio networks, each with a long list of affiliated stations: ABC Contemporary, ABC Entertainment, ABC-FM, ABC-Information, CBS, Mutual Broadcasting System, NBC, RKO, and Mutual Black Network.

Costs are comparatively low for a network radio announcement. The average network charges $2,400 for a 60-second announcement and delivers an average rating of 1.4 to men, 1.3 to women, and 0.7 to teenagers.

Spot Radio. Spot radio programming formats vary widely from market to market. In major markets, such as New York, Los Angeles, and Chicago, there are numerous radio formats appealing to a wide variety of listener interests. Programming ranges from talk shows to various kinds of music formats to total news. Generally, the multiplicity of radio stations in major markets provides something for nearly every listener.

As is the case with spot television, it is extremely difficult to generalize about costs because of the diversity of the medium. In overall terms, however, spot radio selectively purchased against designated target audiences can be an exceptionally cost-efficient medium for reaching these audiences.

Many station groups have developed and make available computerized reach and frequency programs that help planners measure the effect of different combinations of stations in delivering both gross impressions as well as reach and frequency estimates against selected audience segments.

Out-of-Home Media Costs

Out-of-home media come in a wide range of availabilities that differ dramatically in size and location. Out-of-home media are the most local of all media forms, inasmuch as one advertising unit can be purchased in one very specific location geographically. The more popular varieties of out-of-home media are the following.

Poster Panels. A *poster panel* is an outdoor advertising structure on which a preprinted advertisement is displayed. The most widely used poster sizes are: standard, junior, and 3-sheet. The *standard poster* measures approximately 10 feet high by 22 feet long, but dimensions vary from one location to another. The *junior panel* is about one-fourth the size of a standard poster. The *3-sheet poster* is about half the size of the junior panel.

Poster panels are generally sold in packages of Gross Rating Points. For example, a 100-GRP package will deliver in one day exposure opportunities equal to 100 percent of the population of the market. The cost for posters varies tremendously from one market to another, and often from one location to another in a given market. The cost to purchase a 100-GRP package for one month in standard posters in the top 10 markets of the U.S. is approximately $838,000. The same purchase encompassing the top 100 markets is about $2,294,000.

Painted Bulletins. A painted bulletin is an outdoor advertising structure that is painted with the advertising copy. Paints are generally larger than posters and measure, on average, 14 feet high by 48 feet wide. "Paints" are sold both individually and in packages. There are basically two types of paint availabilities: permanent and rotary. In the case of a *permanent paint*, the advertiser buys the specific location for one or more years and the units may vary in size. A permanent paint is usually bought for the specific location's desirability and is priced accordingly. *Rotary paints* are sold individually or in packages. The rotary bulletin is moved from location to location within a market on a set schedule (either 30-, 60-, or 90-day cycles, depending on the market).

The cost for one painted bulletin can range from as low as $500 in smaller markets to more than $3,000 in larger markets for an average month.

Transit. Transit advertising is available on buses, taxi cabs, trains, and in carrier terminals (train stations, airline terminals, etc.) in selected cities. There are numerous sizes and shapes that can be purchased, with advertising costs varying depending on the market, the medium, the size of the advertisement, the length of the purchase, and the scope of the purchase.

Media Buying Problems

As indicated earlier, audience delivery and cost estimating represent major considerations in the development of a media plan. Once the plan has been approved, then it becomes necessary to implement the budgeted effort in the most effective manner possible. Knowledge of how media sell their product is vital both for the development of the plan and its ultimate implementation. This section discusses some of the timing and buying implications associated with various media. Here again, as in the case with cost estimating, the major distinction rests between broadcast and print.

Network Television

One of the major problems the media planner and buyer of network television time must consider is timing. Incorrect timing and wrongly assessing when to buy can lead to severe implementation problems. For example, if the network buyer waits too long before committing the designated budget, all of the availabilities could be exhausted, thus leaving nothing to buy. Generally, the earlier the network buy is initiated, the more likely it is that desired programming in terms of audience delivery and stability will be obtained. The longer the buyer waits before committing to a buy for a specified period of time, the less likely it is that the most desirable programming will be available, but there is the possibility of lower pricing.

The planner must indicate to the network buyer exactly what is expected of the buy so as to ensure deliverability of the plan. For example, if the plan calls for 50 Gross Rating Points a week during the January-February-March quarter in three or four highly selective daytime network serials, the network buyer would do well to buy sooner rather than wait until just before the beginning of the quarter. The need to deliver a specific set of programs and desired weight level dictates an early purchase.

Network television time can be purchased in packages of shows or by individual program. Packages, which mean multiple programs with only a few commercials per program during the course of the schedule, provide maximum programming dispersion and thus tend to generate broader reach for the available budget. In addition, the risk of not delivering the specified weight levels is reduced, since the ultimate outcome of the buy is not based on any one or two individual programs achieving their audience levels. Conversely, networks make individual programs available for sale on a continuity basis. One or two individual shows with regular commercial appearances can be highly effective when the planner can identify specific audience values in those shows that achieve the objectives of the media plan.

Networks also have the flexibility to provide both short- and long-term time commitments. If time is available, network time can be purchased for specific days and time periods, perhaps to support a very short promotion. Such limited time purchases are generally called *short-term buys*. The networks also make available yearly buys that are designated *long-term buys*. The purchase of this time is not cancelable since there is a contractual obligation between the advertiser and the network for the specific commercial time purchased. Therefore, considerable care must be exercised to insure against overcommitting for network time.

In some cases, network regional time becomes available. A *regional network buy* is a situation when an advertiser buys only a portion of the country, with another advertiser buying the remainder. Regional network availabilities can be beneficial to the advertiser seeking certain types of programming identification. However, regional network time availabilities are very difficult to forecast and are, generally, secured only after considerable planning and discussions with the Network Sales Department.

Spot Television

There are 226 Designated Spot Television Markets with 984 television stations in the United States. The number of stations per market, which directly influences spot inventory, ranges from a high of 11 in Los Angeles to many markets with only one or two stations.

Major markets with multiple stations offer a considerable spot inventory from which to select. The multiplicity of spot commercial availabilities in such markets allows the buyer to be somewhat selective as far as programming and timing are concerned. Spot schedules are generally purchased two weeks to two months in advance of the start date of the schedule. Spot time can be bought for specified flight periods or on a continuing basis until canceled. Cancellation notice must be given two weeks prior to the end of a schedule.

Magazines

Once the planner has designated which magazines will carry the approved schedule, the plan implementation tends to be relatively mechanical. Most national publications accept space reservations guaranteeing that advertising space will be available in the desired issues. Space reservations can be made almost any time in advance of the issue. The final date for contracting to appear in a given issue is called the *closing date*, which varies by publication. Closing dates for monthly magazines will generally be 60 to 90 days in advance of issue. Closing dates for weekly publications normally fall about three to seven weeks prior to issue.

National magazines provide regional and test market circulation breakouts for achieving coverage in specified geographic areas. The regional availability can include multiple states or just a limited area such as New York City. The remainder of the circulation carries either another advertiser or editorial material. Magazines also make available test market circulation breakouts that conform closely to television market coverage patterns, thus permitting test translations of national plans into local test areas. Costs and availabilities of such special breakouts must normally be secured from the magazines prior to order since they are subject to change.

Many magazines also make available what are called A and B *copy splits*. This means two different blocks of copy can appear in alternate copies of the magazine in the same issue. These copy splits provide opportunities to test alternative copy approaches or they can be used by different brands when national coverage is desired and half of the circulation is considered adequate for each brand. Some magazines also make available demographic breakouts. Such demographic breaks might include space only in copies going to physicians, or businessmen, or some other breakout provided by the publication.

Media planners, in the course of continuing their education, should keep abreast of the flexibilities provided by the ever-changing publishing industry.

Newspapers

Space closing for ROP space is only a few days before the actual issue. If a special unit is desired, such as a two- or four-color half-page, then additional time in ordering such space is generally required. However, the advance notice time to the newspapers is still relatively short compared with the longer closing dates of national magazines.

Newspapers have been very aggressive in developing special sections geared to various audiences and issues. For example, many food advertisers look for what is called the Best Food Day. Best Food Day in most markets is Wednesday or Thursday, the days that major food chains schedule their advertising. The advertiser is positioned adjacent to the special editorial sections that the consumer is likely to read before going to market. Positions within these sections are generally available at no extra cost.

Other sections that can be advantageous in reaching selected audiences include sports, business, and special features on fashion, good grooming, and home care. In addition to such regular opportunities for positioning, newspapers offer availabilities for special preprints, such as Spectacolor, Hi-Fi, and hard stock inserts. In most cases, the advertiser provides the particular preprint to the newspaper. Such advertising units have to be ordered well in advance to ensure space availability.

Network Radio

Network radio programming tends to offer relatively few format types, such as news and sports and some special events. Network radio is purchased in the same way as network television, namely a contractual obligation for a specified number of commercials over a designated period of time.

Spot Radio

Spot radio provides different buying problems in view of the tremendous selectivity and diversity of programming and stations in many major markets. Rating information is available in most markets, but does not provide the total picture in buying radio. The number of men, women, and teenagers listening at various times to specific radio stations can be identified. However, the format, whether it be contemporary music, country western, stock market reports, music/weather, or sports, can be an important factor influencing station selection. The planner must rely heavily on the buyer's experience in executing a local market radio buy and ensuring a close match between the commercial copy, audience, and station format.

This chapter has examined the essential elements of media costs, accuracy, and related problems in implementing the media plan. There is a high degree of art in good media planning because the audiences of media and the pricing of advertising time/space are in a constant state of change. The professional media planner never stops inquiring and learning. The ability to form sound judgments about alternative media values requires intense concentration on the part of the planner. In the final analysis, those judgments are what distinguish a qualified media professional from a competent numbers manipulator.

QUESTIONS FOR DISCUSSION

1. Explain the main bases upon which broadcast and print media often set their prices.
2. What is the value of analyzing costs *after* a media plan has been implemented?

3. What is meant by the term "perishability of the inventory" in selling television broadcast time?

4. Why do print media costs tend to be more stable and less variable than broadcast media costs?

5. About how much more does it cost to print a four-color ad in newspapers than it does a black-and-white ad? Explain why color costs more.

6. How does the cost efficiency of radio (in general) compare with other media? Briefly explain why this is so.

7. Why would an advertiser want to buy a magazine that makes available A and B copy splits?

8. What is meant by the term "availabilities" in the sale of spot television time?

9. In planning for preprints such as Hi-Fi or Spectacolor, what costs other than typical space costs must be considered?

10. What are the advantages of buying network packages instead of buying time in a number of individual programs for commercials?

13

Setting and Allocating the Budget

One of the most difficult tasks facing advertising and agency planners is that of determining the optimum amount of money to spend for advertising. This is a problem that seems to defy solution despite the time and thought that have been given to attacking it. This amount is called the *appropriation* or the *budget*. We will use the latter term in this book. The main difficulty in determining the budget size is that no one knows precisely how a given amount of money spent for advertising will affect sales or other marketing goals. Media expert Herbert D. Maneloveg summarized the problem as follows:

> Our major problem, I believe, is that we really don't know how much advertising is enough. And we haven't done much about trying to find out. Not until lately. When someone asks about the amount of advertising pressure needed to make a potential consumer aware of the merits of a brand, we fumble and grope. When asked to justify an increase or decrease in advertising budget, we are lost because of an inability to articulate what would happen with the increase or decrease: if sales go up, we credit advertising; if sales go down, we blame pricing, distribution, and competition.[1]

In other words, there is no simple cause and effect relationship between the amount of money spent and the sales results that are supposed to occur because of the expenditure. Some manufacturers have been able

---

[1]Maneloveg, Herbert D., "How Much Advertising is Enough?" *Advertising Age*, June 6, 1966, p. 130.

to learn from experience how much money they should spend to obtain a desired share or sales volume at a given time. But even these manufacturers do not assume that the relationship will remain constant at all times. At some time or other, they and most other advertisers are in the same quandary about how much to spend on advertising.

What further complicates the matter is that each brand usually has a number of competitors whose changing activities make it difficult to anticipate correctly what they will do. The dynamic marketplace situation makes the task of budget setting—including having to estimate probable competitors' activities and allow a portion of money for contingencies—a difficult task for most advertisers.

Finally, advertising is not the only factor that contributes to the sale of a product. Other elements of the marketing mix, such as pricing, sales promotion, personal selling, and packaging, also play a role. But who can separate the precise contribution of advertising from the effects of the other marketing mix elements? Few, if any.

Despite these problems, advertising budgets must be established, and the task is performed based on as much knowledge as is available at the moment. This chapter outlines some of the major methods and problems of setting budgets, along with their advantages and disadvantages.

Setting the Budget

Ogilvy & Mather's Approach to Budgeting

The following, prepared by Ogilvy & Mather, is a brief introduction to the subject of advertising budgeting. It presents a frame of reference for thinking about budgeting and serves as a preparation for studying the various techniques of budgeting that follow.

> One of the most important and perplexing questions confronting advertisers is how much to spend on advertising. If too little is spent, the most brilliant campaign can fail. Conversely, if too much is spent on advertising, money will be wasted no matter how effective the campaign is.

> How much to spend on advertising is a strategic decision. The budget must be viewed as a function of the marketing and selling objectives of the brand or company. Modest budgets and ambitious goals are irreconcilable. Ambitious budgets for modest goals are inexcusable. One must clearly define the role of advertising and its task must be decided before settling on the budget.

> Until planners have positioned the advertising task, they cannot

apply the necessary discipline and available techniques to determine how much money is required.

Here are some factors to consider in determining an advertising/ spending strategy:

1. In what market will the brand compete?
    In the U.S., Mercedes-Benz decided to compete with the $10,000-plus luxury cars as well as luxury imports. This required an advertising budget many times greater. Had Mercedes decided to compete with the top-of-the-line Buicks, Chryslers, etc., even this budget would have been insufficient. Here are some points to remember:
    a. Expanding a market usually requires higher advertising expenditures than gaining competitive share. The reason? It is usually far more difficult to induce consumers to switch to or try another brand.
    b. The broader the market the brand competes in, the larger the advertising budget required. The reason? The brand must talk to more people and its competitive world is more diverse.
    c. Precise definition of a marketing target can save the advertiser money. For example, advertising just to children requires less expenditure than reaching children plus parents; reaching women only can be done more efficiently than reaching all adults.
2. What is the brand's current market position?
    When an advertiser has decided upon the market to compete in, the advertiser will know the product's relative strength compared with competitors. This will help define the planner's task. While all brands seek growth, the difficulty of achieving specific goals relates very importantly to a brand's position in a clearly defined market.
3. How does the advertiser evaluate the competition?
    In evaluating a brand's requirements versus competition, the planner should bear in mind that the market leader can usually retain business by spending relatively less than the brand rated second, third, or fourth. A low-rated brand must spend proportionately more to stay in business. To increase competitive position, a planner should be prepared to spend proportionately more than the brands he or she wants to overtake.
4. Where will the brand be advertised?
    Invariably, all brands have pockets of strengths and weaknesses across the country. Spending decisions must take

these variations into consideration. The same rate of spending in every city or region will not produce the same results. Determining local spending policies requires a great deal of marketing homework. It is not sufficient to simply know the share of market. The planner must try to determine why that share of market exists. Quite often, poor share areas are a result of distribution deficiencies, pricing policies, or sales force weaknesses. Knowing the whys will help the planner judge the contribution that can or cannot be made by advertising. This in turn will help the planner determine spending policies. So it is important to determine the importance and ability of advertising to effect sales change.

Traditional Methods of Setting Budgets

There are a number of widely used methods of determining the budget. Those used most often tend to be simple to understand and quick and easy to compute.

Percent-of-Sales. In the *percent-of-sales* method, an advertising budget is determined by multiplying projected sales revenue for the year by a given percentage. The amount of money available for advertising purposes, therefore, is based directly on the sales achievement of the brand. As sales increase, so does the advertising budget. But as sales decline, the budget also declines.

The heart of this method is the *multiplier*, the percentage by which the sales base is multiplied. In determining which percentage to use, one must consider the cost of goods and the pricing policy of each industry. If a brand costs 15 cents to manufacture and distribute and sells for $1.25, a considerable margin is available for advertising, promotion, and profit.

The first step in setting a budget based on percent of sales is to determine the expenses incurred in manufacturing and distribution. The difference between this cost and the selling price helps determine the margin available for advertising, promotion, and profit. (There are, of course, other costs to be factored in, such as overhead.) Smaller margins may mean a smaller percentage available for advertising.

The key to this method of setting budgets is that of finding the best multiplier. Many times this multiplier is determined arbitrarily. At other times, industry standards may be used as a base. (See Figure 13–1).

Textbooks that discuss the percent-of-sales method of budgeting often give the impression, however, that the method is totally inflexible. This is not true. Often the percent of sales may be only the starting point. After the percentage is multiplied by gross sales, the total may be adjusted to compensate for special marketing situations. When there are special marketing needs, extra dollars are added. Some companies, instead of adding to the total, will raise the multiplier when they are introducing a new product or when they are faced with very heavy competition. In some instances, however, the percentage multiplier remains constant year after year no matter how much sales may vary. When this happens, the multiplier tends to become a historical figure that is rarely questioned.

The multiplier is also affected by product pricing. Sales of low-ticket products such as drugs or supermarket items depend heavily on advertising, while high-ticket items such as appliances, cars, and home furnishings are less dependent on advertising. A rule of thumb for determining whether the multiplier should be large or small is that the more advertising is used as a substitute for personal selling, the higher the multiplier (or the higher the margin to advertising).

Among the advantages of this method are that it is easy to manage and easy to understand. It is self-correcting as sales volume changes, and it may maintain a consistent profit margin. It also is suitable for both financial and marketing group needs.

However, there are many criticisms of the percent-of-sales method. It may well be illogical because advertising is based on sales rather than the other way around. When sales decline, less advertising money will be spent when perhaps more money should be spent. Also, unless the advertising-to-sales ratios are analyzed by area, better sales areas will tend to get better and weaker sales areas will get little relief. This technique also assumes that there is a direct linear relationship between advertising and sales, which is not always true.

Another criticism of this method is that it does not encourage companies to provide the research money needed to find the relationship between advertising and sales. Marketing expert Alfred A. Kuehn offered this comment:

> Perhaps the best of these rules [methods of setting budgets] for an established brand is "budget a percentage of expected sales equal to the industry average." This rule is of particular interest since it is self-adjusting over time, and appears to be a low-risk policy for a firm which does not have a better understanding of the effects of advertising than does its competitors.[2]

On the other hand, if all competitive brands used this method and employed about the same percent multiplier, advertising budget sizes would be approximately proportional to market share, thus limiting investment spending for advertising warfare among competitors.

---

[2]Kuehn, Alfred A., "A Model for Budgeting Advertising," *Mathematical Models and Methods in Marketing*, Homewood, Ill.: Irwin Publishing Company, 1961, pp. 315–316.

FIGURE 13–1.

100 Leaders' Media Expenditures Compared in 1980
In measured media only, ad dollars in thousands

% of Total Dollars

	RANK	COMPANY	TOTAL	Network TV	Newspapers	Spot Radio	General Magazines	Network Radio	Farm Publications	Outdoor	Spot TV
Airlines	55	Trans World Corp.	$52,760.4	33.3	5.8	—	21.8	27.0	12.0	—	0.1
	59	UAL, Inc.	49,286.2	33.0	7.5	—	25.2	17.2	16.5	—	0.6
	71	American Airlines	42,105.2	41.5	9.7	—	26.0	2.5	19.0	—	1.3
	76	Eastern Air Lines	40,340.2	50.0	11.4	—	15.7	4.9	13.2	—	4.8
	87	Delta Air Lines	35,172.6	58.0	2.3	—	13.1	—	22.9	—	3.7
Appliances, TV, Radio	33	RCA Corp.	77,297.3	32.5	31.4	—	8.0	25.7	0.2	1.8	0.4
	35	General Electric Co.	74,296.3	16.3	22.1	—	11.3	44.4	1.9	3.7	0.3
Automobiles	4	General Motors Corp.	295,968.4	17.6	18.7	0.7	6.4	41.7	10.9	1.3	2.7
	6	Ford Motor Co.	247,310.5	9.9	14.5	1.0	12.8	50.8	7.9	2.3	0.8
	9	Chrysler Corp.	165,451.4	12.8	9.9	0.6	7.1	39.5	29.8	0.2	0.1
	34	Toyota Motor Sales	75,128.0	9.3	9.3	—	44.0	30.5	4.8	—	2.1
	49	Volkswagen of America	59,720.3	8.3	36.3	—	21.7	32.5	0.2	—	1.0
	53	Nissan Motor Corp.	54,365.7	12.6	13.6	—	28.3	33.4	10.8	—	1.3
	65	American Motors Corp.	45,896.3	4.5	21.4	—	34.7	38.6	0.7	—	0.1
	89	American Honda Motor Co.	34,910.7	9.1	30.5	1.2	3.7	44.8	7.5	0.9	2.3
	98	Mazda Motors of America	30,116.0	1.9	20.9	—	9.2	67.5	—	—	0.5
Chemicals	62	Union Carbide Corp.	47,831.1	7.3	3.2	5.4	8.8	66.4	8.0	—	0.9
	66	American Cyanamid	44,947.3	0.4	14.6	9.0	30.1	42.9	3.0	—	—
	70	DuPont	43,104.4	1.5	50.3	5.4	5.5	36.5	0.6	0.1	0.1
Communi-cations, Entertainment	26	Time, Inc.	86,773.5	12.6	41.0	—	35.0	10.1	0.4	0.8	0.1
	46	CBS, Inc.	63,493.5	23.6	47.0	—	13.8	8.2	0.2	5.4	1.8
	60	Warner Communications	49,104.5	3.5	7.9	—	19.0	64.0	4.9	0.1	0.6
	78	MCA, Inc.	40,142.9	17.7	4.1	—	24.6	39.8	12.2	0.9	0.7
	81	ABC, Inc.	37,931.1	31.5	47.5	—	13.0	—	0.5	5.4	2.1
	85	Columbia Pictures Industries	36,432.2	0.8	3.2	—	14.1	74.4	7.4	—	0.1
Drugs	28	Sterling Drug	83,517.4	0.5	13.9	0.2	6.5	68.8	2.0	8.0	0.1
	38	Richardson-Vicks	72,242.5	0.5	6.5	—	17.9	69.1	4.6	1.3	—
	50	Schering-Plough Corp.	59,108.4	0.4	19.0	0.5	9.4	59.6	2.1	6.7	2.3
	68	Miles Laboratories	44,116.5	0.1	4.6	—	12.5	81.2	0.4	—	1.2
	72	Squibb Corp.	41,807.6	1.0	9.2	0.7	9.3	60.8	3.1	15.9	—
	84	SmithKline	36,438.8	0.1	19.9	1.4	10.4	61.8	0.1	6.3	—
	90	A. H. Robins Co.	34,726.7	0.2	6.5	—	93.2	0.1	—	—	—
	96	Pfizer, Inc.	30,712.2	0.1	10.4	5.2	4.8	79.1	0.2	0.1	0.1
Food	2	General Foods Corp.	338,717.0	2.9	10.1	—	24.6	59.5	1.6	1.2	0.1
	10	General Mills	161,142.7	2.1	9.3	—	40.6	47.0	0.7	0.2	0.1
	14	McDonald's Corp.	130,862.1	—	1.8	—	54.0	41.0	0.7	0.1	2.4
	18	Dart & Kraft, Inc.	122,841.5	5.4	22.4	—	27.1	39.2	4.5	0.9	0.5
	21	Ralston Purina Co.	114,887.7	1.9	11.8	0.6	17.5	63.8	4.3	—	0.1
	24	Pillsbury Co.	96,895.1	3.2	5.3	—	32.9	55.0	2.9	0.3	0.4
	25	Kellogg Co.	90,486.2	4.6	4.9	—	21.0	66.1	2.8	0.6	—
	30	Consolidated Foods Co.	82,571.0	2.1	15.3	—	26.4	52.4	2.2	1.3	0.3
	36	Norton Simon, Inc.	73,264.2	7.5	23.6	—	27.1	36.5	1.8	0.4	3.1
	37	Nestle Enterprises	72,949.6	5.5	7.1	—	35.1	49.4	1.2	1.4	0.3
	41	Quaker Oats Co.	68,575.1	1.4	13.8	—	16.4	68.0	0.4	—	—
	44	Esmark, Inc.	65,819.1	3.2	13.9	—	14.2	64.6	1.9	2.1	0.1
	45	Nabisco, Inc.	63,923.4	2.1	15.0	—	20.8	61.2	0.9	—	—
	61	H. J. Heinz Co.	47,995.7	5.4	10.3	—	32.3	51.5	0.5	—	—
	63	MortonNorwich	46,895.2	3.6	6.8	—	15.3	66.5	0.2	7.4	0.2
	79	Campbell Soup Co.	39,997.5	7.0	18.2	—	23.6	41.0	2.8	7.3	0.1
	82	CPC International	37,429.9	1.8	13.8	—	32.4	51.3	—	—	0.7
	86	Borden, Inc.	35,820.7	5.0	12.4	0.5	21.6	49.0	6.7	4.4	0.4

% of Total Dollars

	RANK	COMPANY	TOTAL	Network T	Newspapers	Spot Radio	General Magazines	Network Radio	Farm Publications	Outdoor	Spot TV
Food (cont.)	94	Beatrice Foods Co.	31,493.3	8.1	13.5	3.0	46.8	17.0	9.4	1.8	0.4
	97	Standard Brands	30,137.4	12.7	18.1	—	35.3	19.7	12.7	—	1.5
	100	Carnation Co.	29,201.8	7.5	2.3	1.0	10.4	78.2	0.1	—	0.5
Gum, Candy	39	Mars, Inc.	70,290.5	4.0	0.4	—	42.0	52.2	1.1	0.3	—
	57	Wm. Wrigley Jr. Co.	51,143.5	1.1	1.2	—	26.4	66.7	1.7	2.9	—
	88	Hershey Foods Corp.	35,081.8	2.2	8.8	—	26.0	60.8	2.2	—	—
Photographic Equipment	52	Eastman Kodak	54,474.9	6.0	20.4	—	5.9	63.8	0.5	2.8	0.6
	83	Polaroid Corp.	37,194.9	2.5	13.8	—	2.4	80.2	—	1.1	—
Retail Chains	13	Sears, Roebuck & Co.	143,265.9	—	22.4	—	10.9	60.7	1.8	3.7	0.5
	67	K mart Corp.	44,311.0	—	22.4	—	41.7	11.4	19.3	4.9	0.3
	80	J. C. Penney	38,894.0	—	13.1	—	37.7	47.8	0.4	0.8	0.2
Soaps, Cleaners (and Allied)	1	Procter & Gamble	545,723.2	1.4	6.8	—	24.8	66.1	0.8	—	0.1
	16	Unilever U.S.	129,329.1	1.3	11.2	—	29.8	57.3	0.2	—	0.2
	32	Colgate-Palmolive Co.	79,336.1	2.6	9.0	0.2	29.8	50.5	7.8	—	0.1
	56	Clorox Co.	52,509.3	0.1	7.4	—	7.9	84.6	—	—	—
	75	S. C. Johnson & Son	40,411.6	3.6	24.5	—	8.5	57.7	2.6	2.4	0.7
Soft Drinks	11	PepsiCo, Inc.	160,869.9	1.1	1.8	—	36.0	55.2	5.4	—	0.5
	15	Coca-Cola, Inc.	129,481.7	4.2	3.1	—	36.9	44.7	7.7	1.1	2.3
Telephone Service, Equipment	7	American Telephone & Telegraph	180,665.6	10.6	19.1	—	28.1	31.8	6.7	3.3	0.4
	47	International Telephone & Telegraph	63,159.9	6.5	13.8	—	48.6	28.9	1.2	0.1	0.9
Tobacco	3	Philip Morris, Inc.	319,594.7	24.2	24.8	—	7.1	30.5	3.5	—	9.9
	5	R. J. Reynolds Industries	294,124.1	38.5	40.3	—	2.8	3.7	0.2	—	14.5
	31	B.A.T. Industries Ltd.	79,457.0	17.2	41.3	—	8.5	—	0.1	—	32.9
	40	American Brands	69,598.9	24.2	49.2	—	2.1	8.5	0.1	0.4	15.5
	95	Liggett Group	31,386.4	12.0	39.9	—	11.0	30.6	—	—	6.5
Toiletries, Cosmetics	8	American Home Products Corp.	180,288.2	0.8	5.2	0.3	20.2	68.7	2.9	1.9	—
	12	Bristol-Myers Co.	150,996.3	1.7	12.2	—	13.9	70.2	1.8	—	0.2
	19	Johnson & Johnson	120,409.1	4.2	15.3	0.2	4.1	75.1	0.5	0.6	—
	22	Loews Corp.	112,785.2	40.8	34.2	—	1.4	3.9	0.3	—	19.4
	23	Warner-Lambert Co.	98,202.0	2.9	5.8	—	21.7	64.3	0.1	5.0	0.2
	27	Gillette Co.	85,981.7	1.4	14.0	—	15.3	69.2	—	—	0.1
	42	Chesebrough-Pond's	68,428.7	2.8	16.6	—	8.8	71.7	0.1	—	—
	48	Revlon, Inc.	61,897.9	1.1	17.7	—	36.1	40.9	1.7	2.5	—
	54	Beecham Group Ltd.	54,364.5	0.1	8.9	0.9	10.0	80.0	0.1	—	—
	77	Noxell Corp.	40,193.2	0.3	22.4	—	7.4	69.8	0.1	—	—
	92	Jeffrey Martin, Inc.	33,408.1	0.4	0.7	—	34.1	42.5	—	22.3	—
Wine, Beer, Liquor	17	Anheuser-Busch	127,661.6	1.3	4.0	—	19.0	51.2	21.5	2.0	1.0
	20	Seagram Co.	117,339.9	15.4	60.2	—	4.6	9.6	0.3	—	9.9
	29	Heublein, Inc.	82,959.3	6.1	19.8	—	21.6	36.5	7.7	—	8.3
	58	Jos. Schlitz Brewing Co.	50,443.7	0.9	2.9	—	34.5	49.2	11.7	0.1	0.7
	93	Brown-Forman Distillers Co.	31,466.9	8.7	46.4	—	11.3	15.9	—	—	17.7
Miscellaneous	43	U.S. Government	67,862.1	10.7	27.6	1.1	8.4	27.4	18.7	4.8	1.3
	51	Mobil Corp.	55,377.1	10.7	5.0	3.5	59.8	15.6	5.2	—	0.2
	64	Gulf & Western Industries	46,114.1	7.0	12.3	—	27.0	49.2	3.2	0.9	0.4
	69	Greyhound Corp.	43,732.5	5.1	7.1	—	21.7	55.2	5.8	5.1	—
	73	American Express Co.	41,578.8	6.7	14.8	—	27.3	45.0	3.9	2.2	0.1
	74	Kimberly-Clark Corp.	40,527.9	3.8	22.7	—	24.4	44.7	0.8	3.6	—
	91	Mattel, Inc.	33,563.9	3.7	6.2	—	46.2	43.4	0.1	—	0.4
	99	Levi Strauss & Co.	29,947.2	1.0	13.2	—	15.7	50.0	18.9	1.2	—

Source: *Advertising Age*, Sept. 10, 1981, p. 8.

Competitive Spending. The *competitive spending* method depends on setting the budget in relation to the amount of competitive spending. The amount to be spent need not be precisely the same as that of competitors, though at times it is. At times, a brand that has a smaller market share than its competitor may be given an amount equal to or greater than the competitor, as a means of improving the share position.

A major criticism of this approach is that it assumes that competitors know what they are doing or that competitors' goals are the same as one's own. It also assumes, incorrectly, that a simple increase in advertising expenditures will automatically increase sales and/or market share. The products of competitors may be different, or at least consumers may perceive them as different, so that a company's advertising may have to work much harder to make sales than competitors' advertising. Certainly, the marketing goals of one company are not the same as another, and the ability of advertising to create sales also is not the same.

Objective and Task. The *objective and task* method starts with someone setting specific marketing and/or advertising objectives that are then costed out. The total cost represents the budget. Objectives may be sales, share volume levels, revenues expected, income, or profit.

There are two main criticisms of this method. First, it is not always possible to determine how much money it takes to attain any given objective. Second, the method does not consider the value of each objective and the relationship to the cost of obtaining it. Is it really worth all of the money necessary to achieve any given objective?

Expenditure Per Unit (Case-Rate). This system is a variant of the percent-of-sales method. In the *case-rate* method, the budget is generated as a result of sales, but units sold, not dollar sales, are used as the base. Many of the same advantages and disadvantages of the percent-of-sales method apply also to this method. However, there are two additional disadvantages:

1. Unless the method is properly handled, there is a possibility that the control of profits may be lost. This is particularly true if the product or brand has a wide range of sizes or prices. Shell Oil Company, for example, has four types of gasoline ranging from Super-Regular (premium price) to Regular (lowest price). Profitability varies for each. Spending on a cents-per-gallon basis must take into consideration the mix of the line.
2. Working with units and fixed rates of expenditures will not take inflation into account. To overcome this, the case rate must be adjusted from year to year.

Subjective Budgeting. These budgeting systems involve decisions made on a subjective basis. Essentially, the executive whose responsibility it is to determine the budget size uses experience and judgment as a basis for decisions. This is not to say that such executives would not consider some objective factors as well, such as first determining the minimum job that advertising will be required to do, or perhaps considering available profit margins as a basis. But after such considerations, the final figure is decided upon rather subjectively.

One subjective budgeting method is known as "All We Can Afford." While at first glance, this approach may seem illogical or crude, it may be quite realistic if the subjective decision is accurate. On the other hand, a budget made on such a basis is hard to defend, especially when there is reason to believe that if more money were appropriated, the result would be higher sales and higher profits.

Newer Methods of Setting Budgets

Experimental Methods. A number of marketing and advertising professionals feel that the best way to determine the size of an advertising budget is by testing various levels of expenditures to see which will produce the most sales at the lowest total cost. The experimental designs for this purpose may range from a simple before-and-after test in one market to elaborate designs where many markets are tested and compared with control markets. Although the details of such experiments are usually kept secret, occasionally some are publicized.[3, 4]

Essentially, experimental tests involve trying different advertising expenditure levels in different markets. In one example, Anheuser-Busch used three sets of markets (each set consisting of nine individual markets) to test alternative expenditure levels and measure the effects on sales. In one set of markets, advertising expenditures were reduced from 50 percent to 100 percent below the level that ordinarily would have been used in those markets. In another group of markets, the budget was increased by 50 percent to perhaps as much as 300 percent. A third group of markets were control markets where there was no increase or decrease in normal advertising expenditures to provide a base of comparison with the other market groups.

In some experimental situations, advertisers discover that they can reduce advertising expenditures without any effect on sales. In other situations, increases in advertising produce varying degrees of sales increases.

---

[3]McNiven, Malcolm A., "Choosing the Most Profitable Level of Advertising," a case study in *How Much to Spend for Advertising*, Association of National Advertisers, Inc., 1969.

[4]Newell, Thomas M., "What is the Right Amount to Spend for Advertising?" in *Papers from the 1968 American Association of Advertising Agencies Regional Convention*, Palm Springs, California, Oct. 6–9, 1968.

If the experimental method is indeed as effective as some individuals assume it to be, why then is it not used more often to determine budget size? There are a number of reasons. George H. Brown, former director of the U.S. Census Bureau and a marketing expert, cited two problems involved with this method. The first is the relatively high cost of conducting the experiment, which involves finding and measuring a fairly large sample. The second problem is the long time span, perhaps a year or more, that is required. By the time the experiment is completed, the marketing situation may have changed, making the final figures irrelevant. Brown also pointed out that, while the cost may not be considered too high if the payoff is accurate and valuable, the payoff may not be worth the cost.

At present, not many companies use the experimental method, though some who have used it are quite content with it. Unfortunately, most of these companies have not revealed the details of their methods so that no outside evaluation is possible.

The Hendry Method. The detailed mathematical description of this method is not publicly known because companies that want to use it must pay the Hendry Corporation for the privilege. However, some of the essential ideas have been made public. Stanley D. Canter, former senior vice president of Ogilvy & Mather, explained some of these ideas in a speech given to the Association of National Advertisers.[5]

When making a purchase, consumers tend to buy the products and brands they have purchased in the past. But their decision to buy based on past preference contains a degree of uncertainty. The nature of this uncertainty has not been explained, although it can be assumed that consumers may perceive buying as a risk and wish to minimize such risks. This uncertainty represents an opportunity to change purchase habits.

Canter noted: "The degree of uncertainty is a marketing analogy to the properties of entropy in statistical mechanics. In marketing it becomes a measure of brand switching." Therefore, the degree of entropy may be considered the degree of probability that consumers will switch brands.

The relationship between consumers' preferences and their uncertainties can sometimes be shifted one way or another by various marketing strategies, one of which is advertising. However, other marketing strategies—price, distribution, and personal selling—may also play a role in influencing buying.

The additional share of market gained by a given brand due to adver-

---

[5]Canter, Stanley D., "Exposition of the Hendry Advertising Analysis Model," presented at the Association of National Advertisers Workshop on Media Planning, New York, Sept. 30, 1971.

tising is equal to the share of advertising weighted by differences in the effectiveness, multiplied by the entropy of the brand. Figure 13–2 illustrates this.

If the probability of brand switching is zero, then advertising would have no effect on that brand's share of market, and its market share would be due entirely to factors other than advertising. "But as the probability of brand switching increases, the opportunity for advertising to work increases, and a greater proportion of a brand's share of market may be attributable to advertising," noted Canter.

As advertising is increased, profits may also increase to a maximum point beyond which profits will decline. Therefore it is important to look at the relationship between advertising, profits, and market share simultaneously, as shown in Figure 13–3. In this figure, advertising expenditures, profits, and market share are input data that are used for calibration purposes to help position the brand under current marketing conditions on a specific curve, out of a general family of curves describing a generalized relationship between the three variables. That curve is called the *profit profile*. Using the profit profile curve, the marketer can experiment to see how alternative advertising expenditures will affect potential market shares and/or profits. How one determines this curve, however, has not been explained publicly.

When a company comes to Hendry, the first step in determining the advertising budget size is to calibrate the three variables. The third variable may be direct advertising margins (gross sales minus the cost of producing the product).

Once this calibration has been made, Hendry, through its formulas and computer analysis, can then show the relationship between advertising expenditures and market share or profit for that brand. Hendry can

FIGURE 13–2. The Concept of the Hendry Method

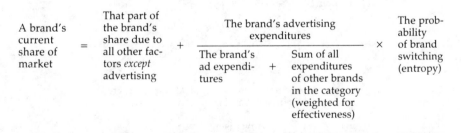

Source: Canter, Stanley D., *Exposition of the Hendry Advertising Analysis Model*, Association of National Advertisers Workshop on Media Planning, New York, Sept. 30, 1971, p. 2.

also show what share of market and profits would result if the advertising level for a brand were increased or decreased. Allocations can be made by sales territories, and a client can learn how much to spend for new product introductions, or what impact advertising expenditures will have upon competitors' profits and share of advertising. Although the details of this method are not known, it is known that some large companies that have used the method have found it successful.

Andrew Kershaw, former chairman of the board of Ogilvy & Mather, has reported some findings using Hendry methods in about 40 different analyses.

1. Advertising always makes a measurable contribution to share of market. On the average, one-quarter of market share points of a brand is attributable to advertising. Some brands depend entirely on advertising, but other brands' advertising contributes much less to share.
2. For every brand, there is a point where additional media expenditures do not result in an increase in market share. While some brands have spent more money than needed, others are getting less than 50 percent of the share they could attain if they spent more for advertising.

FIGURE 13–3. Relationship Between Expenditures, Market Share, and Profit

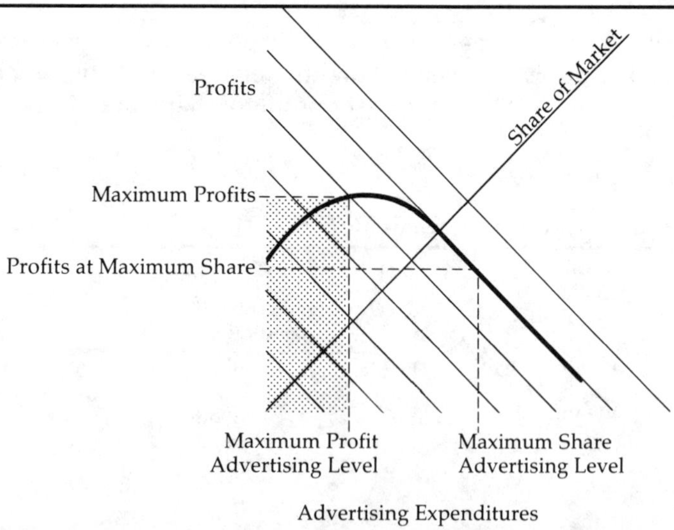

Source: Kershaw, Andrew, "How to Use Our Media Dollars As A More Effective Marketing Tool," Association of National Advertisers Workshop on Media Planning, Sept. 30, 1971, p. 10.

3. Maximum share of market never results in maximum profits. There is evidence that the advertising expenditures that yield maximum share of market do not maximize profits, so the rule would be to spend less than needed to achieve maximum share.
4. Many companies choose to advertise at less than maximum profits. Figure 13–4 shows that 56.5% of brands studied advertise at a budget level that results in maximum profits. More than 4 out of 10 brands spend too little or too much money in advertising to achieve profit maximization.
5. Some product categories spend too much on advertising.
6. Some market definitions based on consumer usage are too narrow and the brand finds itself with a lower market share. This in turn may require more money to be spent to hold or increase market share.
7. It may be far more efficient to adopt a corporate media expenditure policy rather than a brand-oriented one. . . . Thus it is possible to shift media funds from one brand with a lower marginal advertising productivity to another brand with a higher rate of productivity.[6]

FIGURE 13–4. **Proportion of Brands Advertising Below, At, or Above Level that Results in Profit Maximization**

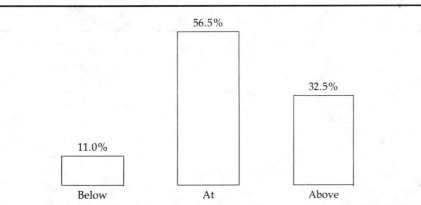

Source: Kershaw, Andrew, "How to Use Our Media Dollars as a More Effective Marketing Tool," Association of National Advertisers Workshop on Media Planning, Sept. 30, 1971, p. 10.

---

[6]Kershaw, Andrew, "How to Use Our Media Dollars as a More Effective Marketing Tool," speech given to the Association of National Advertisers Workshop on Media Planning, New York, Sept. 30, 1971.

Theoretical Methods. An increasing number of theoretical budgeting methods have been discussed in journals of marketing and/or business. Most are based on rather complex mathematical formulas and none have found continuing acceptance in the everyday world of advertising and marketing. This text is not the appropriate place to discuss the alternative theoretical methods, but the reader who wants to know more about them should consult the Selected Readings at the end of this chapter.

Which Methods Are Used Most Often?

Table 13–1, compiled by Andre J. San Augustine and William Foley, gives some indication of the prevalence of methods currently in use.

Factors in Determining the Size of an Advertising Budget

While it may not be possible to determine a budget size scientifically, it may be advisable to approach the task by weighting a number of factors that might affect the budget size. Setting a budget in this manner might be called "atomistic" in that one could think about each factor separately (like a collection of atoms), then assemble these factors into a final budget figure.

In weighting each factor, some will be found to be more important than others, suggesting that priorities for marketing the brand must be determined first. Furthermore, each factor must be judged on the basis of whether one should spend more than, the same as, or less than the

TABLE 13–1. Methods 100 Executives Use to Set Advertising Budgets*

Methods	Consumer Product Companies: Averages (%)	Rank	Nonconsumer Product Companies: Averages (%)	Rank
Percent of anticipated sales	50	1	28	2
All that is affordable	30	2	26	3
Others (not specified)	26	3	10	5
Percent of past years' sales	14	4	16	4
Arbitrary approach	12	5	34	1
Unit anticipated sales	8	6	10	5
Objective and task	6	7	10	5
Unit past years' sales	6	7	4	6
Quantitative models	2	8	0	7
Don't know	2	–	2	–
Total†	156		140	

* Sample consisted of two executives from each of 25 nonconsumer product companies, and 25 consumer product companies. One was a financial executive and the other an advertising executive. The averages are of two percentages representing two executives per company.
†Adds to over 100 percent because of multiple responses

Source: San Augustine, A. J., and Foley, W. F., "How Large Advertisers Set Their Budgets," *Journal of Advertising Research*, October 1975, p. 12.

previous year. Again this is a subjective decision, but it may help the executive arrive at a final figure more easily.

A brief discussion of these factors follows:

Assessing the Task of Advertising. Before deciding on any figure, it is reasonable to determine what role advertising is to play. Must it do the selling job alone, or will it be added to other marketing mix elements such as reduced prices and sales promotion? If advertising must do the selling job alone, the size of the budget may have to be substantial. If it works with other marketing mix elements, the size of the budget may be less.

Important in this consideration is an understanding of the power of advertising to sell the brand. Some brands simply are not sensitive to advertising; perhaps because they are so much like other brands on the market, because they do not have a unique selling proposition, or because it is difficult to be creative in presenting the message through print or broadcast media.

Long- and Short-Term Goals. To some extent advertising may have long- and short-term goals set for it, but when the objective is to build an image, then the budget should be treated as an investment rather than an expense (as one would treat the budget for short-term goals). If both goals are required at the same time, then more money may be required because advertising has been given a dual function. The advertising copy for immediate sales may differ markedly from the copy whose goal is to build an image.

In a sense, however, the concept of dividing an advertising budget into an expense for immediate sales and an investment for long-term image building may be invalid. The reason is that image-building advertising may not consist of special ads that are designed for that purpose. If the brand image is thought of as a "long-term investment in the reputation of a brand," then every ad that is run, no matter whether it opts for immediate or future image, contributes to the long-range goal.

The goals of the company and advertising's relationship with them, then, affect to some degree the amount of money to be spent. Companies may perceive this relationship somewhat differently, so no general principle can be extracted.

Profit Margins Affect Budget Size. There is an assumption in the industry that where there are larger profit margins there will be larger advertising budgets, and the converse is also assumed to be true. Profit margins may be a limiting factor in setting marketing and/or advertising goals—what one would like to do cannot be done simply because there isn't enough money available to do it. It may be ironic that when profit margins must be increased, advertising expenditures also should be increased, but there is little or no money available to do the job.

Degree of Product Usage. Products that are used widely throughout the country may require more money for advertising than those whose usage is limited to a relatively small geographic area. However, some local and regional advertisers may find it necessary to invest heavily in their marketing area due to heavy competitive spending, e.g., fast-food firms and automobile dealers.

Difficulty in Reaching Target Markets. Some markets are so unique that no single medium reaches them well, such as the market for expensive yachts. A number of different media may have to be purchased, requiring more money. Many times, targets are so spread out geographically that mass media may have to be purchased, resulting in enormous message waste. When this occurs, more money is needed to do a reasonable job.

Frequency of Purchase. It is assumed that brands and/or products purchased frequently will require more money for advertising than those that are purchased infrequently. However, an exception occurs when the advertising goals of infrequently purchased brands are such that they require more money to be spent for other reasons than frequency of purchase.

Effect of Increased Sales Volume on Production Costs. If there is a danger of demand exceeding supply because of advertising's power, the consequence may be that a new plant must be built. In that situation, the amount of money spent for advertising may have to be limited until the factory is built or a decision is made to the contrary. The advertiser may want to reduce advertising expenditures for awhile until it is possible to supply the demand.

New Product Introductions. It is widely held that new product introductions take a great deal of additional money to break into the market. How much more depends on the size of the market, the degree of competition, and the desirable qualities of the new brand. A rule of thumb is that it takes at least one-and-a-half times as much as is spent on established brands to introduce the new brand.

Competitive Activity. In markets where competitors are very active in advertising and sales promotion, it may be necessary to match, or even exceed, their expenditures, depending on the marketing goals of the brand in question. While the preceding factors do not indicate exactly how much to spend on advertising, they do serve as decision-making guidelines.

Allocating the Advertising Budget

Once the size of the advertising budget has been determined, then it must be allocated, or apportioned, in some reasonable way. When relating advertising to source of sales, advertising budgets are allocated to geographic areas. Many advertisers, however, particularly on a national level, allocate their budgets on the basis of national media selection with relatively little concern for geographical business skews.

Geographic Allocations

Perhaps the most often used budget allocation technique is to allot at least equal portions to the amount of sales produced by a geographical area. The reasoning behind this method is that one takes a minimal risk in allocating the most dollars to areas where sales are known to have been good. If previous budgets were successful in producing or at least contributing to sales, why would not more money (or an equal amount relative to sales) be equally effective? The concept is not only to keep the risk low, but to optimize whatever monies are available.

If a geographical area contributed 15 percent of total sales, then it may be assumed that it would get 15 percent of the budget. Of course, there may be a problem here. It is possible that it took much more than 15 percent of the previous year's allocation to produce 15 percent sales. In such a case, a different method of allocation could be used, one based on the amount of profit produced by the area in proportion to total profit nationwide. Allocating on the basis of profit is simply another method of distributing effort.

Other methods could be based on the market share contributed by each area, the anticipated sales produced by each area, or some index number that would be a composite of a number of marketing variables, such as population, income, retail sales of the product class, plus other related variables.

In practice, formula methods of allocating budgets tend to be only the starting point, rather than the endpoint, of the allocating procedure. Adjustments usually have to be made to take into consideration special marketing problems. One such problem could be that the media in a particular area may cost much more, proportionally, than in any other part of the country. More money may have to be added to the initial allocation figure to compensate for this problem. Another problem could be that competitors have started to promote more heavily in areas that have been most profitable for the brand in question. Again special adjustments will have to be made to the original allocation.

Media Allocations

A budget allocated by geographic sales territories may not be sufficient to put a marketing/advertising plan into operation—a further allocation may have to be made to media. In fact, one could dispense with allocations to areas and start with allocations to media that reach demographic targets no matter where they are located geographically. Following is a simulated example of how a budget might be allocated to both area and media.

For purposes of illustration, assume that a manufacturer sells a product in five geographic areas of the country. Sales percentages for each of the five areas are shown in Table 13–2, as is a proportional allocation of the budget to each sales area. Also shown is the percentage of network television delivery in each sales area.

Table 13–2 shows that each area received a proportional amount of dollars equal to the percentage of sales made in the area. However, a close look at the relationship of sales and network delivery percentages shows some anomalies. For example, Area A delivered 30 percent of total sales but has only 25 percent of total network delivery. As a result, it may be necessary to allocate some of the budget to local television.

The problem that arises is how to divide the television budget between network and spot so that each area receives an equitable portion of the budget. Ideally, a planner would like the percentage of network television delivery to match sales percentages in each market. Therefore, if a market provides 20 percent of total U.S. sales, then it should receive 20 percent of the budget. Unfortunately, when advertisers use network television, the delivery in some markets is more than needed, while the delivery in other markets is less than needed.

For example, if sales in Market A are 30 percent and the percentage of total U.S. network program delivery is 20 percent, then some way must be found to bring television delivery up to the 30 percent level. This may be done by adding a certain amount of dollars to local spot television. However, if a market accounts for 10 percent of sales and network television delivery is 20 percent of the U.S. total, one cannot easily cut network, market by market. So a technique has been created to take dollars from network television in certain markets and add them to spot television to bring each market up to a percentage equal to its sales.

TABLE 13–2. A Budget Allocated Proportionately to Sales Made by Each Area

Sales Area	Sales Made by Each Area (%)	Budget Goal	Network Delivery* (%)
A	30	$1,500,000	25
B	15	750,000	15
C	10	500,000	20
D	10	500,000	10
E	35	1,750,000	30
Total	100	$5,000,000	100

*Delivery is based on a number of selected network programs that cover targets.

Source: J. Walter Thompson Company, *Allocating Advertising Weight Geographically*, 1973, p. 9.

The technique, outlined step-by-step here, applies to Table 13–3 in particular. The total U.S. budget was set earlier at $5,000,000.

1. The planner should first calculate a budget for each individual market by multiplying the total budget by each market's sales percentage. In Table 13–3, Market A accounted for 30 percent of total sales, so it received 30 percent of the $5,000,000 budget, or $1,500,000.
2. Now the market in which network television is most over-delivered must be found. This can be done by calculating an index number relating sales percentage to network television delivery percentage in each market. The market with the largest index number is most over-delivered. Here is the formula:

$$\text{Index} = \frac{\text{Percentage of network delivery in a market}}{\text{Percentage of sales in the same market}} \times 100$$

3. Using the market with the largest index number as a base (Market C, with a 200 index), divide the total budget by the percentage of television targets delivered in that market. Example: $5,000,000 ÷ .20 = $2,500,000. This represents a revised total network budget, based on the most over-delivered market.
4. Subtract the network budget from the total budget to find the total spent in spot television; in this example, $2,500,000.
5. Multiply the network delivery percentage for each market by the new total budget for network television. Thus, for Market A: .25 x $2,500,000; for Market B: .15 x $2,500,000, etc.
6. To find the spot television budget for each market, subtract the network allocation in each market from the original total budget in each market. Thus, Market A: $1,500,000 − $625,000 = $875,000, for spot television; Market B: $750,000 − $375,000 = $375,000 for spot. Note that Market C receives no spot dollars, because it did not need additional television delivery.

Payout Planning

The Concept. Another kind of budgeting operation that media planners may be involved with is called payout planning. A *payout plan* is a budget used in new product introductions where more money than usual is needed to launch a brand. The extra dollars come not only from the sales made by the brand, but also from allocating the brand's profits to advertising, for a limited time.

The following data may be helpful in explaining the situation before

TABLE 13–3. Allocation of Budget to Network and Spot TV

Sales Area	Sales Made by Each Area (%)	Budget Goal	Total Network Delivery (%)	Index: Network to Sales Delivery	Network Budget	Spot TV (Local) Budget
A	30	$1,500,000	25	83	$ 625,000	$ 875,000
B	15	750,000	15	100	375,000	375,000
C	10	500,000	20	200	500,000	—
D	10	500,000	10	100	250,000	250,000
E	35	1,750,000	30	86	750,000	1,000,000
Total	100	$5,000,000	100		$2,500,000	$2,500,000

Source: J. Walter Thompson Company, *Allocating Advertising Weight Geographically*, 1973, p. 9.

studying the formal portions of a payout plan. A new brand may have the following costs and pricing:

	Per case
Selling price of brand by factory	$12.00
Costs of manufacturing, overhead, and selling the brand	7.00
Amount available for promotion and profit	$ 5.00
Normal amount available for promotion	$ 2.50
Normal amount available for profit	2.50
Full amount available for introducing the new brand: promotion + profit	$ 5.00

So, in new product introductions, the manufacturer may be willing to forego profits for a limited time and invest them in advertising, in addition to the usual advertising investment. This practice of investing both promotion and profit funds is called *full available*.

What is important to understand about this investment is that in the very first months, the brand does not earn enough money to pay for the extra heavy advertising investments that it needs. Therefore, the company, in a sense, invests money (or pays out of its own pocket) to the brand during the early periods of selling. But, as the brand begins to sell more and earn more money, it begins to be in a position to start paying back the investment that the company made. Finally, if everything goes well, the brand will be selling enough of the product to pay back the entire investment and stand on its own as a profit center. When that happens, the full available is divided so that part goes for profits and a portion for advertising.

Explanation of a Payout Plan. Following is an explanation of the payout plan shown in Table 13–4. Each paragraph is keyed to the number at the beginning of each row on the plan. Although payout plans are not generally calculated by media planning personnel, the media planner should be aware of the mechanics insofar as they bear on the final advertising budget.

    1. Time periods. While three time periods are shown on the payout plan, more or fewer could have been used. Furthermore, these time periods could have varied from one to three years in length, or they could have been one to three six-month periods. The timing, therefore, is a matter of judgment and experience on the part of the planner who must estimate how long it will take to pay back the money necessary to get the brand launched in the marketplace.

    2. Size of total market in millions (MM) of cases. A market may be described in any way most suitable to the advertiser. Some prefer to use cases. Others use pounds of the product, packages, or dollars. The data for the number of cases that will be sold is an estimate, based on trend analysis, modified by the judgment and experience of the advertising executive. If these estimates are wrong, then the payout plan will have to be adjusted accordingly.

    3. Average share for the brand. As a new product is introduced and begins to be purchased by wholesalers, retailers, and consumers, it is obvious that the share of market could vary considerably from month to month. So this percentage rep-

TABLE 13–4. A Three-Period Payout Plan

(1) Time periods	Period 1	Period 2	Period 3	Total
(2) Size of total market in millions of cases	10	11	12	
(3) Average share for the brand	12%	18%	25%	
(4) Year-end total share for the brand	15%	25%	25%	
(5) Cases (millions) purchased by pipeline	0.4	0.2	0.1	
(6) Cases (millions) purchased at consumer level	1.2	2.0	3.0	
(7) Total shipments from factory (millions of cases)	1.6	2.2	3.1	
(8) Factory income @ $12 a case*	$19.2	$26.4	$37.2	
(9) Less cost @ $7 a case	$11.2	$15.4	$21.7	
(10) The budget (dollars available for promotion and profit)	$ 8.0	$11.0	$15.5	$34.5
(11) Reallocation of budget to place heavier weight in first period	$14.9	$11.7	$ 7.9	$34.5
(12) Percent of reallocated budget	43%	34%	23%	100%
(13) Allocation of budget to advertising and sales promotion				
To advertising (85%)	$12.7	$ 9.9	$ 6.7	$29.3
To sales promotion (15%)	$ 2.2	$ 1.8	$ 1.2	$ 5.2
Total	$14.9	$11.7	$ 7.9	$34.5
(14) Profit (or loss)	($ 6.9)	($ 0.7)	$ 7.6	—
(15) Cumulative investment	($ 6.9)	($ 7.6)	0	—

*All dollar figures are in millions. Thus 19.2 = $19,200,000.

resents the average for the year rather than the total. Either could have been used, but the more modest percentage is probably safer. Again, this is a crucial estimate which, if incorrect, would require the plan to be adjusted immediately.

4. Year-end total share for the brand. This figure is shown only as a guide to what the executive hopes to achieve at year end. It is not used in the calculations, though it could be substituted for average share, as previously mentioned.

5. Cases purchased by pipeline. The first factory sales could be to pipeline companies such as wholesalers and distributors (depending on how the product is distributed). This group of companies represents a portion of total sales. The amount in the pipeline at any time can be estimated from past experience with similar types of products.

6. Cases purchased at the consumer level. This figure is calculated by multiplying the average share expected times the number of cases expected to be sold in the total market: $(10,000,000 \times 12\% = 1,200,000 \text{ cases})$.

7. Total shipments from factory. Pipeline and consumer purchases are added here: $(400,000 + 1,200,000 = 1,600,000 \text{ cases for Period 1})$.

8. Factory income @ $12 a case. Since the decision was to price a case at $12 each, then this figure is multiplied by the number of cases expected to be sold for each period: (Period 1: $1,600,000 \text{ cases} \times \$12 \text{ a case} = \$19,200,000 \text{ income})$.

9. Less cost of $7 a case. Here $7 (the total manufacturing cost) was multiplied by the estimated number of cases that will be sold: (Period 1: $1,600,000 \times \$7 = \$11,200,000 \text{ cost})$.

10. The budget. Since the budget is composed of dollars allocated both for promotion and for profit (or full available) it is necessary only to subtract the cost of cases sold per period from the selling price to learn what amount of money is available for promotion: (Period 1: $\$19,200,000 - \$11,200,000 = \$8,000,000$). The term promotion as used here does not mean sales promotion, but more broadly, advertising and sales promotion. As a result of the subtraction in each period, there is a given amount of money available in each, which when added together equals $34,500,000.

11. Reallocation of budget. Although $34,500,000 would be available for advertising and sales promotion, the budget as it is shown in paragraph (10) is allocated in a strict mathematical fashion, rather than with an understanding of advertising investment needs. Most of the budget occurs in the third period. On the other hand, most of the money is needed in the first period, where extra heavy expenditures usually

are needed to launch the brand.

12. Percent budget. So the executive has reallocated the budget total ($34,500,000) in the manner felt necessary. As a result, the executive allocated 43 percent of the $34,500,000 to the first period instead of the 23.2 percent that would have been available if the budget were accepted as shown in paragraph 10: ($8,000,000 ÷ $34,500,000 = 23.2%).

13. Allocation of the budget to advertising and sales promotion. This is an arbitrary allocation based on what the executive thinks is needed for each. Some other executive with a different marketing situation and product might think the proportions should be different.

14. Profit or loss. At this point, an investment in the brand must be made. Since the amount of money available for promotion in Period 1 is only $8,000,000 (paragraph 10) and dollars needed for the same period are $14,900,000 (paragraph 11), it will be necessary for the company to invest an additional $6,900,000, which represents a loss for the brand for Period 1. The brand now owes the company $6,900,000 for Period 1.

In Period 2, again the reallocated budget is more than the brand would earn for that period, $11,700,000 vs. $11,000,000. Again the brand loses money; only this time not so much: $700,000. If this amount is added to the amount already owed to the company from Period 1, the cumulative total for period 2 is now $7,600,000. This means that the company has to give the brand $7,600,000 for the extra amount needed above sales dollars up to the end of Period 2.

However, in Period 3, the brand earns enough money ($7,600,000) to pay back the amount given to it by the company. At this point it has made a profit, paid back the money given to it by the company, and presumably will make a profit to keep it going in Period 4. When the brand makes a profit, it *pays out* money to the company. Not shown in this example, but what obviously should be included in real situations, is the inflation factor. Money "loaned" to a brand in year 1 is worth more than face value in succeeding years.

Conclusion

Although media planners have begun to use more scientific tools in budgeting, many areas still require judgment. The area of planning that most seems to defy solution is how to determine the optimum size of an advertising budget. Methods described in this chapter have been used for many years. Though they are considered relatively crude, they are easy and quick to compute, and for that reason they have maintained their popularity over many years. Allocation techniques, on the other hand, can be characterized as logical and reasonable. Some involve decisions based on subjective judgments of what will happen in the marketplace, as the payout plan indicates. But in any case, allocation procedures are more advanced than previous budget-setting methods have been. Perhaps the greatest advances have come in theoretical model building on the relationship between advertising, sales, and share of market. None of these have found their way into everyday use, though the Hendry method may be the one most operational at this time.

QUESTIONS FOR DISCUSSION

1. What is the difference between setting a budget and allocating it?
2. Why is it so difficult to devise an advertising budget using scientific methods?
3. Why is the percent-of-sales method probably the most widely used method of budgeting, considering the fact that it has many limitations?
4. Discuss the question of whether a company that wants larger profit margins should increase or decrease its advertising budget.
5. Often markets are assigned proportions of budgets in direct relation to the amount of sales or market share they produce. Under what conditions might this practice not be advisable?
6. While the objective and task method of budgeting is often considered to be one of the best methods, what limitations does it have?
7. What is the underlying concept of a payout plan?
8. Discuss the question of whether a planner with the third-rated brand on the market ought to copy competitors' budgets.
9. Where, in a payout plan, is it possible to make a judgmental error that could affect the outcome of the plan?

SELECTED READINGS

Alderson, Wroe, "The Theory of Advertising Measurement," in *Papers from the 1957 Regional Conventions*, American Association of Advertising Agencies, pp. 5–16.

Canter, Stanley D., "Exposition of the Hendry Advertising Analysis Model," speech presented to the Association of National Advertisers Workshop on Media Planning, New York, Sept. 30, 1971.

Dean, Joel, "How Much Should You Spend for Advertising?" in *Advertising Plans: Preparation and Presentation*, Vol. III, 1957, Association of National Advertisers, pp. 92–107.

Friedman, Lawrence, "Game Theory Models in the Allocation of Advertising Expenditures," in *Operations Research*, Operations Research Society of America, 1958, pp. 699–709.

Gerhold, Paul, "Measuring the Pro-

ductivity of Advertising Dollars,"
in *Papers from the 1957 Regional Conventions,* American Association of
Advertising Agencies, pp. 17–28.

Kelly, Richard S., and Ahlgren,
Herbert A. (eds.), *The Advertising
Budget,* New York: Association of
National Advertisers, 1967, p. 289.

Kershaw, Andrew, "How to Use Our
Media Dollars as a More Effective
Marketing Tool," speech presented
to the Association of National Advertisers Workshop on Media Planning, Sept. 30, 1971.

Kuehn, Alfred A., "A Model for Budgeting Advertising," in *Mathematical
Models and Methods in Marketing,*
Homewood, Ill.: Irwin Publishing
Company, 1961, p. 315.

Kropp, H. R.; Ehrenberg, A. S. C.;
Butler, Ben, Sr.; Gross, I., "Setting
Budgets and Allocating Advertising
Efforts," in *Advertising Research
Foundation 19th Annual Conference
Report,* New York, 1973, pp. 29–38.

Little, John D., and Ackoff, Russell
L., "How Techniques of Mathematical Analysis Have Been Used to
Determine Advertising Budgets
and Strategy," in Advertising Research Foundation *Fourth Annual
Conference Report,* 1958, pp. 19–24.

Mansfield, Frank W., "Budgeting Your
Advertising for Profit," in *Advertising Plans: Preparation and Presentation,* Vol. III, Association of National

Advertisers, 1957, pp. 108–14.

Mason, Kenneth, "How Much Do You
Spend on Advertising? Product is
the Key," *Advertising Age,* June 12,
1972, pp. 41–44.

McCabe, Thomas B., "How Much to
Spend for Advertising," in *Perspectives in Advertising Management,*
Association of National Advertisers,
New York, 1969, pp. 113–23.

Newell, Thomas M., "What is the
Right Amount to Spend for Advertising?" in *Papers from the 1968 Regional Conventions,* American Association of Advertising Agencies,
New York.

Parrish, T. Kirk, "How Much to Spend
for Advertising," *Journal of Advertising Research,* February 1974, pp. 9–
12.

Peckham, James O., "Can We Relate
Advertising Dollars to Market Share
Objectives?" in Advertising Research Foundation, *12th Annual
Conference Report,* 1966, pp. 53–57.

Schaffir, Kurt H., and Orr, E. W., Jr.,
"The Determination of Advertising
Budgets for Brands," *Journal of Advertising Research,* March 1963, pp.
7–11.

Weinberg, Robert S., "Are We Spending Too Much for Advertising?" in
Advertising Research Foundation,
14th Annual Conference Report, 1968,
pp. 29–36.

14

Testing, Experimenting, and Media Planning

Most of this book deals with the statistical data and subjective judgment that a media planner uses to decide among strategy alternatives. Most of such data comes from syndicated research companies whose services are widely available. This chapter, however, deals with the use of custom-made research to help the planner in making decisions. Such research usually is not under the direct supervision of a media planner, but there are some important facts about research that every media planner should know.

Tests and Experiments

Most of the research used to evaluate alternative media strategies falls under the general heading of tests and experiments. Briefly defined, a *test* is a simple field study of some advertising variable. An *experiment* is a carefully designed study in which the researcher controls and manipulates conditions to see how an experimental variable may affect audience behavior. A more comprehensive explanation of the two kinds of research will be given later.

Why Test or Experiment?

There are a number of reasons why testing or experimenting is necessary. The most important reason was stated above: to help the planner make decisions. Often the planner is faced with alternatives that are seemingly equal, and there might be differences of opinion between the planner and others (such as account executives or clients) about whether to use a given alternative. A way to resolve these differences is through custom-made research.

Another reason for testing or experimenting is to avoid making costly errors; the rising cost of media time and space, plus the proliferation of many new media alternatives, makes this more necessary than ever. Furthermore, clients want more and better proof that they are getting their money's worth in media, and that optimum media strategies are being used.

Finally, although media planners use numerical data in making decisions, they often modify the data with their own judgment, based on personal experience. But often such personal experience may not be broad enough, or the current situation may be vastly different from what it was in the past. Research is needed to answer the question of which strategy may work best.

Tests and Experiments: How They Differ

Because both tests and experiments usually involve field studies, they may seem to be alike. But tests are quite different from experiments.

In advertising or marketing, a test is a simple piece of research in which one measures a variable (or treatment) introduced into the market to see what effect it has. While advertising can be tested in one market, most often it is tested in at least two; each market is given a different treatment. For example, in one market $500,000 could be spent for advertising, while in the other $1,000,000 could be spent, using the same medium in both markets. Results could be measured on the basis of which produced the greatest sales.

When the test was over, it might be seen that the $1,000,000 produced 10 percent more sales than did the smaller figure. Which treatment was better? The answer depends on the decision maker who, on the basis of experience, judgment, or a payout calculation, says one expenditure is better than another. The most important characteristic of the test is its simplicity and its minimal controls. Although some attempts may have been made to see that the two test markets were alike, the nature of testing is such that it is simple and not too much trouble is exerted to control extraneous factors that could affect its outcome. Such rough testing provides guidelines for decision making rather than yielding definitive and projectable results.

An experiment resembles a test in that similar markets are selected for treatments, but great care is exerted to make sure that the markets are equivalent in nature. Usually the same treatments are assigned to two or more test markets, and usually two or more treatments are used. Finally, the treatments must be assigned at random, by using a table of random numbers or, perhaps, in simple cases, the toss of a coin. Furthermore, in measuring the results that occur because of the different treatments, a random sample must be drawn from each test marketing unit, and two or more replications may be made of each advertising treatment.

Once a random sample has been drawn from each of the test markets, the samples are measured through normal survey techniques to determine the effects of the various treatments. Results from experiments are analyzed, however, in a much different manner than in test results. In tests, the percentage of change from one market to the other is probably the most sophisticated analysis made; in experiments, data are cast in the form of analysis of variance, or some other statistical technique that helps tell the experimenter whether there is a cause and effect relationship between the treatment and the result.

The difference between the test and the experiment is that a better basis for decision making exists in the experiment, as noted by Dr. Seymour Banks, former vice president at the Leo Burnett Company, Chicago, when he wrote:

> The importance of experimental design versus mere testing lies in the fact that the existence of an experimental error permits the use of a whole system of logical inference about the meaning of the data. It may well be the case that a test will produce empirically useful information, but there exists no logically defensible system for evaluating results. A test may come up with the true answer, it may not; nobody really can tell which condition is true.[1]

Which Is Better: Test or Experiment?

There are advantages and limitations to both testing and experimenting. The experiment is preferable when the highest degree of objectivity is needed. In evaluating one against the other, the following should be considered:

Experiments are better controlled than tests. This means that special efforts usually have been taken to exclude from the study any extraneous variables that could seriously bias the findings. In addition, experiments are designed or planned to allow statistical inference to be used in making decisions, whereas tests usually are based on some one person's (or group's) judgment. Statistical inference is usually more valid than personal judgment. As a consequence, the results of an experiment may be projected to a large universe, whereas the results of a test usually are restricted to the areas where the test was conducted.

On the other hand, a test may be less expensive than an experiment. Many companies that cannot afford the cost of an experiment still have some way of finding answers to their problems by conducting tests. Furthermore, tests usually take less time to conduct than experiments. Often

---

[1]Banks, Seymour, "Using Experimental Design to Study Advertising Productivity," in *How Much to Spend for Advertising*, Association of National Advertisers, New York, 1969, p. 77.

there just isn't enough time for an experiment, but something needs to be learned. A test may provide this. Then, too, although the test design promises less than an experiment, often what is promised is enough. For example, a planner may simply want some clues, rather than a complete rationale, for a decision. Finally, a test is analyzed on the basis of relatively simple logic and reasoning that can be understood by everybody. Those who use experiments often err by substituting the elegance of their statistics for good, common sense reasoning. The formulas of statistics are means to an end—not the end.

Yet both experiments and tests have limitations. For example, neither may be able to detect small changes that have occurred. Furthermore, when testing alternative advertising expenditure levels in a number of markets, the total sales of a brand may decline because a control market has received no advertising for a period of time. Both tests and experiments may also be so visible that competitors not only know they are going on, but they may deliberately foil the research by reducing the price of their own brands or by introducing another product similar to the one being tested. Sometimes, the sales force of a company can ruin either a test or experiment by working either for it or against it—rather than letting the research commence naturally. When salespeople deviate from their normal handling of a brand, their actions can distort the outcomes of research.

One final consideration about both testing and experimenting: Neither may produce results that are projectable across the country. As Professor Roy H. Campbell of Arizona State University noted: "Research has shown the projection error from three markets to national market shares ranges from 22 percent over-projection to 22 percent under-projection."[2]

Even an experiment may be inadequate, because it does not take competitive action (or reaction) into consideration, a concern expressed by Benjamin Lipstein, senior vice president for research at the advertising agency Sullivan, Stauffer, Colwell & Bayles:

> There is serious question as to whether this classical experiment is valid in the social and economic sciences. The experimental design inference process implies that we can draw conclusions from the experiment which will have application in the larger world. If we arrive at some optimum level of advertising expenditures from test marketing situations, these results when applied to the larger environment of the total economy could well lead to serious error since they do not anticipate competitive reaction to

---

[2]Campbell, Roy H., *Measuring the Sales and Profit Results of Advertising*, Association of National Advertisers, New York, 1969, p. 54.

our presumed optimum level of expenditures. The experiment in no way makes provision for the independent intellectual life of competition.[3]

Lipstein also noted that, while it may be possible to anticipate competitive reactions to a strategy, statistical theory could give no rules on when and how competitors would really react. He concluded that competitive reactions would have to be assessed on the basis of judgment, something the experiment was supposed to have eliminated. Lipstein's alternative to classical experiments was a call for non-manipulative experiments in marketing and advertising, using mathematical model building to estimate what is likely to happen in the real world. These mathematical theories involve the use of nonstationary Markov chains, stability theory, simulation, and adaptative control theory.

What the Media Planner Should Know About Test Marketing

What Is Test Marketing?

Test marketing is the use of controlled tests or experiments (depending on how they are done) in one or more geographical areas to gather certain kinds of information or to gain experience in marketing a brand. In actual practice, test marketing may mean different things to different people. Consultant Alvin Achenbaum pointed out that to research-oriented people, test marketing means a precise method for gaining information or experience.[4] At the other extreme, test marketing can mean to some entrepreneurs: "Let's try something out in the marketplace." Between these two extremes exist many other possibilities.

Test marketing is most often done for new brands in existing product categories or for extensions of a product line. Even in new product testing, the media portion of the test is usually not the first consideration because the brand first has to be developed, packaged, and priced; selling strategies must be determined; and starting dates must be decided upon. In a sense, then, media planning assumes the same relationship in test marketing that it does in an existing brand strategy: Marketing considerations must be decided first.

---

[3]Lipstein, Benjamin, "Advertising Effectiveness Measurement, Has It Been Going Down a Blind Alley?" in *Papers from the American Association of Advertising Agencies Regional Meetings*, New York, 1969, p.2.

[4]Achenbaum, Alvin A., "Market Testing: Using the Marketplace as a Laboratory," in *Handbook of Marketing Research*, Robert Ferber (ed.), New York: McGraw-Hill, 1974, pp. 4–32.

It is important for a media planner to have a good basic understanding of test marketing because the planner may be involved in it when translating national media plans to a local level. Although it is beyond the scope of this book to provide all the details of test marketing, the following discussion covers the more essential facts for planners.

Purposes of Test Marketing

Because most market testing deals with new products, it should be obvious that the risks of making a wrong decision in introducing a new product could be costly. The number of new products that fail each year always is assumed to be high. Essentially test marketing is conducted to reduce the risk of failure by providing top management with knowledge gained from advertising in a limited geographical area. Management then can project test findings to a larger geographical area. The major objectives of test marketing are to estimate the brand market share that is likely to occur once the brand is introduced nationally and to evaluate alternative marketing and advertising strategies that also may be effective on a national basis.

Specifically, the purpose of test marketing is to help planners work out the mechanics of a market introduction while learning the local market share and effects of various strategies. If problems exist, then it is better to learn them ahead of time and solve them before national introduction. By spending a relatively small amount of money in a local market, one has less to lose than after national introduction. Once top management learns the local brand shares, then it may try to project those findings to the national market, using local shares as a predictive device. At that point, management may decide not to go ahead because there is not enough profit in the brand. In such a case, the investment in the test is considerably less than it would have been had the brand been introduced nationally without test marketing.

Despite the fact that a brand's local share can be learned from test markets, a growing number of marketing experts feel that the data cannot be projected nationally, because a few markets simply cannot accurately reflect the national market. Because the number of test markets used tends to be no more than three, the populations found in those markets may not be representative of the national universe. As a consequence, statistical inference usually cannot be used to analyze results. Furthermore, biases of many kinds tend to creep into test marketing operations. For example, in some tests higher distribution levels are present in test markets than could be expected on a national level. Or extra sales efforts are used locally that could not be expected nationally. Sometimes the expenditure of dollars for advertising is excessive at the local level and could not be duplicated nationally. Finally, markets change, people's attitudes change, and the economy may change so that, by the time a test marketing operation has been completed, the national universe, as well as the local universe, is far different than it was in the initial findings.

One must not conclude, however, that test marketing results can never predict national shares and/or profits. A sizable number of experts still feel that test marketing is here to stay and believe firmly in its underlying concepts. Their attitudes towards test marketing are based on the following arguments.

1. It is possible to improve the projectability of local market shares to national shares if better controls are exercised and more than just a few markets are used.
2. Market testing is better than no testing at all. It helps reduce the odds on failure, and it is the best that is available.
3. It has been successful in predicting market shares many times. The track records for some companies using market testing in predicting national share have been excellent.

A study made by Market Facts, Inc., and reported by Verne B. Churchill, Jr., showed that 52 percent of the respondents said their test marketing results were "very predictive"; and in controlled test marketing, the percentage saying results were very predictive was even higher.[5] So it would be incorrect to state that test marketing is totally invalid as a means of predicting national share, although almost all marketing experts agree that there is room for improvement in the degree of control that could be exercised to produce more meaningful results.

On the other hand, there is less disagreement about the use of market testing for determining alternative strategies. The test market seems to be a laboratory that can help the planner decide which courses of action to use nationally. However, most of the same limitations that apply to market share prediction should also apply to alternative strategy prediction.

Number of Test Markets to Use

Although most marketing experts would agree that more markets should be used in testing, few actually are used. In Churchill's research, 67 percent (or 36 out of 54) used no more than three markets, as shown in Table 14–1.

The reason more markets are not used is the prohibitively high cost. Even though management can be shown that the results of an experiment

---

[5]Churchill, Verne B., Jr., "New Product Test Marketing—An Overview of the Current Scene," an address before the Midwest Conference on Successful New Marketing Research Techniques, March 1971, p. 4; report published by Market Facts, Inc., Chicago, 1971.

TABLE 14–1. Number of Markets Used in Testing

Number of markets used	Breakdown of respondents (%)
1	21
2	24
3	22
4	15
5	7
6 or more	11
Total	100

Source: Churchill, Verne B., Jr., "New Product Test Marketing—An Overview of the Current Scene," Report by Market Facts, Inc., Chicago, 1971, p. 4.

might be considerably enhanced through the use of more markets, there is still a great deal of reluctance to spend the extra money. Using fewer than three markets could be considered inadequate for predicting national share, but some kinds of information may be learned from two or even one market. But the results usually are not representative of the entire country. Cost and degree of accuracy are considerations in determining the number of markets that should be used. No simple rules exist for deciding on a number of markets.

Kinds of Markets to Include

There are a number of criteria used in selecting test markets. The primary one is that a market should be representative of the universe. Since the markets selected are really samples from the universe, the more they are like the larger area, the better. This would mean that the markets selected should have the same demographic distribution of population as the country (if the universe is the entire country).

Peoria, Illinois, is among those markets that have a population distribution that closely matches the population distribution of the entire country, as shown in Table 14–2. Because of this similarity, Peoria is often used as a single test market. At times it is used in combination with others. Yet, despite this similarity, there should be some question about the lifestyle of Peoria inhabitants compared with lifestyles in other areas of the country.

Other criteria for a test market are:

1. Its economy should be independent rather than dependent on a nearby market.
2. Competition in the market should be similar to what a brand would expect nationally, and distribution opportunities in the number and kinds of retail outlets should be similar to the national level.

TABLE 14–2. Peoria Compared with the National Population (1971)

Population	Metro Peoria	Total U.S.A.
Male	49.2%	49.2%
Female	50.8%	50.8%
Children under 18 yrs. of age	35.5%	35.8%
Age Brackets:		
Under 5 years	11.5%	11.3%
5–19 yrs.	26.6%	27.2%
20–34 yrs.	19.1%	18.7%
35–44 yrs.	13.1%	13.4%
45–64 yrs.	20.4%	20.1%
65 & over	9.3%	9.3%
Employment:		
Employed Males	53.1%	49.2%
Employed Females	21.8%	23.2%
Unemployed Males	46.9%	50.8%
Unemployed Females	78.2%	76.8%
By occupation:		
Business and Professional	9.6%	11.2%
Salaried and Semiprofessional	7.8%	8.4%
Skilled	63.7%	59.6%
Unskilled	18.9%	20.8%
Median Family Income	$5,998	$5,660
Median School Years (males, 25 yrs. & over)	10.2 yrs.	10.6 yrs.
Median Age (total population)	29.4 yrs.	30.3 yrs.

Source: Sederberg, Kathryn, "The Anatomy of a Test Market: How It Works in Peoria," *Advertising Age*, Nov. 1, 1971, p. 147.

3. There should be diversification of industry in the community, and there should not be a strong franchise for other brands.[6]

Media availability should also be investigated to ensure that the market is representative of the average market in the universe. There is one other requirement: Markets should be randomly dispersed so that, in conjunction with large-sized markets, the competitors would find it difficult to disrupt the effects of the test.

Market Sizes

There is a difference of opinion about the optimum market size for test markets. One expert feels that the range should be from 100,000 to 1,000,000 population. Another expert employs a rule-of-thumb that the size should be about 2 percent to 3 percent of the national population. Achenbaum

[6]Sederberg, Kathryn, "Anatomy of a Test Market: How It Works in Peoria," *Advertising Age*, Nov. 1, 1971, p. 147.

feels that the total population involved in test marketing should be not less than 20 percent of the United States because anything less would affect the amount of statistical sampling variance.[7] Probably the size of each market is not as important as the kinds or numbers of markets used. Size, however, may be an important consideration controlling the cost of the test. Larger markets could be expected to have relatively higher media costs.

What to Test

A number of marketing variables can be tested in addition to sales volume or share at a profitable level. These include tests of advertising media weights, various price levels, store promotion plans, trial and repeat buying rates, creative approaches, package sizes and assortments, brand names, brand awareness and/or attitude changes, and alternative media strategies.

Research Designs Used in Test Marketing

Research design refers to a plan of actions to be taken in the testing. This plan, or design, is carefully worked out in such a way so as to obtain certain kinds of information. Most often research design refers to experimental situations where the test data results will lend themselves to statistical manipulation.

Research design can be very simple, such as observing a market, introducing an experimental variable, and then observing it again to learn what effects the variable had on the market. Or, the design can be simple to the extent that two or more markets, presumably similar in demographic characteristics, are tested at the same time, with each one getting a different treatment. However, more complex designs sometimes are used in test marketing experiments.

Use of Control Markets. Before conducting test marketing, the planner must design the test in such a way as to guarantee its validity. *Validity* means that the test measures what it is supposed to measure and not something else. If, for example, advertising is introduced into a test market as an experimental treatment, the planner will want to know to what extent advertising had any effect on the outcome.

One method of assuring the planner of the internal validity of the test is to use a control market along with a test market. A *control market* is one that does not receive any experimental treatment while the test market

---

[7]Achenbaum, Alvin A., "Market Testing: Using the Marketplace as a Laboratory," in *Handbook of Marketing Research*, Robert Ferber (ed.), New York: McGraw-Hill, 1974, pp. 4–32.

does. The control market, therefore, must be selected carefully so that it shares all the demographic and economic characteristics of the test market. If the research objective is to measure advertising's effect on sales, then advertising will be used in the test market only. Sales then are measured in both kinds of markets. If sales rise higher in the test market than in the control market, one may conclude that advertising had a significant effect on sales. But if sales rise to about the same degree in both markets, then advertising had little or no effect.

The design of a test and control market for a new brand is shown in Figure 14–1. This kind of test can involve more than a single variable. For example, different spending levels may be tested in different test markets and compared with the control group. In addition, market shares of all groups may be tested simultaneously for the total of all test groups and compared with the control group.

Randomized Block Design. A *randomized block design* is one where subjects to be measured are first grouped together into blocks. Each subject is carefully chosen so he or she will be much like every other subject in that block. The selection process, however, is done on a random basis so that every person with the same characteristic has an equal chance of being chosen. Randomized blocks are designed to prevent situations where differences within the sample affect the outcome, rather than differences due to the treatments.

The matching or grouping of subjects can be on the basis of age, such as people aged 18 to 34; or income, people earning $10,000 or more a year; or store volume, grocery stores with less than $500,000 income. Once subjects are placed into blocks, the experimenter can compare the results of treatments among the blocks. If subjects are not combined into blocks, then the experimenter may not be able to find significant results because

FIGURE 14–1. How Test and Control Markets Are Used

	Time Period 1→	Time Period 2→	Time Period 3→	
Test Market	Sales of new brand measured (no advertising)	Advertising introduced	Sales of new brand measured again	Sales of both markets compared on basis of percentage of change.
Control Market	Sales of new brand measured (no advertising)	No advertising	Sales of new brand measured (no advertising)	

the differences might be too small to be measured. This problem may be overcome if the experiment uses a very large number of subjects, but randomized blocks aid the experimenter in reducing the number of subjects to be used in an experiment.

Latin Square Designs

A *Latin square* is a block divided into a number of cells containing coded letters and so arranged that a letter appears only once in each row and column. This design technique is more precise than the randomized block because it helps control the problem of two rather than one source of variation within markets that could not be controlled by careful selection.

An example of a Latin square used in a marketing experiment is shown in Table 14–3, where two variables were controlled, and three different treatments were applied. The two variables were geographic variation and competitive expenditures. It is assumed in this design that each control or treatment is independent of the others and therefore will not affect the others in any way.

The problem illustrated in Table 14–3 is: If Brand X should spend three varying amounts of money for advertising, which would produce the most sales, or brand awareness, or other marketing variable? In order to make the experiment projectable to the entire country, different expenditure levels were tried in different parts of the country, and also where different competitive spending levels took place. By controlling for both variables, the experiment thereby eliminated them as possible reasons for variations in sales that were found through the experiment.

The method of eliminating the effects of both variables is to add the rows and average out the effect of regions. By adding the columns, it is possible to average out the effects of competitive spending levels. By adding the expenditure levels for Brand X (or treatments), it is possible to average out the effects of both regions and competitive activity to obtain a determination which Brand X spending level was best.

TABLE 14–3. A Latin Square Design Applied to a Test Marketing Situation

Degree of Competitive Spending	Regions of the United States		
	East	Central	West
Low spending levels	A	C	B
Medium spending levels	C	B	A
High spending levels	B	A	C

Treatments: A = high spending level for Brand X
　　　　　　　B = medium spending level for Brand X
　　　　　　　C = low spending level for Brand X

Source: Lipstein, Benjamin, "The Design of Test Market Experiments," *Journal of Advertising Research*, December 1965, p. 6.

Factorial Design. A *factorial design*, based on a factor as an independent variable, is one where it is possible to measure the effects of different kinds of treatments, but with the added value of determining whether the factors interact, or whether they are independent of each other. In conceptual terms, experiments may be designed to determine the influence of two or more independent variables on a dependent variable. *Independent variables* are those which the experimenter controls, manipulates, or varies. *Dependent variables* are the yield, or the effect variables; they vary depending on the independent variable.

An example of differing treatments in an experiment could be the effects of old versus new packaging, or an old package price versus a new price. The goal is to determine whether price and package changes are related to each other or are independent.

Other Test Marketing Designs

Achenbaum suggested a *checkerboard design* as a valid means of obtaining data in test marketing.[8] He described this design as requiring three basic elements:

1. Dividing a universe into groups of markets. These markets should be randomly selected and be about equal in size. An example might be to select three television market groups from each of Nielsen's ten geographical areas.
2. The use of alternative strategies in groups of three. Perhaps one group would receive 80 percent of a current spending level while the second group would receive 100 percent and the third group might receive 120 percent. Achenbaum would also use local media such as newspapers, spot television, and local magazines as the testing media. Three complete media plans at each spending level would then be produced.
3. Then, through syndicated retail auditing services, measure results over a period of a year. The key to the success of this plan is representativeness, good control, and ease of measurement (because it uses Nielsen areas).

Other testing designs are *minimarkets*, where a test is conducted in a very small area, usually for testing a new product introduction; or *in-store tests*, used to test marketing variables within a store. Stores may be divided into two groups with each group being given a different treatment. And finally, there are *CATV* (Community Antenna Television) *tests*, where

---

[8]Achenbaum, Alvin A., Jr., "Market Testing: Using the Marketplace as a Laboratory," in *Handbook of Marketing Research*, Robert Ferber (ed.), New York: McGraw-Hill, 1974, pp. 4, 47, 48.

two randomly matched groups of homes that have cable television can receive different treatments. At present, about one in three homes have cable television. But if expectations are correct, the number will be substantially larger in the future.

Media Testing

Media play an important role in most test marketing operations. Although the objective of a market test may be to learn whether certain marketing actions will result in a given level of sales or profits, usually other parts of a test are directly related to the selection and use of media. These other parts may have different objectives, such as learning which spending levels or which media mix to use.

How Planners Test the Plan

A media planner's initial responsibility in test marketing is to create a national media plan, then reduce this plan in size to fit the individual markets that are to be tested. (The reduction process is called *media translation*, and will be explained in detail later.) Meanwhile, the planner may have a number of different objectives to test, which are described here.

Testing a Complete Media Plan. A national media plan may be developed for a new product that has not been marketed before. While the marketing part of a test is to learn a brand's sales or market share that may be developed on a national scale, alternative forms of the national media plan may be tested to see which will best fulfill the brand's media needs later on.

Testing Alternative Spending Levels. A special part of media planning information is testing how much money should be spent on media. The following kinds of spending plans could be tested:

1. High spending vs. current spending levels
2. Low spending vs. current spending levels
3. High spending vs. low spending levels
4. Allocation spending tests to determine how much to allocate, either by dollars or Gross Rating Points, to various geographic markets and/or media. In testing allocation weights, the tester may use various kinds of weighted BDIs and CDIs to help arrive at spending levels.

Testing Alternative Schedules. At times it is important to know whether a media plan should use flighting, continuity, or pulsing. Although experience provides planners with some basis for judgment, there are times when a test may provide more objective information than that based on experience."

Testing Alternative Media Mixes. One could test the results obtained from any single medium or any combination: television vs. magazines, television vs. newspapers, national vs. local media, etc. Media mix testing could also include the comparison of various dayparts in broadcast media: Should a media plan use an exclusive daypart, such as primetime, or a combination of dayparts, such as daytime and early or late fringe? These are only a few of the possible combinations that could be tested.

Testing Alternative Commercial Lengths or Ad Sizes. In these tests, one could test 60-second vs. 30-second commercials, or 30-second vs. 10-second commercials, or 60-second commercials vs. a full page print ad.

It should be noted that there are times when media tests are made for reasons other than that of predicting sales share. It may be important to learn how media and advertising work, and media may play an integral role in such learning experiences.

Requirements for Media Testing

There are a number of criteria for selecting test markets that apply specifically to media. For example, there should be enough media options available in the test markets to replicate the national media that will be used later. As a result, certain very small markets may be unsuitable for testing purposes. But there are other considerations as well.

Media Availability. A test market must have a balance of media alternatives available. For example, if television is to be part of a national media plan, then there ought to be at least three TV stations in the test market because there probably would be at least three TV stations in most major markets when the plan is implemented nationally. In the same manner, if radio is to be used in the national plan, then one radio station in the test market should not dominate the market, because it is highly unlikely that, when translated nationally, most markets would have a single dominant station in them.

Spill-in and Spill-out. One of the qualities of a test market medium is the degree to which it is isolated from other markets. Media from markets outside the test area often *spill into* the test market, that is, people in the test market are exposed to media originating from another market. Sometimes it works the other way, when media from the test market *spill out* into adjacent markets.

The degree to which media in a test market spill out messages to markets outside the test area can be a serious problem. Spill-out is generally undesirable for a number of reasons. The first is that consumers who live outside the test market area may hear or see advertising for a product but may be unable to buy it because it does not yet have national distribution. These consumers may become irritated at their inability to buy the advertised brand, and may not respond to later advertising because of their annoyance at not being able to find the brand on store shelves during the testing period.

A marketer can attempt to avoid the problem by distributing the brand in the broader spill-out area, but this in turn may cause another problem: Will the supply of the brand be adequate? At times only a limited amount of a brand is available for testing purposes, perhaps just enough for the test, but not for spill-out.

There is another way to get around the problem of poor distribution in spill-out areas: Print and broadcast advertisements can specifically tell consumers where to purchase the brand, thereby averting the animosity that could occur when there is no distribution in a spill-out area.

The reverse problem to spill-out is *spill-in*, which occurs when media originating in another market spill into the test market. The more that people in the test market are exposed to media from another market, the greater is the variation in the reach and frequency pattern from the pattern ordinarily expected. For example, if a schedule of 100 GRPs produces a 50 reach and a 2.0 frequency in an *average* market, it will produce lower reach and higher frequency in a market where there is a proportionately high level of spill-in.

Some areas of the United States have more spill-in markets than others. Markets in the Northeast, for example, tend to have large spill-in (although Portland, Maine, is an exception). Meanwhile, Phoenix and Tucson (southwestern markets) have relatively little spill-in.

Media Costs. When a market becomes known as a good test area, the local media may sometimes raise their advertising rates to take advantage of their popularity, making it more expensive to test media in such a popular area. Some experts feel that persons responsible for the media portion of testing should not worry about higher media costs in certain markets because there are other more important considerations to watch for—spill-in, spill-out, quality, availability, etc. In translating a national media plan to a test market, the objective should be not to translate costs downward from a national plan, but to translate the delivery (e.g., reach and frequency) into the test market regardless of the cost. If a test market cannot generate the kinds of reach and frequency effects that are necessary, then some other market should be selected.

Test Area Coverage. In selecting test markets for media planning, enough markets (whether ADIs or DMAs) should be used to cover at least 95 percent of the test areas (sales districts, territories, etc.) that the company typically uses. This assumes that the test is being made to correspond to a specific company's sales area. At times, this correspondence is not necessary, depending on what the client wants to learn from the test.

Network Delivery. Another consideration for test market selection, especially when the test is supposed to represent the entire United States, is that the daypart usage in the test market should closely match the planned national daypart usage of television or radio.

Number of Markets. As discussed previously, the number of markets used in testing should be more than two or three. Yet despite consensus that as many as five, six, or more are desirable, only one is often used. When a single market is used, it is assumed that the "one" is a Little U.S.A. market (to be discussed later). Dangers of projecting from one market are well recognized.

There has been a trend for some time now to test in very large markets such as New York, Los Angeles, or Chicago, on the assumption that these markets are more representative of the United States than smaller markets. A marketer might also try a test in an entire geographic region, such as the West Coast, where a number of various-sized population centers exist. The regional approach could be much easier to use than a single isolated market because the planner can more easily simulate the national media plan in the area. Regional editions of national magazines may be available, whereas in a single market no local editions of a national magazine may exist. The regional test would be less likely to be affected by local strikes, bad weather, or high competitive reactions to the test. Sometimes network buys in a region such as the West Coast may be relatively inexpensive and flexible, but for most regions regional network buys may be difficult, if available at all.

Other reasons why regional test markets may be preferred to individual and isolated markets are that it may be easier to obtain distribution in a region as well as easier to compare market data with media coverage. In local test markets, the media coverage may far exceed market coverage measurements. Finally, in auditing sales, it may be easier and less costly to audit sales in large regions than in isolated markets.

On the other hand, there are three good reasons for not using regional tests: The cost may be prohibitive; there could be a large amount of wasted media impressions because not everyone in the region is being tested; and a regional test is not really a laboratory or sample test, but a small-scale introduction. If the product is not well accepted, the risks of large-scale failure have not been eliminated in the testing procedure.

Sometimes media considerations are not an important part of test marketing. While media usually are an important part of test marketing, there are occasions where the purpose of the test does not involve media. As one media planner noted: ". . . our client was interested only in finding out if he could sell the product to the trade. In this instance, the actual media schedules were not important."[9]

---

[9]Yovovich, B. G., "Quality of Local Media Can Be a Determining Factor," *Advertising Age*, Feb. 4, 1980, p. S-2.

Media Translations

Media translation was defined earlier as a process for reducing national media plans to fit the needs of individual test markets. This is an adjustment technique, and there are several ways to make such adjustments. Each technique is based on a different philosophy of operations.

Little U.S.A. versus As Is Philosophy

There are at least two philosophies regarding media translations in test marketing. One is the Little U.S.A. concept; the other the As Is concept. The *Little U.S.A.* concept is based on the idea that some test markets are so much like the country as a whole, that what one finds in one market can easily be projected to the national market. Therefore, if a media plan calls for the use of one primetime network minute per week with a 20 national rating, the test market translation would be a 20 rating on some local program, or a number of spot commercials with 20 Gross Rating Points in that market, regardless of the local rating for that network vehicle in the test market. Another way of using the Little U.S.A. concept would be to translate it in direct proportion to the weight that would be delivered on a national basis. The measurement could be the average number of impressions to be delivered per household nationally, translated to a proportion the local market should have received.

In the *As Is* concept, the exact media weight of the national plan is delivered into specified markets. Using the same example as above, with a primetime network program rated 20, the planner might find that this program delivers a higher or lower rating in the test market, since national media deliver varying levels of advertising weight from market to market. If the primetime program happens to deliver, for example, an 18

TABLE 14–4. National Media Plan—Little U.S.A. Method

Media Used	Spot Markets (Women GRPs)	Total U.S. (Women GRPs)	Test Market Translation (Women GRPs)
Network TV		400	400
Magazines		100	100
Spot TV (60% of U.S. covered)			
Average spot*	100	60**	60 (National average)
Total		560	560

*A markets received 150 GRPs, B markets 100 GRPs, and C markets 50 GRPs, but the average for all markets is 100.

**Average calculations are as follows:　100 GRPs in 60% of U.S.　=　60
　　　　　　　　　　　　　　　　　　0 GRPs in 40% of U.S.　=　　0
　　　　　　　　　　　　　　　　　　Weighted average　　　=　60

rating in the chosen test market, then 18 GRPs should be purchased in the test market.

The decision to use Little U.S.A. or As Is is generally related to how representative the test area is relative to the national plan. If the As Is translation method would result in delivering an abnormally high (or low) level of media weight, some adjustment toward the Little U.S.A. should be considered.

Table 14–4 shows how a Little U.S.A. media translation would be made. A national media plan has been devised in which network and spot television and national magazines would be the only media used. The spot television plan covers markets that include 60 percent of U.S. households. In order to make a Little U.S.A. translation, average delivery is scheduled in local test markets as shown in Table 14–4.

Using the same data, the As Is translation would first require the planner to determine how many GRPs were to go into individual markets. Whereas the Little U.S.A. technique used the average delivery, this technique requires much more detailed planning in order to know what local delivery might be. In making this translation, it may not be possible to buy GRPs precisely as planned, so some media get more and others less than the national plan, as shown in Table 14–5.

Note that, under the As Is approach, only 380 GRPs were purchased in network TV while 120 GRPs were purchased in magazines in the test market. The reason is that this combination of national media delivers the desired levels of GRPs in the test market. Although the difference between the two translation techniques may not seem like much, it is the difference between average and actual plan deliveries.

Translations in Radio and Television

There are a number of ways to translate a national media plan in radio and television. One way is the *cut-in*, in which a local commercial is

TABLE 14–5. National Media Plan—As Is Method

Media Used	Spot Markets (Women GRPs)	Total U.S. (Women GRPs)	Test Market Translation (Women GRPs)
Network TV		400	380
Magazines		100	120
Spot TV (60% U.S. coverage)			
Average spot	100	100	
A markets	150		
B markets	100		
C markets*	50		50
Total		600	550

*The GRPs of C markets were used because test markets were C markets in character.

inserted in a network or transcribed program in place of some other commercial originally scheduled in a market for the same advertiser. This is possible when the client already has purchased a commercial on a network, and simply replaces it with the test market commercial by cutting in only in the test market. The remainder of the country would see the national commercial. A cut-in is considered to be an excellent way to translate for broadcast media because it keeps the program environment the same as in the national plan and it provides the exact national weight in a local market. Local stations, however, charge high fees for mechanically inserting substitute commercials. Also, national advertising for some other product may suffer because it was replaced with the cut-in.

If a cut-in is not feasible, then the planner will have to substitute local announcements for the network commercials. This may be a problem because the spot announcement times chosen must provide the same kind of target audience and the same audience sizes that the network program in that market would provide. In order to use spot television, the only times available at a reasonable cost may be fringe times. Since fringe time spots do not produce as high ratings as would primetime network programs, some kind of compensation might be used. Planners add Gross Rating Points to those of the theoretical plan level as a form of compensation. The degree of additional spot weight over the theoretical plan level is usually determined by the research experience of each advertiser. There is no single set of industry standards that applies to such translation methods.

When a primetime spot is used (instead of a primetime network program) then the additional Gross Rating Point compensation may not be as high as the amount of compensation used with fringe spot. In deciding on any compensation, two factors should be considered: compensation for loss of reach and compensation for loss of program environment. Of course, it is assumed that any spots used will aim for a selected target audience.

Compensations will vary in different markets, depending on the relationship of audience sizes between primetime and fringe times. Daytime spots, on the other hand, may be used in lieu of daytime network programs without compensation since they may be purchased either within or next to the kinds of network programs used in the national media plan.

When a national media plan calls for spot television, no compensation may be necessary; spots are simply scheduled in the same number, same number of Gross Rating Points, length, placement, reach, and frequency called for in the national plan.

In translating network radio, the method is identical to that used for translating daytime network television. For spot radio, the translation method would be identical to spot television.

Translations in Print

Translation of newspapers is direct and simple, because the national media plan would spell out all details for local markets.

Magazines may or may not require special translations. If regional, metropolitan, or special test market editions of a magazine exist, then there is little difficulty in making a translation.

But if a national magazine has none of the above editions, three alternatives exist for translation: using Sunday supplements adjusted to deliver the same number of impressions in a local market that a national magazine would have delivered, using local magazines that are similar to those in the national plan and adjusting differences through compensation, and using ROP color in newspapers with some kind of compensation. The last alternative may be the poorest choice because the reproduction of ROP color in newspaper advertisements is not the same as color printed in most national magazines. But it would be possible to make some kind of compensation for the differences if that were the only viable alternative.

The first alternative, using Sunday supplements in lieu of national magazines, may be relatively easy to translate. An example of how this could be done is shown in Table 14–6. If the data on target audience delivery is not known in any given market, it could be estimated by working from known data. The number of circulation units delivered into Market X can usually be obtained from the publisher, who also can furnish the national number of readers per copy for the magazine. Multiply circulation by readers-per-copy to find the readers in Market X. However, these would be total audience readers, not target audience members. The same could be done for readers of Sunday supplements or

TABLE 14–6. Translation of National Magazine Impressions to Sunday Supplements

Problem:	How many Sunday supplement ads are needed to deliver the same number of national magazine impressions that would be delivered by a national magazine in Test Market X?
Solution:	1. Find the number of target audience members of a national magazine delivered into Test Market X (either from published data or by estimate). Suppose the magazine delivers 100,000 readers in Market X.
	2. Assume that the national media plan called for 6 national ads in that market for a year. Find the total number of impressions in Market X: (100,000 impressions × 6 ads = 600,000).
	3. Find the number of target audience members delivered by one ad in a Sunday supplement in Market X. Assume it would be 75,000 readers.
	4. Calculate the number of Sunday supplement ads that would be needed to deliver 600,000 target impressions: 600,000 ÷ 75,000 = 8 ads.
	5. If the media planner judges that supplements have a lower "value" than magazines, the number of insertions needed in the test market can be increased to compensate: For example, scheduling 9 or 10 insertions in supplements rather than 8.

similar magazines, and a translation then could be worked out. At times, the audience data could be further reduced by multiplying it by known recognition scores for a product category and comparing it with the substitute medium's noted score projection.

If a national media plan calls for Sunday supplements in a select group of test markets, then translation is easily done by using the local supplement or test insertions in the nationally syndicated supplements. On the other hand, if there is no Sunday supplement in a given market, then one could buy ROP color ads in the local newspaper. In the latter situation, some form of compensation would be required. In some markets, syndicated national supplements make test market breakouts available.

In summary, whenever a direct translation can be made, it is preferable to simulating a national medium in a local market. Almost any simulation will require some kind of compensation based at times on arbitrary rather than empirical means.

Conclusions

Testing and experimenting to find the best media strategy is a reasonable and relatively objective way of finding answers, as opposed to using simple judgment and experience. Yet there are countervailing forces that work against them. The high cost of research, the pressure of time, and the failure to control extraneous factors that could bias the outcomes all affect the continued use of these methods. But it is likely that as time progresses, more companies will pay the cost, take the time, and place competent persons who understand experimental research in positions of authority so that experiments will be used more for solving problems. At present the number of persons engaged in this kind of research is not large compared with the number of companies for whom media strategies are being devised in a single year.

QUESTIONS FOR DISCUSSION

1. Generally, what are the values of testing and experimenting?
2. What are the differences between a test and an experiment?
3. Does an experiment, even if carefully designed and conducted, guarantee an answer that will solve a problem? Briefly explain.
4. Why do some marketing experts feel that the results of test marketing may not be projectable to the entire country?
5. Although Peoria, Illinois, may have demographics similar to the demographics of the entire country, why is there still some question that it may not be representative of the country?
6. What is the value of using statistical inference in market testing?

7. What is the main difference between the Little U.S.A. and the As Is philosophies of media translation?
8. What are the main reasons for not using an entire geographic region, such as the West Coast, for a media translation?
9. Why may it be important to test in very large metropolitan centers such as New York, Los Angeles, or Chicago, apart from other testing?
10. Explain how one can translate a network television program to a local area.
11. Explain the purposes of compensation in media translations.

SELECTED READINGS

Achenbaum, Alvin A., "Market Testing: Using the Marketplace as a Laboratory," in *Handbook of Marketing Research*, Robert Ferber (ed.), New York: McGraw-Hill, 1974, pp. 4–47.

Advertising Age, "Test Marketing Full of Inconclusive, Contradictory Evidence, Berdy Says," Nov. 16, 1964, p. 37.

Advertising Age, "Test Marketing," Feb. 4, 1980, pp. S-1, 5–28.

Banks, Seymour, "Using Experimental Design to Study Advertising Productivity," in *How Much to Spend for Advertising?* edited by Malcolm A. McNiven, New York: Association of National Advertisers, 1969, pp. 72–89.

Banks, Seymour, *Experimentation in Marketing*, New York: McGraw-Hill, 1965.

Becknell, James C., Jr., "Use of Experimental Design in the Study of Media Effectiveness," *Media/Scope*, August 1962, pp. 46–49.

Brown, George H., "Measuring the Sales Effectiveness of Alternative Media," in *Advertising Research Foundation, 7th Conference Report*, 1961, pp. 43–47.

Campbell, Roy H., *Measuring the Sales and Profit Results of Advertising*, New York: Association of National Advertisers, 1969.

Canter, Stanley, "The Evaluation of Media Through Empirical Experiments," in *Advertising Research Foundation, 11th Conference Report*, 1965, pp. 39–44.

Casey, Richard F., "Tests for Test Marketing," in *Papers from the 1962 Regional Conventions*, American Association of Advertising Agencies, Western Region Meeting, Oct. 22, 1962.

Edwards, Allen L., *Experimental Design in Psychological Research*, New York: Holt, Rinehart and Winston, 1960, 398 pp.

Giges, Nancy, "Advertisers Take Harder Look at Test Market Ways," *Advertising Age*, Oct. 12, 1972, p. 3.

Hardin, David K., "A New Approach to Test Marketing," *Journal of Marketing*, October 1966, pp. 28–31.

Honomichl, Jack J., "Market Facts' Success with Controlled Market Tests Attracts Nielsen," *Advertising Age*, Oct. 8, 1973, p. 3.

Keshin, Mort, "Media Planners' Role in Test Marketing," *Media/Scope*, December 1967, pp. 14–17.

Kroeger, Albert R., (ed.), "Test Marketing: The Concept and How It is Changing," Part I in *Media/Scope*, December 1966, p. 63: Part II, January 1967, p. 51.

Lasman, L. L., "Determining the Proper Advertising Mix for a Consumer Product," *NAEA 1964 Summer Meeting Digest*, pp. 21–25.

Lipstein, Benjamin, "The Design of Test Marketing Experiments," *Journal of Advertising Research*, December 1965, pp. 2–7.

Lipstein, Benjamin, "Advertising Effectiveness Measurement: Has It Been Going Down a Blind Alley?" in *Papers from the 1969 American Association of Advertising Agencies Annual Meeting*, April 25, 1969, White Sulphur Springs, W.V.

Marketing Insights, "Test Marketing, The Most Dangerous Game in Marketing," published by *Advertising Age*, Oct. 9, 1967, pp. 16–17.

Media Decisions, "The Media Testers," September 1971, p. 52.

Orman, Allen, "Which Marketing Alternative Should We Test in the Market?" in *Marketing Insights*, published by *Advertising Age*, Jan. 22, 1968.

Sederberg, Kathryn, "Anatomy of a Test Market: How it Works in Peoria," *Advertising Age*, Nov. 1, 1971, p. 144.

Sherak, Bud, "Controlled Sales and Marketing Tests," paper delivered to the Advertising Research Foundation Conference, March 15, 1967.

"Testing! Anywhere, U.S.A.," *Sponsor*, March 8, 1965, pp. 28–34.

15

Use of the Computer
in Media Planning

In the early 60s, predictions were widespread that computers were going to dramatically change the practice of media planning. It was predicted that computers would be able to do complex media data analysis, create improved media schedules, determine which media and strategies were the best, and in general, raise the level of media planning operations. After more than two decades of use, computers have not quite lived up to their predictions, even though large amounts of money, time, and effort have been expended on them. Why were these predictions mostly incorrect? More importantly, what is the role of the computer in the future of media planning? Explanations of the answers to these and other questions about the use of computers are the purpose of this chapter. The main objective, however, is to place the use of computers in a proper perspective for the media planner by showing not only its best potential uses, but some of the continuing problems that need solutions.

What Does a Computer Do?

A computer is essentially an electronic calculator that can add, subtract, multiply, and divide at lightning-like speeds. It can also store information in its memory units, and when this is called forth, it can be manipulated arithmetically in many ways. Because the four arithmetic functions are part of many formulas needed to solve complex mathematical problems, the computer, if fed the correct data and programmed correctly, can solve the problem quickly.

Specifically in media planning, a computer can do a number of things that help the planner.

Construct media schedules. Through special programming, the computer can create a schedule showing the names of vehicles, gross number of exposures delivered, and the amount of money spent by time period.

Assess alternative media plans. A computer can be given alternative media plans that were either created by computer or by hand and evaluate them in terms of reach and frequency, and/or cost-per-thousand. The planner then can either select the best of available alternatives or improve one or more.

Analyze marketing and/or media data. The computer can scan a great deal of marketing and/or media data quickly and organize them into a meaningful arrangement. It can compute index numbers of demographic segments of a market and then arrange the data in rank order and quickly calculate reach and frequency of any given number of media combinations. It can analyze media expenditures by competitors into percentage of dollars spent in various media by various brands in a given market.

Control Billing and Management. A computer can be used to tabulate bills and/or payments and analyze other operations within the agency or media department.

Media planning, therefore, poses a special kind of problem that requires the use of the four arithmetic functions. Theoretically, the computer should be able to devise media strategy and solve media problems if the correct data and programs are fed into it. At the heart of the problem, however, is the question of whether it is possible to first create a mathematical model that can solve media strategy problems.

Media Models

A *model* is a simplified representation of reality, or in the case of media planning, a description of a process. But it is more than a simple description because it must explain logical relationships, both quantitative and qualitative, between parts of the process and the whole. In order to help the model builder better perceive the relationships, models are usually expressed in symbolic or mathematical form. These symbols make it relatively easy to see at a glance the entire spectrum of actions and their relationships.

In media planning, most models are predictive, in the sense that if a planner uses the model, certain outcomes should result. Therefore the model can be used to predict and control the outcomes. Other than simply describing or predicting what happens, a model's value is based on helping one understand a process or reality. This occurs because a good model builder should spell out the relationships, state underlying assumptions on which the model is based, and trace the logic of relationships through parts of the model.

Three Well-Known Media Models

There are a number of media models in existence. Three of the most popular models are *linear programming, simulation,* and a formula model called *beta binomial.* Each model has a number of different variations.

Linear programming is an optimizing model, while simulation is nonoptimizing. Beta binomial is a formula model. An *optimizing model* is one created to search for and find an optimum solution to a media problem. Given the costs of media and other requirements for selection, the model can, through the use of a computer, compile a list of vehicles that meet the constraints. The *nonoptimizing model,* on the other hand, assesses media plans that already have been conceived. Each kind of model has its advantages and limitations.

Linear Programming

A *linear programming* model can be used to deliver a list of media vehicles that represent the best of all alternatives subject to certain requirements or constraints. Typically, the model maximizes the total number of exposures subject to a cost constraint or minimizes costs subject to an exposure constraint for each vehicle on a recommended list.

The model is based on a mathematical technique developed by economist Wassily W. Leontief in the 1920s. Further developments were made by George B. Dantzig, who is credited with devising the simplex method of linear programming that is used in media models today. In essence, the model allocates a scarce resource, the budget, to alternative media.

To use the model in computer planning, the planner must set up specific constraints that become a criterion function for making selections. For example, this function gives a set of weights to each vehicle based on its ability to deliver large numbers of targets. However, other constraints usually are added to help the computer decide which media to recommend, such as a set of weights that accounts for qualitative differences between vehicles. Some vehicles have a better image, are more believable, or have more authority than others. Still another set of weights is usually applied to different ad forms, such as a half-page print ad versus a 30-second TV commercial. The three weights are all part of the criterion function called by such names as Rated Exposure Units (REU) or Rated Exposure Values (REV). Another important constraint is the advertising budget. Obviously the planner cannot accept a decision that costs more money than is available. Still another constraint could be derived from marketing/media objectives, such as an objective to reach at least 70 percent of all women, or planning for year-round continuity, or using at least two different programs, etc. The computer output can be either an analysis of alternative media in terms of REUs, or a schedule, or a summary of a schedule. With linear programming, a media planner can have a computer print out a summary of the media plan, then change one or more of the constraints, and have the computer print out alternative schedules.

Some of the major advantages of linear programming are:

1. It provides a mathematical basis for what otherwise is a subjective decision.
2. It requires the planner to state assumptions and quantify them, a practice not usually required in non-computerized planning. Such a practice forces one to establish written relationships. If they are wrong, then they should be immediately visible and can be changed.
3. It allows the user to feed audience data that was obtained from different sources into a computer, thus saving time and money.
4. It delivers alternative decisions quickly because it allows the user to examine a number of schedules based on varied constraints.
5. It allows the planner to scan thousands of alternatives quickly.
6. Finally, the computer can find and accumulate many more Rated Exposure Units from among a list of media vehicles than can a group of individuals doing the same thing by hand.

Major disadvantages can outweigh linear programming's advantages:

1. The model does not take reach and frequency into account.
2. It cannot handle the myriad of discount structures one finds in the real world where some rates are determined only by negotiation.
3. It requires a great deal of data that must be constantly updated. The results do not conform to reality.

Simulation

A *simulation model* attempts to reproduce, or simulate, the probable reading or viewing of individuals in the real world to such an extent that it is possible to predict how they will be exposed to media in the future. The model is quite different from linear programming in that it is nonoptimizing, and it contains relatively few, if any, algorithms. The simulation model measures the reading or viewing habits of individuals in a sample population, yielding data in the form of reading and viewing probabilities.

In addition, the model takes into consideration the value of each individual in the marketplace. Obviously some persons are more likely to buy a brand of product than others. Therefore, media vehicles that have large numbers of prospects in their audiences are more heavily weighted than those media with smaller numbers of prospects.

Essentially, then, when programmed through a computer the model provides the planner with an estimate of exposure delivery of specific media vehicles that have already been chosen and scheduled by time periods. The computer also can rank each vehicle in terms of its ability to deliver target audiences at the lowest unit cost. But the model does not produce a media schedule nor can it answer the question of how good a media plan is. If a planner devises two or more media plans and uses the model, the computer will print out the reach and frequency and cost-per-thousand for each plan. But the ultimate decision about which is better rests on the planner's judgment.

Elaborate simulation models have been made that do more than simply provide basic reach and frequency data. In some models, the data are modified by impact evaluation variables. One such variable is vehicle appropriateness. This model assumes that some vehicles are more appropriate for carrying advertisements than others. Perhaps television is more appropriate than newspapers to carry dishwasher detergent ads. Television then might be assigned a weight of 1.10 while newspapers might be assigned a weight of 0.75. The determination of how much weight to assign each media class is usually decided by consensus vote of experts, since there is little objective data on which to base weights.

Another impact variable might be to weight ad forms differently. A 60-second TV commercial, therefore, would be given a different weight than a 30-second commercial, or a full-page, black-and-white newspaper ad. The assignment of weights to different ad forms is another area where there is little objective evidence, so decisions on how much weight to give each form is usually done by consensus vote.

Other simulation models take the value of repetition into consideration. A model created by Dennis Gensch required six repeat exposures of an ad in a given vehicle before that ad could have maximum impact. In addition, Gensch's model allowed for memory decay of ad messages.[1] The decision on how to draw a decay curve usually is based on subjective judgment, plus any objective evidence that is available.

Some people believe that the simulation model generally has a number of advantages over a linear programming model. They feel that the simulation model usually includes fewer simplifying assumptions which, when converted into mathematics, tend to emasculate the media selec-

---

[1]Gensch, Dennis H., *Advertising Planning*, Amsterdam: Elsevier Scientific Publishing Company, 1973, pp. 94–95.

tion problem. As Simon Broadbent noted, the linear programming model may solve a problem, but it may not be the correct problem, while simulation models may come closer to the real problem. Simulation models also are more flexible, theoretically, so that they may be extended into time, if suitable data become available.

Simulation models, nevertheless, have some disadvantages. Broadbent noted that they "suffer because they are restricted to only one heuristic method of obtaining a solution."[2] To overcome this problem, Gensch recommended that a simulation model assessment of a schedule be followed by a heuristic program. Since the simulation model may include judgmental weights applied to impact variables, the media planner could use the same data bank to first evaluate a schedule and then, through heuristic programming, find a number of alternative schedules that are better. But the simulation does not find the best schedule, and this is one of its limitations. Finally, many simulation models devised in the past do not have an effectiveness function, though some of the newer ones do.

Formula Models

At present, neither linear programming nor simulation models are used very much in media planning. Rather models based on formulas are used almost exclusively for calculating the reach, frequency, and frequency distributions of any number of media vehicles. The planner generally pre-selects a number of alternative media vehicles that could deliver the target demographics, and then uses the computer to calculate the reach and other information via the formulas. At times, the planner may even have a computer do an optimization run in which the computer will compare all vehicles submitted and rank them according to optimum reach, frequency, etc.

There are a number of different kinds of formula models available for doing the above calculations. A media planner who wants to know the net reach of a combination of media vehicles could, theoretically, have their audiences measured directly, but at great expense of time, effort, and money. Planners have sought for some kind of formula that could be used to estimate the reach and frequency of alternative vehicles using as few measurements as possible. If, for example, the duplications of every combination of two vehicles being considered were measured, it would be possible to project reach for those two and extend them to a large number of insertions. To validate such formula use, planners have compared observed measurements with estimated measurements to see how large an error results. The best formulas have relatively small degrees of

²Broadbent, Simon, "Media Planning and the Computer by 1970," in *Thomson Medals and Awards for Advertising Research, 1965,* Report, London: The Thomson Organization Ltd., p. 68.

error. Some of the observed measurement data used for comparisons have come from old research such as Alfred Politz's measurement of audience accumulation of *Life* magazine in 1952.

Perhaps the best known and most widely used formula is the *beta binomial model,* which comes from the area of probability statistics. While a typical binomial curve looks much like the curve in a normal distribution, a beta curve closely approximates a typical reach curve. Through the use of the beta function in statistics, it is possible to make survey measurements of audiences of two media vehicles and extend the data to more issues of the same two. In addition, it is possible to calculate a frequency distribution using the beta function.

Richard A. Metheringham devised an early formula for estimating the reach and frequency of vehicles using the beta function, but his version contained a problem: It was possible for the reach level to decline after a certain number of vehicles and insertions had been calculated. At that point, the addition of just one more insertion might result in a decrease of reach, something that does not happen in real life where reach continues to increase, if only by a very small amount.

Newer formulas have resolved the problem of declining reach and reproduce data that corresponds fairly well with observed measurements. The beta binomial model, with varying kinds of modifications, is now being used widely.

The advantages of formula models over others are two-fold: They do not promise as much and therefore less can go wrong in using the results for planning; they estimate reach and frequency fairly well. Disadvantages center around the use of different versions of these models that sometimes produce different results. Some slight differences may be expected, but when the differences are large, the formulas are suspect. Bernard Guggenheim, vice president of support operations at the Campbell-Ewald advertising agency in Detroit, points to an experiment using different formula models in which he found differences in answers that were too great to be acceptable. His findings using one of these models compared with a standard analysis is shown in Table 15–1. Guggenheim called for validation of computer formula models by the Advertising Research Foundation—something that has not been done as yet.

TABLE 15–1. Differences in the Reach of Women Aged 18 to 49

	291 GRPs Late Fringe	245 GRPs Prime, Plus Day
Reach of standard spot system	67.0%	59.3%
Reach of Version B	55.4	67.9
Difference between versions	−11.6%	− 8.6%

Source: Guggenheim, Bernard, "My Black Box Is Better than Your Black Box," *Marketing and Media Decisions,* November 1979, p. 88.

Table 15–2 is an example of a printout of a formula-derived estimation of reach, frequency, and frequency distribution.

Other Uses for Computers in Media Planning

While estimating reach and frequency is certainly one of the most important functions that computers can fulfill for media planners, it certainly is not the only one. Computers are used for many other media planning activities and new uses are continually being found, meaning that computers will probably be used more rather than less in the future. Some of the new computer uses fall directly within the area of media planning, while others may affect marketing and/or creative planning.

Many advertising agencies do not own a computer outright, but rather work with on-line, time-sharing companies such as Telmar and IMS. An agency may have one or more terminals in its offices which can connect to a central computer in some other city. Recently, time-sharing companies have produced small, desk-top, hand computers with special media programs built into them that can calculate some of the same

TABLE 15–2. An Example of Reach and Frequency Calculations Based on a Formula Model

Reach and Frequency of Three Vehicles

Targets: Upscale adults

Vehicles: 3 insertions in CCC
          4 insertions in BBB
          5 insertions in AAA

Total popu-lation	Gross impres-sions	Net reach	Avg. fre-quency	Median fre-quency	Coverage (%)	CPM Gross im-pressions	CPM Net reach
29,356	81,726	20,643	3.96	3.80	70.32	$5.32	$21.07

Total cost is: $434,900.

Frequency	Number	Number in group plus all higher frequency levels	Population (%)
0	8,713		
1	3,285	20,643	70.32
2	2,277	17,358	59.13
3	3,170	15,081	51.37
4	5,322	11,911	40.57
5	2,588	6,589	22.45
6	1,106	4,001	13.63
7	1,210	2,895	9.86
8	687	1,685	5.74
9	699	998	3.40
10	121	299	1.02
11	91	178	0.61
12	87	87	0.30

Source: Interactive Market Service (IMS)

things that the larger computers can. But these small hand computers cannot handle very complex media planning problems.

Here is a partial list of some of the general uses for a computer as an aid in media planning.

Helping the planner evaluate alternatives. One media planning principle widely accepted today is that media vehicles selected should represent the best of all alternatives. But the planner cannot very well examine many alternatives by hand. Through the use of a computer, the planner can expand the number of alternatives to be explored at relatively low cost and with minimum effort. The organization of data by a computer also helps the planner study the output with less effort than if it had to be done by hand. Evaluations are made on the basis of reach, frequency, cost-per-thousand, and frequency distributions both of vehicles and ads in vehicles.

Helping the planner find alternatives to be evaluated. Through the use of heuristic programming, the computer can develop many alternative schedules quickly. These then may be analyzed by the computer through the simulation process.

Saving time and effort in media analysis. The best use of computers at this time is in the area of media analysis. There are so many computations that must be made that huge quantities of time must be alloted for this task if it is done by hand. The computer prints out many kinds of analyses quickly and in convenient order for the media planner. Perhaps one of the major unrealized values in this area is that if the inputs into the computer are correct, then the output is likely to be free from computational or recording errors.

Serving as a learning tool. If planners continue to use computers for media planning they will be forced to be more thoughtful about the underlying assumptions under which they operate. If initial outputs of computers are wrong, the model builder or planner modifies the assumptions and discards erroneous ones. The use of a computer motivates the planner to reevaluate assumptions continually and learn as a result.

Simulating test markets. Another, but limited, use of computers in media planning has been test market simulations in which media strategy plays a role. The test market simulation model is much like the media simulation model, but the former is more comprehensive. It not only attempts to predict consumer exposure to media, but also probable purchase rates, brand-switching rates, attitude changes, and, eventually, market share. Since media play a role in these models, the planner may want to see what responses could be obtained from changes in advertising in much the same way a test marketing experiment allows investigation of advertising changes.

Finding targets with automatic interaction detection (AID). Computers have been used to find the best prospective market segments. The Automatic Interaction Detector technique is one means of dividing a

FIGURE 15–1. Use of AID to Find Best Target Markets

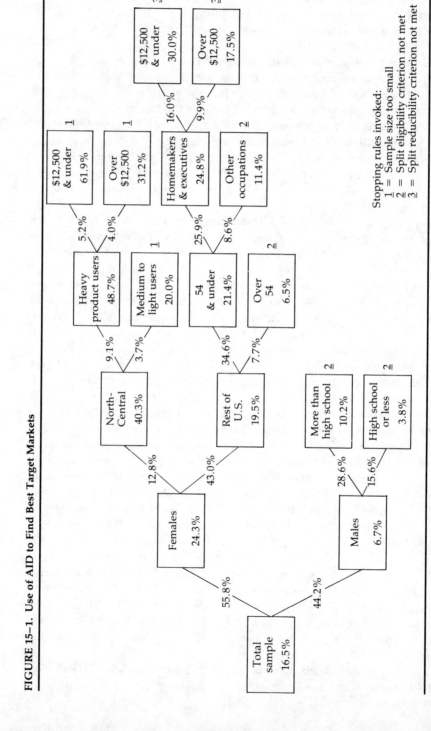

Stopping rules invoked:
1 = Sample size too small
2 = Split eligibility criterion not met
3 = Split reducibility criterion not met

Source: Assael, Henry, "Segmenting Markets by Group Purchasing Behavior: An Application of the AID Technique," *Journal of Marketing Research*, May 1970, p. 154.

market into subgroups on the basis of product usage until the best targets appear.

The method starts with a national sample of individuals chosen because they are representative of the universe, or the entire United States. Then, through an analysis of purchase rates and demographics, the computer is programmed to determine the average product buying rate for each person, identify the most powerful demographic predictor of usage, divide the universe into high and low purchase groups on the basis of the predictor, and continue to subdivide each group until no more meaningful subdivisions can be made.

Henry Assael, professor of marketing at New York University, explained how the process works:

> In operation, the program splits the sample into two subgroups to provide the largest reduction in the unexplained sum of squares of the dependent variable. This is accomplished as follows: group means are determined for each classification of all independent variables, and all dichotomous groupings of each variable are examined. . . . The division will take place at the point of greatest discrimination in group means.[3]

The result looks like a decision tree. Figure 15–1 shows that the best target market, other things being equal, would be females, living in the North Central states, who are heavy users of Brand X, and whose annual income is $12,500 and under. A second group, but much larger in number, would be females in the remainder of the U.S., who are homemakers or executives under 55.

Cross tabulation of demographic market segments. In the past, media planners were handicapped in analyzing marketing data because few cross tabulations were possible. Probably the most frequent cross tabulation was for age and sex. Beyond that, few data were available. The computer, however, makes it possible to obtain multiple cross tabulations to whatever extent the planner would like. As a result, the planner now can look at the relationships of a number of demographic variables at one time. This technique, in addition to AID, provides better opportunities to find the most precise target to whom to direct media.

Other specific examples of computer uses in media planning are shown in Case Studies 15–1 through 15–11. These examples by no means represent all computer planning systems used today. Most of the larger agencies have developed their own proprietary systems for specific uses in planning media for their clients.

---

[3]Assael, Henry, "Segmenting Markets by Group Purchasing Behavior: An Application of the AID Technique," *Journal of Marketing Research*, May 1970, pp. 153–154.

CASE STUDY 15-1
Analysis of Sales Related to Advertising Per Market

Description. This is a breakout of sales or shipments to various markets and advertising dollars spent in those markets. Various ratios are calculated in the form of index numbers that relate population to sales, population to advertising dollars, and advertising dollars to case shipments.

How the analysis is used in planning. This analysis may be used to determine market weights for allocating dollars to markets proportionately. Markets that have the largest percentage of sales (relative to population) usually are assigned higher advertising weights than others.

Example

District	U.S. Pop. (MM)	U.S. Pop. (%)	Shipments (M)	Shipments (%)	Shipments Index	Advertising $(M)	Advertising (%)	Adv. $/M Pop. $	Adv. $/M Pop. Index	Adv. $/Case $(M)	Adv. $/Case Index
Boston	11.5	5.3	36.2	3.6	68	150.3	3.9	13.12	73	4.15	107
New York	17.6	8.1	49.2	4.9	60	240.2	6.2	13.68	76	4.88	126
Philadelphia	7.5	3.5	10.7	1.1	31	105.7	2.7	14.17	78	9.88	254
Syracuse	3.7	1.7	16.8	1.7	98	59.2	1.5	16.08	89	3.52	91
Buffalo	3.2	1.5	7.1	0.7	47	44.9	1.2	13.91	77	6.33	163
***Division	43.4	20.1	120.0	12.0	60	600.3	15.4	13.84	77	5.00	129
Baltimore	5.4	2.5	10.2	1.0	41	75.3	1.9	14.05	78	7.38	190
Wash. DC	7.1	3.3	28.0	2.8	85	103.5	2.7	14.56	81	3.69	95
Charlotte	8.5	3.9	80.5	8.0	204	236.3	6.1	27.85	154	2.94	76
Atlanta	8.8	4.1	64.0	6.4	157	200.7	5.1	22.91	127	3.14	81
Jacksvle	8.9	4.1	10.4	1.0	25	117.3	3.0	13.14	73	****	290
Louisville	4.7	2.2	60.3	6.0	276	169.5	4.3	36.07	200	2.81	72
***Division	43.3	20.1	253.4	25.2	126	902.5	23.1	20.82	115	3.56	92
Pittsburgh	4.7	2.2	14.6	1.5	67	70.8	1.8	15.07	83	4.85	125
Cleveland	5.1	2.3	12.7	1.3	54	76.2	2.0	15.05	83	6.00	154
Detroit	9.4	4.3	11.2	1.1	26	130.7	3.4	13.96	77	****	300
Cincinnati	6.1	2.8	35.6	3.5	125	117.5	3.0	19.12	106	3.30	85
Indianapolis	4.7	2.2	28.3	2.8	131	92.4	2.4	19.85	110	3.27	84
Chicago	8.8	4.1	22.4	2.2	55	114.5	2.9	12.99	72	5.11	132
Milwaukee	4.7	2.2	17.4	1.7	80	64.5	1.7	13.74	76	3.71	95
***Division	43.4	20.1	142.2	14.2	70	666.7	17.1	15.35	85	4.69	121
St. Louis	5.7	2.6	37.8	3.8	142	120.5	3.1	21.10	117	3.19	82
Kansas City	4.8	2.2	42.3	4.2	190	127.9	3.3	26.70	148	3.02	78
Okla. City	5.7	2.7	65.3	6.5	244	186.4	4.8	32.42	180	2.85	73
Dallas	5.1	2.4	52.4	5.2	220	154.3	4.0	30.08	167	2.95	76
Houston	6.8	3.2	34.4	3.4	109	117.9	3.0	17.30	96	3.43	88
Memphis	4.5	2.1	59.2	5.9	283	166.0	4.3	36.91	204	2.80	72
New Orleans	5.2	2.4	54.4	5.4	226	159.6	4.1	30.81	171	2.93	76
***Division	37.9	17.5	345.8	34.5	196	1032.7	26.5	27.27	151	2.99	77
Mpls.	5.4	2.5	11.6	1.2	46	67.6	1.7	12.46	69	5.83	150
Omaha	4.6	2.1	28.1	2.8	131	91.5	2.3	19.89	110	3.26	84
Denver	8.3	3.9	45.4	4.5	117	146.7	3.8	17.60	97	3.23	83
Seattle	6.5	3.0	35.8	3.6	119	116.2	3.0	17.99	100	3.25	84
San Fran	8.6	4.0	14.3	1.4	36	102.9	2.6	12.01	67	7.19	185
Los Angeles	14.6	6.7	7.0	0.7	10	170.6	4.4	11.70	65	****	627
***Division	48.0	22.2	142.2	14.2	64	695.4	17.8	14.50	80	4.89	126
*Total U.S.	216.0	100.0	1003.6	100.0	100	3900.0	100.0	18.06	100	3.89	100

Source: J. Walter Thompson

CASE STUDY 15–2
Allocation of Network Delivery on a Market-by-Market Basis

Description. This is an analysis of network delivery on a market-by-market basis. It shows how a number of network television shows deliver an audience locally. In the example below, the network shows are listed at the top and analyzed. Then a market by market delivery analysis is shown.

How the analysis is used in planning. The media planner does not know how much of each program's audience is delivered into any particular market unless this kind of analysis is done. The planner does know each market's sales potential, however. With this analysis, it is possible to learn whether good markets are being underdelivered and poor markets are overdelivered. The planner may use spot television on top of network to balance weights in some markets.

Example

Actual Program		Comml. Units	Cost/Comml. Unit	Total Sched. Cost	Estimated Program Rating	
Name	Net.				Avg.	GRP
All in Family	C	4	25,000	100,000	16.5	66.0
Waltons	C	4	25,000	100,000	18.5	74.0
Rhoda	C	2	150,000	300,000	17.4	34.8
Bob Newhart	C	2	150,000	300,000	11.1	22.2
Totals		12		800,000		197
Average			66,666		16.4	

Audience Analysis

Pro Rata: % TV Households
Ranked on: % TV Households

Rank	Market Name	% US TVHH	% Target Mkt	Pro Rata Cost/ Market	Gross Aud. Total (000)	Comml. Delvy. Sched. (%)	GRPs Wkly	Schedule GRPs	Index
1	New York	8.90	8.70	71,192	5,464	5.8	16	130	66
2	Los Angeles	5.19	5.05	41,535	3,148	3.3	16	129	65
3	Chicago	3.89	3.92	31,121	3,343	3.5	22	177	90
4	Philadelphia	3.25	3.28	26,018	3,288	3.5	26	208	106
5	Boston	2.41	2.46	19,265	2,136	2.2	23	180	91
6	San Francisco	2.36	2.34	18,872	1,850	1.9	21	164	83
7	Detroit	2.18	2.35	17,429	2,209	2.3	24	195	99
8	Washington, DC	1.83	2.04	14,667	1,931	2.0	25	196	99
9	Cleveland	1.77	1.85	14,172	1,724	1.8	24	193	98
10	Pittsburgh	1.54	1.50	12,331	1,658	1.7	29	230	117
Subtotal		33.33	33.50	266,602	26,752	28.2	20	166	84
Remainder		66.67	66.50	533,398	68,260	71.8	27	213	108
Total		100.00	100.00	800,000	95,012	100.0	24	197	100

Source: Interactive Market Systems (IMS)

CASE STUDY 15–3
Demographic Analysis of a Brand's Users

Description. This is a breakdown of data normally found in Simmons Market Research Bureau reports. Usually, the data are cross-tabulated as in the example below, which has degree of usage (in columns) cross-tabulated with age and income classes.

How the analysis is used in planning. The planner may want to study at close-hand the most significant data about a brand's users. The planner may have found that age and income are the most important demographics (from SMRB data), but wants to have a closer look at these demographics and their relationship with usage. The ultimate aim is to select a precise target market.

Example

Demographic Analysis of Users of Product A

	Total	Total Users	Heavy Users	Medium Users	Light Users
Total	68,386	9,161	3,202	4,101	1,857
% Table	100.0	13.4	4.7	6.0	2.7
% Col.	100.0	100.0	100.0	100.0	100.0
Age 18–34	23,923	4,274	1,406	1,819	1,049
% Table	35.0	6.2	2.1	2.7	1.5
% Col.	35.0	46.7	43.9	44.4	56.5
Age 35–49	18,305	2,352	904	1,096	353
% Table	26.8	3.4	1.3	1.6	0.5
% Col.	26.8	25.7	28.2	26.7	19.0
Age 50+	26,158	2,534	892	1,187	455
% Table	38.3	3.7	1.3	1.7	0.7
% Col.	38.3	27.7	27.9	28.9	24.5
Income $0–8	28,480	2,943	847	1,572	524
% Table	41.6	4.3	1.2	2.3	0.8
% Col.	41.6	32.1	26.5	38.3	28.2
Income $8–10	9,086	1,297	536	490	271
% Table	13.3	1.9	0.8	0.7	0.4
% Col.	13.3	14.2	16.7	11.9	14.6
Income $10+	30,820	4,921	1,819	2,040	1,062
% Table	45.1	7.2	2.7	3.0	1.6
% Col.	45.1	53.7	56.8	49.7	57.2

Source: Telmar

CASE STUDY 15–4
Magazine Reach and Frequency Calculations
for Various Numbers of Issues

Description. This is an analysis of magazine alternatives to show reach over a number of different issues. Also cost-per-thousand data for four color and/or black-and-white ads may be shown (as in the example below).

How this analysis is used in planning. This kind of analysis is useful in planning where it is important to know how many target audience members may be reached. Typically, media plans are made on a month by month basis where the reach is known for any given month, but not for a number of months combined. These data, therefore, provide the longer range time element for decision-making purposes.

Example

Age 18 to 34
Population (000) = 60643
Unweighted Pop. = 5433

Total Audience

Magazine		1 Issue	3 Issue	4 Issue	12 Issue	15 Issue	18 Issue	36 Issue	45 Issue	52 Issue
AAA	Reach (%)	17.20	28.53	31.56	42.51	44.57	46.20	52.04	53.79	54.90
	Gross (000)	10,433	31,299	41,732	125,196	156,495	187,794	375,588	469,485	542,516
	GRPs	17	52	69	206	258	310	619	774	895
	4C CPM GI	5.63	5.63	5.63	5.63	5.41	5.32	5.18	5.07	4.96
	BL CPM GI	6.48	6.48	6.48	6.48	6.22	6.12	5.96	5.83	5.70
BBB	Reach (%)	14.88	23.85	26.23	34.91	36.58	37.91	42.76	44.24	45.18
	Gross (000)	9,023	27,069	36,092	108,276	135,345	162,414	324,828	406,035	469,196
	GRPs	15	45	60	179	223	268	536	670	774
	4C CPM GI	4.61	4.61	4.61	4.61	4.42	4.36	4.24	4.15	4.07
	BL CPM GI	5.30	5.30	5.30	5.30	5.09	5.01	4.88	4.77	4.69
CCC	Reach (%)	14.62	25.75	28.85	40.36	42.55	44.30	50.54	52.41	53.59
	Gross (000)	8,866	26,598	35,464	106,392	132,990	159,588	319,176	398,970	461,032
	GRPs	15	44	58	175	219	263	526	658	760
	4C CPM GI	2.27	2.27	2.27	2.27	2.18	2.13	2.09	2.04	2.00
	BL CPM GI	2.61	2.61	2.61	2.61	2.50	2.45	2.40	2.35	2.29
DDD	Reach (%)	4.84	8.95	10.18	15.08	16.09	16.91	20.00	20.97	21.60
	Gross (000)	2,934	8,802	11,736	35,208	44,010	52,812	105,624	132,030	152,568
	GRPs	5	15	19	58	73	87	174	218	252
	4C CPM GI	9.82	9.82	9.82	9.82	9.42	9.28	9.03	8.83	7.61
	BL CPM GI	11.29	11.29	11.29	11.29	10.84	10.67	10.39	10.16	8.75

Source: Interactive Market Systems (IMS)

CASE STUDY 15–5
Reach and Frequency of Alternative Media Packages

Description. This is a report of the reach and frequency of a number of alternative vehicle packages. The example below shows that the first package consisted of six insertions of vehicle AAA, four of FF, six of BBB, and two of GGG. The package developed a net reach of 76.21 percent and a frequency of 4.7. Other data such as cost-per-thousand, gross impressions, and total cost are also shown. This package, then, may be compared with other packages.

How this analysis is used in planning. The planner usually selects a number of vehicles that he or she feels will best reach the target audience. The planner uses audience analysis data from the syndicated services to determine which package group will reach the largest number of targets at the lowest unit cost. This analysis is a help in making vehicle selection decisions.

Example

Population: 50,833

Schedule		Total Uses	Total Cost	Net Reach	% Net Reach	CPM Net	Gross Imprs.	CPM Gross	Avg. Freq.
6 AAA	6 BBB								
4 FF	2 GGG	18	593,000	38,739	76.21	15.31	182,084	3.26	4.7
6 AAA	6 BBB								
2 E	4 FFF	18	595,000	38,406	75.55	15.49	174,678	3.41	4.5
6 AAA	2 GGG								
6 H	4 BBB	18	586,000	38,338	75.42	15.28	174,148	3.36	4.5
6 AAA	6 BBB								
4 CC	2 EEE	18	599,000	38,112	74.97	15.72	177,406	3.38	4.7
6 AAA	6 BBB								
4 CCC	1 DDD	17	595,000	37,903	74.56	15.70	181,194	3.28	4.8
6 AAA	4 FFF								
2 GGG	6 HHH	18	578,000	32,341	63.62	17.87	123,092	4.70	3.8

Source: Telmar

CASE STUDY 15–6
Optimization of Reach and Frequency

Description. This analysis takes a number of media vehicle alternatives and calculates all possible combinations of them until those with the highest reach (optimum) for a given budget are found. This is done in a series of steps by the computer.

How this analysis is used in planning. The media planner may have found, through prior planning, a number of media vehicles that reach the target audience very well. However, some of these vehicles in combinations with selected others may produce more reach at a lower unit cost than others. The computer does the calculations and prints out the optimum combination. The planner then must decide whether this combination meets all other objectives before deciding to use it.

Example

Master Optimization

271 Schedules Evaluated
Schedule: Known Optimal
8 insertions cost $243,250

Total Population	Gross Impr.	Net Reach	Average Frequency	%–Cover	CPM–GI	CPM–NR
17,711	36,043	11,470	3.1422	64.7655	6.75	21.21
1 DDD						
1 BBB						
5 AAA						
1 CCC						

Other Schedules (Not Optimal)
8 insertions cost $242,250

Total Population	Gross Impr.	Net Reach	Average Frequency	%–Cover	CPM–GI	CPM–NR
17,711	32,577	11,373	2.8645	64.2137	7.44	21.30
1 EEE						
1 DDD						
1 BBB						
4 AAA						
1 CCC						

Source: Interactive Market Systems (IMS)

CASE STUDY 15–7
Reach and Frequency and Frequency Distribution

Description. This is a basic analysis of a package of media vehicles to show reach, frequency, and frequency distribution. The frequency distribution is shown in two forms: One is an incremental form that shows, for each insertion, the number and percentage exposed individually. The other is cumulative, showing the number and percentage of targets exposed for all levels up to the one in question.

How this analysis is used in planning. In order to make decisions about which media to use and how the media attains objectives, this analysis is necessary. The frequency distribution is especially useful for demonstrating how many people will be exposed to a given number of advertising impressions. Frequency distributions are also necessary to calculate "*effective* reach and/or frequency."

Example

Media Name	Number of Uses	Unit Cost	Average Audience	CPM	Percent Coverage
AAA	4	35,000	12,894	2.71	25.37
BBB	3	36,500	14,662	2.49	28.84
CCC	2	16,500	2,580	6.40	5.08
DDD	1	26,000	5,538	4.69	10.89

Total Cost	$ 308,500
Total Uses	10
Net Reach	34,159
Percent Net Reach	67.20
CPM Net Reach	9.03
Gross Impressions	106,260
CPM Gross Impressions	2.90
Average Frequency	3.11

Insertion Level	Exposed		Exposed at Least	
	(%)	(000)	(%)	(000)
0	32.80	16,673	100.00	50,833
1	19.39	9,854	67.20	34,160
2	13.88	7,054	47.82	24,306
3	10.36	5,266	33.94	17,252
4	7.77	3,952	23.58	11,986
5	5.76	2,927	15.80	8,033
6	4.14	2,103	10.05	5,107
7	2.83	1,437	5.91	3,004
8	1.77	902	3.08	1,567
9	0.95	484	1.31	665
10	0.36	181	0.36	181

Source: Telmar

CASE STUDY 15–8
Magazine Audience Analysis with In-Home, Out-of-Home Weighting

Description. This analysis shows magazine audience delivery broken down by in-home and out-of-home and total audience segments. In addition, it is possible to weight the out-of-home segment (or in-home) as desired.

How this analysis is used in planning. Many planners feel strongly that out-of-home magazine audiences should be given less weight than in-home audiences because the former do not have an opportunity to see a given magazine regularly. This analysis helps the planner see just what a list of magazines actually delivers on a weighted basis (out-of-homes weighted 50 percent in sample).

Example

Target Market: Men 18–34, Household Income $15,000+, A Counties
Population = 7295 (000)
Percent of Base = 10.07

In-Home	Cost	Weight	(000)	% Covg.	% Comp.	CPM
Magazine AAA	21,300	100.00	134*	1.8	13.3	158.96
Magazine BBB	41,590	100.00	1,024	14.0	17.5	40.62
Magazine CCC	49,750	100.00	149*	2.0	6.6	333.89
Magazine DDD	13,390	100.00	23**	0.3	6.8	582.17
Magazine EEE	20,670	100.00	101*	1.4	17.5	204.65
Magazine FFF	13,440	100.00	452	6.2	24.0	29.73
Total (With Out-of Home Discounted 50%)						
1. Magazine AAA	21,300	100.00	247	3.4	13.8	86.23
2. Magazine BBB	41,590	100.00	1,347	18.5	16.8	30.88
3. Magazine CCC	49,750	100.00	159	2.2	6.4	312.89
4. Magazine DDD	13,390	100.00	31	0.4	7.2	431.94
5. Magazine EEE	20,670	100.00	175	2.4	17.7	118.11
6. Magazine FFF	13,440	100.00	529	7.3	19.7	25.41
Total Audience						
Magazine AAA	21,300	100.00	361	4.9	14.1	59.00
Magazine BBB	41,590	100.00	1,671	22.9	16.5	24.89
Magazine CCC	49,750	100.00	169*	2.3	6.3	294.38
Magazine DDD	13,390	100.00	39**	0.5	7.4	343.33
Magazine EEE	20,670	100.00	250	3.4	17.9	82.68
Magazine FFF	13,440	100.00	606	8.3	17.3	22.18

Source: Interactive Market Systems (IMS)

CASE STUDY 15–9
Reach and Frequency Table

Description. This is a table showing the reach, frequency, and effective reach for a given level of GRPs for primetime in network television programs. The effective reach shown in the example is of two different levels: from 3 to 8 and from nine-plus.

How this analysis is used in planning. Early in the planning process, the person in charge may want some quick analyses of how many GRPs will deliver various kinds of reaches and frequencies. Such a table is a handy method for finding the answers quickly. By analyzing more or fewer GRPs, it is possible to increase or decrease reaches or effective reaches quickly.

Example

Prime Network Average 4/Week Reach Table

4/Week GRPs	Average Frequency	Total Reach	3–8 Reach	9+ Reach
50	1.1	44	0	0
100	1.7	58	10	0
150	2.2	68	22	0
200	2.7	74	34	0
250	3.1	80	42	1
300	3.6	83	50	2
350	4.1	86	54	4
400	4.5	88	56	8
450	5.0	90	57	13
500	5.6	90	58	17

Source: J. Walter Thompson

CASE STUDY 15–10
Spot TV Planning Guide

Description. An analysis of the ability of spot TV to reach various target markets at different levels of coverage. In the example below, the top analysis shows coverage of 50 percent of the U.S. and the bottom, 100 percent. Note also that this analysis can show network TV delivery in conjunction with spot television and the delivery of various dayparts.

How this analysis is used in planning. A media planner usually considers a number of alternative strategies before settling on a final decision. In order to make the wisest decision, it must be known how various alternatives would affect delivery results. This analysis helps in such a respect.

Example

Plan: 1
Spot Universe 50.0%

	W 18+				W 18–34				W 18–49			
	Reach	Freq.	GRPs	Adj.	Reach	Freq.	GRPs	Adj.	Reach	Freq.	GRPs	Adj.
Grand Total	92	21.4	1970	1003	93	17.4	1621	835	93	19.1	1774	909
Total Network	85	6.9	587	360	89	5.9	527	326	90	6.2	560	344
Tot. Nite Net.	83	5.6	466	305	88	4.9	431	282	89	5.1	452	295
Total Spot	84	16.5	1383	643	88	12.4	1094	509	90	13.5	1214	565
Day Network	33	3.7	121	55	30	3.2	96	44	32	3.4	108	49
Prime Network	77	4.6	354	258	82	4.0	326	238	85	4.0	338	247
Late Nite Net.	45	2.5	112	47	59	1.8	105	44	57	2.0	114	48
Day Spot	63	15.5	977	472	85	9.3	787	380	92	9.6	880	425
Early Fringe	71	5.7	406	171	67	4.6	307	129	69	4.8	334	140

Total U.S. 100.0%

	W 18+				W 18–34				W 18–49			
	Reach	Freq.	GRPs	Adj.	Reach	Freq.	GRPs	Adj.	Reach	Freq.	GRPs	Adj.
Grand Total	89	14.4	1279	681	91	11.8	1075	580	92	12.7	1167	627
Total Network	85	6.9	587	360	89	5.9	527	326	90	6.2	560	344
Tot. Nite Net.	83	5.6	466	305	88	4.9	431	282	89	5.1	452	295
Total Spot	42	16.5	692	321	44	12.5	548	254	45	13.5	607	283
Day Network	33	3.7	121	55	30	3.2	96	44	32	3.4	108	49
Prime Network	77	4.6	354	258	82	4.0	326	238	85	4.0	338	247
Late Nite Net.	45	2.5	112	47	59	1.8	105	44	57	2.0	114	48
Day Spot	32	15.3	489	236	43	9.2	394	190	46	9.6	440	213
Early Fringe	36	5.6	203	85	34	4.5	154	64	35	4.8	167	70

Source: Interactive Market Systems (IMS)

CASE STUDY 15–11
Weekly Radio Planning Guide

Description. This analysis shows a typical radio buy delivery for one week in a given market. It shows the number of stations, commercials, reach, and frequency ranked by amount of reach per station.

How this analysis is used in planning. This analysis would most likely be requested by the radio buyer as he or she contemplates the amount of delivery to be achieved in a given market. In the example below, a reach goal of 40 percent of the market is given. The analysis therefore should tell the buyer how many stations he needs to achieve the 40 percent goal level.

Example

Rad-Buy Radio Planning System (1 Week)

Metro Anytown   Total 18+
ARB Jan.–Feb.   Target Pop. (00): 115,476

Schedule: 3 spots Mon.–Fri. 6 am–7 pm
Buy Schedule: Until 60.0% of each station's cume is reached

Station Order: Rank by Reach
Market Goal: Reach 40.0% of Target

	By Station				Cumulative	
	No. of Spots	Gross Imps. (00)	% Net Reach	Average Frequency	Net Reach	Average Frequency
WAAA-AM	18	31,014	11.53	2.33	11.53	2.33
WBBB-AM	21	29,484	11.11	2.30	21.67	2.42
WCCC-AM	12	26,928	10.53	2.22	29.96	2.53
WDDD-AM	18	25,866	9.54	2.35	36.41	2.69
WEEE-AM	15	14,775	5.58	2.29	39.73	2.79
WFFF-FM	9	14,616	5.54	2.28	42.87	2.88

Source: Telmar

Thoughts on the Use of Computers in Media Planning

Few people would disagree that computers are playing an increasingly important role in the media planning process. The use of computers saves time and frees the planner from a great deal of lengthy hand-computations and routine paperwork that was formerly required. This freedom, theoretically, should mean that the planner would have more time to concentrate on making judgments and evaluating the quantified data. It should allow the planner more time to make creative, rather than mechanical, decisions. If such is the case, then computers help planners do a better job.

Some experts, however, are concerned about the possibility that planners could develop a blind acceptance of computerized data to such an extent that it could lessen the amount of judgment that goes into planning. These experts point out that no matter how valid formula models are, they do not justify uncritical acceptance of the data without being modified by experience and judgment. They fear that computer printouts may carry an aura of unwarranted credibility. The sight of page after page of computerized numbers printed in neat columns on computer paper could have a numbing effect on a planner.

Part of this problem exists because media models usually are not the concern of most media planners. The evaluation of such models is usually left to a few persons in an advertising agency, such as a research director or department head. The planner may assume that because someone has justified the use of the computer model, then it must be valid.

Other experts, however, feel that there is little cause for concern. Richard C. Anderson, former director of media resources at Needham, Harper & Steers, Chicago, pointed out that there are at least four problems that a computer cannot answer in the media planning process. Therefore, planners will *always* have to modify computer printouts with a great deal of personal judgment. The four unanswerable problems are:

1. A computer cannot tell the planner which medium is most suitable for the message. Such a decision has to be made by the planner in cooperation with creative strategists.
2. The computer cannot analyze environments of media and tell which is best for the message being disseminated. While attempts have been made to quantify qualitative media values, there are few persons who accept such numbers as being valid in the planning process.
3. The computer cannot tell the planner when to switch to some other medium. This is a decision that has to be made by watching marketing results and synthesizing a great deal of other information before making a decision.
4. The computer cannot tell the planner how to reach the consumers with an unexpected message in an unexpected place. Anderson said that there is a time to take a leap into the unknown and this decision is more a matter of gut feeling than fact.

No one can tell you when to make this judgment call, but when it works, you have a final bit of assurance that the computer cannot dominate you. It could be a decision to take a TV maker's $4,000,000 budget, which is struggling to be seen on the tube against competitors with far more dollars to spend, and taking the same money and putting it all into one, single print medium with frequency and merchandising events to help it along.[4]

Other experts agree with Anderson. The computer will not eliminate judgment in media planning because the numbers must be interpreted first before they can be used. (See Figure 15–2.) As long as one of the major requirements for good planning is subjective judgment added to quantifiable computer data, there will be no danger of developing media planning automatons.

The computer can aid in the planning process. But it should not be the only contributor to planning. As the price of media space and time rises, and as clients spend more money in media, there will be a need for more and better media plans. The computer should be an important aid

---

[4]Anderson, Richard C., "Do Computers Leave Room for Judgment?" *Advertising Age,* Jan. 14, 1980, pp. 47–48.

FIGURE 15–2. Interpreting the Numbers

Source: Surmanek, Jim, "More to Buying Media than Number Review," *Advertising Age*,
       May 21, 1979, p. 66.

in this process. Planners might better use computers if they could spend
more time learning about programmed models. They should learn the
underlying assumptions on which the models are based as well as their
strengths and limitations. As clients ask for more accountability for decisions, a valid model will help explain those decisions that are based on
computer usage. Computers will never replace planners, but they will
certainly help them more than they have in the past.

QUESTIONS FOR DISCUSSION

1. What value is there in creating a model of media planning?
2. What is the main advantage of using the beta binomial formula in estimating the reach and frequency of vehicles?
3. Why would AID data be better than using a single demographic variable in target identification?
4. Briefly explain the purpose of a computer optimization run.
5. Explain some of the major concerns about the use of computers in media planning.

SELECTED READINGS

Abelson, Robert P., and Bernstein, Alex, *The Simulation of a Test Market*, New York: Simulmatics Corporation, August 1962.

Alpert, Lewis, "Measuring Effects of Simulation," in *Advertising Research Foundation 18th Annual Conference Proceedings*, 1972, pp. 48–50.

Assael, Henry, "Segmenting Markets by Group Purchasing Behavior: An Application of the AID Technique," *Journal of Marketing Research*, May 1970, pp. 153–58.

Atwater, H. B., Jr., "Mathematical Models to Improve Advertising Decisions," in *Perspectives in Advertising Management*, Association of National Advertisers, April 1969, pp. 75–88.

Bass, Frank M., and Lomsdale, Robert T., "An Exploration of Linear Programming in Media," *Journal of Marketing Research*, May 1966, pp. 179–88.

Broadbent, Simon, "Media Planning and the Computer by 1970," in *Thomson Medals and Awards for Advertising Research*, London, 1965, pp. 63–86.

Broadbent, Simon R., "A Year's Experience of the LPE Media Model," in *Advertising Research Foundation 1965 Conference Proceedings*, pp. 51–56.

Brown, Douglas B., and Warshaw, Martin R., "Media Selection by Linear Programming," *Journal of Marketing Research*, February 1965, pp. 83–88.

Brown, Douglas B., "A Practical Procedure for Media Selection," *Journal of Marketing Research*, August 1967, pp. 262–69.

Charles, A.; Cooper, W. W.; DeVoe, J. K.; Learner, D. B.; and Reinceke, W., "A Goal Programming Model for Media Planning" and "Note on Goal Programming Model for Media Planning," *Management Science*, April 1968, pp. 423–36.

Day, Ralph L., "Linear Programming in Media Selection," *Journal of Advertising Research*, June 1962, pp. 40–44.

Dobbins, Robert, and Shiffman, Philip, "What Kind of Mathematical Models, If Any, Are Useful for Day-to-Day Activity or Long-Range Planning?" *Media Decisions*, January 1972, p. 52.

Ferguson, Robert D., and Sargent, F., *Linear Programming*, New York: McGraw-Hill, 1958.

Fleck, Robert A., Jr., "How Media Planners Process Information," *Journal of Advertising Research*, April 1973, pp. 14–18.

Friedman, Lawrence, "Constructing a

Media Simulation Model," *Journal of Advertising Research*, August 1970, pp. 33–39.

Gensch, Dennis H., "A Computer Simulation Model for Selecting Advertising Schedules," *Journal of Marketing Research*, May 1969, pp. 203–14.

Gensch, Dennis H., *Advertising Planning*, New York: Elsevier Scientific Research Publishing Company, 1973.

Gensch, Dennis H., "Media Factors: A Review Article," *Journal of Marketing Research*, May 1970, pp. 216–25.

Gensch, Dennis H., "Computer Models in Advertising Media Selection," *Journal of Marketing Research*, November 1968, pp. 414–24.

Headen, R. S.; Klompmaker, J. E.; and Teel, J. E., "TV Audience Exposure," *Journal of Advertising Research*, 1976, pp. 49–52.

Jones, P. I., "The Future Use of Computers in Media Planning—Research and Planning, A Dichotomy?" in *Thomson Medals and Awards for Advertising Research*, London, 1965, pp. 103–24.

Kaplan, R. S., and Shocker, A. D., "Discount Effects on Media Plans," *Journal of Advertising Research*, June 1971, pp. 37–43.

Keshin, M., Lyman, R. F.; Ross, K.; and St. Georges, J., *Some Important Things I Believe A Young Account Executive Should Know About Electronic Data Processing*, American Association of Advertising Agencies, January 1969.

Knowlton, Arch, "Using the Computer to Select and Appraise Media," in *Perspectives in Advertising Management*, Association of National Advertisers, April 1969, pp. 178–84.

Kotler, Philip, "Toward an Explicit Model for Media Selection," *Journal of Advertising Research*, March 1964, pp. 34–41.

Kotler, Philip, "Computerized Media Planning: Techniques, Needs and Prospects," in *Occasional Papers in Advertising*, Urbana, Ill., American Academy of Advertising, 1965.

Landis, Jack B., "Improving Media Schedules via Computers" *Computer Operations*, January–February 1968, pp. 22–25.

Learner, D., and Godfrey, M., "Mathematical Methods of Media Selection," *A Report of the Sixth Meeting of the Advertising Research Foundation Operations Research Discussion Group*, New York, December 1961.

Liebman, L., and Lee, E., "Reach and Frequency Estimating Services," *Journal of Advertising Research*, 1974, pp. 23–25.

Little, John D., and Lodish, L. M., "A Media Planning Calculus," *Operations Research*, February 1969, pp. 1–35.

Maneloveg, Herbert, "A Year of Linear Programming Media Planning for Clients," in *Advertising Research Foundation 8th Annual Conference Report*, New York, October 1962.

Moran, William T., "Practical Media Models: What Must They Look Like?" Paper presented at the Midwest Conference of the Advertising Research Foundation, Chicago, November 1962.

Schreiber, Robert J., "A Practical Procedure for Media Selection: Comments," *Journal of Marketing Research*, May 1968, pp. 221–24.

Schreiber, Robert J., "Instability in Media Exposure Habits," *Journal of Advertising Research*, April 1974, pp. 13–17.

St. Georges, Joseph, "How Practical is the Media Model?" *Journal of Marketing Research*, July 1963, pp. 31–33.

Stasch, Stanley, "Linear Programming and Media Selection: A Comment," *Journal of Marketing Research*, May 1967, pp. 205–7.

Stasch, Stanley, "Linear Programming and Space-Time Considerations in Media Selection," *Journal of Advertising Research*, December 1965, pp. 40–46.

Surmanek, James, "More to Buying Media Than Number Review," *Advertising Age*, May 21, 1979, pp. 64, 66.

Teng-Pin-Yu, Tom, "The National Media Simulation Model," *Computer Operations*, September–October 1967, pp. 11–12.

Wilson, C. L., et al, "Mathematical Programming for Better Media Selections," American Association of Advertising Agencies, *Papers from the Regional Conventions, 1961*.

Zangwill, W. I., "Media Selection by Decision Programming," *Journal of Advertising Research*, September 1965, pp. 30–36.

16
The Future

Everything you have read in the preceding 15 chapters applies to the state of the art of advertising as it now exists. The future of advertising is shaping up as something quite different from what we have been accustomed to. There will be enormous changes in the years ahead—in our society as a whole, in media availability, and in media consumption patterns. Moving at great speed is technological evolution that will affect how people consume various media and how advertisers reach consumers with their advertising.

Casey Stengel once said: "Predictions are a very tricky business. Especially if they involve the future." But predictions must be made so that advertisers and media planners can cope with change and pave the way for a better understanding of what might happen. All media plans are written for the future, even if that future is only three months to a year away. The astute media planner is constantly trying to foretell what will happen—what costs will be, which TV programs will be viewed and at what levels, which radio stations will garner what kinds of audiences, which magazines will perform as they have in the past, and on and on. Therefore, attempting to predict what media will be like 10 years hence can only be an aid to the media planner, so the planner can take advantage of the change and harness the opportunities it might present.

Population Changes

Let's first make some predictions about people. America is undergoing substantial changes. Inflation, skyrocketing energy costs, the availability —or unavailability—of energy, unemployment, and the continuing international skirmishes in which our government finds itself embroiled are making people wonder what kind of future they and their children face. All of these events affect the fundamental values of Americans, and to a great extent affect the demographic composition of the population.

The U.S. Census indicates that the population will not grow much in numbers in the decade of the 1980s, but it will grow older. The total U.S. population will increase by only 22,000,000 from 1980 to 1990—a 10 percent increase, compared with 13 percent from 1960 to 1970. Table 16–1 compares today's population bulges with those expected in 1990. Hardly any change is expected in the number of people aged under 25. With a decreasing birth rate and people living longer, the population profile will be older. The 1970 median age was 28. For 1980 it was 30.2, and for 1990 the projected median age is 32.8.

In coming years, there will be smaller family units, but more of them. While the total population will not increase much, and the number of persons per household will actually decline (from more than 3 to close to 2.5), the number of people living alone will grow. The percentage of single-person households will grow from 23 percent now, to 26 percent 10 years from now.

Minority populations will increase, especially Hispanics. The United States is now experiencing a wave of immigration from Mexico, the Caribbean, and South America. According to the U.S. Census, there are now over 12,000,000 Hispanic Americans. Their number has grown at an even faster rate than that of American Blacks—three times as fast in the past eight years and almost ten times as fast during the 1960s. These census estimates do not include the illegal population which is conservatively estimated to include more than 7,000,000 undocumented Hispanic aliens. It's possible that by the end of the decade, Hispanics will represent 25 percent of the U.S. population—and a much higher proportion in certain geographic centers, such as the Southwest.

The population will continue to shift geographically. More and more Americans are moving to the Sunbelt states. During the 1970s, two fifths of the U.S. population growth occurred in three states: California, Florida, and Texas. There is no evidence that this trend will change. Big, overcrowded, cold northern cities will lose population to the warmer climate cities.

The economic pie will be sliced differently in the years ahead. The 1980s will usher in a period of economic extremes. The now comfortable

TABLE 16–1. U.S. Population Projections by Age (Millions)

Age	1980	1990	Increase	
			Millions	(%)
Total	223	246	23	10
65+	25	30	5	20
45–64	44	46	2	5
25–44	62	78	16	26
Under 25	92	92	–	–

middle class will have to strive to "stay ahead". . . staying ahead of inflation and the tax collector. Disposable income will erode as income and sales taxes continue to inch up. And the real income left after these deductions will buy less and less as inflation raises prices at a faster rate than real income increases. If the inflationary spiral abates, we could, of course, see an easing that would stimulate the economy.

Energy costs will take a bigger bite. How big, no one knows. But the past trend is indicative: In 1970, the average fuel cost per BTU was 30.4 cents; in 1973, it was 41.9 cents; in 1977, $1.08. Energy costs have a ripple effect on much of the economy: industrial production, home heating, and transportation. Food scientists at Cornell University estimate that the 240 percent increase in American corn yields between 1946 and 1970 was accompanied by a 310 percent increase in the cost of energy used to produce that corn.

So, in the coming years we will see an older population, smaller family units, a higher percentage of minority population, a continuing geographic movement to the Sunbelt, and less disposable income for the masses. All of these factors will have a marked effect on what people will be like, and the population will move from a *basically* poor/middle class/ upperclass structure to a new market segmentation.

Table 16–2 provides a picture of what American consumers will be like by the end of the 1980s. People will fit into one of four segments.

The younger haves. These are people who are essentially now in college—for the most part the readers of this textbook. The college student today is looking at a world where it will be far more difficult to make a living—especially one that is considered a good living. "Me" is becoming increasingly more important: my career, my future, my possessions, my body, my health. The younger haves, skeptical of tomorrow, will favor going into debt

TABLE 16–2. The Market Segmentation of 1990

		Younger	
	Affluent		Underclassed
	Educated		Disenfranchised
	Careful		Disillusioned
	Cautious		
Haves			*Have-nots*
	Affluent		Poorest of the Poor
	Free-spending		Need more government
	Less cautious		assistance and
	Less careful		intervention
		Older	

today for what they want tomorrow. They will expect more from life, from relationships, and from themselves. And this demand for more will make this group very careful—reading the specs, looking for performance and value.

The younger have-nots. This group exists now. It is the same group that challenges the economic and social status quo. It is a group that will live in a society with moral and political commitments to social welfare programs. The younger have-nots will continue to be an underclassed, disenfranchised, and disillusioned segment of the population. There could well be negative social consequences as a result of this group's actions.

The older haves. The focus on "me" will not be limited to the younger haves. The older haves will be more concerned with themselves than with their children and grandchildren. They will not especially be concerned with building an estate for their heirs and retiring into a moderate-expense way of life.

In 1990, those aged 50 and older will be the same people who were the free spirits of the 1960s. Their outlook on life was formed in a relatively optimistic social environment. The older haves will be self-indulgent spenders, less cautious about spending than the younger haves. This assumes that those now approaching this age category are preparing for it. If the economy sputters there could be a dramatic change in how the "older haves" view money.

The older have-nots. This group will be the most economically disenfranchised in America.

Advertising in the 1980s

Advertising and marketing will confront a changed consumer, and increasingly complex, specialized, and expensive media. The great technological advances now becoming operational, especially in television, coupled with changes in the family, the economy, and society as a whole, will usher in a decade of media selectivity never known before. The remainder of this chapter will explore the changes in the major media (magazines, newspapers, radio, out-of-home, and television) and demonstrate how media planning must adapt to these changes.

Magazines

It is predicted that magazines will grow in the 1980s at a slow but steady pace. Circulation, in general, will keep pace with population increases. Right now the average adult spends about half an hour a day reading magazines. There is no evidence that time spent reading will decline. But *what* is read will change.

The greatest growth in magazines is expected in special interest magazines and special editions of existing magazines. We've seen much evidence of this already. Magazines such as *Omni, Money, Panorama,* and *Games* have debuted in just the last few years. These, and other "lifestyle" publications, are carving a unique niche in the total circulation pie. Mass audience publications are losing circulation. Many large circulation publications are producing more and more demographic and geographic editions that appeal to specific segments of the population. The result of all of this change is an increasingly fragmented medium where a specific publication will reach only a specific, and oftentimes small, audience.

Costs are increasing. Production and editorial costs, ink, paper, and postage are problems that all publishers must deal with. Publishers have the advantage of being able to increase advertising costs and cover prices to offset production costs. Cover and subscription prices will continue to increase. By the end of the decade it will not be uncommon for single issue cover prices to reach $3 and even $4, which appears extraordinarily high relative to today's family income level, but which will be commonplace in the 1990s. The higher prices will limit circulation levels.

In the last decade, in order to maintain a more competitive edge over broadcast media, publishers did not increase advertising costs in the same proportion as production costs. Readers helped absorb a substantial amount of the production cost. But advertisers will see a change in this pattern. In order to maintain circulation at a level that allows the publication to be a viable alternative for advertisers, publishers will have to balance carefully the cost of advertising and the cost to the reader. Advertisers will be in a better position than readers to absorb most of the cost. (Remember, inflation is biting into consumers' real income and consumers must make careful decisions about their discretionary income and how much they will pay for the privilege of reading magazines.)

Russell Hall editorial reports show that most national magazines have an advertising to editorial ratio of about 55/45. This is already an increase over 10 years ago when advertising constituted no more than 50 percent of all pages in an issue. By the end of the decade, 60 out of every 100 magazine pages will be advertising.

There is no research showing the perceived value of a magazine with a preponderance of advertising. Some magazines, such as *Seventeen* and *Harper's Bazaar,* are in fact often purchased by readers very much for their advertising. But whether or not readers think they are getting a better, or worse, value when advertising makes up the majority of pages is not important. What is important is the idea of "clutter." Will an advertisement be read in a cluttered environment? If readership of advertising declines, will more pages of advertising in a given magazine be necessary to effectively communicate with the reader? These questions have not been answered, and unfortunately, there is no research on the drawing boards right now that addresses the issue. The astute media planner, however, must keep these questions in mind when evaluating magazines in the future.

Newspapers

As with magazines, consumers spend about half an hour a day reading a newspaper. This will continue. Circulation will increase in a fairly direct proportion to population increases. And as people move around geographically, newspaper circulation will follow—from the central city to the suburbs to the Sunbelt.

Newspaper publishers will continue to develop special interest and geographic sections. The *Chicago Tribune* coined the phrase "Sectional Revolution" to describe all the new sections of many large daily newspapers that were created to attract new readers, to better serve the readers' interests in specific subjects, and to offer advertisers an opportunity to position ads in a specific editorial environment.

By the end of the decade, it is likely that newspapers will develop daily suburban editions. The editing would occur on location in suburbs and be relayed to the center city operations for make-up. The totally made-up newspaper would then be relayed back to the suburban printing facility using cathode ray equipment. The suburban editions (suburban section plus the center city portions) would then be printed and distributed in the outlying areas. Big city news would be incorporated into suburban editorial. These localized sections and editions will serve to target consumers in an even more precise manner than now—and, of course, will also fragment audiences further.

Newspapers will also be troubled by the rising costs of paper, printing, distribution, and editorial. Publishers will continue to raise advertising rates to pay for these increased production costs, and they will also increase cover prices to the readers.

Newspapers will continue to be an important medium for advertisers, because of their immediacy in delivering advertising, their retail orientation, and schedule flexibility. They are now the second most local of major media (out-of-home being the most local) and with the advances in sectional and geographic editions, newspapers will become more local in nature and therefore more efficient in reaching small segments of the population.

The printed newspaper is now available on your TV set. Two techniques, now in test operation, make this possible.

Teletext printed messages are carried along with the normal broadcast signal. The subscriber is supplied with a key-pad and a decoder attached to the TV set. This equipment enables the user to access the

Teletext signal and receive specifically requested data, such as classified advertising, airline schedules, theater reviews, restaurant listings, etc.

Viewdata takes Teletext a step further and allows the viewer to interact with the TV set (not unlike QUBE). With Viewdata, the subscriber requests specific information (using specialized equipment), such as a catalog listing, and then can order the merchandise directly from the TV set by punching certain codes on the TV attachment. The advertiser then sends the merchandise and the invoice directly to the consumer.

Clearly, the viewer who subscribes to the Teletext or Viewdata systems can preempt programming or commercials at any time to use the systems—a real threat to broadcasting.

The Electronic Newspaper

Such publishers as the New York Times Company and Dow Jones & Company have been supplying professional and business customers with data electronically through news-retrieval services. As the cost for computers declines, general-interest newspapers are testing the viability of having all their news broadcast on TV. Many newspapers have already converted their production operations to electronics, with computers and display screens in newsrooms and press rooms. Extending the technology to delivering news to homes would be relatively simple.

There are a number of experiments now in operation in the United States. The *Ledger & Times* in Murray, Kentucky, feeds its text onto a cable TV screen that can be seen by any cable viewer tuning in. Knight-Ridder newspapers is aggressively testing Viewdata. Gannett Company, the nation's largest circulation newspaper chain, plans to establish a satellite network to transmit new information services. The New York Times Company and the Times-Mirror Company are among the chains buying cable TV systems—for investment and for possible transmission of news directly to viewers.

It is too early to tell the effect that the new technologies will have on the printed newspaper. Although Americans are becoming increasingly more video-conscious, it would appear that the newspaper (in the material fashion) will continue to be published and read at breakfast and on the train. Any reduction in printed circulation probably will not surface until cable penetration reaches extraordinarily high levels, and the consumer becomes accustomed to "reading" TV.

Out-of-Home Media

Several facts suggest that demand for out-of-home media will increase in the 1980s. Advertisers will continue to feel the pressures of government restrictions on broadcast copy. There will be lower billboard capacity due to attrition. Land development and construction will eliminate some portion of existing locations, while local zoning laws will limit deployment of new boards. The result of all this interplay will be a net loss of available units.

Some new technology will make out-of-home more attractive and more effective. Computerized painting of painted boards, for example, will serve to speed up production, ensure uniformity of design across multiple showings, and help control production costs. Panographics, which are billboards illuminated from behind the design, will be available on a broadscale basis.

Other forms of outdoor in existence today show signs of significant growth. Advertising displays in shopping malls, at bus shelters, on trash cans, on top of taxi cabs and the sides of buses, and around stores and other gathering places are all increasing in number.

The out-of-home media are changing and will continue to change, shifting from the traditional billboard medium to a great variety of unique and localized options. This fragmentation of the creative unit will provide new opportunities for reaching very selective markets with even greater effectiveness.

Radio

People will have a continuing need for radio, especially when TV viewing is impractical, such as when getting ready in the morning, going to and from work and the store, while working, studying, relaxing. But, as stated earlier, the population is getting older, and this graying of the population could have an adverse effect on overall radio listening levels. The heaviest listening segment is comprised of people under 30 years old, and this segment is declining as a percentage of the population.

Broadcasters will have to adapt to the population changes in order to retain the nearly three and a half hours a day each individual spends with radio. Different formats must be developed to hold the 30- to 40-year-olds. The possibility of specialized programming for those over 50 also exists, as does possible programming for the sick and those with poor vision.

Radio is now the most fragmented of the major media. To reach large numbers of people, it is necessary to purchase a long list of stations in a given market. This is considered by some media planners as a disadvantage. Planners often characterize radio as a frequency medium (as opposed to reach) because budgets are often too slim to purchase a significant number of announcements on each radio station *and* a long list of stations to increase reach. But what now works for radio will work even harder in the future. What works is radio's fragmentation—its ability to attract very selective audiences that have specific demographic and lifestyle patterns.

Advertising rates will increase, but at a slower rate than the other major media. This will give radio a relative cost advantage over other major media forms.

Television

The most dramatic changes are happening in television. The TV medium that was born in the 1950s has matured. By the end of the 1980s, nine out of ten people will have color sets. Half of all homes will have three or more TV sets—75 percent of homes will have two or more sets.

The television public appears to have an insatiable appetite for more and better viewing options. It is this hunger for programming that is encouraging the development of imaginative systems for delivering greater diversity and choice. The lesson learned in the 1970s is that consumers are willing to pay to satisfy their appetite. It is not unreasonable to assume that, like Dick Tracy, we could have TV sets the size of a watch snapped to our wrists.

Cable penetration will continue to climb. Currently, over 35 percent of homes are wired with cable. Projections to the end of the decade vary, but most advertisers and advertising agencies believe penetration will be somewhere between 50 percent to 60 percent.

Let's review the history of cable. Community Antenna Television (CATV, now referred to simply as Cable) began in the late 1940s as a means of providing a television signal, or an improved signal, to households in areas unable to receive "over-the-air" signals. These households were generally located in mountainous regions where the topography interfered with normal transmission. The cable operator built a high antenna designed to receive signals from the closest television stations. These signals were then transmitted to households subscribing to the service via coaxial cables. One cable system was capable of transmitting a maximum of 12 channels (approximately 70 percent of the systems in operation today still offer no more than 12 channels).

Early cable operators were rarely involved in television programming. They were entrepreneurs and engineers who seized the opportunity to provide a needed service and enjoy a handsome return on their investment. Some of the more innovative cable operators broadcast local community events. Nearly all systems provided a 24-hour weather channel. Advertising on the weather channel took the form of a printed reminder to shop at the local grocery store or drug chain.

It was soon realized that the quality of transmission guaranteed by CATV would be of some value to urban apartment dwellers. This resulted in Manhattan Cable in New York and other urban cable systems. Cable television, however, remains primarily a rural phenomenon. Only 29 percent of television households in Nielsen A and B counties have cable, versus more than five out of ten homes in C and D counties.

In November 1975, Home Box Office (HBO) began using a satellite to transmit first-run movies to cable operators across the U.S. Cable operators received the signal via a disc antenna ("Earthstation") and retransmitted it to their subscribers. The cable industry learned that satellites could be used to distribute quality programming over great distances faster and more efficiently than transmitting the same program over land.

The ready accessibility of quality programming is rapidly changing the cable industry from a transmitter of signals (with an emphasis on engineering) to a transmitter of television programming (with an emphasis on entertainment and information).

This change in industry emphasis is stimulating the growth of both cable systems and cable subscribers. As shown in Table 16–3, households subscribing to cable represented seven percent of total U.S. television households in 1970. In 1980, the percentage of households with cable TV has more than tripled. By 1990, it is anticipated that approximately six out of ten homes will have cable capacity.

Cable operators can now offer over 50 channels to their subscribers. Future technology employing fiber optics will permit each household to receive a limitless number of channels. Of course, each household will pay for this chance to view additional channels, and most of these homes will pay an extra subscription fee for at least one pay channel.

What kind of programming? Cable programming can be divided into two basic segments: basic programming and pay programming. Basic programming is the standard service available at the normal subscription rate. In addition to installation charges, there is a basic monthly rate each subscriber pays to the cable operator. Basic programming consists of local television signals and two types of additional programming:

News/Community Programming—24-hour national and international news, state news, community news, live coverage from the House of Representatives, stock market reports, local school system, comparative shopping information, and classified advertising.

TABLE 16–3. Growth of Cable Television

Year	Cable Systems	Total Subscribers (thousands)	U.S. TV Households (%)
1952	70	14	—
1970	2,490	4,500	7
1975	3,506	9,800	12
1979	4,150	14,100	18
1981	—	29,300	36
1990	—	—	50–60

Source: Television Digest's *Cable & Station Coverage Atlas;* A. C. Nielsen; Turner Communications; Ogilvy & Mather.

Information/Entertainment Programming—sports, news "super-stations," children, special audience, and religious programs.

Pay programming is an option available to subscribers for an additional monthly fee—on top of the basic fee. It normally consists of movies, specials, and sports. Pay networks do not currently accept advertising. Table 16–4 lists the 34 cable networks in operation in 1981, all of which are transmitted to cable operators via satellite and which are, in turn, transmitted to television households subscribing to basic and/or pay programming.

All this increased programming availability, especially recently released movies, could have an adverse affect on the local movie theater. It's conceivable that movie house attendance will decline, or change in demographic composition to exclude many of those able to afford a pay cable package.

Within the not-too-distant future, at least 60 cable channels will be offered in some areas. Future technology, employing fiber optics, will permit each household to receive a limitless number of channels. Each household will, of course, pay for this chance to view additional channels and additional programming. Most of these homes will pay an extra subscription fee for at least one channel. It is not unreasonable to assume that an added basic part of the household budget in the 1980s will be the cost for TV progamming—perhaps $500 or more per year.

In addition, cable can open the home to a variety of special electronic services, ranging from burglar and fire alarms to newspapers and data banks.

Those homes that do not buy cable may become users of subscription TV. Subscription TV does not require cable tie-on. It is broadcast over the air with an electronically scrambled signal. Subscribers are supplied with a device that unscrambles it.

In its most advanced form, subscription TV can convert the home into a satellite receiving station. The subscriber purchases or rents a receiving dish that translates a signal directed from a communications satellite. This is not a Buck Rogers fantasy. Comsat has been moving in this direction for years. Subscribers will be able to receive programs completely bypassing the traditional station. This is a whole new concept for the broadcast industry and an obvious threat to the three TV networks.

Viewing will not be an exclusively passive activity. Two-way systems, like QUBE, will become a reality in many areas. The QUBE system permits the TV audience to interact with television programs. Viewers can add their input by pushing buttons on a special device. The outcome of the combined votes is tallied by computer and it becomes part of the program—instantly.

Adding to the television addiction of the 1980s will be a host of new

TABLE 16–4. Cable Networks

| Network | Number of Cable | | % U.S.** | | |
	Systems	Homes*	TV House-holds	Cable House-holds	Adver-tising
AP News Cable	340	3,000,000	3.9	16.7	No
Appalachian Community Service Network	35	250,000	.3	1.4	No
Black Entertainment Television (BET)	375	3,710,000	4.9	20.6	Yes
Cable News Network	261	2,314,000	3.0	12.9	Yes
Cable Satellite Public Affairs Network (C-Span)	750	6,000,000	7.9	33.3	No
Calliope	300	1,500,000	2.0	8.3	Yes
CBS Cable	N/A	N/A	N/A	N/A	Yes
Christian Broadcasting Network	2,500	7,500,000	9.8	41.7	Yes
Cinemerica Satellite Network	N/A	2,500,000	3.3	13.9	Yes
English Channel	400	4,500,000	5.9	25.0	Yes
Entertainment and Sports Programming Network (ESPN)	632	4,035,859	5.3	22.4	Yes
Galavision	28	13,500	—	—	No
Home Box Office (HBO)	2,000	5,000,000	6.6	27.8	No
Home Theater Network	120	82,000	—	—	No
KTVU	140	700,000	.9	3.9	Yes
Las Vegas Entertainment Network	N/A	1,500,000	2.0	8.3	Yes
Modern Satellite Network (MSN)	369	2,300,000	3.0	12.8	Yes
Movie Channel	372	407,000	.5	2.3	No
National Christian Network	50	N/A	N/A	N/A	No
Nickelodeon	489	2,518,360	3.3	14.0	No
Premiere	N/A	N/A	N/A	N/A	No
PRISM	55	140,000	.2	.8	No
PTL Television Network	235	3,000,000	3.9	16.7	No
Rainbow	N/A	N/A	N/A	N/A	No
Reuters Newsview	325	3,500,000	4.6	19.4	No
Satellite Program Network (SPN)	468	2,839,639	3.7	15.8	Yes
Showtime	735	1,100,000	1.4	6.1	No
Superstations	3,551	14,714,369	N/A	N/A	Yes
Telefrance	486	5,350,000	7.0	29.7	Yes
Trinity Broadcasting Network	300	3,500,000	4.6	19.4	No
UPI Newstime	150	700,000	.9	3.9	No
USA Network	1,028	4,779,826	6.3	26.6	Yes
WGN	986	3,864,644	5.1	21.5	Yes
WOR	385	2,753,000	3.6	15.3	Yes
WTBS	2,040	7,396,725	9.7	41.1	Yes

*These estimates are based on reports published by *Cablevision* Magazine, several industry newsletters, trade media articles, as well as information received directly from the cable networks.

**The percent of U.S. TV households is based on an A. C. Nielsen estimate of 76,310,740 (January 1980).

The percent of cable TV households is based on an industry estimate of 18,000,000 for year-end 1980. Current projections indicate, however, that based on a growth rate of 200,000 new cable homes per month, yearend totals will approach 18,700,000 cable households.

N/A: Not available or not applicable.

video systems that will tie the viewers to the TV set. Home video cassette recorders will be found in over 14,000,000 households by 1990. They will make it possible for viewers to squeeze more out of the TV schedule through taping for more convenient or multiple viewings. Video discs, looking much like shiny phonograph records, are less costly than cassettes. They were tested in 1979 and were introduced nationally in 1980. The major advantage of discs, besides the lower cost, is their capacity to be hooked up with stereo systems—perfect video and audio fidelity. The continued growth in video games and home computers will also place some additional demand on the television set.

The combined effect of all these viewing options will tend to drive up time spent with TV to unprecedented levels. As Larry Cole, senior vice president of Ogilvy & Mather, states: "We will move from the *Age Of Me*, to the *Age Of Eye.*"

There is a good chance that there will be less government regulation over stations and programming. This will result in a greater number of stations, more varied programming, and therefore greater segmentation. It is almost mind-boggling to imagine what a TV listing will look like in 1990. The average *TV Guide* will have to devote at least two pages to each hour's listing of programs.

The television medium will become considerably more fragmented and the share of viewing to the three networks will decline, especially in primetime. Currently, about 75 percent of viewing is devoted to network stations. Cassettes, subscription TV, and video discs do not now have a significant impact on overall TV viewing. A change will not occur overnight, but by 1990 it is predicted that the networks will lose 20 share points to new viewing options.

Viewing time will be redistributed most dramatically among cable homes, where it is anticipated that viewing to network stations will decline most severely. Cable stations, subscription services, videocassette recorders, and discs will have a greater impact on viewing patterns than the combined effect of three decades of the networks' "new seasons."

As shown in Table 16–5, in 1980, 80 percent of homes were equipped with only basic TV, subscription was only a minor factor, and 20 percent

TABLE 16–5. Cable Homes

	1980 (%)	1985 (%)	1990 (%)
Basic TV only	80	51	34
Subscription	—	6	4
Basic Cable	14	23	25
Pay Cable	6	19	37
Total	100	100	100

of homes had cable—14 percent had basic cable and 6 percent subscribed to pay cable. By 1985, only about half of all homes will remain solely basic TV. About 6 percent will subscribe to a subscription facility, 23 percent to basic cable, and almost 20 percent will opt for cable plus at least one pay channel. By 1990, about one-third of all homes will have only standard TV capability. A modest 4 percent of homes, unable to obtain cable hook-up, will have subscription TV. One out of four homes will be wired to basic cable, and 37 percent will subscribe to a pay cable system.

Each of these four household classifications will have a unique viewing pattern and, therefore, a different influence on national audience potential. In primetime, for example, the households with only standard TV capacity will continue to view broadcast staions just as they do today (see Table 16–6). Homes with other options will drift away from traditional programming in varying degrees. Subscription homes will devote 25 percent of active primetime viewing to the pay channel and less than 75 percent to broadcast stations. Cable homes that do not subscribe to the pay option will devote 16 percent of primetime viewing to cable channels. The homes with pay cable will tend to experience the most radical change. It is estimated that these households will devote over a third of primetime viewing to special cable programming—25 out of 100 hours to pay cable.

The net result of this interplay will be an overall share gain of almost 20 points to these new viewing options, with a corresponding share loss to broadcast stations—primarily the network affiliated stations. The share of viewing to each TV option might look something like that shown in Table 16–7.

As can be appreciated, the television medium of the future will bear little resemblance to the orderly, narrow, three-network-dominated medium of the post-World War II years. The public wants programming. It has little concern with who the suppliers are. Through the 1950s, the 1960s, and the 1970s, the network-owned lines fed the nation events and programs that the networks either produced or purchased from independent producers. With communications satellites and cable TV, a new

TABLE 16–6. 1990 Primetime Share of Viewing

	Broadcast Stations (%)	VCR (%)	Subscription (%)	Basic Cable (%)	Pay Cable (%)
Basic TV Only	98	2	—	—	—
Basic TV & Subscription*	73	1	25	—	—
Basic TV & Basic Cable	82	2	—	16	—
Basic TV & Cable & Pay Cable	61	1	—	12	25

*Totals less than 100% due to rounding of numbers.

door has opened that can provide a boundless supply of new viewing options. Consequently, the networks as we know them today are likely to change from station programmers to program suppliers. If this occurs, networks of the future will not pay stations to carry a program schedule. They will sell the programs to the stations just as Home Box Office now sells programs to cable operators. There may not be any networks at all. Stations may be free to purchase individual programs off satellites from any supplier and be free to telecast on a discretionary basis.

Media Planning

Media planners will have their hands full trying to come to grips with a bigger total audience that will become more and more splintered. As an outgrowth of rapidly developing marketing sophistication and an increasingly personalized media environment, marketing and media planning goals will become more precise, with definitions of consumers in much greater detail than we have today.

In addition to more and better traditional consumer data, research will have to provide a greater understanding of who the best prospects are and how to reach them. For example, women aged 25 to 54 who are working and in a household with a total income of $25,000 are good prospects if they characterize current Brand Z users. But women currently using a category brand, or intending to buy, are even more descriptive of a prime prospect. Research will provide greater insight into media usage patterns to reach these individuals and others who will influence a purchase.

An increasingly fragmented audience, coupled with a media inflation spiral that appears to have no end, will make it more important than ever to get every ounce of effectiveness out of each advertising dollar by developing new media techniques and applications. A vast amount of testing and trial of new media will occur in the 1980s. The new technologies will enable advertisers and agencies to measure alternatives and concepts with greater precision than ever. Two-way systems such as QUBE can be

TABLE 16–7. Average Share of TV Viewing

	1980 (%)	1990 (%)
Broadcast	98	80
Pay Cable	1	9
Basic Cable	1	8
VCR	—	2
Subscription	—	1
Total	100	100

employed for a multitude of purposes. Measurements of attitudes or actual purchases could occur instantaneously.

Each component of a media plan might be scheduled as part of a unique pattern to achieve a designated effective reach goal against each specialized segment of the target audience. The average media plan could have a very unorthodox appearance when it includes some daytime serials, pay cable adult movies, sports cable network, demographic editions of magazines and newspapers, and some syndicated network radio.

A new generation of sophisticated computerization will permeate all facets of media planning and media buying. There will be more research, more media outlets, more complex analyses to conduct, more extensive tracking of results—more details than ever. All media professionals will have to have a greater understanding of computer technology, while not losing touch with basic tools and responsibilities.

Changing Dynamics

The first important consideration is that current solutions to the problems of the future will not work. All media dynamics must be reassessed: reach, frequency, frequency distribution, audience accumulation, target audience, etc.

Average Rating

If you buy Kansas City spot TV in late fringe now, you will be purchasing one or more of the four TV stations in the market and delivering, on average, a 5.5 household rating, as shown in Table 16–8.

Now consider the ratings report of the future. As Table 16–9 shows, it will contain many more stations.

The media planner in 1990 might find 18 different stations broadcasting in the Kansas City market. Perhaps 10 to 15 of these stations will accept advertising. The planner will have to choose among programs that will be delivering an average of a 1.4 rating. Four programs (or announce-

TABLE 16–8. Late Fringe TV—Kansas City

Station	DMA/HH Rating
KBMA	3
KCMO	6
KMBC	5
WDAF	8
Total	22
Average	5.5

ments) will have to be purchased to equal the 5.5 Gross Rating Points one can now buy with one program.

Reach/Frequency

If 400 Gross Rating Points are planned today, it can be anticipated that it would be necessary to purchase 25 announcements with an average of a 16 rating each. These 25 announcements, on the average, will reach 87 percent of the designated audience an average of 4.6 times each. In the future, that viewing audience will be splintered across 10, 20, 30, or more channels with each channel delivering a smaller average rating than to-day. To deliver 400 Gross Rating Points, more announcements will have to be purchased, and probably more stations, as shown in Table 16–10.

This raises the following questions:

TABLE 16–9. Kansas City TV in 1990

Station	DMA/HH Rating
A	0.1
B	3.1
C	1.3
D	1.3
E	2.2
F	0.5
G	0.1
H	0.7
I	1.2
J	1.8
K	2.3
L	0.7
M	0.9
N	1.7
O	0.4
P	3.2
Q	2.0
R	2.7
Total	26.2
Average	1.4

TABLE 16–10. Reach/Frequency

	Now	Future
Number Announcements	25	200
Average Rating	16	2
Gross Rating Points	400	400
Reach/Frequency	87/4.6	87/4.6 (?)
		90/4.4 (?)
		80/5.0 (?)

- Will the reach/frequency be the same?
- Is it conceivable that reach could be higher because new programming will attract light and non-TV viewers?
- Is it possible that reach will be lower because there will be more viewers watching pay TV?

Audience Accumulation

When one thinks of audience accumulation, one generally thinks of magazines because it takes time for magazines to build their total readership through pass-along. Television and radio are now thought of as "instantaneous" media vehicles. This will probably change. Reach accumulation in the future could be the same over a long period of time, but it is possible that it could take longer to accumulate a total broadcast audience because many people will record a program for later viewing. If the advertiser plans a sale that ends June 30, it should anticipate that some viewers will see the commercials in July, August, or even later. Table 16–11 illustrates the problem.

Target Audience

Many advertising people subscribe to a viewing theory that might be called "least objectionable program"—viewers first decide to watch TV, then tune in a specific program. In the future, the program might be the first decision made. People will seek out programs they really want to watch, and there will be many more programs available. Programs will appeal to very specific segments of the population based both on demographic characteristics and lifestyle orientation. When broadcast media are purchased now, audience information is available only for certain demographic breaks. In the future, research will have to provide not only narrower demographic breaks, but also lifestyle and, quite possibly, product consumption information.

New Media Jargon

Media planners certainly will have new challenges in the decades to come. There will be bigger audiences, but they will be more splintered. *When* a person will be exposed to advertising will become as important as *what* they are exposed to. There will be greater selectivity in television, magazines, newspapers, radio, and out-of-home.

Media jargon will have to keep pace with these changes. Planners will have to shift from *average quarter hour rating* to *accumulated program rating. Homes using TV* will be antiquated and eventually will be replaced by *Homes Using Electronic Media. Cost-per-thousand* will probably change to *cost-per-hundred* because there will be smaller target audiences to reach. *Reach* will change to *eventual reach* and eventually to *reach when needed*. *Frequency* will become divided into *initial frequency* (when the commercial is first seen), *eventual frequency*, and *repeat frequency* (for those who record a program and view it a second time). Will part of a newspaper's or magazine's delivery be called *electronic delivery* for those subscribers who veiw the periodical on their TV screen? If *Time* magazine's experiment of creating a "talking magazine," which uses an electronic device reacting to an electronically treated page, is successful, will these readers need to be called *reader/listeners*? Table 16–12 lists some of the potential new terms.

Summary

The 1980s will offer advertisers both opportunities and obstacles. A more fragmented media world results in greater audience selectivity, and greater selectivity results in less waste. In light of the increasing cost of media, the less waste in a media plan the better.

More viewing, reading, and listening options should inevitably lead to higher interest, deeper involvement, and higher attentiveness—to both

TABLE 16–11. Audience Accumulation in TV—100 GRPs Per Week

| Week | Now | Future | |
		Same (?)	Longer (?)
1	59	59	50
2	78	78	65
3	85	85	75
4	87	87	80
5	—	—	85
6 Mos. Later	—	—	87

TABLE 16–12. Possible New Media Jargon

Today	Future
RTG – Rating	APR – Accumulated Program Rating
HUT – Homes Using TV	HUEM – Homes Using Electronic Media
CPM – Cost-Per-Thousand	CPC – Cost-Per-Hundred
R – Reach	ER – Eventual Reach
	RWN – Reach When Needed
F – Frequency	IF – Initial Frequency
	EF – Eventual Frequency
	RF – Repeat Frequency
IMP – Impressions	IWN – Impressions When Needed
	ITL – Impressions Too Late
Circ – Circulation	ED – Electronic Delivery
Rdrs – Readers	RL – Reader/Listeners

the media and the advertising within the media. There is a good chance that if advertisers react to this segmentation with personalized and localized advertising messages, their media budgets can be used with greater discrimination and far more effectiveness.

The key to all is research. With more precise research, the media planner can make better decisions.

Glossary

A Counties—As defined by A. C. Nielsen Company, all counties belonging to the 25 largest metropolitan areas. These metro areas correspond to the *SMSA (Standard Metropolitan Statistical Area)* and include the largest cities and consolidated areas in the United States.

A.B.C. (Audit Bureau of Circulations)—An organization that provides certified statements of net paid circulation of magazines and newspapers, supported jointly by advertisers, agencies, and media.

A.B.P. (Associated Business Publications)—A trade association of business (industrial, trade, and technical) publications.

Accordion Insert—An advertisement not printed by the publisher, but inserted in a magazine, folded in such a way as to appear as an accordion fold.

Accumulation—A method of counting audiences wherein each person exposed to a vehicle is counted once, either in a given time period such as four weeks for broadcast, or for one issue in print.

ADI (Area of Dominant Influence)—Geographical market definition wherein each county is assigned exclusively to only one television market as defined by Arbitron.

Adjacencies—The specific time periods that precede and follow regular television programming, usually two minutes. These are commercial break positions between programs that are available for local or spot advertisers. There is no such thing as a network adjacency; only spot adjacencies are available.

Adnorm—A term used by Starch to indicate readership averages by publication, by space size and color, and by type of product for ads studied by Starch in a two-year period. It is used to provide a standard of comparison for individual ads against averages of similar types of ads.

Advertising Allowance—Money paid under contract by the manufacturer or his representative to a wholesaler or a retailer for the express purpose of being spent to advertise a specified product, brand, or line. Usually used for consumer advertising. (See *Cooperative Advertising, Promotion Allowance.*)

Advertising Page Exposure—A measurement of physical opportunity to observe a print ad. Defined as the act of opening a spread of facing pages wide enough to glance at any advertising.

Advertising Weight—The amount of advertising planned for, or used by, a brand. While it is not limited to a particular measurement, it is most frequently stated in terms of the number of messages or impressions delivered or broadcasts/insertions placed over a period of time.

Agate Line (usually simplified to Line)—A unit of space by which newspaper and other print advertising space is sold. One agate line represents a space 1 column wide and $\frac{1}{14}$ of an inch high. This is a measure of area, not shape — a 210 line ad can be 1 column × 210 lines, 2 columns × 105 lines, or 3 columns × 70 lines.

Aided Recall—A measurement technique in which respondents are helped to remember portions or all of ads by having an interviewer provide clues. (See *Unaided Recall.*)

Alternate Week Sponsor—An advertiser who purchases full or participating sponsorship every other week of a network program for a full 52-week broadcast year. Each sponsor purchasing at least two minutes in a given program episode will receive billboard commercial time on his week of sponsorship.

AM (Amplitude Modulation)—AM is the standard broadcast transmission system used by the majority of licensed radio stations. The term is commonly used to differentiate between AM and FM radio.

Arbitron—A television and radio rating service used to measure viewing/listening audiences. Arbitron publishes both a monthly radio network rating report and TV and radio reports for selected individual markets (no network TV).

Audience—The number of people or households who are exposed to a medium. Exposure measurements indicate nothing about whether audiences saw, heard, or read either the advertisements or editorial contents of the medium.

Audience Composition—The demographic makeup of people represented in an audience with respect to income group, age, sex, geography, etc.

Audience Duplication—In broadcast, a measurement of the number of listeners or viewers reached by two or more programs, or by the same program over repeated telecasts, sponsored by the same advertiser. In print, the measurement of the overlap of potential exposure between different issues of the same magazine or among issues of different magazines.

Audience Flow—Changes in audience of broadcast programs. May be reported on a minute-by-minute basis, by five-minute intervals, or from show to show.

Audience Holding Index—A measurement of the retentive power or audience loyalty of a given program. A. C. Nielsen, for 30-minute programs, uses an index based on the percentage of homes tuned to the same program 25 minutes after the first measurement. It is a simple measure of the ratio of average audience rating to total audience rating of a given program.

Audience, Potential—In broadcasting, the number of sets in use in the time period to be studied, or the number of set owners. In print, the total audience of an issue.

Audience, Primary—In a study of audience accumulation, the noncumulative potential audience of an advertising message. In print, all readers who live in households where someone subscribes to, or purchases, the magazine. May be called primary readership.

Audience Profile—The characteristics of the people who make up the audience of a magazine, TV show, newspaper, radio show, etc., in terms of age, family size, location, education, income, and other factors.

Audience, Secondary—Pass-along readers who read a publication they did not purchase. These readers should be taken into account in determining the total number of readers of a particular publication.

Audience Turnover—The average number of times that a television program receives new audience members in a four-week period. Calculated by dividing reach by the average rating.

Audilog—The diary that members of Nielsen's local rating panels fill out to show what they are viewing on television.

Audimeter—An electronic device developed by the A. C. Nielsen Company that records set usage and tuning on a minute-by-minute basis. Nielsen has a national sample of approximately 1,200 Audimeter homes which are used to measure television usage and program audiences.

Audit Report (White Audit)—Official document issued by the A.B.C. detailing its findings as a result of an audit. (Printed on white paper to differentiate it from semi-annual publishers' statements printed on colored paper). Audit reports are issued annually covering the 12-month period of the two previous publisher's statements (See *Publisher's Statement*.) If the auditor's findings differ from the information in the publisher's statements, the discrepancies are reported and explained in the audit report.

Availability—A specific period of broadcast commercial time offered for sale by a station or network for sponsorship.

Average Audience (AA)—In broadcasting, the number of homes/persons tuned in to a TV program for an average minute (a Nielsen network TV measurement). In print, the number of persons who looked into an average issue of a publication.

Average Frequency—The number of times the average home (or person) reached by a media schedule is exposed to the schedule. This is measured over a specific period of time, e.g., four weeks in broadcast media.

Average Net Paid—Average circulation per issue arrived at by dividing the sum total paid circulation for all the issues of the audit period by the total number of issues.

B Counties—As defined by A. C. Nielsen Company, all counties not included under A that are either over 150,000 population or in a metro area over 150,000 population according to the latest census.

Back-to-Back Scheduling—Two or more commercials run one immediately following the other.

BAR (Broadcast Advertising Reports)—An organization that monitors network TV activity and spending by brand as well as non-network activity in selected markets and reports to subscribers the position, length, and advertised brand of all announcements broadcast during a given week. Also reports network radio.

Barter—Acquisition by an advertiser of sizable quantities of spot time or free mentions at rates lower than card rates from broadcast stations in exchange for

b

operating capital or merchandise. While direct negotiation between the advertiser and station is possible, it is more common for barter to be arranged through a middleman, a barter agency, or a film producer or distributor, who may have procured the time through an exchange of film or taped shows.

Base Rate—See *Open Rate*.

Billboard—An identifying announcement of sponsorship at the beginning, end, or breaks of radio and television sponsored programs. Billboards are not sold, but usually are a bonus, based on the advertiser's volume or commitment with the program or the broadcaster. Usually 5 to 10 seconds in length. Also, an outdoor poster.

Black & White (B&W, B/W)—Printing with black ink on white paper (or vice versa); no color. Also known as monotone.

Blanket Coverage—Total coverage by television and radio of a given geographic area.

Bleed—An advertisement in which part or all of the illustration or copy runs past the usual margins out to the edge of a page. Bleed insertions are generally sold at a premium price, usually 15 percent over the basic rate.

Brand Development Index (BDI)—The number of cases, units, or dollar volume of a brand sold per 1,000 population. It is calculated by dividing the percentage of sales in a market by the population percentage in the same market.

Broadside—A promotion piece consisting of one large sheet of paper, generally printed on one side only.

Brochure—An elaborate booklet, usually bound with a special cover.

Bulk Circulation—Sales in quantity lots of an issue of a magazine or newspaper. The purchases are made by individuals or concerns and the copies are usually directed to lists of names supplied by the purchasers. In the A.B.C. report, bulk circulation is listed separately from single-copy sales.

Bulk Sales—Sales of copies of a publication in quantity to one purchaser to be given free by him. Many advertisers do not consider bulk sales to be a valuable part of a publication's circulation.

Bulldog Edition—An edition that is issued and on sale earlier than regular editions. Usually applies to morning newspapers. There are also Bulldog Sunday editions that go on sale Saturday night.

Business Building Test—A test run by a specific brand designed to determine if a marketing or advertising plan change will produce enough additional business for the brand to pay the required costs of the change.

Business Paper—A publication directed to a particular industry, trade, profession, or vocation. A *horizontal* business paper is designed to reach all groups in a broad trade or industry regardless of location or occupational title. A *vertical* publication is for a specific profession, trade, or occupational level within or across various industries.

C

C Counties—As defined by A. C. Nielsen Company, all counties not included under A or B that either have over 35,000 population or are in a metropolitan area of over 35,000 population according to the latest census.

CATV—Community Antenna (or cable) TV services that deliver high quality TV signals to homes via coaxial cable. Also called *cable television*.

C.C.A. (Controlled Circulation Audit)—An organization that audits the circulation statements of publications that are sent free to selected lists.

Cable TV—A system of broadcasting television whereby programs are first tuned-in by a Community Antenna and then distributed to individual homes by cables. Cable operators often receive programs transmitted by satellites and then transmitted by cable to their subscribers.

Cancellation Date—The last date on which it is possible to cancel advertising. Such dates occur for print, outdoor, and broadcasting.

Car Card—A standard 11" high siderack card, generally with poster-like design, placed in buses, street cars, and subways. Common sizes are 11" × 28", 11" × 42", 11" × 56".

Card Rate—The cost of time and space quoted on a rate card.

Case Allowance—An allowance or discount a manufacturer or wholesaler gives to a retailer on each case of product purchased in return for which the retailer is to use the money to advertise the product.

Cash Discount—A deduction allowed by print media (usually 2 percent of the net) for prompt payment (e.g., within 15 to 30 days), generally passed along by the agency to the advertiser to encourage collections.

Cash Refund Offer—A type of mail-in offer used by a brand, or group of brands, which offers cash to the consumer upon providing proof of purchase.

Category Development Index (CDI)—Means the same as *Marketing Development Index*. Essentially, the percentage of total U.S. sales of a product category related to population percentage in a geographical market.

Center Spread—An advertisement appearing on the two facing center pages of a publication.

Checking Copy—A copy of a publication sent to an advertiser and agency as proof that the advertisement appeared as ordered.

Circulation—In print, the number of copies of a vehicle distributed based on an average of a number of issues. In broadcast, the number of television or radio households that tune in to a station a minimum number of times within a specified time period (such as once a week or once a day). In outdoor, the total number of people who have an opportunity to see a given showing of billboards within a specified time, such as a 24-hour period.

City Zone—A geographic area that includes the corporate limits of the central city of the market plus any contiguous areas that have substantially the same built-up characteristics of the central city. This provides a method of reporting newspaper circulation according to A.B.C. standards.

Class A, B, C Rates—Rates for the most desirable and costly television time, usually between 6 pm and 11 pm are called Class A rates; the next most costly is Class B; and so on. Each station sets its own time classifications.

Class Magazine—A publication that reaches select high-income readers in contrast to magazines with larger circulations, generally referred to as *mass magazines*.

Clear Time—Process used by an advertiser to reserve a time period with a local station and by a network to check with its affiliates on the availability of a time period.

Clearance—Obtaining a time period for a program or commercial on a station or obtaining approval to use advertising from clients, legal and/or medical counsel, or network continuity departments.

Closing Date—The final date to commit contractually for the purchase of advertising space. Generally, cancellations are not accepted after the closing date, although some publications have a separate cancellation date, which may fall before the closing date. Also used in connection with supplying ad material to the publication.

Coaxial Cable—Usually abbreviated to *cable*. The mechanical facility used by broadcasters for the transmission of programming from city to city or from a cable organization to individual homes. The cable is actually owned by A.T.& T. and, in turn, is rented to the user. Sometimes, microwave broadcasting operations are utilized instead of these cables. More generally, coaxial cable is any electrical cable capable of carrying large information loads with minimal distortion. (See *CATV, Cable TV*.)

Combination Rate—A discounted rate offered to encourage use of two or more stations, newspapers, magazines, etc., having common ownership. Occasionally, an advertiser has no choice but to buy the combination as space/time may not be sold separately.

Commercial Audience—The audience for a specific commercial as determined by a survey that elicits information about what program viewers were doing just before, during, and after the commercial. The commercial audience is operationally defined as those people who were physically present in the room with the TV set at the time the commercial was on.

Commercial Break—In broadcasting, an interruption of programming in which commercials are broadcast.

Commercial Delivery—That part of the audience actually exposed to a particular commercial.

Confirmation—Broadcast media statement that a requested time slot is available to a prospective client.

Consecutive Weeks Discount—A discount granted to an advertiser who uses a minimum number of weeks of advertising on a station or network without interruption.

Consumer Magazine—A magazine whose editorial content appeals to the general public, or a specific segment or layer of the public. Differentiated from trade or business magazines.

Continuity—A method of scheduling advertising so that audiences have an opportunity to see ads at regular intervals. There are many patterns that could be used, from advertising once each day of the year to once a month.

Controlled Circulation Publications—Publications that confine or restrict their distribution to special groups on a free basis. Some controlled circulation is solicited, while most is non-solicited.

Cooperative Advertising—Advertising run by a local advertiser in conjunction with a national advertiser. The national advertiser usually provides the copy and/or plates and also shares the cost with the local retailer. In return, the national advertiser receives local promotion for its product. The name of the local advertiser and its address appear in the ad.

Co-Sponsorship—The participation of two or more sponsors in a single broadcast program where each advertiser pays a proportionate share of the cost.

Cost Efficiency—The effectiveness of media as measured by a comparison of audience, either potential or actual, with cost and expressed as a cost-per-thousand.

Cost-Per-Thousand (CPM)—A figure used in comparing or evaluating the cost efficiency of media vehicles. CPM is the cost to deliver 1,000 people or homes and is calculated by dividing the cost by the audience delivery and multiplying the quotient by 1,000.

Cost Ratio—Term used by Daniel Starch & Staff. The cost ratio is an adjustment made to the score obtained on each readership measure. The score is translated into per dollar terms (based on the magazine's reported primary circulation and the cost of the ad in terms of size, color, etc.) and then stated as a percentage of the average per dollar scores of all ads studied in the same issue. (See *Noted, Starch Method.*)

Coupon Insert—An IBM-type coupon attached to a carrier unit that is bound into the subscription copies of a magazine much like a normal page is inserted. Several configurations are available depending on the size of magazine, the manner in which it is bound, and the number of coupons to be carried.

Couponing—Distribution of coupons by a manufacturer through the mail, by household calls, or through media, offering a price reduction at the store on a product.

Coverage—A term used to define a medium's geographical potential. In newspapers, the number of circulation units of a paper divided by the number of households in a given area. In magazines, the percentage of a given demographic market reached by a magazine. In radio/television, the percentage of television households that can tune in to a station (or stations) because they are in the signal area. In outdoor, the percentage of adults who pass a given showing and are exposed in a 30-day period. In previous years, coverage meant the same as reach. Today, the meaning will depend on which medium is being discussed.

Cume—A broadcast term that is Nielsen's shorthand for net cumulative audience of a program or of a spot schedule (radio or TV) in four weeks' time. Based on total number of unduplicated TV homes or people reached.

Cumulative Audience—The net unduplicated audience of a campaign, either in one medium or a combination of media. Sometimes called *reach* or *cume*.

Cut-In—Different broadcast copy or format that is used to replace an originating commercial in a network program in a specific market or region. Frequently used in test markets.

Cycle—An interval within a contract year at the end of which, upon proper notice, an advertiser may cancel network stations and/or facilities. Weekly and multi-weekly program cycles usually are 13 weeks in length, while co-sponsored program cycles usually encompass 13 major broadcasts. Also refers to the 13-week periods used as a base for talent and use fee payments.

d

D Counties—Essentially rural counties in the Nielsen classification system of A, B, C, D counties.

Daypart—A part of the broadcast day, so designated for analytical purposes. In TV, the dayparts are usually daytime (morning and afternoon), early fringe, primetime, and late fringe. In radio, they are morning, daytime, afternoon, evening.

Direct Mail Advertising—Letters, folders, reprints, or other material sent through the mails directly to prospective purchasers.

Direct Response Advertising—Advertising material reproduced in quantity and distributed directly to prospects, either by mail, house-to-house delivery, bag stuffers, magazines and newspapers, or television. Allows prospect to respond directly to the advertiser rather than going through a retailer or other middleman.

Directory Advertising—Advertising in a directory. Popularly used to signify any advertising that consumers may deliberately consult, i.e., department store or food advertisements.

Discount—A reduction from regular rates when an advertiser contracts to use quantities of advertising. Discounts in print may consider amount of space bought and frequency of insertion. Discounts in network broadcasting may be based upon number of dayparts used, frequency or weight, and length of contract; in local broadcasting, discounts will consider number of spots per week, length of contract, or purchase of plans or packages.

DMA (Designated Market Area)—Geographical market definition wherein each county is assigned exclusively to only one television market as defined by Nielsen.

Double Truck—A two-page spread in newspapers where the editorial or advertising runs across the gutter of the spread.

Downscale—A general description of a medium's audience of lower socio-economic class members.

Drive Time—The times of day (both morning and afternoon) when most people drive to or from work (about 6 to 10 am and 3 to 7 pm).

Duplication—The number or percentage of people in one vehicle's audience who also are exposed to another vehicle. Also audiences who are counted more than once in measurements, such as those who view the same TV program more than once a month.

e

Earned Rate—The rate that an advertiser has earned based on volume or frequency of space or time used to obtain a discount.

Effective Reach/Frequency—The reach of a medium or media schedule at a pre-determined level of frequency (as opposed to total reach).

Efficiency—See *Cost Efficiency*.

Ethnic Media—A catch-all term for those newspapers, magazines, and radio and television stations that direct their editorial and/or language to specific ethnic groups.

Expansion Plan—An outline of the media to be used and timing thereof for a brand that plans to apply a theoretical national plan to portions of the country subsequent to testing and prior to actual national application. The expansion areas are the geographical units in which the product is to be sold.

Exposure—"Open eyes facing a medium." Practically, however, measurements are based on respondents who either say with assurance that they have looked into a given magazine, or that, after looking at a list of magazines, say that they have looked into those they checked on the list. In broadcast, those who are sitting in the room while a television or radio program is being broadcast.

Exposure, Depth of—The value credited to an increased number of broadcast commercials or multi-page spreads in the form of heightened consciousness of an advertisement. While the audience for such media usage generally does not increase proportionally with the amount of additional investment made, the depth of exposure tends to provide adequate compensation.

Exposure, Opportunity of—The degree to which an audience may reasonably be expected to see or hear an advertising message.

f

Facing—Used in outdoor advertising to refer to the number of billboards used in one display. A single facing is one billboard. A double facing is two billboards either joined or with less than 25 feet between them. A triple facing is three billboards, etc. Also, the number of packages in a store facing out from the front row of a shelf.

Farm Publication—A publication devoted to general agricultural topics edited for farm families or farmers.

Field Intensity Map—A broadcast coverage map showing the quality of reception possible on the basis of signal strength. Sometimes called a *contour map*.

Field Intensity Measurement—The measurement of a signal delivered at a point of reception by a radio transmitter in units of voltage per meter of effective antenna height, usually in terms of microvolts or millivolts per meter.

Fifteen and Two—The usual terms on which advertising media is ordered by advertising agencies for their clients, i.e., 15 percent commission is allowed by the media on the gross cost, plus 2 percent discount on the net amount for prompt payment.

Fifty-Fifty Plan—In cooperative advertising, the equal sharing by a manufacturer and a dealer of the cost of a manufacturer's advertisement appearing over a dealer's name.

Flat Rate—An advertising rate that does not include any discounts.

Flighting—A method of scheduling advertising for a period of time, followed by a period of no advertising, followed by a resumption of advertising.

FM (Frequency Modulation)—FM is a radio broadcast band in the broadcast spectrum different from that used by AM stations. There is no static in FM radio reception.

Forced Combination—Morning and evening newspapers owned by the same publisher that are sold to national advertisers only in combination. Some forced combinations are morning and evening editions of the same newspaper.

Four-Color (4/C)—Black and three colors (blue, yellow, red). Standard color combinations used by practically all publications offering color advertising.

Fractional Showing—In outdoor, a showing of less than 25, offered in certain areas.

Franchise Position—A specified position in a publication (e.g., back cover, inside front cover) for which an advertiser is granted a permanent franchise (or right to use) as long as he continues to use it. Franchise positions are sometimes specific locations such as "opposite punched hole recipe page" in *Better Homes & Gardens*. Some positions are negotiated for specific issues, while others may be granted by frequency of use (i.e., six out of twelve issues). If a given position is not used one year, it usually must be renegotiated to regain it.

Free Publication—A publication sent without cost to a selected list of readers. Circulation may or may not be audited by C.C.A., but cannot qualify for A.B.C. audit unless at least 70 percent of circulation is paid.

Frequency—The average number of times an audience unit is exposed to a vehicle. Usually referred to as *average frequency*.

Frequency Discount—A discount given for running a certain number of insertions irrespective of size of advertisement within a contract year. Similar discounts are available in broadcasting, but may be of two types: frequency per week as well as total number of announcements in a contract year.

Frequency Distribution—An array of reach according to the level of frequency delivered to each group.

Fringe Time—Time periods preceding and following peak set-usage periods and adjacent network programming blocks. Usually represents for television, Class B or C time — 4:30–7:30 pm, or after 11 pm EST.

Full Position—Preferred position for a newspaper advertisement, generally following and next to reading matter, or top of column next to reading matter. When specifically ordered, it costs more than a run-of-paper (R.O.P.) position.

Full-Program Sponsorship—A regular program sponsored by only one advertiser.

Full Showing—In car card advertising, usually denotes one card in each car of a line in which space is bought. In New York subways, a full showing consists of two cards in each car; a half showing is two cards in every other car. In outdoor poster advertising, a full or 100-intensity showing indicates use of a specified number of panels in a particular market.

g

Gatefold—A special space unit in magazines, usually consisting of one full page plus an additional page or part of a page that is an extension of the outer edge of the original page and folds outward from the center of the book as a gate.

General Editorial Magazine—A consumer magazine not classified as to specific audience.

Geographic Split Run—A split run where one ad is placed in all of the circulation which falls within a specified geographic area and another ad is placed in other geographic areas or the balance of the country.

Grid Card—A rate card in which a broadcast station's spots are priced individually, with charges related to the audience delivered.

Gross Audience—The combined audience of a combination of media or a campaign in a single medium. For example, if Medium A and Medium B have audiences of 7,000,000 and 6,000,000, respectively, their gross audience is 13,000,000. To go from gross audience to net audience, one must subtract all duplicated audiences.

Gross Impressions—The sum of audiences of all vehicles used in a media plan. This number represents the message weight of a media plan. The number is sometimes called the "tonnage" of the plan, because it is so large. (See *Gross Audience*.)

Gross Rate—The published rate for space or time quoted by an advertising medium, including agency commission, cash discount, and any other discounts.

GRP (Gross Rating Points)—A measure of the total gross weight delivered by a vehicle (or vehicles). It is the sum of the ratings for the individual announcements or programs. A rating point means an audience of 1 percent of the coverage base. Hence 150 Gross Rating Points means 1.5 messages per average home. Gross Rating Points are duplicated ratings. Also, reach times frequency equals GRPs.

Gutter—The inside margins of facing pages; the point at which a saddle stitched publication is bound.

Half-Page Spread—An advertisement composed of two half-pages facing each other in a publication.

h

Half Run—In transportation advertising, a car card placed in every other car of the transit system used. Also called a *half service*. Can also apply to publications that offer advertising in half of their circulation.

Half Showing—One half of a full showing of car cards; a 50-intensity showing of outdoor posters or panels.

Hiatus—A period of time during which there is no advertising activity.

Hi-Fi Preprinted Insert—A full-page, four-color rotogravure advertisement printed by a supplier on coated newsprint and furnished to a newspaper in roll form for insertion in lieu of a page of standard newsprint. As the roll is fed into the newspaper, the newspaper prints normal editorial/advertising matter on the reverse side and, in some cases, a column of type of the advertisement itself. The advertiser pays the supplier for producing the ad and the newspaper for distributing the ads (usually B&W space rates plus an insertion charge). Generally, the cost is twice as expensive as R.O.P. color. Because there is no accurate cut-off on Hi-Fi pages, the copy and illustration has a repeating "wallpaper" design in order to insure full ad exposure.

Hitchhike—An isolated commercial for a sponsor's secondary product (not advertised in the main body of the show) which is given a free ride following the end of the program.

Holding Power—The degree to which a program retains its audience throughout a broadcast. It is expressed in a percentage determined by dividing the average audience by the total audience.

Holdover Audience—The audience a program acquires from listeners or viewers who tuned to the preceding program on the station and remained with the station.

Home Service Book—A publication with editorial content keyed to the home and home living. Examples of this are *Better Homes & Gardens* and *House Beautiful.*

Horizontal Cume—The cumulative audience rating for two programs in the same time period on different days.

Horizontal Half-Page—A half-page advertisement running horizontally across the page. (See *Vertical Half-Page.*)

Horizontal Trade Publications—A business publication editorially designed to be of interest to a variety of businesses or business functions.

H.U.T. (Households Using TV)—A term used by Nielsen and referring to the total number of TV households using their television sets during a given time period. Can be used for the total U.S. or a local market.

i

ID—A 10-second "identification" commercial on radio or TV.

Impact—The extent and degree of consumer awareness of an advertisement within a specific medium, and the degree to which a medium and an ad within that medium affect the ad's audience.

Illuminated Panel—See *Panels.*

Impressions—See *Gross Impressions.*

Impression Studies—Starch provides studies of print ads and TV commercials called, respectively, "Starch Reader Impression Studies" and "Starch Viewer Impressions Studies," which try to evaluate the kind of impression made by the ad.

Imprint—Used in cooperative poster advertising programs. Sometimes the local dealer pays a portion of the cost of the poster space and the parent company pays the remaining portion. The dealer's name—the imprint—is placed on the bottom portion of the poster design (about ⅕ of the total copy area) so that his store is listed as the place to buy the product advertised.

Index—A percentage that relates numbers to a base. Used to show what is above average (101 or greater), average (100), or below average (99 or less).

Industrial Advertising—Advertising of capital goods, supplies, and services directed mainly to industrial or professional firms that require them in the course of manufacturing.

Inherited Audience—The carry-over from one program to another on the same station of a portion of the preceding program's audience. (See *Holdover Audience.*)

In-Home—Refers to that portion of media exposure (reading, listening, or viewing) done in the home.

Insert—A special page printed on superior or different paper stock by the advertiser and forwarded to the publisher to be bound into the publication or to be inserted loose. Usually used for fine color work.

Insertion—An advertisement in a print medium.

Insertion Order—Authorization from an advertiser or agency to a publisher to print an advertisement of specified size on a given date or dates at a definite rate. Copy instructions, cuts, or complete plates may accompany the order or be sent later.

Instantaneous Rating—The size of a broadcast audience at a given instant (or point in time) expressed as a percentage of some base. Usually determined by an electronic device for a single market or a small number of markets.

Intensity—In outdoor advertising, the strength of combinations of poster locations throughout a city in terms of coverage or repetition opportunities. A 100 showing has a 100 intensity. A 100 showing (therefore, a 100 intensity) varies from city to city.

Interim Statement—Sworn circulation statement of a publisher made quarterly to the A.B.C. at the publisher's option and issued unaudited but subject to audit. A situation that might call for an interim statement would occur when a community served by more than one newspaper loses one of them through consolidation or discontinuance and its circulation is absorbed by the other newspaper. (See *Publisher's Statement.*)

Island Position—A newspaper or magazine advertisement entirely surrounded by editorial matter or margin.

Isolated 30—A 30-second commercial surrounded only by programming.

Issue Life—The time during which a publication accrues its total readership. For a weekly, this is generally five weeks. For a monthly, three months.

Junior Page—In print, a page size that permits an advertiser to use the same engraving plates for small and large page publications. The ad is prepared as a full-page unit in the smaller publication, appears in the larger publication as a junior page with editorial around it.   **j**

Junior Panel—A small-scale version of the 24-sheet poster. Also called *six-sheet poster.*

Junior Spread—An advertisement appearing on two facing pages that occupies only part of each page.

Keying an Advertisement—Identification within an advertisement or coupon that permits inquiries or requests to be traced to a specific advertisement.   **k**

Keyline—An assembly of all elements of a print ad pasted on a board. It is camera-ready art that is photographed in order to make the negative that in turn is used to make the printing plate. Also called *mechanical.*

Lead-In—Words spoken by announcer or narrator at the beginning of some shows to perform a scene-setting or recapitulation function. Also a broadcast program positioned before another program.   **l**

Lead-Out—In relation to audience flow, the program following an advertiser's program on the same station.

Linage—A newspaper term denoting the number of (agate) lines in an ad or an ad schedule. Also, amount of total space run by a publication in certain categories, e.g., retail grocery linage.

List Broker—In direct mail advertising, an agent who rents prospect lists, compiled by one advertiser, and sold by the agent to another advertiser. He receives a commission for his services.

List House—In direct mail advertising, an agent who sells prospect lists compiled by the organization to an advertiser.

Listener Diary—Method of TV or radio research whereby audience keeps continuing record of viewing or listening in a diary.

Listening Area—The geographic area covered by a station's signal, usually divided into primary and secondary areas.

Little America (or Little U.S.A.) Concept—A test market media plan translation method that equalizes the media weight in the test area with the weighted average of the media weight that will be delivered by the national plan in all areas of the country.

Live Time—The time that the actual performance of a program is transmitted by interconnected facilities directly to the receiving stations at the moment of performance.

Live Time Delay—A delay that coincides with the local live time. Usually occurs when the station is non-interconnected and thus unable to take a live feed.

Lloyd Hall Editorial Analysis (now called Russell Hall)—A study of the number of editorial pages a magazine devotes to various categories of product interest over a period of time. For example, the number of pages a magazine devotes to articles on food, home furnishings, fiction, news. This information is frequently used in analyzing the editorial content of a magazine before advertising is placed in it.

LNA-BAR (Leading National Advertiser-Broadcast Advertiser Reports)—A monthly analysis of television commercial allocations and gross time billing by brand, station line-ups, and program production talent estimates. A second volume reports network radio stations, line-ups by programs and advertisers.

Local Advertising—Advertising by local retailers (as opposed to national advertisers advertising in local markets), usually at a lower rate than that charged national advertisers.

Local Channel Station—A radio station that is allowed just enough power to be heard near its point of transmission and is assigned a channel on the air wave set aside for local channel stations (usually 250 watts).

Local Media—Media whose coverage and circulation are confined to or concentrated in their market of origin. Usually, they offer different sets of rates to the national advertiser and the local advertiser.

Local Rate—Rate charged by a medium to the local retail trade.

Local Time—Availabilities or times of broadcasting quoted in terms of local time rather than Eastern Standard Time.

Locally Edited Supplement—Sunday magazine supplement similar in character to syndicated magazine supplements but owned and edited by the newspaper distributing it. Such supplements are available in most of the larger cities throughout the country. Certain of them have banded together into groups for purposes of more efficient soliciting of national advertising and they offer group rates to advertisers who buy all the papers.

Loyalty Index—Frequency of listenership to a particular station.

Magazine Supplement—A magazine section of a Sunday or daily newspaper distributed either locally or nationally.

Mail-In Premium—A premium offered at the point-of-sale in a retail store to be obtained by the consumer by mailing a box top, coin, or label to the manufacturer.

Mail Order Advertising—Type of advertising in which the complete sales transaction is handled through advertising and by mail.

Mail Survey Map—A broadcast coverage map prepared by tabulating cumulative, unsolicited mail received during a certain period or by tabulating listener response to a special order or contest run during a certain period.

Makegood—An announcement or advertisement run as a replacement for one that was scheduled but did not run, or that ran incorrectly.

Market-by-Market Allocation (MBM)—The MBM system of media/marketing planning, which allocates a brand's total available advertising dollars against current and/or potential business on an individual TV market basis. MBM spends all advertising dollars (national and local) available in each market in proportion to current and/or anticipated business in the market. The result of MBM planning is to spend more accurately against anticipated sales and thereby generate greater business for a brand.

Market Development Index—See *Category Development Index, Market Index*.

Market Index—The factor chosen to measure relative sales opportunities in different geographic or territorial units. Any quantitative information that makes it possible to estimate this might be used as a market index. A General Market Index is a factor developed that influences the purchase of a specific product or groups of related products. Sometimes called *Market Development Index* or *Category Development Index*.

Market Outline—The measurement of the share of market based on total purchases of a particular brand or groups of similar brands within a product category during a specific time period.

Market Pattern—The pattern of a product's sales in terms of the relation between the volume and concentration either by total market or by individual market. A *thick market pattern* is one in which a high portion of all people are prospects for a product. A *thin market pattern* is one in which a low portion of all people are prospects for a product.

Market Potential—That portion of a market that a company can hope to capture for its own product.

Market Profile—A demographic description of the people or the households in a product's market. It may also include economic and retailing information about a territory.

Market Share—A product's share of an industry's sales volume.

"Marriage" Split—Occurs when more than one advertiser buys the total circulation of a magazine and each of the advertisers runs its ad in only a portion of that circulation. For example, an advertiser with distribution in the western U.S. and one with distribution in the eastern U.S. may split an ad in a magazine that permits this. In this case, the advertiser with distribution in the West would use only that part of the magazine's circulation which reaches the West and the other advertiser would use the remainder.

Masked Identification Test—A method of assessing an ad's effectiveness by finding the percentage of respondents who can identify the advertiser or brand when all identifying marks are concealed.

Mass Magazine—Magazine of a general nature that appeals to all types of people in all localities.

Maxiline—The maximum milline rate for a newspaper. (See *Miniline*.)

Maximil/Minimil—Milline rates for newspapers offering sliding scale discounts. The maximil is the milline computed on the maximum line rate. The minimil is computed on the lowest line rate available.

Mechanical—See *Keyline*.

Media Records—A detailed report of advertising volume by selected brands in selected daily and Sunday newspapers in selected cities.

Media Strategy Statement—Prepared by an agency, outlining the specific media that it believes best accomplish the brand's marketing objectives (as outlined in the market strategy statement) within the funds available.

Media Translation—The process of reducing a national advertising media plan to local level in order to test a product or campaign locally. It also can mean the expansion of a local advertising campaign to a national level.

Media Weight—The total impact of an advertising campaign in terms of number of commercials, insertions, reach and frequency, advertising dollars, etc.

Medium—Any media class used to convey an advertising message to the public, such as newspapers, magazines, direct mail, radio, television, billboards, etc.

Message Weight—Refers to the gross number of advertising messages delivered by a vehicle or group of vehicles in a schedule.

Metro Area—A well-defined county or group of counties comprising the central core of a market (usually based on governmental lines).

Middle Break—Station identification at about the halfway point of a show.

Milline Rate—A means of comparing rates of newspapers. It is the cost of one agate line per million circulation. The milline rate is computed by multiplying the line rate by 1,000,000 and then dividing by the circulation. The factor of 1,000,000 is used merely to provide an answer in convenient terms of dollars and cents rather than in fractions of a cent.

Miniline—The milline rate for a newspaper at its minimum rate. (See *Maxiline*.)

Minimil Rate—This represents the minimum cost of one line of advertising per million circulation at the lowest rate available after deducting all space or frequency discounts. (See *Maximil/Minimil*.)

Minimum Depth—Most newspapers have minimum depth requirements for advertising. In general, an ad must be at least one inch high for every column it is wide. For example, if an advertiser wants an ad to run that is eight columns wide, it must be at least eight inches high.

Minute-by-Minute Profile—Nielsen minute-by-minute program audience data. Used to study audience gains and losses during specific minutes of the program and to aid in placing commercials at times in which they receive maximum audiences.

Monitor—To check timing, program, and commercial content of individual broadcasts of radio and/or television shows.

MRI—Mediamark Research, Inc. A company that measures magazine audiences using the recent-reading technique.

Multi-Network Area Rating—This rating, which is tabulated by Nielsen, measures a program's performance in 70 cities with three or more TV stations.

Multistation Lineup—Buying more than one station in a market.

National Advertising Rates—Rates for newspaper space charged to a national advertiser as distinguished from local rates applying to local retailers. National advertising rates are generally higher than local rates.

National Media—Media that are national in scope.

National Plan—A media plan that is national in scope, as opposed to a local plan covering less than the entire U.S.

National Rating—A rating of all households or individuals tuned in to a program on a national base. Sometimes the base is all television or radio households in the country. Other times, the base is only those households that can tune in to the program because they are in the signal area of a station carrying the program.

NCH (Nielsen Clearing House)—A company that handles the administrative work associated with processing coupons.

NCS (Nielsen Coverage Service)—This provides station coverage and circulation information rather than program audience measurements. The data are reported for each station in terms of total daytime and total evening audiences over the span of the day, week, and month, on a county-by-county basis.

Net Paid Circulation—A term used by A.B.C. audit reports and publishers' statements referring to circulation that has been paid for at not less than 50 percent of the basic newsstand or subscription price.

Net Plus—The net cost of a print ad, commercial, or program with an earned discount added on.

Net Unduplicated Audience—The combined cumulative audience for a single issue of a group of magazines or broadcasts.

Net Weekly Audience—In broadcast research, the number of families tuned in at least once to a program aired more than once a week.

Network—Two or more stations contractually united to broadcast programs, e.g., network programs.

Network Affiliate—A broadcast station that is part of a network and therefore offers network programs.

Network Franchise—A brand's right to retain the sponsorship of a program at the sponsoring brand's discretion. This right is acquired by agreeing to sponsor a program on a continuing basis.

Network Identification—Acknowledgment of a network affiliation at the end of a network broadcast.

Network Option Time—Time on network affiliates for which the network has selling priority. Also called *network time*.

n

Newspaper Distributed Magazine—A supplement inserted into a Sunday newspaper.

Newspaper Syndicate—A business concern that sells special material (columns, photographs, comic strips) for simultaneous publication in a number of newspapers.

Nielsen—The A. C. Nielsen Company is the world's largest research company, with worldwide operations. It operates a wide variety of syndicated services: NTI—a national television rating service using Audimeters to collect set-tuning data; Food & Drug Index—a service collecting information on retail sales movement by means of store audits; NMS—a service collecting audience data by personal interview and diaries for television programs, publications (magazines and newspapers); NSI—a local television rating service.

Nielsen Market Section Rating—A Nielsen report on television ratings by zone breakdowns. The rating breakdowns are: Territory; County-Size Groups; Age of Housewife; Age of Household Head; Size of Family; Time Zone.

Nielsen Rating—TV program rating that uses set-tuning data from Audimeters. The Nielsen rating is used to refer to households who have viewed a program five or more minutes. This audience definition is also referred to as the *total audience* as opposed to the *average audience*, which is the audience of the average minute of a program.

90-Day Cancellation—All poster advertising is cancellable on 90 days' notice to the plant. This means that the advertiser or his agency must notify the poster plant owner of cancellation 90 days prior to the contract posting date.

Noted—The basic measure of the Starch method for testing print ads. The Noted Score represents the percentage of respondents (claimed readers of the issue) who say they saw the ad when they first read or looked into that magazine issue: i.e., claimed recognition of the ad.

NSI (Nielsen Station Index)—A service that measures local TV station ratings.

NTI (Nielsen Television Index)—A report on network television viewing.

O

O & O Station—A station owned and operated by a network.

Obtained Score—This is a Gallup-Robinson term for the actual percentage of respondents who prove recall of a print ad before the score is adjusted for color and size or converted to an index score. It is the basis for the final score.

Off Card—The use of a special rate not covered by a rate card.

Offensive Spending—Advertising activity intended to secure new business.

One-Time Rate—The highest rate charged by a medium not subject to discounts. Sometimes called *open* or *transient rate*.

Open End—A broadcast that leaves the commercial spots blank to be filled in locally.

Open End Transcription—A recorded program usually sold on a syndicated basis in various cities and produced so that local commercial announcements may be inserted at various points throughout the show.

Open Rate—In print, the highest rate charged to an advertiser on which all discounts are placed. Also called *base rate*, or *one-time rate*.

Option Time—Network option time is that time reserved by the networks in contract with their affiliates and for which the network has prior call under certain conditions for sponsored network programs. Station option time is that time reserved by the local stations for local and national spot shows.

Orbit—A scheduling method used by stations that consists of rotating an advertiser's commercial among different programs and/or time periods.

O.T.O.—One-time-only, a spot that runs only once; bought outright or as a makegood.

Outdoor Advertising—Display advertising (billboards, posters, signs, etc.) placed out-of-doors, along highways and railroads, or on walls and roofs of buildings.

Outdoor Advertising Plant—A company that builds and maintains outdoor displays consisting of painted bulletins and/or poster panels.

Overlapping Circulation—Duplication of circulation when advertising is placed in two or more media reaching the same prospects. Sometimes desirable to give additional impact to advertising.

P4C—Abbreviation for Page/Four Color. Other abbreviations are P2C (Page/Two-Color), PB&W (Page/Black and White), 3/5P4C (3/5 Page/Four-Color), 2C (Second Cover), BC (Back Cover), etc.

P

Package—A combination of programs or commercials offered by a network for sponsorship as an entity at one price. Spot TV is sometimes sold as a package. Also, a program property in which all elements from script to finished production are owned and controlled by an individual or organization, commonly known as a *packager*.

Packaged Goods—Mostly food, soap, and household products that are marketed in the manufacturer's package, wrapper, or container.

Package Enclosure—A premium enclosed in a package.

Package Insert—Separate advertising material included in packaged goods.

Package Plan—A plan by which an advertiser purchases a certain number of TV or radio announcements per week, in return for which he receives a lower rate per announcement from the station. The advertiser agrees to run the specific number of announcements each week and cannot split them up over a period of time.

Package Plan Discount—In spot television, a discount based upon frequency within a week; e.g., "5-plan," "10-plan."

Packager—An individual or company producing a broadcast program or series of programs that are sold as complete units.

Painted Bulletin—This structure is approximately 50' long by 15' high and has a molding around the outer edges similar to a poster panel, but the copy message is painted on the face of this structure as contrasted to the poster panel.

Painted Display—In outdoor, a display painted on a bulletin structure or wall, which may be illuminated, and sold as an individual unit. The three standard structures are the Deluxe Urban Bulletin, the Standard Highway Bulletin, and the Standard Streamliner Bulletin. In addition to these are the Semispectacular (embellished painted bulletin) and the Painted Wall.

Painted Wall—An outdoor advertising unit, purchased individually, usually situated on a high-traffic artery or in a neighborhood shopping area.

Panel—A fixed sample of respondents or stores selected to participate in a research project who report periodically on their knowledge, attitudes, and activities. This is in contrast to the technique of using fresh samples each time. (See *Store Panel*.) Also a master TV or radio control board, usually in a master control room.

Panels—Regular and illuminated units of outdoor advertising. A *regular panel* is a billboard that is not lighted at night. An *illuminated panel* is a billboard that is lighted from dusk until midnight.

Panographics—An outdoor bulletin that is lit from behind the display.

Pantry Audit—A consumer survey to tabulate brands, items, and varieties of grocery store products in the home.

Parallel Location—An outdoor advertising location in which the poster panel is parallel to the road.

Participation—A station or network may program a segment of time to carry *participation announcements* sold to various advertisers for commercial use. The announcements are usually :10, :30, or :60, but may be longer. Participations are announcements inside the context of programs as opposed to sponsorship or to chain or station breaks which are placed between programs.

Participation Program—A commercial program co-sponsored by a number of advertisers. Or, a program in which the audience participates; e.g., quiz show.

Pass-Along Reader—A person who reads a publication that he or a member of his family did not purchase. These readers must be taken into account in determining the total numbers of readers of a particular issue or a particular publication. (See *Audience, Secondary*.)

Pay TV—A television system providing programs available only to subscribing homes. Signals are generally transmitted via coaxial cables or telephone lines, and the subscriber is usually charged on a sliding scale for the number of programs actually tuned in.

Penalty Costs—In test market and expansion operation, this refers to the premium paid for local replacement media compared with the national media that the brand would be using under their national plan.

Penetration—The percentage of total homes in a specified area owning at least one TV set.

Penetration Study—The study of the effectiveness of advertising on the public.

Percent Composition—The percentage of a medium's total audience that is part of a specific demographic group. Example: If there are 10,000,000 women who read Magazine A, and 5,000,000 are 18 to 34 years old, then 50 percent of the total audience is composed of women 18 to 34.

Percent Coverage—In print media: the total audience of a publication as a percent of the total population. Or, the circulation of a publication as a percent of total homes. In broadcast media: the number of homes that are able to receive a signal of specific strength, but which do not necessarily tune to the station(s). Or, all homes in counties which meet a minimum circulation criterion (e.g., 50 percent).

Per Inquiry Advertising (P.I. Advertising)—An agreement between a media owner and an advertiser in which the owner agrees to accept payment for advertising on the basis of the number of inquiries or completed sales resulting from advertising, soliciting inquiries, or direct sales.

Persons Using Radio (PUR)—The percentage of an area's population (over age 12) listening to a radio at any given time.

PIB (Publisher's Information Bureau, Inc.)—PIB Service is a monthly analysis of both advertising space and revenue in general magazines, national farm magazines, and newspaper sections. It is designed to give convenient summaries of national advertising expenditures by advertisers and by media.

Piggyback—The back-to-back scheduling of two or more brand commercials of one advertiser in network or spot positions.

Pilot (Pilot Film)—A sample of a proposed TV series used for demonstration.

Plan Rate—The rate paid by an advertiser who purchased a TV or radio package plan. The rates are lower than if the spots were purchased individually since the advertiser agreed to run a specific number of spots each week.

Plant Operator—The company that owns and maintains poster panels in any given market. The plant operator rents space on its poster panels to advertisers in 30-day units. It leases or owns the land on which the poster panel is erected.

Position—An advertisement's place on a page and the location of the page in the publication. A preferred position is an especially desirable position obtained by paying an extra charge, or granted to an advertiser who has placed a heavy schedule in a publication, occasionally rotated among advertisers who have contracted for space above a specified minimum. In broadcast, programs or time spots considered most desirable by advertisers.

Post-Test—Study of the response to finished advertising after it has been published and telecast in media. Post-tests rely on normal patterns of behavior to expose respondents to advertising.

Poster—A product sign intended to be displayed on a store window, or on an inside wall, large enough to be legible at a reasonable distance.

Poster Frame—In point-of-purchase advertising, a frame holding a blowup of an advertisement or poster. Layers of advertisements may be mounted on one frame, and the top one torn off to reveal a new one.

Poster Panel—A standard surface on which outdoor advertisements are mounted. The poster panel is the most widely used form of outdoor advertising. The standard panel measures 12' × 25' long, is usually made of steel with a wood, fiberglass, or metal molding around the outer edges. The 24-sheet poster is actually posted on this structure.

Poster Plant—The company that builds and services poster panels and hangs poster sheets on them displaying illustration and/or message of advertiser.

Poster, Regular—A non-illuminated poster.

Poster Showing—Poster advertising is sold in packages called *showings*. A 100 showing (synonymous with *Gross Rating Points*) produces an audience circulation in one day that is equivalent to the total population in the market.

Potential Audience—See *Audience, Potential*.

Pre-emption—Recapture by the station or network of an advertiser's time in order to substitute a special program of universal value. For example, when the President speaks, he pre-empts the show regularly scheduled at that time.

Preferred Position—A position in a magazine or newspaper which is regarded as excellent in terms of its ability to generate a large readership. Preferred position is usually located next to editorial material that has a high interest among the publication's readers.

Preprint—A reproduction of an advertisement before it appears in a publication.

Pre-Test—Study of advertisements or commercials prior to distribution via regular media channels. Advertising may be studied in rough or finished form; pretesting relies on some special means of exposing respondents to the advertisement other than the regular media planned—portfolios, dummy magazines, etc.

Primary Audience—See *Audience, Primary*.

Primary Households—Households into which a publication has been introduced by purchase, either at the newsstand or by subscription, rather than by pass-along.

Primary Readers—The readers of a publication who reside in primary households.

Primary Service Area—In AM or standard broadcasting, the area in which a station signal is strongest and steadiest. Defined by Federal Communications Commission rules as the area in which the ground wave (the primary wave for broadcast transmission) is not subject to objectionable interference or objectionable fading. No similar term is officially used in TV broadcasting, although television engineering standards recognize three zones of signal service, existing in concentric rings from the transmitting tower: City Grade Service, A Contour, B Contour.

Primetime—Time periods covering peak broadcast set usage and highest ratings. Also is used as synonym for highest rate classification time periods—Class A or better. For network television, usually considered as 8:00-11:00 pm EST.

Product Protection—Protection that an advertiser wants and sometimes gets against adjacency in a medium to advertising of a competitive product. Has special interest in television advertising.

Program Basis—A Nielsen cost estimate of a television show that takes into consideration the length-of-commitment discount as determined by whether the program is normally telecast every week, less-than-weekly, more-than-weekly, or one-time-only. This discount is determined by the number of telecasts of the show and not the number used by a specific advertiser. Also, this basis disregards other programs sponsored by an advertiser that affect its discount structure.

Program Coverage—The number (or percentage) of television households that can receive a program over one or more stations, because they are in the signal area of some station carrying the program.

Program Delivery (Rating)—Percentage of sample contacted who tuned to a particular program at a particular time.

Program Station Rating—A rating based on the television homes located in the area in which a program was telecast that permits an unbiased comparison of different programs regardless of variation in the number of homes capable of receiving the programs.

Programming, Counter—A technique used by the networks to regulate audience flow by offering a program of a different type from that broadcast by a strong competitor in the same time period.

Promotion Allowance—Money received by a wholesaler or a retailer from a manufacturer or his representative for sales promotion other than advertising. (See *Advertising Allowance*.)

Psychographic—A term that describes consumers or audience members on the basis of some psychological trait, characteristic of behavior, or lifestyle.

Publisher's Statement—A notarized statement made by the publisher regarding total circulation, geographic distribution, methods of securing subscriptions, etc. These are often issued between audited statements, especially when market conditions have changed.

Pure Program Ratings—A measurement of audience size in which estimates are made excluding program pre-emptions that have occurred during the survey period.

q

Qualified Issue Reader—A respondent who qualifies to be interviewed about advertisements in a magazine on the basis of having read the study issue of a magazine. Requirements for such qualification vary: for Starch interviews, readers have merely to claim they looked into the issue when shown the cover; for Gallup & Robinson studies, respondents must prove reading by correctly describing some article when shown the cover and Table of Contents.

Qualified Viewer—Respondent who has demonstrated viewing of a TV program (on the basis of recall of at least one part of the episode), thus becoming eligible or qualified for interview about commercials aired on that show.

Quantity Discount—A graduated discount on quantity purchases scaled to the number of cases in a single order; or, a periodic refund based upon the value of purchases over a period of time.

Quintile—The division of any sample of respondents into five equal sized groups ranging from the heaviest to the lightest amount of exposure to the medium. Samples may also be divided into tertiles, quartiles, deciles, etc.

Quota—A pre-determined media goal in a market. Goals can be established in dollars spent, number of spots to be purchased, or GRPs to be achieved. Used as a target for the agency time buyer in implementing a media plan.

r

Radio Rating Point—One percent of the homes in the measured area whose sets are tuned to a station, used for making comparisons of spot stations.

Rate Card—A listing put out by a medium containing advertising costs, mechanical requirements, issue dates, closing dates, cancellation dates, and circulation data. Rate cards are issued by both print and broadcast media.

Rate Class—In broadcast media, the time charge in effect at a specified time.

Rate Differential—Among newspapers, the difference between the national and the local rates.

Rate Holder—A minimum sized advertisement placed in a publication during a contract period to hold a time or quantity discount rate. Also, an ID spot bought by the advertiser for the same reason.

Rate Protection— A guarantee that an advertiser's current rate under the old rate card will be protected for a period, usually from three to six months, should a new rate be introduced.

Reach—The number of different persons or homes exposed to a specific media vehicle or schedule at least once. Usually measured over a specific period of time, e.g., four weeks. Also known as *cume, cumulative, unduplicated,* or *net audience.*

Reach, Cumulative—The total number of homes reached by a medium during a specific time period.

Reader Impression Studies—Studies carried out by Starch over and above their regular Readership Study to find out something of what the advertisement meant to respondents who "noted" the ad.

Reader Interest—Expression of interest by readers in advertisements they have read. Sometimes evaluated by unsolicited mail. Sometimes evaluated by the numbers of people who can remember having read material with interest. Also, an evaluation of the relative level of general interest in different types of products.

Reader Traffic—The movement from page to page by readers of a publication.

Readers—People who are exposed to a print vehicle.

Readers-Per-Copy—The average number of readers of a magazine per copy of circulation. When multiplied by a magazine's circulation, the result equals its audience.

Readership—The degree to which print vehicles have been seen (not necessarily read) by members of the publication's audience.

Readership or Audience—The total average number of persons who are exposed to a publication as distinguished from the circulation or number of copies distributed.

Read Most—Starch ad readership measurement term referring to magazines or newspaper readers who read 50 percent or more of the copy of a specific advertisement.

Rebate—A refund that reduces the contract price for merchandise. A term frequently used for advertising allowances. Also given to advertisers by a certain media vehicle as a result of an advertiser's exceeding the contract minimum and earning a greater discount.

Recent Reading—A measurement technique for magazines in which survey respondents check a list of magazines they have read recently.

Recognition—The technique used to determine whether a person saw or heard a given print advertisement or broadcast commercial by actually showing the ad or commercial (or playing it) and inquiring whether he or she saw or heard it at a previous date in a specific medium. This technique was pioneered and is still being used by Starch.

Recordimeter—An electro-mechanical device utilized by the A. C. Nielsen Company in conjunction with the *Audilog.* It measures the amount of time that a radio or TV set is turned on during the day, but cannot distinguish among stations as does the *Audimeter.*

Regional Edition—A geographical section of a national magazine's circulation that can be purchased by an advertiser without having to purchase the rest of the magazine's circulation (as is required in a split run.) A higher premium is usually paid for regional editions and demographic editions.

Regional Network—A network of stations serving a limited geographic area.

Regular Panel—See *Panels*.

Remnant Space—Magazine space sold at reduced price to help fill out regional editions.

Remote—A broadcast originating outside the regular studio. Also called *remote pickup*.

Remote Control—Broadcasting a program from a point removed from the regular studios of the station.

Renewals—In print: refers to magazine or newspaper subscriptions which people extend past their expiration dates. In outdoor advertising: extra posters over and above the quantity actually needed to post the exact number of panels in a showing. They are shipped to the plant operator and, if one of the posters on display is damaged, the plant operator has a complete poster design on hand to replace immediately the damaged poster.

Rep—Publisher's or broadcast station's sales representative.

Replacement Media—Local media that are being used to replace national media in a test market or expansion area, e.g., local rotogravure supplements, comic sections, black-and-white daily newspapers.

Response Function—An effect of an ad in a medium, sometimes called *impact*. These effects may be attitude change, degrees of brand awareness, or sales.

Retail Trading Zone—The area beyond the city zone whose residents regularly trade to an important degree with retail merchants in the city zone. These are defined by the Audit Bureau of Circulation.

Returns Per Thousand Circulation—A gauge of the effectiveness of media used in support of promotions computed by dividing the total number of returns by the circulation of the publication to which the returns are attributable. (See *Keying an Advertisment*.)

Roll-Out—A marketing strategy technique in which a brand is introduced in a limited geographical area. If it succeeds in that area, it is then introduced in adjacent areas and, if successful, in other adjacent areas until the entire country is covered.

ROP (Run of Press)—A newspaper advertisement for which a definite position is not specified is inserted as run-of-press (or run-of-book), but usually in the general news sections. The term is also used in connection with color newspaper advertising to distinguish color advertising in the main portion of the paper from that placed in the magazine section (*Sunday supplement*).

R.O.S. (Run of Schedule)—A broadcast commercial for which a definite time is not specified. For example, a nighttime commercial during primetime may be run at any time during this period. Also, the time at which an announcement runs may vary from week to week, depending upon other requirements.

Roster Recall—Method of research in which a list of radio or TV programs is submitted to respondents for recall.

Rotating Painted Bulletins—Moving the advertiser's copy from one painted bulletin to another, usually every 30 days. This service is available in a limited number of cities. Offers advertiser an opportunity to cover a large area or a given market (over a long period of time) with a limited number of painted bulletins.

Rotation—The practice in store management of moving the older stock forward when restocking shelves or cases. The practice, in retail advertising, of scheduling a branded product or gruop of products to be featured at intervals throughout the year to maintain a desired stock balance. Also, the process of continuing a series of advertisements over and over again in a regular order.

Rotogravure (Roto)—Printing process where an impression is produced by sunken or deep etched letters or pictures in a copper printing plate. The ink is held in indentation in the plates, not on the surface as in offset, or on the tops of dots or letters as in letterpress.

Runs—In television film syndication, the number of times a film has been telecast in a given area. The number of times a film may be run according to an advertiser's lease. A rerun among television film syndicators is an available program previously telecast in an area.

Russell Hall—See Lloyd Hall.

S

Sales Promotion—Those sales activities that supplement both personal selling and marketing, coordinate the two, and help to make them effective; for example, displays.

Satellite Station—A station that relays TV signals to areas that are beyond the usual coverage area of the parent TV station.

Saturation—A level of advertising weight several times above normal coverage and frequency levels standard for the market or product involved. Saturation implies simultaneous achievement of wide coverage and high frequency designed to achieve maximum impact, coverage, or both.

Saturation Showing—In outdoor, a showing of maximum intensity, designed to surpass complete coverage (the 100 showing) with repeat impressions. Often a 200 showing.

Scatter Plan—The use of announcements in a number of different network TV programs.

Schedule—A list of media to be used during an advertising campaign. A list of a product's advertising to be included in a media vehicle during a specific time. The chronological list of programs broadcast by a station. Also called a *flow-chart*.

Secondary Audience—See *Audience, Secondary*.

Secondary Service Area—The distant area in which a broadcast station's signal is subject to interference of fading, but can still be received.

Sectional Magazine—A magazine that is distributed only sectionally and not nationally (such as *Sunset*, which is confined to the western states). Also called *regional magazine*.

Selective Magazine—A magazine which, because of its nature and editorial content, appeals only to a certain type of audience.

Self-Liquidating Point-of-Purchase Unit—One for which the retailer wholly or partially pays.

Self-Liquidating Premium—A premium whose total cost is recoverable in the basic sales transaction.

Self-Mailer—A folder, booklet, or other direct mail piece that provides space for addressing, postage, and sealing, and therefore requires no separate envelope for mailing.

Semi-Liquidator—Premium offered to the consumer whose cost is partially recovered by the manufacturer or merchant offering the inducement.

Sets-in-Use—The total number of sets tuned in to some program at a given time of day and day of week. At one time sets-in-use was equivalent to H.U.T., but today, its meaning is limited to sets, not households. (See *H.U.T.*).

Share or **Share of Audience**—The audience for a program as a percentage of all households using the medium at the time of the program's broadcast.

Share of Market—The percentage of the total sales of a specified class of products that is held by or attributed to a particular brand at a given time.

Share of Mind—The percentage of the relevant population (or a sample of that population) who indicate awareness of, or preference for, the various brands within a product group. Specific meaning varies considerably with the method of measurement. It may be a test of salience or a test of total recall, aided or unaided. Usually refers to consumer awareness of brands in comparison with like measures of awareness for competing brands.

Shelter Magazines—Magazines dealing editorially with the home such as decorating, maintenance, gardening, etc. Additionally, these magazines carry a considerable amount of food editorial matter. An example is *Better Homes & Gardens*.

Shopper—A newspaper published in a local community and containing mainly local news, shopping hints and suggestions, and advertisements. Sometimes called a *shopping newspaper*.

Short Rate—The additional charge incurred when an advertiser fails to use enough media time or space to earn the contract discount envisaged at the time of the original order.

Showing—In outdoor advertising, the number of posters offered as a unit in terms of 100 intensity and variations thereof. In transit advertising, the number of cards included in a unit of sale. (See *Poster Showing*.)

SIC (Standard Industrial Classification)—A classification system set up by the U.S. Bureau of the Budget to define business establishments by type of activity. Used to facilitate analysis of business paper markets.

Simmon's Data—Print and broadcast media audience exposure and product-usage data reported by the Simmons Market Research Bureau.

Sliding Rate—A space or time rate in a medium that decreases as the amount of space or time used by an advertiser increases over a period of time.

Six-Sheet Poster—See *Junior Panel*.

SMSA (Standard Metropolitan Statistical Area)—An area that consists of one or more entire counties meeting specified criteria pertaining to population, metropolitan character, and economic and social integration between outlying counties and the central county, determined by the Bureau of the Budget with the advice of the Federal Committee on Standard Metropolitan Areas composed of representatives of the major federal government statistical agencies.

Space Position Value—In outdoor, an estimate of the effectiveness of a particular poster location. The factors considered are the length of approach, the speed of travel, the angle of the panel to its circulation, and the relation of the panel to adjacent panels.

Space Schedule—A schedule sent to the advertiser by the agency, showing the media to be used, the dates on which advertising is to appear, size of advertisements, and cost of space.

Special—A one-time TV show generally employing known talent and usually running an hour or longer. Also called *spectacular*.

Spill-In (or Spill-Out)—The degree to which programming is viewed in adjacent ADI (or DMA) areas. Depending on the perspective, this is either spill-in or spill-out. Milwaukee television programming spills out of the Milwaukee DMA and spills into the Madison, Wisconsin, area, and vice versa.

Split Run—The running of two or more versions of an ad in alternate copies of the same magazine or newspaper. There are also split runs in which one version of the ad appears in newsstand copies and one in mail subscription copies. Splits may also occur geographically.

Split Run Test—Research designed to test the effectiveness of various copy elements, prices, or types of offers by placing them in alternate copies of an issue. The various forms of the advertisement are evaluated by means of coupon or inquiry returns, or by orders placed for trial offers.

Sponsor Identification (SI)—The extent to which a program's sponsor is identified or its product or service remembered. The percentage of listeners or viewers who correctly associate a program with the sponsor or his product is the Sponsor Identification Index (SII).

Sponsor Rating—A rating determined by applying the Sponsor Identification Index to the total audience rating.

Sponsor Relief—Occurs when an advertiser on a regular television program wishes to suspend activities for an off-season period, and requests contractual relief from the TV networks.

Sponsorship—The purchase of more than one announcement in a program (usually a majority of commercials) by one advertiser.

Spot—A time period filled entirely by a commercial or public service message and sold separately from the adjacent time periods. Such announcements may be placed between network programs or within local programs. Also, to buy time (programs and/or announcements) on a market-by-market basis from stations through their representatives.

Spot Announcement—Commercial placed upon individual stations, radio and TV. Often referred to as *spots*. Technically, spots should be referred to as *announcements*.

Spot Programming—The process by which an advertiser secures the rights to a television program and places it on stations in selected markets without regard to network affiliation. The advertiser may own the television program outright, have rights to the program for a specific length of time, or have the rights to the program in only a certain part of the country.

Spot Radio—The use of stations in selected markets without regard to network affiliation. May involve spot announcements or complete programs.

Spot Schedule—A local spot announcement buy or a standard form that agencies submit showing specific times, adjacencies, etc., of a brand's current spot announcements in a market.

Spot Television—The use of stations in selected markets without regard to network affiliation. May involve spot announcements or complete local programs.

Spread—An advertisement appearing on any two facing pages of a publication.

SRDS (Standard Rate & Data Service, Inc.)—A service that publishes the rates and discount structures of all major media. It also publishes market research studies, often on media or market areas.

Staggered Schedule—Several advertisements scheduled in two or more publications, arranged so that the dates of insertion are alternated or rotated.

Standby Space—An order accepted by some magazines to run an advertisement whenever and wherever they wish, at an extra discount. Advertiser forwards plate with order. Helps magazine fill odd pages or spaces.

Starch Method—A term that refers to the recognition method used by Daniel Starch & Staff in their studies of advertising readership.

Station Break—A time period between two programs when a station announces the call letters, channel number, and also broadcasts commercials.

Station Log—The official, chronological listing of a radio or television station's programming and commercial announcements throughout the day.

Station Rep—A sales organization or person representing individual stations to national advertisers. Short for station representative.

Store Check—An in-the-field personal review of merchandise movement conducted in retail outlets by non-store personnel.

Store Distributed Magazine—Any one of several magazines (e.g., *Family Circle*, *Woman's Day*) whose primary channel of distribution is retail grocery stores.

Store Panel—A selected sample of stores used repeatedly for market research to collect data on retail sales movement, e.g., A. C. Nielsen Company's food store panel. (See *Panel*).

Sunday Newspaper Supplement—Any printed matter that is inserted in a Sunday edition of a newspaper on a continuing basis and is not part of the newspaper itself. Two main publications fitting into this category are magazine supplements and comic sections. A supplement may be either syndicated nationally or edited locally.

Sweeps—Both Arbitron and Nielsen survey all television local markets three times yearly (November, March, and May). These are called *sweep months*.

Syndicated Program—A method of placing a TV or radio program on a market-by-market basis as opposed to the line interconnected network system of program transmission.

Syndicated Sunday Magazine Supplement—A magazine supplement that is distributed through a group of newspapers and is owned by a single publisher. The distributing newspapers pay the publisher for the privilege of distributing the supplement which in turn helps to build circulation for the distributing newspapers. There are only two syndicated supplements: *Parade* and *Family Weekly*.

t

Target Audience—The desired or intended audience for advertising as described or determined by the advertiser. Usually defined in terms of specific demographic (age, sex, income, etc.), purchase, or ownership characteristics.

Tear Sheets—Actual pages of advertising as they appeared in an issue of any publication, used to serve as proofs of insertion.

Telecast—A broadcast, program, or show on television.

Telephone Coincidental Survey—In research, the interview method in which telephone calls are made while a particular activity, usually a broadcast program, is in progress.

Test Market—A given marketing area, usually a metropolitan census region, in which a market test is conducted. Sometimes used as a verb to refer to introduction of a new product.

Test Market Translation—The use of local media that are available in a specific market to replace the national media included in a brand's national plan. The theoretical national plan must be reproduced as carefully and as accurately as possible in the test market since sales results will be used by company management to determine whether or not the product should be expanded to national distribution.

30-Sheet and Bleed Posters—The 30-sheet poster offers advertisers 25 percent more billboard space than the 24-sheet poster. Bleed posters cover the entire metal face of the billboard and are difficult to handle, as the posters quite often have to be trimmed to fit the billboard after they are put up.

3-Sheet Poster—Approximately 84″ high by 43″ wide and used primarily in areas where there is not enough room to build a standard 24-sheet poster panel. Usually, a 24-sheet poster company does not handle 3-sheet posters.

Through-the-Book—A technique of determining a print medium's audience size by having respondents go through a stripped-down issue with an interviewer to learn which articles are most interesting. After this preliminary examination, respondents are asked whether they are sure they looked into the magazine. Only those who answer positively are counted as readers.

Tie-In—Advertisement run by retail outlets in a newspaper referring to or associating with another ad in the same newspaper. Tie-ins are paid for by the retail outlets running them.

Total Audience—Audience viewing all or any part of a program in excess of five minutes. For programs of less than ten minutes duration, households viewing one minute or more are included. Also total number of unduplicated readers of a magazine.

Total Audience Rating—The sum of all exposures to several issues of the same publication or several issues of different publications.

Total Net Paid—Total of all classes of a publication's circulation for which the ultimate purchasers have paid in accordance with the standards set by the Audit Bureau of Circulations' rules. Includes single copy sales, mail subscriptions, and specials.

TPT (Total Primetime)—A television research project of Gallup & Robinson evaluating all paid commercials aired during the evening period when national network programming is shown; i.e., both program commercials and station breaks. Offers data both on percentage of commercial audience able to recall the commercial, plus an estimate of actual audience in station coverage. At date of report, such operations were confined to the Philadelphia metro area.

Traceable Expenditures—Published reports on advertising expenditures by media for different advertisers. Currently, traceable expenditures are available for consumer magazines, farm publications, supplements, newspapers, spot TV, network TV (gross time only), and outdoor.

Trade Advertising—Advertisements of consumer items directed to wholesalers and retailers in the distribution channel.

Trade Magazine—See *Business Paper*.

Trade Paper—Publication covering the commercial activities of wholesale and retail outlets, but many reach the sales departments of manufacturers. Trade papers include all publications that offer a manufacturer the opportunity to reach those who will sell the product for him, either from the standpoint of the retail or wholesale level.

Trading Area—The area surrounding a city set up by the Audit Bureau of Circulations whose residents would normally be expected to use the city as their trading center.

Traffic Count—The evaluation of outdoor poster circulation by an actual count of traffic passing the poster.

Traffic Flow Map (Outdoor)—An outline map of a market's streets scaled to indicate the relative densities of traffic.

Traffic Pattern—Comparisons of customer count to establish averages. How customers behave as to shopping time, hour of day, day of week, frequency.

Transient Rate—Same as *one-time rate* in buying space.

Transit Advertising—Advertising on transportation vehicles such as buses, subways, street cars, etc. Uses poster-type ads.

Translator—An independent TV station that picks up programs from a given station and rebroadcasts them to another area on the upper 13 UHF channels (chs. 70-83). Translators serve from several hundred to, in several instances, up to 50,000 TV homes.

Truline Rate—A rate concept sometimes used at the local level. It is computed by multiplying the agate line rate by 1,000,000 circulation and dividing it by the retail trading zone circulation.

Turnover—The ratio of a weekly rating to a four-week reach. This ratio serves as an indication of the relative degree to which the audience of a program changes. The greater the turnover in the audience, the higher the ratio.

TVAR (TV Advertisers Report)—A bi-monthly report from Trendex that gives indices of TV audience characteristics in three categories: audience composition, program selection, and sponsor identification.

24-Sheet Poster—An outdoor poster that is 8'-6" high and 19'-6" long. In the early days of advertising, the poster consisted of 24 individual panels pasted together to form an advertisement. Today about 10 to 12 panels are used, depending on the type of artwork and copy used.

U

UHF (Ultra High Frequency)—Television channels 14-74.

Unaided Recall—The process of determining whether a person saw or heard a given ad or commercial or brand sometime after exposure with only minimal cueing such as mention of product class (not brand).

Upscale—A general description of a medium's audience indicating upper socio-economic class membership.

V

Vehicle—A particular component of a media class, e.g., a particular magazine or broadcast program.

Vertical Cume—In broadcast research, a cumulative rating for two or more programs broadcast on the same day.

Vertical Discount—Broadcast media discount earned through maintenance of specified frequency during given time period, e.g., six spots per week.

Vertical Half-Page—A half page where the long dimension of the ad is vertical. (See *Horizontal Half-Page.*)

Vertical Publication—A business publication that appeals to a specific trade, industry, business, or profession.

VHF (Very High Frequency)—Television channels 2-13. Generally, VHF stations have the greatest range of coverage, whereas UHF stations cover a much smaller area.

Viewer Impression Studies—A service of Daniel Starch & Staff that provides qualitative data about TV commercials. It is based on interviews with respondents who have seen a commercial in the context of normal at-home viewing. Viewers are asked probing questions about the communication of the commercial and its meanings.

Viewers Per Set (VPS)—The average number of persons watching or listening to a program in each home.

Volume Discount—A discount given for running a certain volume of space in a publication. An advertiser might use many small insertions to make up the required number of pages.

W

Waste Circulation—The audience members of a magazine or newspaper who are not prospects for a particular advertised product. Circulation in an area where an advertiser does not have distribution of his product.

Women's Service Magazine—Magazine appealing directly to women (housewives specifically), and whose editorial contents are designed to further their knowledge as homemakers.

Index